The Illustrated Souls of Black Folk

The Illustrated Souls of Black Folk

W. E. B. Du Bois

Edited and Annotated by
Eugene F. Provenzo Jr.

with a Foreword by

Manning Marable

An Annotated, Illustrated, Documentary Edition

Paradigm Publishers
Boulder • London

Copyright © 2005 Paradigm Publishers

The text of *The Souls of Black Folk* used in this edition has been reprinted by arrangement with David Graham Du Bois.

Published in the United States by Paradigm Publishers, 3360 Mitchell Lane Suite C, Boulder, CO 80301 USA.

Paradigm Publishers is the trade name of Birkenkamp & Company, LLC, Dean Birkenkamp, President and Publisher.

ISBN 1-59451-030-X (cloth)
ISBN 1-59451-031-8 (pbk)

Library of Congress Cataloging-in-Publication Data has been applied for.

Printed and bound in the United States of America on acid free paper that meets the standards of the American National Standard for Permanence of Paper for Printed Library Materials.

10 09 08 07 06 05   1 2 3 4 5 6

To

BURGHARDT AND YOLANDE

The Lost and the Found

Herein Is Written

Foreword

The Souls of Black Folk has remained the most influential text about the African-American experience for a century.[1] Even Du Bois's contemporaries, whether agreeing or dissenting from the book's various arguments, understood its unique power as a work of literature. In the book's most important quote: "The problem of the twentieth century is the problem of the color-line," Du Bois presciently set forth what would be the most important social issue in American culture for his generation and the generation that followed him.

Why was the book so important? I believe that Du Bois had given the emerging black middle class a lyrical language of racial reform. *Souls* was to the black American petit bourgeoisie what *The Communist Manifesto* had once been for sectors of the European proletariat under industrial capitalism in the late nineteenth century: a framework for understanding history, a philosophical statement establishing group identity and social location within society's unequal hierarchy, and an appeal for collective action and resistance to oppression and exploitation.

In *Souls*, culture and politics are inextricably linked, as part of the process of group self-awareness and affirmation. As the cultural studies theorist Stuart Hall has explained, "Du Bois used language and ideas to hammer out a strategy for political equality, and to sound the depths of the black experience in the aftermath of slavery." *The Souls of Black Folk,* for the first time in history, tried to paint for white America "a vivid portrait of black people in the decades after emancipation in 1862—how they lived and who they really were—and thus to enlighten white America (still profoundly attached to myths of black inferiority) as to the true meaning of being black in post–Civil War America."[2]

Du Bois reflected shortly after the publication of *Souls* how he had deliberately employed throughout the text "a personal and intimate tone of self-revelation. In each essay I sought to speak from within—to depict a world as we see it who dwell therein."[3]

---

[1] This foreword draws on the introduction I wrote to *The Souls of Black Folk, 100th Anniversary Edition* by W. E. B. Du Bois (Boulder, Colorado: Paradigm Publishers, 2004).

[2] Stuart Hall, "Tearing Down the Veil," *Guardian* (London), February 22, 2003.

[3] W. E. B. Du Bois, "The Souls of Black Folk," *Independent*, vol. 57, no. 2920 (November 17, 1904), p. 1152

Foreword

This edition of *The Souls of Black Folk*, edited by Eugene F. Provenzo Jr., expands and elaborates on Du Bois's work in ways that resonate with the original intention and purpose of the book. By annotating the work, and drawing on period documents and sources, as well as photographs and illustrations, Provenzo extends Du Bois's "desire to speak from within—to depict a world as we see it who dwell therein." In doing so, he takes a classic and revolutionary work in American history, and not only makes it more accessible, but enriches it in ways that one is confident that Du Bois would heartily agree with and applaud.

—Manning Marable

Preface

One can legitimately ask why there is a need to publish a new edition of W. E. B. Du Bois's masterpiece, *The Souls of Black Folk*. There are already numerous editions available, including an annotated version by the distinguished African-American scholar Henry Louis Gates Jr.[1] In part, this edition is intended to celebrate the 100th anniversary of the publication of the book. Like Gates's edition of *The Souls of Black Folk*, this edition is annotated and also includes a critical introduction. It also provides pictorial and documentary sources to supplement the text.

I have drawn on period documents and sources, as well as illustrations and photographs, to supplement this text. Of greatest interest to me are the materials from *The Exhibit of the American Negroes* that was part of the 1900 Paris International Exposition. It is, in fact, the thesis of this work that much of the information and conceptualization of *The Souls of Black Folk* is a direct outgrowth of Du Bois's involvement with this pioneering and largely unheralded exhibit of sociological, cultural, and literary artifacts. As will be demonstrated in this work, echoes of the Paris exhibit can be found throughout *The Souls of Black Folk*.[2]

I believe that there is a great deal that is new that can be said about *The Souls of Black Folk*. I also believe that different perspectives can prove helpful in looking at Du Bois and his work. I am a historian by training, and a cultural theorist and "cultural archeologist" by practice. Du Bois has particularly caught the attention of literary scholars in recent years, and while their insights are useful, they are by no means complete. The reader can be the judge of whether or not I have something new to contribute.

Finally, I am interested in creating an edition of *The Souls of Black Folk* that can be of particular use to scholars and students. I hope this work, through the inclusion of extensive illustrated materials and photographs, as well as original documents and sources from the period (written by both Du Bois and his contemporaries), will provide the reader

---

[1] W. E. B. Du Bois, *The Souls of Black Folk*, edited by Henry Louis Gates Jr. and Terri Hume Oliver (New York: W. W. Norton & Company, 1999).

[2] For a detailed account of *The Exhibit of the American Negroes*, see Eugene F, Provenzo Jr., *The Exhibit of the American Negroes, 1900 (Paris Exposition Universelle)* (Walnut Creek, CA: Altamira Press, in press).

with a deeper understanding of Du Bois's work and its significance not only as an historical document, but also as one of the most important political and cultural texts of the twentieth century.

In this special edition, each section or chapter of Du Bois's original work is accompanied by, not only annotations and illustrations, but also by a selected set of documents at the end. I have chosen these materials because of their relevance to the information and arguments made by Du Bois. In doing so, I hope to extend the reader's access to related documents and resources, as well as add to the richness of this already engaging text.

I would like to thank the many people who have helped and encouraged me in my work on this project. Dean Birkenkamp at Paradigm Publishers has shown particular imagination and enthusiasm for this project. In doing so, he gives one faith in the enterprise of publishing and the creation of new books. Also special thanks go to Dianne Ewing, Michael Peirce, Beth Davis, and Alison Sullenberger at Paradigm Publishers.

Asterie Baker Provenzo has provided her usual superb editorial support and critical insight—without her help I would be a much poorer scholar.

John P. Renaud helped with the index. His enthusiasm, insight and precision are always appreciated.

Terry and George Moneo are thanked for their technical help.

Steve Robinson, Special Collections, W. E. B. Du Bois Library, University of Massachusetts was extremely helpful in obtaining mages for this work. He and his colleagues are thanked for their effort, as is Frederick T. Courtwright of the Permissions Company.

Special thanks go to David Du Bois for giving us permission to use the Blue Heron edition of *The Souls of Black Folk*, as well as other select materials. His ongoing support of projects such as this represents an important continuation of his stepfather's intellectual legacy.

Finally, I would like to dedicate my work on this edition to my colleague and friend Carlos Diaz. He serves as a bold reminder of what is best about our profession and the ideal of diversity in American culture. I would suggest that all who read this book consider his advice (words that could have easily been written by Du Bois): "Let nothing that is human be alien to you."

Eugene F. Provenzo Jr.
University of Miami
Fall 2004

Introduction

Courage and the Sociological Imagination: W. E. B. Du Bois's *The Souls of Black Folk*

Eugene F. Provenzo Jr.

Every act of sociological research is ultimately an act of courage and an act of imagination. Nowhere is this clearer than in the work of the sociologist and political activist, W. E. B. Du Bois, and in particular, his 1903 work *The Souls of Black Folk*. In this Introduction, I wish to examine Du Bois's courage and imagination as a scholar and as a social activist. In doing so, I hope to reveal an additional dimension to our understanding of one of the most complex and important figures in American political activism and social thought.

Du Bois did many remarkable things. He overcame poverty and prejudice to become one of the best-educated persons of his era. He attended Fisk and Harvard as an undergraduate, the University of Berlin and Harvard University for graduate school, and in 1896 became the first black Ph.D. in the United States with his groundbreaking study *The Suppression of the African Slave Trade*.[1] He was a founder of the Niagara Movement and the National Association for the Advancement of Colored People. He was perhaps the most competent American Sociologist of his generation—ignored and underappreciated in this regard because of the color of his skin and his increasingly radical political orientation. In 1910, he became the founding editor for *The Crisis*—the first mass-circulated magazine of social research and social uplift for African-American people. He was a critical leader in the Pan African movement and one of the founders of African Nationalism. More so than perhaps any other figure in the late nineteenth and early twentieth centuries, he laid the foundation for the founding of the modern field of African-American Studies. He was a talented novelist, and occasionally even an inspired poet. He was literally a man for all seasons, a man

---

[1] W. E. B. Du Bois, *The Suppression of the African Slave Trade* (Cambridge: Harvard University Press, 1896).

whose force and intellect transcended the limitations of prejudice and race, and who continues to reach out and affect the lives and thoughts of others, long after his death.[2]

Du Bois was also very human. His marriage to Nina Gomer (?–1950) was not a particularly happy one. His relationship with her was tragically affected by the death of his two-year-old son Burghardt in 1899. While he was a good financial provider for his family, he tended to intimidate his daughter Yolande (1900–1960) with whom he had, at best, an awkward relationship. By all accounts, Du Bois was often haughty and aloof—some would say, particularly when he was younger, conceited—and lacked the common touch.[3] He was clearly elitist, and while

[2] For background on Du Bois the best starting point is his first autobiography, *Dusk of Dawn: An Essay Toward and Autobiography of a Race Concept*, introduction by Irene Diggs (New Brunswick, N.J.: Transaction Books, 1984), which was first published in 1940. A second autobiography, which included much of the same material as *Dusk of Dawn*, is *The Autobiography of W. E. B. Du Bois: A Soliloquy on Viewing My Life from the Last Decade of Its First Century* (New York: International Publishers, 1968). This second autobiography appeared five years after Du Bois died. Thus, he did not have editorial control over its final content. The major scholarly and biographical studies of Du Bois include: Francis Broderick, *W.E.B. Du Bois, Negro Leader in a Time of Crisis* (Palo Alto, CA: Stanford University Press, 1959); Elliott Rudwick, *W.E.B. Du Bois: A Study in Minority Group Leadership* (Philadelphia: University of Pennsylvania Press, 1960); Elliott Rudwick, *W.E.B. Du Bois* (New York: Atheneum, 1968); Virginia Hamilton, *W.E.B. DuBois* (New York: T. Y. Crowell, 1972); Virginia Hamilton, *Black Titan: W.E.B. Du Bois* (Boston: Beacon Press, 1970); David Levering Lewis, *W. E. B. Du Bois: Biography of a Race* (New York: Henry Holt and Company, 1993); and David Levering Lewis, *W. E. B. Du Bois: The Fight for Equality and the American Century, 1919–1963* (New York: Henry Holt and Company, 2000). Du Bois's correspondence has been published in a three-volume collection under the title *The Correspondence of W.E.B. Du Bois* (Amherst: University of Massachusetts Press, 1973–78). Invaluable for any work on Du Bois is Herbert Aptheker's *Annotated Bibliography of the Published Writings of W.E.B. Du Bois* (Millwood, N.Y.: Kraus-Thomason Organization, 1973). For an intriguing assessment of the importance of *The Souls of Black Folk* see: Stanley Crouch and Playthell Benjamin, *Reconsidering the Souls of Black Folk: Thoughts on the Groundbreaking Classic Work of W. E. B. Du Bois* (Philadelphia: Running Press, 2002).

[3] Du Bois has been criticized by Cornel West in his article "W. E. B. Du Bois: An Interpretation," included in Kawame Anthony Appiah and Henry Louis Gates, editors, *Africana: The Encyclopedia of the African and African American Experience* (New York: Basic/Civitas Books, 1999) as being disconnected to "suffering, yet striving ordinary blackfolk." (West, 1994, 1967). Although as a student at Fisk, he spent several summers living and teaching in rural black

enormously perceptive about most things, could occasionally be beguiled and misled. His admiration for the Soviet dictator Stalin, for example, now seems naïve.[4]

Taking all of this into account, he was the clearest voice of his era to address the problems of racial prejudice and injustice in the United States. Prior to 1903, Du Bois had written numerous articles,[5] several government reports,[6] and two seminal books: *The Suppression of the African Slave Trade* (1896)[7] and *The Philadelphia Negro* (1899).[8] He

---

Tennessee and lived in black communities and neighborhoods throughout his life, he was largely disconnected from ordinary blacks. As West explains, Du Bois's "...inability to immerse himself in black everyday life precluded his access to the distinctive black tragicomic sense and black encounter with the absurd. He certainly saw, analyzed, and empathized with black sadness, sorrow and suffering.... His own personal and intellectual distance lifted him above them even as he addressed their plight in his progressive writings" (West, 1994, 1967). I believe that this is a potentially unfair assessment of Du Bois. Du Bois spent his life working in Black institutions, living and researching in Black neighborhoods and working at a grassroots level with activist groups such as the National Association for Colored People. While aloof by nature, I am not convinced from his writings that he was as separated from everyday Black life to the degree suggested by West.

[4] In 1953 Du Bois, for example, wrote admiringly about Stalin: "Let all Negroes, Jews and Foreign-born, who have suffered in America from prejudice and intolerance, remember Joseph Stalin. This son of a slave in Georgia, as Commissar of Nationalities, fought prejudice and particularism and helped build the first modern state which outlawed race discrimination." See: "Joseph Stalin," March 7, 1953; microfilm reel no. 69, frame no. 748; W. E. B. Du Bois Papers, University of Massachusetts, Amherst. Quoted in Meyer Weinberg, editor *The World of W. E. B. Du Bois* (Westport, CT: Greenwood Press, 1992), p. 183. Also see: "On Stalin," *National Guardian*, March 16, 1953, reprinted in David Levering Lewis, editor, *W. E. B. Du Bois: A Reader* (New York: Henry Holt, 1995), pp. 796–797.

[5] See for example: "The Strivings of the Negro People," *Atlantic Monthly*, August 1897, Vol. LXXX, pp. 194–198; "The Study of Negro Problems," *Annals of the American Academy of Political and Social Science*, January 1898, Vol. XI, pp. 1–23; "The Negro and Crime," *Independent*, May 18, 1899, Vol. LI, pp. 1355–1357.

[6] See for example: *The Negroes of Farmville, Virginia: A Social Study*, U. S. Labor Department *Bulletin*, Vol. III, No. 14, January 1898 (Washington: Government Printing Office), pp. 1–38; and *The Negro in the Black Belt: Some Social Sketches: Bulletin of the Department of Labor*, Vol. IV, May 1899 (Washington: Government Printing Office), pp. 401–417.

[7] *The Suppression of the African Slave Trade to the United States of America, 1638–1870* (Cambridge: Harvard, 1897).

[8] *The Philadelphia Negro* (New York: Lippincott, 1899).

came to national attention in 1903 with the publication of what was to become his most well-known book *The Souls of Black Folk.*[9] The book included fourteen essays, nine of which had been previously published in magazines such as *The World's Work, The Dial, The Atlantic Monthly,* and *The Annals of the American Academy of Political and Social Science.* James Weldon Johnson, the gifted poet and novelist, and friend and colleague of Du Bois at the National Association for the Advancement of Colored People, described the book's impact as being "greater upon and within the Negro race than any other single book published in this country since *Uncle Tom's Cabin.*"[10]

David Levering Lewis has described *The Souls of Black Folk* as "one of those events epochally dividing history into a before and an after. Like fireworks going off in a cemetery,... an electrifying manifesto, mobilizing a people for bitter, prolonged struggle to win a place in history."[11]

The Souls of Black Folk did many things. It described the future of race issues in American culture more clearly than any other work from its period. Its assertion that, "the problem of the Twentieth Century is the problem of the color-line,"[12] remains perhaps the most prophetic statement made by a social scientist in the United States during the period prior to the First World War. The book brought to the attention of its readers important metaphors and images that would dominate the debate over race and culture in the twentieth century. The notion of a "Talented Tenth," an educated African-American elite who would act as a vanguard of leadership in the black community, was an idea that was revisited from a previous article.[13] While in retrospect, a seemingly obvious approach, the book in fact represented a powerful counter-

---

[9] *The Souls of Black Folk: Essays and Sketches* (Chicago: A. C. McClurg, 1903).

[10] Quoted by David Levering Lewis, *W. E. B. Du Bois: Biography of a Race, 1868–1919* (New York: Henry Holt and Company, 1993), p. 277.

[11] Ibid.

[12] The declaration was first publicly made by Du Bois while attending the Pan-African Association's conference in London in July of 1900. See: *Report of the Pan-African Conference, held on 23rd, 24th, and 25th July 1900, at Westminister Town Hall, Westminister, S. W.* [London]. Headquarters 61 and 62, Chancery Lane, W.C., London, England [1900], pp. 10-12 included as Document Number 1 (Forethought), pp. 7–8 of this book. Also note the placard from the Georgia Negro Exhibit that is illustrated on page 4 of this work.

[13] See: "The Talented Tenth." *The Negro Problem: A Series of Articles by Representative American Negroes of Today. Contributions by Booker T. Washington, W. E. Burghardt Du Bois, Paul Laurence Dunbar, Charles W. Chesnutt and others* (New York: James Pott), pp. 33–75.

argument and strategy for dealing with the assumption that black Americans were somehow inferior and needed to be led by the white mainstream, and more specifically, the Anglo-Saxon culture. The idea of African-Americans as being "gifted with second-sight," of possessing a "double-consciousness... of always looking at one's self through the eyes of others, of measuring one's soul by the tape of a world that looks on in amused contempt and pity," is perhaps the most famous image from the book. According to Du Bois, every black possessed "two souls, two thoughts, two unreconciled strivings, two warring ideals in one dark body; whose dogged strength alone keeps it from being torn asunder."[14] As David Levering Lewis has pointed out, the idea of double-consciousness was both revolutionary and mystical.[15] It was also a concept that was profoundly democratic and practical, one which through a process of evolution would make it possible "for a man to be both a Negro and an American, without being cursed and spit upon by his fellows, without having the doors of Opportunity closed roughly in his face."[16]

The major themes and images found in *The Souls of Black Folk* have been analyzed in detail by many different authors.[17] As already mentioned, the idea of the "color line" being the "problem of the twentieth century," the concept of the "Talented Tenth" and "double-consciousness" are three of these major themes. The book is also rightly cited as the seminal work calling for a rejection of the assimilationist model put forward by Booker T. Washington in his 1895 Atlanta Compromise speech.[18] Any of these points would probably have made the book significant, but there are other elements at work in it as well that need to have attention paid to them—many of them overlooked by scholars.

Charles Lemert, for example, has pointed out that *The Souls of Black Folk*, while widely recognized for its importance as a cultural and literary work, has been largely neglected in terms of its sociological

---

[14] Lewis, *op. cit.*, p. 282, makes the point that the idea of "double-consciousness" was not original to Du Bois, but shows up in the work of Goethe, Chesnutt, and Emerson.

[15] Lewis, *op. cit.*, p. 281. Lewis explains: "Because he dwelt equally in the mind and heart of his oppressor as in his own best psyche, the African-American embraced a vision of the commonweal at its best. But the gift was also double-edged—always potentially enervating—because the African-American only saw him/herself reflected from a white surface."

[16] See page 15 of this work for this quote.

[17] See for example: W. E. B. Du Bois, *The Souls of Black Folk*, edited by Henry Louis Gates Jr. and Terri Hume Oliver (New York: Norton, 1999).

[18] See Document Number 4, Chapter III, pp. 81–84 included in this work.

Advertisement for *The Souls of Black Folk* included in the June 1911 issue of *The Crisis* magazine.

dimensions.[19] I believe that his point is well taken, although I would extend his argument even further, maintaining that *The Souls of Black Folk* has been insufficiently appreciated as an historical study, as well as a pioneering work in personal biography, policy analysis, and even ethno-musicology. Such a claim may appear to be overstated, but I believe my point is demonstrated simply by looking at the subject matter of the book's chapters.

Chapter II, for example, "The Dawn of Freedom," is widely considered the most important early essay to appear on the history of the Freedman's Bureau, one that David Levering Lewis describes as "decades ahead of its time." Chapter IV, "On the Meaning of Progress," is a classic biographical essay describing the experience of a beginning teacher working in the impoverished schools of rural Tennessee. It can be looked at as a pioneering work in the field of Educational Sociology/Anthropology and Participant Observation. In this chapter, Du Bois describes his personal experience teaching for two summers in the hills of rural Tennessee, and then going back later to visit the place where he had taught nearly twenty years earlier. In doing so, he reflects on the lives of his students and their families, and in the context of their experience, on "the meaning of progress."

In Chapter V, "Of the Wings of Atalanta," Du Bois asks how the pursuit of wealth and commerce, rather than Truth, Beauty and Justice, was leading American culture and, more particularly the South, to lose its moral compass and bearing. Chapter VI, a discussion of the education of black Americans alludes to the idea of the "Talented Tenth" and Du Bois's belief that social and political advancement of African-Americans will only come through the education of its most talented and capable individuals.

Chapters VII and VIII is a thoughtful policy analysis of the conditions of the Negro Black Belt, in particular, Dougherty, Georgia. Published, like many of the chapters in *The Souls*, as a magazine article, it provided not only detailed descriptions of life in the Black Belt based on surveys, observations, and interviews, but even on a detailed photographic record of the region and its people.[20]

---

[19] See: Charles Lemert, Foreword to *The Souls of Black Folk* (Boulder, Colorado: Paradigm Publishers, 2004), pp. vii–viii; and Phil Zuckerman, editor, *The Social Theory of W. E. B. Du Bois* (Thousand Oaks, CA: Pine Forge Press, 2004).

[20] See Eugene F. Provenzo Jr., "The Souls of Black Folk," Photographs by A. Radclyffe Dugmore, text by W. E. B. DuBois, edited by Eugene F. Provenzo Jr. *Society*, Vol. 28, #5, July/August 1991, pp. 74–80.

Chapter IX looks at the function of prejudice in American culture and its consequences for African-Americans in terms of social and economic issues. As is so often the case in *The Souls of Black Folk*, Du Bois is prophetic in much of what he has to say. In the very first words of the chapter, for example, he outlines the significance of European and Colonial domination for world culture and the new century, which had just begun:

> The world-old phenomenon of the contact of diverse races of men is to have new exemplification during the new century. Indeed, the characteristic of our age is the contact of European civilization with the world's underdeveloped peoples. Whatever we may say of the results of such contact in the past, it certainly forms a chapter in human action not pleasant to look back upon. War, murder, slavery, extermination and debauchery,—this has again and again been the result of carrying civilization and the blessed gospel to the isles of the sea and the heathen without the law.[21]

One can see in a statement like this the first glimmerings of what would evolve, on the part of Du Bois, into a profound critique of Colonialism and the hegemony of European culture on world culture.

In Chapter X, "Of the Faith of the Fathers," Du Bois provides an analysis of the African-American church. He follows this in Chapter XI with an intensely personal reflection on the early death of his son Burghardt. Chapter XII is a bibliography of Alexander Crummell—one of the founders of the American Negro Academy—and a personal hero and mentor for Du Bois. Chapter XIII is a short story dealing with the consequences of racial prejudice, and Chapter XIV, "Of the Sorrow Songs," represents one the first careful analyses of Negro Spirituals and their cultural significance, and is arguably one of the most important essays written up until that time dealing with the significance of music in the cultural and social identity of a people.

Prophetic, eclectic, encyclopedic, and intensely personal, *The Souls of Black Folk* could uncritically be dismissed as a hodgepodge of random essays strung together to meet the needs of a Chicago publisher. In "The Afterthought" included at the end of the book, Du Bois speculated that his small volume might easily fall "still-born into the universe."[22] The book, however, was an immediate success, going into its third printing before the end of its first year of publication.[23] What explains the success

---

[21] See page 213 of this work for this quote.
[22] See page 343 of this work for this quote.
[23] Lewis, *op. cit.*, p. 291.

of the book? Why does it endure over a hundred years after its first publication?

I believe the answer to these questions lies in the book's imagination and its courageous stand. When he wrote *The Souls of Black Folk* Du Bois had been active as a scholar for nearly ten years. As Phil Zuckerman has pointed out, he was a pioneer in the field of Sociology—at a level that should have made him widely recognized as a founder of the field. In the ten or twelve years prior to the publication of *The Souls of Black Folk*, Du Bois, as much as any person up until that time, pioneered the fields of urban sociology, rural sociology, criminology, and religion. In addition, it is clear that he was already well on his way to becoming the first great social theorist of race.[24]

In *The Souls of Black Folk*, Du Bois clearly demonstrated the new models of thinking and research that make him, according to Zuckerman, a founding figure in the field of Sociology. For myself, Du Bois demonstrates a sociological imagination that goes well beyond his pioneering work in Sociology. Du Bois's great accomplishment is that he draws together, as an essentially interdisciplinary scholar (and arguably the first scholar of African-American Studies), the multiple and interwoven threads that represented black culture and society at the beginning of the twentieth century. In doing so, as the fine Hegelian scholar that he was, he created a synthesis.

He had actually done something similar just a few years before. In 1900, he had gone to Paris, where together with Thomas Calloway he placed on display "The Exhibit of American Negroes" for the 1900 Universal Exposition.[25] The exhibit, largely forgotten today, was an attempt to show the condition of black life and culture in the United States since the time of Emancipation. Du Bois described the materials sent to Paris as: "...an honest straightforward exhibit of a small nation of people, picturing their life and development without apology or gloss, and above all made by themselves. In a way this marks an era in the history of the Negroes of America."[26]

The exhibit had four purposes: first, it was concerned with showing the history of the American Negro; second, it attempted to describe "his present condition"; third, "his education"; and fourth "his literature."[27] In

---

[24] See the Introduction, pp. 1–17 to Phil Zuckerman, editor, *The Social Theory of W. E. B. Du Bois* (Thousand Oaks, California: Pine Forge Press, 2004).

[25] See the editors's forthcoming book on the Negro Exhibit at the 1900 Paris Exposition (Altamira Press, in press).

[26] William Edgar Burghardt Du Bois, "The American Negro at Paris," *The American Monthly Review of Reviews*, Vol. XXII, November 1900, #5, p. 577.

[27] Du Bois, "The American Negro at Paris," p. 577.

many regards, *The Souls of Black Folk* had the same purpose. Essentially, Du Bois was trying to describe the condition of African-Americans at the dawn of the new century. He attempted to understand through a critical sociological and cultural lens the meaning of being black in the United States.

As an act of sociological and cultural imagination Du Bois did many things that were unique in *The Souls of Black Folk*. Some were small things that had a cumulative effect. At the beginning of each chapter, for example, he employed the device of pairing a few lines of Negro spiritual with a verse of European poetry by figures such as Browning or Tennyson. As David Levering Lewis has explained: "He twined them in this manner in order to advance the then-unprecedented notion of the creative parity and complementarity of white folk and black folk alike. Du Bois meant the cultural symbolism of these double epigraphs to be profoundly subversive of the cultural hierarchy of his time."[28] In the brief passages of music included at the beginning of each chapter, and in Chapter XIV where he examined the cultural meaning of the "sorrow songs," Du Bois gave voice to a people whose voices—at least in the venue of contemporary writing—had been largely misrepresented or ignored.

Du Bois's approach in *The Souls of Black Folk* combined passionate argument and reasoning with historical, sociological, and cultural analysis in the same text. His descriptions of black leadership in the United States, combined with his personal experience and perceptions, created a voice that was unlike any that had spoken before within the African-American community.

This "gift" of Du Bois to his people, and to the larger American consciousness, was further distinguished by its extraordinary courage. Essentially, Du Bois used the book not only to challenge traditional ideas about the Black experience, but to challenge the foundation of African-American leadership—specifically Booker T. Washington and the "Tuskegee Machine."

The story is well-known and is played out in Chapter III, in *The Souls of Black Folk*, "Of Mr. Booker T. Washington and Others." After a somewhat hesitant embrace of Washington's "Atlanta Exposition Speech" (eventually known as the "Atlanta Compromise"), Du Bois rejected what James Anderson has described as "the logical extension of an ideology that rejected black political power while recognizing that the

---

[28] Lewis, *op. cit.*, p. 278.

South's agricultural economy rested on the backs of black agricultural workers."[29]

Specifically, in *The Souls of Black Folk* Du Bois argues that as a result of Washington's policies three things were happening to African-Americans: 1. they were losing political power, 2. they were losing their civil rights, and 3. they were increasingly losing access to higher education. According to Du Bois, these developments were:

> ...not, to be sure, direct results of Mr. Washington's teachings; but his propaganda has, without a shadow of doubt, helped their speedier accomplishment. The question then comes: Is it possible, and probable, that nine millions of men can make effective progress in economic lines if they are deprived of political rights, made a servile caste, and allowed only the most meagre chance for developing their exceptional men? If history and reason give any distinct answer to these questions, it is an emphatic *No*.

Washington, argued Du Bois, was confronted by a triple paradox:

> 1. He is striving nobly to make Negro artisans business men and property-owners; but it is utterly impossible, under modern competitive methods, for workingmen and property-owners to defend their rights and exist without the right of suffrage.
> 2. He insists on thrift and self-respect, but at the same time counsels a silent submission to civic inferiority such as is bound to sap the manhood of any race in the long run.
> 3. He advocates common-school and industrial training, and depreciates institutions of higher learning; but neither the Negro common-schools, nor Tuskegee itself, could remain open a day were it not for teachers trained in Negro colleges, or trained by their graduates.

Du Bois argues that American Blacks needed to strive for the rights they were being denied. As he explained at the conclusion of Chapter III:

> By every civilized and peaceful method we must strive for the rights which the world accords to men, clinging unwaveringly to those great words which the sons of the Fathers would fain forget: "We hold these truths to be self-evident: That all men are created equal; that they are endowed by their Creator with certain unalienable rights; that among these are life, liberty, and the pursuit of happiness."[30]

---

[29] James Anderson, *The Education of Blacks in the South* (Chapel Hill, NC: University of North Carolina Press, 1988), p. 44.

[30] See page 80 of this work for this quote.

This represents the second aspect of Du Bois's accomplishment in *The Souls of Black Folk*—his willingness to confront the entrenched system of power that backed Booker T. Washington and the Tuskegee Machine. In doing so, he performed an act of profound courage—one that almost certainly made his own life more difficult and challenging. Like Cordelia in *King Lear*, he suffered in his personal life from telling the truth, even though he did so in order to advance a more important end—the freedom of his people.

In summary, *The Souls of Black Folk* is a revolutionary work. It is such because of its methods and the meaning of its words as well as the imagination and courage of its author. As such, it deserves our attention as a pivotal document in American intellectual and social history.

The Illustrated, Annotated, Documentary Edition that follows is intended to provide the reader with a broader foundation for reading and interpreting Du Bois's masterpiece. It is hoped that important new dimensions are brought to the reader about Du Bois and his work as a scholar and social and cultural leader. I hope it is a work that Du Bois would be pleased with—one which advances our understanding of race and culture in American society.

Fifty Years After

Late in the nineteenth century, there developed in Chicago a movement to build a literary and publishing center in the Mid-west. [1] The Brownes, father and son, editors for A. C. McClurg & Company, began looking about for young and unknown authors. I had just published my first two books: a history of the *Suppression of the African Slave Trade to America,* which appeared as the first volume of the new Harvard Historical Studies in 1896. [2] My *Philadelphia Negro* was published by the University of Pennsylvania in 1899. [3] I had also written a few essays which had been accepted by the *Atlantic Monthly,* the *Dial* and some other periodicals. [4]

The McClurg editors wrote me about 1900, asking if I did not have material for a book which they could consider. I was at the time just embarking at Atlanta University on what I hoped to make my life work; it was to be a broad and exhaustive study of the Negro Problem in the United States. I outlined this project to the editors, but they naturally wanted something more limited and aimed at a popular audience. I therefore undertook to assemble some of my published and unpublished essays, adding a few new ones.

They liked the proposed book and offered publication. I hesitated because I was sure that with more time and thought I could do a better job; in so many respects this was incomplete and unsatisfactory. But finally I plucked up courage and sent the manuscript off, and fifty years ago, *The Souls of Black Folk* appeared. It was well received and for the next generation it ran into a number of editions.

Several times I planned to revise the book and bring it abreast of my own thought and to answer criticism. But I hesitated and finally decided to leave the book as first printed, as a monument to what I thought and felt in 1903. I hoped in other books to set down changes of fact and reaction.

---

[1] Preface to the Jubilee Edition of *The Souls of Black Folk*, published in 1953 by the Blue Heron Press—the last edition to appear prior to this edition in the Premier Americana Series.

[2] *The Suppression of the African Slave Trade to America to the United States of America, 1638-1870: Harvard Historical Studies Number 1* (1896).

[3] *The Philadelphia Negro: A Social Study* (Philadelphia, PA: University of Pennsylvania, 1899).

[4] These included "The Evolution of Negro Leadership," *Dial*, 31 (July 16, 1901): 53–55.

In the present edition I have clung to this decision, and my thoughts appear again as then written. I have made less than a half-dozen alterations in word or phrase and then not to change my thought as previously set down but to avoid any possible misunderstanding today of what I meant to say yesterday.[5]

As I reread these messages of more than half a century ago, I sense two matters which are not so much omission on my part as indications of what I then did not know or did not realize: one is the influence of Freud and his coworkers in their study of psychology; the other is the tremendous impact on the modern world of Karl Marx.

As a student of James, Santayana and Royce, I was not unprepared for the revolution in psychology which the Twentieth Century has brought; but *The Souls of Black Folk* does not adequately allow for unconscious thought and the cake of custom in the growth and influence of race prejudice.

My college training did not altogether omit Karl Marx. He was mentioned at Harvard and taken into account in Berlin. It was not omission but lack of proper emphasis or comprehension among my teachers of the revolution in thought and action which Marx meant. So perhaps I might end this retrospect simply by saying: I still think today as yesterday that the color fine is a great problem of this century. But today I see more clearly than yesterday that back of the problem of race and color, lies a greater problem which both obscures and implements it: and that is the fact that so many civilized persons are willing to live in comfort even if the price of this is poverty, ignorance and disease of the majority of their fellowmen; that to maintain this privilege men have waged war until today war tends to become universal and continuous, and the excuse for this war continues largely to be color and race.

W. E. B. Du Bois

---

[5] Du Bois's changes in the 1953 Blue Heron edition largely focused on removing what could be viewed as potentially anti-Semitic references resulting from his use of "Jews" as a synonym for immigrants or business people. Less than ten changes were made in the text that addressed this and other problems.

The Sorrow Songs

"I walk through the churchyard
"To lay this body down
"I know moon-rise, I know star-rise;
"I walk in the moonlight, I walk in the star-light;
"I'll lie in the grave and stretch out my arms,
"I'll go to judgment in the evening of the day
"And my soul and thy soul shall meet that day
"When I lay this body down."

Negro Song.

They that walked in darkness sang songs in the olden days — Sorrow Songs — for they were weary at heart. And so before each thought that I have written I have set a phrase, a haunting echo of these weird old songs in which the soul of the black slave spoke to men. Ever since I was a child these songs have stirred me strangely. They came to me out of the South unknown to me, one by one, and yet at once I knew them as of me and of mine. Then in after years when I came to Nashville I saw the great temple builded of these songs towering over the pale city. To me

Manuscript draft of Chapter XIV, "The Sorrow Songs," from *The Souls of Black Folk.* Courtesy of the Special Collections and Archives, W .E. B. Du Bois Library, University of Massachusetts, Amherst, and David Graham Du Bois.

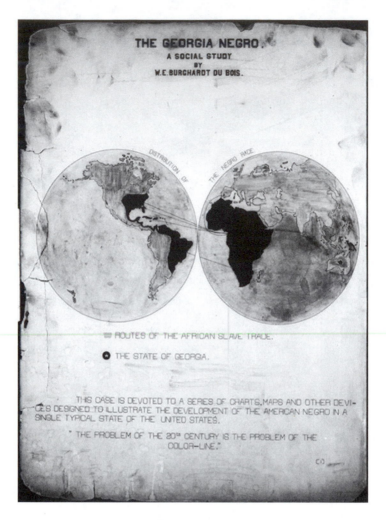

The first page of the Exhibit of the Georgia Negro, compiled by Du Bois and his students at Atlanta University for the Exhibit of the American Negroes at the 1900 Paris International Exposition. Courtesy of the Library of Congress. At the base of the page is the quote: "The problem of the 20th century is the problem of the color-line"—certainly the most important quote from *The Souls of Black Folk* and perhaps the most significant single quote in African-American history. The declaration was first publicly made by Du Bois while attending the Pan-African Association's conference in London in July of 1900 where he made the address "To the Nations of the World" (see "Documentary Source Number 1 on pages 7–8 of this work). Immediately following this conference Du Bois went on to Paris where he supervised the mounting of the Exhibit of American Negroes in Paris. The quote is included in the "Forethought" and Chapter 2 of *The Souls of Black Folk*.

The Forethought

Herein lie buried many things which if read with patience may show the strange meaning of being black here at the dawning of the twentieth century. This meaning is not without interest to you, Gentle Reader; for the problem of the twentieth century is the problem of the color line.[1] I pray you, then, receive my little book in all charity, studying my words with me, forgiving mistake and foible for sake of the faith and passion that is in me, and seeking the grain of truth hidden there.

I have sought here to sketch, in vague, uncertain outline, the spiritual world in which ten thousand thousand Americans live and strive. First, in two chapters I have tried to show what Emancipation meant to them, and what was its aftermath. In a third chapter I have pointed out the slow rise of personal leadership, and criticized candidly the leader[2] who bears the chief burden of his race today. Then, in two other chapters I have sketched in swift outline the two worlds within and without the Veil, and thus have come to the central problem of training men for life. Venturing now into deeper detail, I have in two chapters studied the struggles of the massed millions of the black peasantry, and in another have sought to make clear the present relations of the sons of master and man. Leaving, then, the white world, I have stepped within the Veil,[3] raising it that you may view faintly its deeper recesses,—the meaning of its religion, the passion of its human sorrow, and the struggle of its greater souls. All this I have ended with a tale twice told but seldom written, and a chapter of song.

Some of these thoughts of mine have seen the light before in other guise. For kindly consenting to their republication here, in altered and extended form, I must thank the publishers of the *Atlantic Monthly*, *The World's Work*, *The Dial*, *The New World*, and the *Annals of the American Academy of Political and Social Science*. Before each chapter, as now printed, stands a bar of the Sorrow Songs,[4]—some echo of haunting melody from the only American music which welled up from black souls

---

[1] See the caption on the preceding page for an explanation of the origins of this quote. Du Bois's July 1900 pamphlet "To the Nations of the World," wherein he first used this quote, is included in its entirety in the documents section at the conclusion of this work (pages 7–8).

[2] The "leader" whom Du Bois is referring to in this case is Booker T. Washington.

[3] This is a reference to *Exodus* 34:33–35 and *Isaiah* 25:7 which prophesizes that God will destroy "the veil that is spread over all nations."

[4] Du Bois is referring to the traditional black spiritual or religious folksong.

in the dark past. And, finally, need I add that I who speak here am bone of the bone and flesh of the flesh of them that live within the Veil?[5]

W.E.B Du B.

ATLANTA, GA., FEB. 1, 1903.

Title header for the editorial section "Along the Color Line" *The Crisis* magazine, August 1912, written by W. E. B. Du Bois.

---

[5] A reference to *Genesis* 2:23 where Adams says of Eve: "This at last is bone of my bone and flesh of my flesh; she shall be called Woman because she was taken out of Man."

Document Number 1 ("Forethought")

The following address made by W. E. B. Du Bois at the Pan-African Conference held in London in July 1900 is the first known instance of Du Bois publicly using the phrase "The problem of the twentieth century is the problem of the colour line,..." The address is remarkably prophetic and indicative of issues and themes of global racism and postcolonialism that Du Bois would continue to address throughout his career.

*   *   *

To the Nations of the World[6]

In the metropolis of the modern world, in this the closing year of the nineteenth century, there has been assembled a congress of men and women of African blood, to deliberate solemnly upon the present situation and outlook of the darker races of mankind. The problem of the twentieth century is the problem of the colour line, the question as to how far differences of race, which show themselves chiefly in the colour of the skin and the texture of the hair, are going to be made, hereafter, the basis of denying to over half the world the right of sharing to their utmost ability the opportunities and privileges of modern civilisation.

To be sure, the darker races are today the least advanced in culture according to European standards. This has not, however, always been the case in the past, and certainly the world's history, both ancient and modern, has given many instances of no despicable ability and capacity among the blackest races of men.

In any case, the modern world must needs remember that in this age, when the ends of the world are being brought so near together, the millions of black men in Africa, America, and the Islands of the Sea, not to speak of the brown and yellow myriads elsewhere, are bound to have great influence upon the world in the future, by reason of sheer numbers and physical contact. If now the world of culture bends itself towards giving Negroes and other dark men the largest and broadest opportunity for education and self-development, then this contact and influence is bound to have a beneficial effect upon the world and hasten human progress. But if, by reason of carelessness, prejudice, greed, and injustice, the black world is to be exploited and ravished and degraded, the results must be deplorable, if not fatal, not simply to them, but to the high ideals of justice; freedom, and culture which a thousand years of Christian civilisation have held before Europe.

---

[6] Source: *Report of the Pan-African Conference, held on 23rd, 24th, and 25th July 1900, at Westminister Town Hall, Westminister, S. W.* [London]. Headquarters 61 and 62, Chancery Lane, W.C., London, England [1900], pp. 10–12.

And now, therefore, to these ideals of civilisation, to the broader humanity of the followers of the Prince of Peace, we, the men and women of Africa in world congress assembled, do now solemnly appeal:

Let the world take no backward step in that slow but sure progress which has successively refused to let the spirit of class, of caste, of privilege, or of birth, debar from like liberty and the pursuit of happiness a striving human soul.

Let not mere colour or race be a feature of distinction drawn between white and black men, regardless of worth or ability.

Let not the natives of Africa be sacrificed to the greed of gold, their liberties taken away, their family life debauched, their just aspirations repressed, and avenues of advancement and culture taken from them.

Let not the cloak of Christian missionary enterprise be allowed in the future, as so often in the past, to hide the ruthless economic exploitation and political downfall of less developed nations, whose chief fault has been reliance on the plighted faith of the Christian church.

Let the British nation, the first modern champion of Negro freedom, hasten to crown the work of Wilberforce, and Clarkson, and Buxton, and, Sharpe. Bishop Colenso, and Livingstone, and give, as soon as practicable, the rights of responsible government to the black colonies of Africa and the West Indies.

Let not the spirit of Garrison, Phillips, and Douglas wholly die out in America: may the conscience of a great nation rise and rebuke all dishonesty and unrighteous oppression toward the American Negro, and grant to him the right of franchise, security of person and property, and generous recognition of the great work he has accomplished in a generation toward raising nine millions of human beings from slavery to manhood.

Let the German Empire, and the French Republic, true to their great past, remember that the true worth of colonies lies in their prosperity and progress, and that justice, impartial alike to black and white, is the first element of prosperity.

Let the Congo Free State become a great central Negro State of the world, and let its prosperity be counted, not simply in cash and commerce, but in the happiness and true advancement of its black people.

Let the nations of the World respect the integrity and independence of the free Negro States of Abyssinia, Liberia, Hayti, etc., and let the inhabitants of these States, the independent tribes of Africa, the Negroes of the West Indies and America, and the black subjects of all nations take courage, strive ceaselessly, and fight bravely, that they may prove to the world their incontestable right to be counted among the great brotherhood of mankind.

Thus we appeal with boldness and confidence to the Great Powers of the civilised world, trusting in the wide spirit of humanity, and the deep sense of justice of our age, for a generous recognition of the righteousness of our cause.

ALEXANDER WALTERS (Bishop), President, Pan African Association.
HENRY B. BROWN, Vice-President.
H. SYLVESTER WILLIAMS, General Secretary.
W. E. BURGHARDT DU Bois, Chairman Committee on Address.

W. E. B. Du Bois, portrait by J. E. Purdy. Courtesy of the Library of Congress (LC-USZ62-28485). This photograph was taken in 1904, just shortly after the publication of *The Souls of Black Folk*.

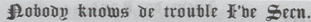

Nobody knows de trouble I've Seen.

(This song was a favorite in the Sea Islands. Once when there had been a good deal of ill feeling excited, and trouble was apprehended, owing to the uncertain action of the Government in regard to the confiscated lands on the Sea Islands, Gen. Howard was called upon to address the colored people earnestly. To prepare them to listen, he asked them to sing. Immediately an old woman on the outskirts of the meeting began "Nobody knows the trouble I've seen," and the whole audience joined in. The General was so affected by the plaintive melody, that he found it difficult to maintain his official dignity.)

Oh, no-bod-y knows de trou-ble I've seen, No-bod-y knows but

Je-sus, Nobod-y knows de trouble I've seen. Glory Hal-le-lu-jah!

Some-times I'm up, sometimes I'm down; Oh, yes, Lord;
Al-though you see me goin' 'long so, Oh, yes, Lord;

Some-times I'm al-most to de groun', Oh, yes, Lord.
I have my tri-als here be-low, Oh, yes, Lord.

2 One day when I was walkin' along, Oh yes, Lord—
    De element opened, an' de Love came down, Oh yes, &c.
    I never shall forget dat day, Oh yes, &c.
    When Jesus washed my sins away, Oh yes, &c.
CHO.—Oh, nobody knows de trouble I've seen, &c.

"Nobody Knows the Trouble I've Seen," as included in *Religious Folk Songs of the Negro: As Sung on the Plantations* (Hampton, VA: Hampton Institute Press, 1909), p. 9.

I

Of Our Spiritual Strivings

O water, voice of my heart, crying in the sand,
    All night long crying with a mournful cry,
As I lie and listen, and cannot understand
    The voice of my heart in my side or the voice of the sea,
O water, crying for rest, is it I, is it I?
    All night long the water is crying to me.

Unresting water, there shall never be rest
    Till the last moon droop and the last tide fail,
And the fire of the end begin to burn in the west;
      And the heart shall be weary and wonder and cry like the sea,
    All life long crying without avail,
    As the water all night long is crying to me.

ARTHUR SYMONS.[1]

Between me and the other world there is ever an unasked question: unasked by some through feelings of delicacy; by others through the difficulty of rightly framing it. All, nevertheless, flutter round it. They approach me in a half-hesitant sort of way, eye me curiously or compassionately, and then instead of saying directly How does it feel to be a problem? They say, I know an excellent colored man in my town; or I fought at Mechanicsville;[2] or Do not these Southern outrages make your blood boil? At these I smile, or am interested, or reduce the boiling to a simmer, as the occasion may require. To the real question, How does it feel to be a problem? I answer seldom a word.

---

[1] "O water, voice of my heart, crying in the sand,"… This is the complete text of the poem, "The Crying of Water," by the Welsh poet Arthur Symons (1865–1945). As pointed out by David Levering Lewis, Du Bois introduces each chapter of *The Souls of Black Folk* with the lines of a Western poet contrasted against the content of a black spiritual—an implicit recognition of the integrity and validity of each work.

[2] Mechanicsville: The site of a June 1862 Civil War battle; located Northeast of Richmond, Virginia.

And yet, being a problem is a strange experience,—peculiar even for one who has never been anything else, save perhaps in babyhood and in Europe. It is in the early days of rollicking boyhood that the revelation first bursts upon one, all in a day, as it were. I remember well when the shadow swept across me. I was a little thing, away up in the hills of New England, where the dark Housatonic[3] winds between Hoosac and Taghkanic to the sea. In a wee wooden schoolhouse, something put it into the boys' and girls' heads to buy gorgeous visiting-cards—ten cents a package—and exchange. The exchange was merry, till one girl, a tall newcomer, refused my card,—refused it peremptorily, with a glance. Then it dawned upon me with a certain suddenness that I was different from the others; or like, mayhap, in heart and life and longing, but shut out from their world by a vast veil. I had thereafter no desire to tear down that veil, to creep through; I held all beyond it in common contempt, and lived above it in a region of blue sky and great wandering shadows. That sky was bluest when I could beat my mates at examination-time, or beat them at a foot-race, or even beat their stringy heads. Alas, with the years all this fine contempt began to fade; for the words I longed for, and all their dazzling opportunities, were theirs, not mine. But they should not keep these prizes, I said; some, all, I would wrest from them. Just how I would do it I could never decide: by reading law, by healing the sick, by telling the wonderful tales that swam in my head,—some way. With other black boys the strife was not so fiercely sunny: Their youth shrunk into tasteless sycophancy, or into silent hatred of the pale world about them and mocking distrust of everything white; or wasted itself in a bitter cry, Why did God make me an outcast and a stranger in mine own house? The shades of the prison-house closed round about us all; walls strait and stubborn to the whitest, but relentlessly narrow, tall, and unscalable to sons of night who must plod darkly on in resignation, or beat unavailing palms against the stone, or steadily, half hopelessly, watch the streak of blue above.

After the Egyptian and Indian, the Greek and Roman, the Teuton and Mongolian, the Negro is a sort of seventh son,[4] born with a veil and gifted with second-sight in this American world,—a world which yields him no true self-consciousness, but only lets him see himself

---

[3] The Housatonic River runs through Du Bois's hometown of Great Barrington, Massachusetts. Du Bois lived in Great Barrington until 1885 when his mother died in late March at the age of fifty-four. The following fall he began his Freshman year at at Fisk University in Nashville, Tennessee.

[4] In black folklore seventh sons are believed to have supernatural powers, including the ability to see the future and to perceive individuals from the spirit world.

"Am I Not a Man and a Brother?" This engraving of a slave in chains was published in 1835 as the header for a broadside on which appeared John Greenleaf Whittier's poem "My Countrymen in Chains!" The illustration and the motto date back to the Abolitionist movement in eighteenth-century England. In 1787, the Quaker-led "Society for Effecting the Abolition of the Slave Trade" met in London and a committee was charged with preparing the design for a "Seal." Later that year, the design and motto illustrated above was approved by the society. Josiah Wedgewood, the pottery manufacturer, who was a member of the Society, manufactured a jasper-ware cameo/medallion of the image. In 1788, a shipment of the cameos was sent to Benjamin Franklin in Philadelphia. Courtesy of the Library of Congress. The image was published in many different versions prior to the Civil War.

Mountain road in the Berkshires, c. 1908. Detroit Publishing Company. Courtesy of the Library of Congress. Du Bois's youth was spent in Great Barrington, Massachusetts, at the edge of the Berkshire Mountains.

through the revelation of the other world. It is a peculiar sensation, this double-consciousness, this sense of always looking at one's self through the eyes of others, of measuring one's soul by the tape of a world that looks on in amused contempt and pity. One ever feels his twoness,—an American, a Negro; two souls, two thoughts, two unreconciled strivings; two warring ideals in one dark body, whose dogged strength alone keeps it from being torn asunder. [5]

The history of the American Negro is the history of this strife,—this longing to attain self-conscious manhood, to merge his double self into a better and truer self. In this merging he wishes neither of the older selves to be lost. He would not Africanize America, for America has too much to teach the world and Africa. He would not bleach his Negro soul in a flood of white Americanism, for he knows that Negro blood has a

---

[5] The idea of "double-consciousness" is among the most important ideas developed by Du Bois in *The Souls of Black Folk*. Its significance is analyzed in detail in Dickson D. Bruce Jr.'s, "W.E.B. Du Bois and the Idea of Double Consciousness," *American Literature: A Journal of Literary History, Criticism, and Bibliography*, 64, #2, (June 1992), 299–309.

message for the world. He simply wishes to make it possible for a man to be both a Negro and an American, without being cursed and spit upon by his fellows, without having the doors of Opportunity closed roughly in his face.

This, then, is the end of his striving: to be a coworker in the kingdom of culture, to escape both death and isolation, to husband and use his best powers and his latent genius. These powers of body and mind have in the past been strangely wasted, dispersed, or forgotten. The shadow of a mighty Negro past flits through the tale of Ethiopia the Shadowy and of Egypt the Sphinx. Through history, the powers of single black men flash here and there like falling stars, and die sometimes before the world has rightly gauged their brightness. Here in America, in the few days since Emancipation, the black man's turning hither and thither in hesitant and doubtful striving has often made his very strength to lose effectiveness, to seem like absence of power, like weakness. And yet it is not weakness, —it is the contradiction of double aims. The double-aimed struggle of the black artisan—on the one hand to escape white contempt for a nation of black artisan—on the one hand to escape white contempt for a nation of mere hewers of wood and drawers of water, and on the other hand to plough and nail and dig for a poverty-stricken horde—could only result in making him a poor craftsman, for he had but half a heart in either cause. By the poverty and ignorance of his people, the Negro minister or doctor was tempted toward quackery and demagogy; and by the criticism of the other world, toward ideals that made him ashamed of his lowly tasks. The would-be black *savant* was confronted by the paradox that the knowledge his people needed was a twice-told tale to his white neighbors, while the knowledge which would teach the white world was Greek to his own flesh and blood. The innate love of harmony and beauty that set the ruder souls of his people a-dancing and a-singing raised but confusion and doubt in the soul of the black artist; for the beauty revealed to him was the soul-beauty of a race which his larger audience despised, and he could not articulate the message of another people. This waste of double aims, this seeking to satisfy two unreconciled ideals, has wrought sad havoc with the courage and faith and deeds of ten thousand thousand people,—has sent them often wooing false gods and invoking false means of salvation, and at times has even seemed about to make them ashamed of themselves.

Away back in the days of bondage they thought to see in one divine event the end of all doubt and disappointment; few men ever worshipped Freedom with half such unquestioning faith as did the American Negro for two centuries. To him, so far as he thought and dreamed, slavery was indeed the sum of all villainies, the cause of all sorrow, the root of all prejudice; Emancipation was the key to a promised land of sweeter

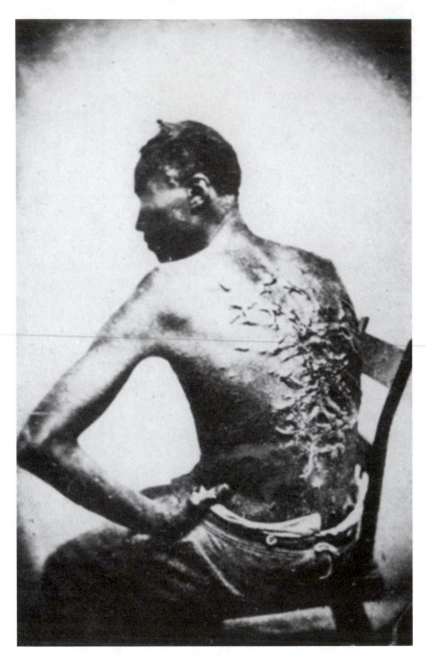

"Overseer Artayou Carrier whipped me. I was two months in bed sore from the whipping. My master come after I was whipped; he discharged the overseer. The very words of poor Peter, taken as he sat for his picture." Baton Rouge, Louisiana, April 2, 1863. Photograph by Matthew Brady. Courtesy of the National Archives and Records Administration.

beauty than ever stretched before the eyes of wearied Israelites. In song and exhortation swelled one refrain—Liberty; in his tears and curses the God he implored had Freedom in his right hand. At last it came,—suddenly, fearfully, like a dream. With one wild carnival of blood and passion came the message in his own plaintive cadences:—

> "Shout, O children!
> Shout, you're free!
> For God has bought your liberty!"[6]

Years have passed away since then,—ten, twenty, forty; forty years of national life, forty years of renewal and development, and yet the swarthy spectre sits in its accustomed seat at the Nation's feast. In vain do we cry to this our vastest social problem:—

> "Take any shape but that, and my firm nerves
> Shall never tremble!"[7]

The Nation has not yet found peace from its sins; the freedman has not yet found in freedom his promised land. Whatever of good may have come in these years of change, the shadow of a deep disappointment rests upon the Negro people,—a disappointment all the more bitter because the unattained ideal was unbounded save by the simple ignorance of a lowly people.

The first decade was merely a prolongation of the vain search for freedom, the boon that seemed ever barely to elude their grasp,—like a tantalizing will-o'-the-wisp, maddening and misleading the headless host. The holocaust of war, the terrors of the Ku-Klux Klan, [8] the lies of

---

[6] These lines are taken from the traditional African American spiritual "Shout O Children."

[7] Macbeth Act 3, Scene 4, Lines 102–103. Du Bois is representing American society as guilty and blood-stained, like the main character in Shakespeare's play.

[8] The Ku Klux Klan was founded in 1865 in Pulaski, Tennessee. The Klan terrorized both blacks and Republican whites who opposed the tradition of white supremacy and power. Members of the organization wore white robes and masks and burned crosses as part of their campaign of assault, murder, and rape. In 1871 violence perpetrated by the Klan was so great that Republicans in Congress authorized President Ulysses S. Grant to use federal troops to subdue the Klan. Within a few years the power of the Klan was broken. A generation later, however, the Klan's power was revived, and it once again became a powerful force at the beginning of the twentieth century.

carpet-baggers, advice of friends and foes, left the bewildered serf with no new watchword beyond the old cry for freedom. As the time flew, however, he began to grasp a new idea. The ideal of liberty demanded for its attainment powerful means, and these the Fifteenth Amendment[9] gave him. The ballot, which before he had looked upon as a visible sign of freedom, he now regarded as the chief means of gaining and perfecting the liberty with which war had partially endowed him. And why not? Had not votes made war and emancipated millions? Had not votes enfranchised the freedmen? Was anything impossible to a power that had done all this? A million black men started with renewed zeal to vote themselves into the kingdom. So the decade flew away, the revolution of 1876 came, and left the half-free serf weary, wondering, but still inspired. Slowly but steadily, in the following years, a new vision began gradually to replace the dream of political power,—a powerful movement, the rise of another ideal to guide the unguided, another pillar of fire by night after a clouded day. It was the ideal of "book-learning"; the curiosity, born of compulsory ignorance, to know and test the power of the cabalistic letters of the white man, the longing to know. Here at last seemed to have been discovered the mountain path to Canaan; longer than the highway of Emancipation and law, steep and rugged, but straight, leading to heights high enough to overlook life.

Up the new path the advance guard toiled, slowly, heavily, doggedly; only those who have watched and guided the faltering feet, the misty minds, the dull understandings, of the dark pupils of these schools know how faithfully, how piteously, this people strove to learn. It was weary work. The cold statistician wrote down the inches of progress here and there, noted also where here and there a foot had slipped or someone had fallen. To the tired climbers, the horizon was ever dark, the mists were often cold, the Canaan was always dim and far away. If, however, the vistas disclosed as yet no goal, no resting-place, little but flattery and criticism, the journey at least gave leisure for reflection and self-examination; it changed the child of Emancipation to the youth with dawning self-consciousness, self-realization, self-respect. In those sombre forests of his striving his own soul rose before him, and he saw himself,—darkly as through a veil; and yet he saw in himself some faint revelation of his power, of his mission. He began to have a dim feeling

---

[9] The XV Amendment to the Constitution was ratified March 10, 1870. It grants voting to all citizens, stating specifically: "Section 1. The right of citizens of the United States to vote shall not be denied or abridged by the United States or by any State on account of race, color, or previous condition of servitude. Section 2. The Congress shall have power to enforce this article by appropriate legislation."

that, to attain his place in the world, he must be himself, and not another. For the first time he sought to analyze the burden he bore upon his back, that dead-weight of social degradation partially masked behind a half-named Negro problem. He felt his poverty; without a cent, without a home, without land, tools, or savings, he had entered into competition with rich, landed, skilled neighbors. To be a poor man is hard, but to be a poor race in a land of dollars is the very bottom of hardships. He felt the weight of his ignorance,—not simply of letters, but of life, of business, of the humanities; the accumulated sloth and shirking and awkwardness of decades and centuries shackled his hands and feet. Nor was his burden all poverty and ignorance. The red stain of bastardy, which two centuries of systematic legal defilement of Negro women had stamped upon his race, meant, not only the loss of ancient African chastity, but also the hereditary weight of a mass of corruption from white adulterers, threatening almost the obliteration of the Negro home.

A people thus handicapped ought not to be asked to race with the world, but rather allowed to give all its time and thought to its own social problems. But alas! while sociologists gleefully count his bastards and his prostitutes, the very soul of the toiling, sweating black man is darkened by the shadow of a vast despair. Men call the shadow prejudice, and learnedly explain it as the natural defence of culture against barbarism, learning against ignorance, purity against crime, the "higher" against the "lower" races. To which the Negro cries Amen! And swears that to so much of this strange prejudice as is founded on just homage to civilization, culture, righteousness, and progress, he humbly bows and meekly does obeisance. But before that nameless prejudice that leaps beyond all this he stands helpless, dismayed, and well-nigh speechless; before that personal disrespect and mockery, the ridicule and systematic humiliation, the distortion of fact and wanton license of fancy, the cynical ignoring of the better and the boisterous welcoming of the worse, the all-pervading desire to inculcate disdain for everything black, from Toussaint to the devil,—before this there rises a sickening despair that would disarm and discourage any nation save that black host to whom "discouragement" is an unwritten word.

But the facing of so vast a prejudice could not but bring the inevitable self-questioning, self-disparagement, and lowering of ideals which ever accompany repression and breed in an atmosphere of contempt and hate. Whisperings and portents came home upon the four winds: Lo! we are diseased and dying, cried the dark hosts; we cannot write, our voting is vain; what need of education, since we must always cook and serve? And the Nation echoed and enforced this self-criticism, saying: Be content to be servants, and nothing more; what need of higher culture for half-men? Away with the black man's ballot, by force or

"Two members of the Ku-Klux-Klan in their disguises." *Harper's Weekly*, December 19, 1868. In April of 1871 Congress passed the Ku Klux Act which gave the president the right to suspend the writ of habeas corpus in counties where disturbances occurred. In doing so, the Klan was effectively eliminated as a political force in the United States.

"Oh Carry Me Back to Ole Virginny," Printed by Robertson, Seibert & Shearman, New York, c. 1859. Courtesy of the Library of Congress. Slavery was often depicted prior to the Civil War as being far more benevolent than is demonstrated by the historical evidence.

fraud,—and behold the suicide of a race! Nevertheless, out of the evil came something of good,—the more careful adjustment of education to real life, the clearer perception of the Negroes' social responsibilities, and the sobering realization of the meaning of progress.

So dawned the time of *Sturm und Drang*: storm and stress to-day rocks our little boat on the mad waters of the world-sea; there is within and without the sound of conflict, the burning of body and rending of soul; inspiration strives with doubt, and faith with vain questionings. The bright ideals of the past,—physical freedom, political power, the training of brains and the training of hands,—all these in turn have waxed and waned, until even the last grows dim and overcast. Are they all wrong,— all false? No, not that, but each alone was over-simple and incomplete,— the dreams of a credulous race-childhood, or the fond imaginings of the other world which does not know and does not want to know our power. To be really true, all these ideals must be melted and welded into one. The training of the schools we need to-day more than ever,—the training of deft hands, quick eyes and ears, and above all the broader, deeper, higher culture of gifted minds and pure hearts. The power of the ballot we need in sheer self-defence,—else what shall save us from a second slavery? Freedom, too, the long-sought, we still seek,—the freedom of life and limb, the freedom to work and think, the freedom to love and aspire. Work, culture, liberty,—all these we need, not singly but together,

"Worse than Slavery." Cartoon by Thomas Nast, *Harper's Weekly*, October 24, 1874.

not successively but together, each growing and aiding each, and all striving toward that vaster ideal that swims before the Negro people, the ideal of human brotherhood, gained through the unifying ideal of Race; the ideal of fostering and developing the traits and talents of the Negro, not in opposition to or contempt for other races, but rather in large conformity to the greater ideals of the American Republic, in order that some day on American soil two world-races may give each to each those characteristics both so sadly lack. We the darker ones come even now not altogether empty-handed: There are to-day no truer exponents of the pure human spirit of the Declaration of Independence than the American Negroes; there is no true American music but the wild sweet melodies of the Negro slave; the American fairy tales and folklore are Indian and African; and, all in all, we black men seem the sole oasis of simple faith and reverence in a dusty desert of dollars and smartness. Will America be poorer if she replace her brutal dyspeptic blundering with light-hearted but determined Negro humility? or her coarse and cruel wit with loving jovial good-humor? or her vulgar music with the soul of the Sorrow Songs?

Merely a concrete test of the underlying principles of the great republic is the Negro Problem, and the spiritual striving of the freedmen's sons is the travail of souls whose burden is almost beyond the measure of their strength, but who bear it in the name of an historic race, in the name of this the land of their fathers' fathers, and in the name of human opportunity.

And now what I have briefly sketched in large outline let me on coming pages tell again in many ways, with loving emphasis and deeper detail, that men may listen to the striving in the souls of black folk.

Thomas Nast's cartoon "The Man with the (Carpet) Bags," *Harper's Weekly*, November 9, 1872.

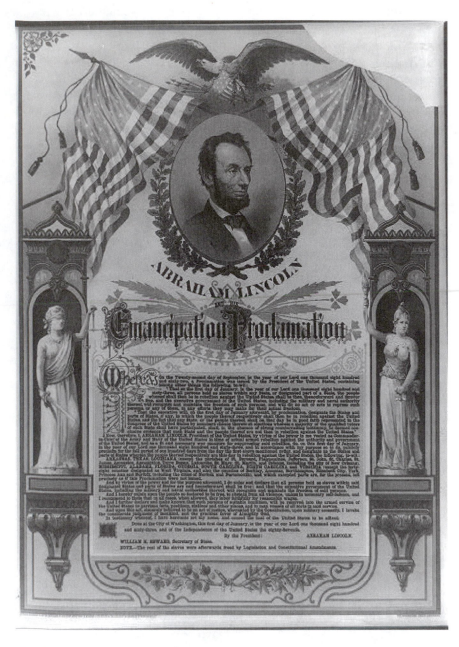

Abraham Lincoln and his Emancipation Proclamation. The Strobridge Lith. Co., Cincinnati, c. 1888. Courtesy of the Library of Congress.

Document Number 2, Chapter I

The Emancipation Proclamation was issued by President Abraham Lincoln on January 1, 1863. It proclaimed "that all persons held as slaves" within the rebellious states "are, and henceforward shall be free." The Emancipation Proclamation applied only to states that had seceded from the Union. Slavery remained intact in the loyal border states. It also expressly exempted parts of the Confederacy that had already come under Northern control. More than any other political act up until this time, the Emancipation Proclamation captured the imagination of African Americans by transforming the Civil War from a conflict over the Union to a war of liberation. Du Bois makes repeated reference to the Emancipation Proclamation and "Emancipation" throughout *The Souls of Black Folk.* By actual reading the document one becomes more aware of its limitations and the very specific political purposes it served for Lincoln and his cabinet.

*   *   *

The Emancipation Proclamation[10]

By the President of the United States of America:

A PROCLAMATION

Whereas on the 22nd day of September, A.D. 1862, a proclamation was issued by the President of the United States, containing, among other things, the following, to wit:

"That on the 1st day of January, A.D. 1863, all persons held as slaves within any State or designated part of a State the people whereof shall then be in rebellion against the United States shall be then, thenceforward, and forever free; and the executive government of the United States, including the military and naval authority thereof, will recognize and maintain the freedom of such persons and will do no act or acts to repress such persons, or any of them, in any efforts they may make for their actual freedom.

"That the executive will on the 1st day of January aforesaid, by proclamation, designate the States and parts of States, if any, in which the people thereof, respectively, shall then be in rebellion against the United States; and the fact that any State or the people thereof shall on that day be in good faith represented in the Congress of the United States by members chosen thereto at elections wherein a majority of the qualified voters of such States shall have participated shall, in the absence of strong countervailing testimony, be deemed conclusive evidence that such State and the people thereof are not then in rebellion against the United States."

---

[10] Source: National Archives and Records Administration website located at: http://www.archives.gov/

Now, therefore, I, Abraham Lincoln, President of the United States, by virtue of the power in me vested as Commander-In-Chief of the Army and Navy of the United States in time of actual armed rebellion against the authority and government of the United States, and as a fit and necessary war measure for supressing said rebellion, do, on this 1st day of January, A.D. 1863, and in accordance with my purpose so to do, publicly proclaimed for the full period of one hundred days from the first day above mentioned, order and designate as the States and parts of States wherein the people thereof, respectively, are this day in rebellion against the United States the following, to wit: Arkansas, Texas, Louisiana (except the parishes of St. Bernard, Palquemines, Jefferson, St. John, St. Charles, St. James, Ascension, Assumption, Terrebone, Lafourche, St. Mary, St. Martin, and Orleans, including the city of New Orleans), Mississippi, Alabama, Florida, Georgia, South Carolina, North Carolina, and Virginia (except the forty-eight counties designated as West Virginia, and also the counties of Berkeley, Accomac, Northhampton, Elizabeth City, York, Princess Anne, and Norfolk, including the cities of Norfolk and Portsmouth), and which excepted parts are for the present left precisely as if this proclamation were not issued.

And by virtue of the power and for the purpose aforesaid, I do order and declare that all persons held as slaves within said designated States and parts of States are, and henceforward shall be, free; and that the Executive Government of the United States, including the military and naval authorities thereof, will recognize and maintain the freedom of said persons.

And I hereby enjoin upon the people so declared to be free to abstain from all violence, unless in necessary self-defence; and I recommend to them that, in all cases when allowed, they labor faithfully for reasonable wages.

And I further declare and make known that such persons of suitable condition will be received into the armed service of the United States to garrison forts, positions, stations, and other places, and to man vessels of all sorts in said service.

And upon this act, sincerely believed to be an act of justice, warranted by the Constitution upon military necessity, I invoke the considerate judgment of mankind and the gracious favor of Almighty God.

"The First Vote." *Harper's Weekly*, November 16, 1867

My Lord, what a Morning.

1. My Lord, what a morning, My Lord, what a morn-ing, My

Lord, what a morn-ing, When de stars be-gin to fall.

Fine.

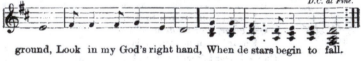

You'll hear de trumpet sound, To wake de na-tions un-der-
You'll hear de sin-ner moan, To wake, &c.

D.C. al Fine.

ground, Look in my God's right hand, When de stars begin to fall.

2 You'll hear de Christians shout, To wake, &c.
    Look in my God's right hand, When de stars, &c.
You'll hear de angels sing, To wake, &c.
    Look in my God's right hand, When de stars, &c.
Cho.—My Lord, what a morning, &c.

3 You'll see my Jesus come, To wake, &c.
    Look in my God's right hand, When de stars, &c.
His chariot wheels roll round, To wake, &c.
    Look in my God's right hand, When de stars, &c.
Cho.—My Lord, what a morning, &c.

"My Lord What a Morning," as included in *Religious Folk Songs of the Negro: As Sung on the Plantations* (Hampton, VA: Hampton Institute Press, 1909), p. 4.

II

Of the Dawn of Freedom[1]

Careless seems the great Avenger;
History's lessons but record
One death-grapple in the darkness
'Twixt old systems and the Word;
Truth forever on the scaffold,
Wrong forever on the throne;
Yet that scaffold sways the future,
And behind the dim unknown
Standeth God within the shadow
Keeping watch above His own.

LOWELL [2]

The problem of the twentieth century is the problem of the color-line,—the relation of the darker to the lighter races of men in Asia and Africa, in America and the islands of the sea. It was a phase of this problem that caused the Civil War; and however much they who marched South and North in 1861 may have fixed on the technical points, of union and local autonomy as a shibboleth,[3] all nevertheless

---

[1] A slightly different version of this chapter was originally published by Du Bois as "The Freedman's Bureau," *Atlantic Monthly*, March 1901, pp. 354–65.

[2] "Careless seems the great Avenger," is taken from a poem by the American poet James Russell Lowell (1819–1891) titled "The Present Crisis." In 1910, when Du Bois became the Director of Publications and Research for the National Association for the Advancement of Colored People (NAACP), he, and the members of the organization's board, took Lowell's poem and used it as the title for their magazine *The Crisis*.

[3] Shibboleth is a belief or practice that is commonly adhered to but which some people feel to be inappropriate or out of date; it comes from an incident described in the *Bible*, Judges 12:4-6, where the Emphraimites from the West,

"Emancipation," by Thomas Nast. *Harper's Weekly*, January 24, 1863, pp. 56–57.

knew, as we know, that the question of Negro slavery was the real cause of the conflict. Curious it was, too, how this deeper question ever forced itself to the surface despite effort and disclaimer. No sooner had Northern armies touched Southern soil than this old question, newly guised, sprang from the earth,—What shall be done with Negroes? Peremptory military commands this way and that could not answer the query; the Emancipation Proclamation seemed but to broaden and intensify the difficulties; and the War Amendments made the Negro problems of today.[4]

It is the aim of this essay to study the period from 1861 to 1872 so far as it relates to the American Negro. In effect, this tale of the dawn of

---

invaded Gilead. Defeated by the Gileadites, the escaping Emphraimites, when captured, could not pronounce shibboleth the same way as the Gileadites, thus revealing that they were part of the unsuccessful invading force.

[4] Three Constitutional Amendments come out of the Civil War: the Thirteenth Amendment ratified December 6, 1865, abolished slavery; the Fourteenth Amendment, ratified July 28, 1868, mandated due process and equal protection under the law to all citizens; and the Fifteenth Amendment, ratified February 3, 1870, provided male citizens with the right to vote regardless of race, color, or previous condition of servitude.

Freedom is an account of that government of men called the Freedmen's Bureau,—one of the most singular and interesting of the attempts made by a great nation to grapple with vast problems of race and social condition.[5]

The war has naught to do with slaves, cried Congress, the President, and the Nation; and yet no sooner had the armies, East and West, penetrated Virginia and Tennessee than fugitive slaves appeared within their lines. They came at night, when the flickering camp-fires shone like vast unsteady stars along the black horizon: old men and thin, with gray and tufted hair; women with frightened eyes, dragging whimpering hungry children; men and girls, stalwart and gaunt,—a horde of starving vagabonds, homeless, helpless, and pitiable, in their dark distress. Two methods of treating these newcomers seemed equally logical to opposite

"The Fifteenth Amendment," no date. Courtesy of the Library of Congress.

---

[5] The Freedman's Bureau, or the United States Bureau of Refugees, Freedmen and Abandoned Lands, was established as part of the War Department on March 3, 1865, as a federal agency to provide assistance with rations, clothing, medicine, and education to freed slaves. Originally created for just one year, it was kept in operation until 1872.

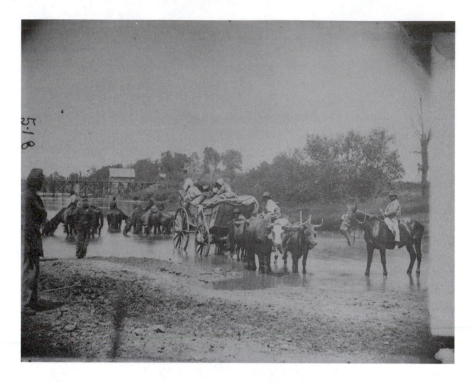

Timothy H. O'Sullivan. Fugitive African Americans Fording the Rappahannock River. Rappahannock, Virginia, August 1862. Courtesy of the Library of Congress.

sorts of minds. Ben Butler,[6] in Virginia, quickly declared slave property contraband of war, and put the fugitives to work; while Fremont,[7] in Missouri, declared the slaves free under martial law. Butler's action was approved, but Fremont's was hastily countermanded, and his successor, Halleck, saw things differently.[8] "Hereafter," he commanded, "no slaves should be allowed to come into your lines at all; if any come without your knowledge, when owners call for them deliver them." Such a policy was difficult to enforce; some of the black refugees declared themselves free men, others showed that their masters had deserted them, and still others were captured with forts and plantations. Evidently, too, slaves

---

[6] Benjamin F. Butler (1818–1893) was a Union General and politician who was most well known as the officer in charge of the occupation of New Orleans. After several defeats he became governor of Massachusetts in 1883.

[7] John C. Fremont (1813–1880) was a Union General, and for a short time, the Radical Republican candidate for President in 1864.

[8] Henry H. Halleck (1815–1872) was a Union military officer who succeeded Fremont.

were a source of strength to the Confederacy, and were being used as laborers and producers. "They constitute a military resource," wrote Secretary Cameron,[9] late in 1861; "and being such, that they should not be turned over to the enemy is too plain to discuss." So gradually the tone of the army chiefs changed; Congress forbade the rendition[10] of fugitives, and Butler's "contrabands" were welcomed as military laborers. This complicated rather than solved the problem, for now the scattering fugitives became a steady stream, which flowed faster as the armies marched.

Then the long-headed man with care-chiselled face who sat in the White House saw the inevitable, and emancipated the slaves of rebels on New Year's, 1863. A month later Congress called earnestly for the Negro soldiers whom the act of July 1862[11] had half grudgingly allowed to enlist. Thus the barriers were levelled and the deed was done. The stream of fugitives swelled to a flood, and anxious army officers kept inquiring:

Abraham Lincoln, head-and-shoulders portrait, facing slightly left. Copy daguerreotype of a post-1860 albumen photograph created circa 1864. Courtesy of the Library of Congress.

---

[9] Simon L. Cameron (1799–1889) known as the "Czar of Pennsylvania" was Secretary of War, March 1861–January 1862. Corrupt army appointments and contracts led Lincoln to remove him from office and appoint him the ambassador to Russia, a post he held until November 1862.

[10] Surrender.

[11] The Militia Act of July 17, 1862, specifically authorized the President to be able to enlist African-Americans to provide labor in any of the military services with the promise of emancipation for his "mother, wife and children."

"Morning Mustering of the 'Contraband' at Fortress Monroe." *Frank Leslie's Illustrated Newspaper,* November 2, 1861.

"What must be done with slaves, arriving almost daily? Are we to find food and shelter for women and children?"

It was a Pierce of Boston who pointed out the way,[12] and thus became in a sense the founder of the Freedmen's Bureau. He was a firm friend of Secretary Chase; and when, in 1861, the care of slaves and abandoned lands devolved upon the Treasury officials, Pierce was specially detailed from the ranks to study the conditions. First, he cared for the refugees at Fortress Monroe; and then, after Sherman[13] had captured Hilton Head, Pierce was sent there to found his Port Royal experiment of making free workingmen out of slaves.[14] Before his experiment was barely started, however, the problem of the fugitives had

---

[12] In February 1862, Edward L. Pierce (1829–1897) a Boston abolitionist, was sent to the Sea Islands of South Carolina to address the "contraband negro" situation. In April 1862, a military order freeing blacks in the Sea Islands was issued.

[13] William Thomas Sherman (1813–1879). Union General who lead the Port Royal Expedition (September 19, 1861–March 15, 1862). Often referred to as "the other General Sherman," he should not be confused with William Tecumsah Sherman (1820–1891).

[14] On January 15, 1862, General Thomas Sherman asked that the War Department send teachers to Port Royal, South Carolina, to educate ex-slaves who had been abandoned on plantations now occupied by Union forces. The idea behind the experiment was, not only to help them become literate, but also help them find work as freed men and women.

assumed such proportions that it was taken from the hands of the over-burdened Treasury Department and given to the army officials. Already centres of massed freedmen were forming at Fortress Monroe, Washington, New Orleans, Vicksburg and Corinth, Columbus, Ky., and Cairo, Ill., as well as at Port Royal. Army chaplains found here new and fruitful fields; "superintendents of contrabands" multiplied, and some attempt at systematic work was made by enlisting the able-bodied men and giving work to the others.

Then came the Freedmen's Aid societies, born of the touching appeals from Pierce and from these other centres of distress. There was the American Missionary Association, sprung from the *Amistad*,[15] and now full-grown for work; the various church organizations, the National Freedmen's Relief Association, the American Freedmen's Union, the Western Freedmen's Aid Commission,—in all fifty or more active organizations, which sent clothes, money, school-books, and teachers southward. All they did was needed, for the destitution of the freedmen was often reported as "too appalling for belief," and the situation was daily growing worse rather than better.

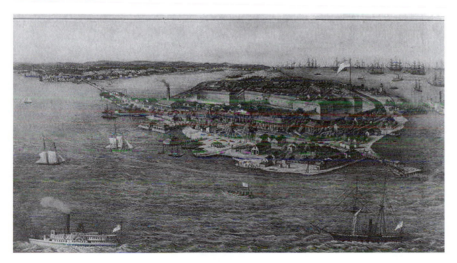

"Old Point Comfort, & Hygeia Hotel, Va. in 1861 & 1862—The key to the South," Lithography and print by E. Sachse & Co, 1862. Courtesy of the Library of Congress.

---

[15] The *Amistad* was a slave ship on which illegally captured slaves were being transported to Principe in 1839. Overcoming their captors off the coast of Cuba, they attempted to return to Africa. In Connecticut, when they landed, they were seized by the United States brig *Washington* and taken to Hartford, Connecticut, where they were imprisoned. After an appeal to the Supreme Court they were freed and sent back to Africa.

"Sherman's march to the sea," drawn by F.O.C. Darley, 1883. Courtesy of the Library of Congress.

And daily, to it seemed more plain that this was no ordinary matter of temporary relief, but a national crisis; for here loomed a labor problem of vast dimensions. Masses of Negroes stood idle, or, if they worked spasmodically, were never sure of pay; and if perchance they received pay, squandered the new thing thoughtlessly. In these and other ways were camp-life and the new liberty demoralizing the freedmen. The broader economic organization thus clearly demanded sprang up here and there as accident and local conditions determined. Here it was that Pierce's Port Royal plan of leased plantations and guided workmen pointed out the rough way. In Washington the military governor, at the urgent appeal of the superintendent, opened confiscated estates to the cultivation of the fugitives, and there in the shadow of the dome gathered black farm villages. General Dix[16] gave over estates to the freedmen of Fortress Monroe, and so on, South and West. The government and benevolent societies furnished the means of cultivation, and the Negro turned again slowly to work. The systems of control, thus started, rapidly grew, here and there, into strange little governments, like that of General Banks[17] in Louisiana, with its ninety thousand black subjects, its fifty

---

[16] John A. Dix (1798–1879), Union general who had served prior to the Civil War as a Senator and as Secretary of the Treasury. After the war, he was a minister to the French government and then the Governor of New York from 1872–1874.

[17] Nathaniel P. Banks (1824–1908). Union general.

thousand guided laborers, and its annual budget of one hundred thousand dollars and more. It made out four thousand pay-rolls a year, registered all freedmen, inquired into grievances and redressed them, laid and collected taxes, and established a system of public schools. So, too, Colonel Eaton,[18] the superintendent of Tennessee and Arkansas, ruled over one hundred thousand freedmen, leased and cultivated seven thousand acres of cotton land, and fed ten thousand paupers a year. In South Carolina was General Saxton,[19] with his deep interest in black folk. He succeeded Pierce and the Treasury officials, and sold forfeited estates, leased abandoned plantations, encouraged schools, and received from Sherman, after that terribly picturesque march to the sea, thousands of the wretched camp followers.[20]

Three characteristic things one might have seen in Sherman's raid through Georgia, which threw the new situation in shadowy relief: the Conqueror, the Conquered, and the Negro. Some see all significance in the grim front of the destroyer, and some in the bitter sufferers of the Lost Cause. But to me neither soldier nor fugitive speaks with so deep a meaning as that dark human cloud that clung like remorse on the rear of those swift columns, swelling at times to half their size, almost engulfing and choking them. In vain were they ordered back, in vain were bridges hewn from beneath their feet; on they trudged and writhed and surged, until they rolled into Savannah, a starved and naked horde of tens of thousands. There too came the characteristic military remedy: "The islands from Charleston south, the abandoned rice-fields along the rivers for thirty miles back from the sea, and the country bordering the St. John's River, Florida, are reserved and set apart for the settlement of Negroes now made free by act of war." So read the celebrated "Field-Order Number Fifteen."[21]

All these experiments, orders, and systems were bound to attract and perplex the government and the nation. Directly after the Emancipation Proclamation, Representative Eliot had introduced a bill creating a Bureau of Emancipation; but it was never reported. The following June a committee of inquiry, appointed by the Secretary of War, reported in

---

[18] John Eaton(1829–?). Union officer who was assigned responsibility for "Contraband" blacks early in the Civil War. His organizational schemes became models for the Freedman's Bureau.

[19] Rufus Saxton Jr. (1824–1908). Union general.

[20] William Tecumsah Sherman (1820–1891). Union general responsible for a "scorched earth policy" carried out in Georgia at the end of the war.

[21] General Sherman's Special Field-Order Number Fifteen was issued in January 1865. It promised forty acres in land to freed slaves who agreed to move to areas such as the Sea Islands of Georgia.

Death of Capt. Ferrer, the Captain of the Amistad, July, 1839.

Don Jose Ruiz and Don Pedro Montez, of the Island of Cuba, having purchased fifty-three slaves at Havana, recently imported from Africa, put them on board the Amistad, Capt. Ferrer, in order to transport them to Principe, another port on the Island of Cuba. After being out from Havana about four days, the African captives on board, in order to obtain their freedom, and return to Africa, armed themselves with cane knives, and rose upon the Captain and crew of the vessel. Capt. Ferrer and the cook of the vessel were killed; two of the crew escaped; Ruiz and Montez were made prisoners.

Barber, John W., compiler. "A History of the *Amistad* Captives: Being a Circumstantial Account of the Capture of the Spanish Schooner *Amistad*..." New Haven, CT.: E.L. & J.W. Barber, 1840. Courtesy of the Library of Congress.

favor of a temporary bureau for the "improvement, protection, and employment of refugee freedmen," on much the same lines as were afterwards followed. Petitions came in to President Lincoln from distinguished citizens and organizations, strongly urging a comprehensive and unified plan of dealing with the freedmen, under a bureau which should be "charged with the study of plans and execution of measures for easily guiding, and in every way judiciously and humanely aiding, the passage of our emancipated and yet to be emancipated blacks from the old condition of forced labor to their new state of voluntary industry."

Some half-hearted steps were taken to accomplish this, in part, by putting the whole matter again in charge of the special Treasury agents. Laws of 1863 and 1864 directed them to take charge of and lease abandoned lands for periods not exceeding twelve months, and to "provide in such leases, or otherwise, for the employment and general welfare" of the freedmen. Most of the army officers greeted this as a welcome relief from perplexing "Negro affairs," and Secretary Fessenden, July 29, 1864, issued an excellent system of regulations, which were afterward closely followed by General Howard.[22] Under Treasury agents, large quantities of land were leased in the Mississippi Valley, and many Negroes were employed; but in August, 1864, the new

---

[22] Oliver Otis Howard (1830–1909) was a Union General who was appointed Commissioner of the Freedman's Bureau in 1865. He helped found Howard University in 1869, serving as its president from 1869 to 1874.

regulations were suspended for reasons of "public policy," and the army was again in control.

Meanwhile Congress had turned its attention to the subject; and in March the House passed a bill by a majority of two establishing a Bureau for Freedmen in the War Department. Charles Sumner,[23] who had charge of the bill in the Senate, argued that freedmen and abandoned lands ought to be under the same department, and reported a substitute for the House bill attaching the Bureau to the Treasury Department. This bill passed, but too late for action by the House. The debates wandered over the whole policy of the administration and the general question of slavery, without touching very closely the specific merits of the measure in hand. Then the national election took place; and the administration, with a vote of renewed confidence from the country, addressed itself to the matter more seriously. A conference between the two branches of Congress agreed upon a carefully drawn measure which contained the chief provisions of Sumner's bill, but made the proposed organization a department independent of both the War and the Treasury officials. The bill was conservative, giving the new department "general superintendence of all freedmen." Its purpose was to "establish regulations" for them, protect them, lease them lands, adjust their wages, and appear in civil and military courts as their "next friend." There were many limitations attached to the powers thus granted, and the organization was made permanent. Nevertheless, the Senate defeated the bill, and a new conference committee was appointed. This committee reported a new bill, February 28, which was whirled through just as the session closed, and became the act of 1865 establishing in the War Department a "Bureau of Refugees, Freedmen, and Abandoned Lands."[24]

This last compromise was a hasty bit of legislation, vague and uncertain in outline. A Bureau was created, "to continue during the present War of Rebellion, and for one year thereafter," to which was given "the supervision and management of all abandoned lands and the control of all subjects relating to refugees and freedmen," under "such rules and regulations as may be presented by the head of the Bureau and approved by the President." A Commissioner, appointed by the President

---

[23] Charles Sumner (1811–74), United States Senator from Massachusetts. A highly vocal abolitionist, he attacked the fugitive slave laws, denounced the Kansas-Nebraska Act of 1854, and on May 19–20, 1856, delivered his famous antislavery speech called "The Crime against Kansas." In the speech he specifically singled out Senator Andrew Pickens Butler of South Carolina. Sumner was assaulted two days later on the floor of the Senate by Butler's nephew Preston S. Brooks.

[24] See document Number 1 included at the end of this chapter.

and Senate, was to control the Bureau, with an office force not exceeding ten clerks. The President might also appoint assistant commissioners in the seceded States, and to all these offices military officials might be detailed at regular pay. The Secretary of War could issue rations, clothing, and fuel to the destitute, and all abandoned property was placed in the hands of the Bureau for eventual lease and sale to ex-slaves in forty-acre parcels.

Thus did the United States government definitely assume charge of the emancipated Negro as the ward of the nation. It was a tremendous undertaking. Here at a stroke of the pen was erected a government of millions of men,—and not ordinary men either, but black men— emasculated by a peculiarly complete system of slavery, centuries old; and now, suddenly, violently, they come into a new birthright, at a time of war and passion, in the midst of the stricken and embittered population of their former masters. Any man might well have hesitated to assume charge of such a work, with vast responsibilities, indefinite powers, and limited resources. Probably no one but a soldier would have answered such a call promptly; and, indeed, no one but a soldier could be called, for Congress had appropriated no money for salaries and expenses.

Less than a month after the weary Emancipator passed to his rest, his successor assigned Major-Gen. Oliver O. Howard to duty as Commissioner of the new Bureau.[25] He was a Maine man, then only thirty-five years of age. He had marched with Sherman to the sea, had fought well at Gettysburg, and but the year before had been assigned to the command of the Department of Tennessee. An honest man, with too much faith in human nature, little aptitude for business and intricate detail, he had had large opportunity of becoming acquainted at first hand with much of the work before him. And of that work it has been truly said that "no approximately correct history of civilization can ever be written which does not throw out in bold relief, as one of the great landmarks of political and social progress, the organization and administration of the Freedmen's Bureau."

On May 12, 1865, Howard was appointed; and he assumed the duties of his office promptly on the 15th, and began examining the field of work. A curious mess he looked upon: little despotisms, communistic experiments, slavery, peonage, business speculations, organized charity, unorganized almsgiving,—all reeling on under the guise of helping the freedmen, and all enshrined in the smoke and blood of the war and the cursing and silence of angry men. On May 19 the new government—for

---

[25] Du Bois is referring to the assassination of Lincoln and his succession by Andrew Johnson (1808–1869).

a government it really was—issued its constitution; commissioners were to be appointed in each of the seceded states, who were to take charge of "all subjects relating to refugees and freedmen," and all relief and rations were to be given by their consent alone. The Bureau invited continued cooperation with benevolent societies, and declared: "It will be the object of all commissioners to introduce practicable systems of compensated labor," and to establish schools. Forthwith nine assistant commissioners were appointed. They were to hasten to their fields of work; seek gradually to close relief establishments, and make the destitute self-supporting; act as courts of law where there were no courts, or where Negroes were not recognized in them as free; establish the institution of marriage among ex-slaves, and keep records; see that freedmen were free to choose their employers, and help in making fair contracts for them; and finally, the circular said: "Simple good faith, for which we hope on all hands for those concerned in the passing away of slavery, will especially relieve the assistant commissioners in the discharge of their duties toward the freedmen, as well as promote the general welfare."

No sooner was the work thus started, and the general system and local organization in some measure begun, than two grave difficulties appeared which changed largely the theory and outcome of Bureau work. First, there were the abandoned lands of the South. It had long been the more or less definitely expressed theory of the North that all the chief problems of Emancipation might be settled by establishing the slaves on the forfeited lands of their masters,—a sort of poetic justice, said some. But this poetry done into solemn prose meant either wholesale confiscation of private property in the South, or vast appropriations. Now Congress had not appropriated a cent, and no sooner did the proclamations of general amnesty appear than the eight hundred thousand acres of abandoned lands in the hands of the Freedmen's Bureau melted quickly away. The second difficulty lay in perfecting the local organization of the Bureau throughout the wide field of work. Making a new machine and sending out officials of duly ascertained fitness for a great work of social reform is no child's task; but this task was even harder, for a new central organization had to be fitted on a heterogeneous and confused but already existing system of relief and control of ex-slaves; and the agents available for this work must be sought for in an army still busy with war operations,—men in the very nature of the case ill fitted for delicate social work,—or among the questionable camp followers of an invading host. Thus, after a year's work, vigorously as it was pushed, the problem looked even more difficult to grasp and solve than at the beginning. Nevertheless, three things that year's work did, well worth the doing: it relieved a vast amount of physical suffering; it transported seven thousand fugitives

"Auction & Negro Sales, Whitehall Street." Photograph by George Barnard, fall of 1864. Courtesy of the Library of Congress.

from congested centres back to the farm; and, best of all, it inaugurated the crusade of the New England schoolma'am.

The annals of this Ninth Crusade are yet to be written,—the tale of a mission that seemed to our age far more quixotic than the quest of St. Louis[26] seemed to his. Behind the mists of ruin and rapine waved the

---

[26] A reference to the French King Louis IX (1215–1270), who went on the Seventh Crusade to the Holy Land, often referred to as the "Children's Crusade."

calico dresses of women who dared, and after the hoarse mouthings of the field guns rang the rhythm of the alphabet. Rich and poor they were, serious and curious. Bereaved now of a father, now of a brother, now of more than these, they came seeking a life work in planting New England schoolhouses among the white and black of the South. They did their work well. In that first year they taught one hundred thousand souls, and more.

Evidently, Congress must soon legislate again on the hastily organized Bureau, which had so quickly grown into wide significance and vast possibilities. An institution such as that was well-nigh as difficult to end as to begin. Early in 1866 Congress took up the matter, when Senator Trumbull, of Illinois,[27] introduced a bill to extend the Bureau and enlarge its powers. This measure received, at the hands of Congress, far more thorough discussion and attention than its predecessor. The war cloud had thinned enough to allow a clearer conception of the work of Emancipation. The champions of the bill argued that the strengthening of the Freedmen's Bureau was still a military necessity; that it was needed for the proper carrying out of the Thirteenth Amendment, and was a work of sheer justice to the ex-slave, at a trifling cost to the government.[28] The opponents of the measure declared that the war was over, and the necessity for war measures past; that the Bureau, by reason of its extraordinary powers, was clearly unconstitutional in time of peace, and was destined to irritate the South and pauperize the freedmen, at a final cost of possibly hundreds of millions. These two arguments were unanswered, and indeed unanswerable: the one that the extraordinary powers of the Bureau threatened the civil rights of all citizens; and the other that the government must have power to do what manifestly must be done, and that present abandonment of the freedmen meant their practical re-enslavement. The bill which finally passed enlarged and made permanent the Freedmen's Bureau. It was promptly vetoed by President Johnson as "unconstitutional," "unnecessary," and "extrajudicial," and failed of passage over the veto. Meantime, however, the breach between Congress and the President began to broaden, and a modified form of the lost bill was finally passed over the President's second veto, July 16.

The act of 1866 gave the Freedmen's Bureau its final form,—the form by which it will be known to posterity and judged of men. It extended the existence of the Bureau to July 1868; it authorized

---

[27] Louis Trumbull (1813–1869) Senator from Illinois who led the movement to extend the power and influence of the Freedman's Bureau over the veto of President Johnson.

[28] The Thirteenth Amendment ended slavery in the United States.

"All ages in class at primary school for Freedmen," *Harper's Weekly*, June 23, 1866, p. 392.

additional assistant commissioners, the retention of army officers mustered out of regular service, the sale of certain forfeited lands to freedmen on nominal terms, the sale of Confederate public property for Negro schools, and a wider field of judicial interpretation and cognizance. The government of the unreconstructed South was thus put very largely in the hands of the Freedmen's Bureau, especially as in many cases the departmental military commander was now made also assistant commissioner. It was thus that the Freedmen's Bureau became a full-fledged government of men. It made laws, executed them and interpreted them; it laid and collected taxes, defined and punished crime, maintained and used military force, and dictated such measures as it thought necessary and proper for the accomplishment of its varied ends. Naturally, all these powers were not exercised continuously nor to their fullest extent; and yet, as General Howard has said, "scarcely any subject that has to be legislated upon in civil society failed, at one time or another, to demand the action of this singular Bureau."

To understand and criticise intelligently so vast a work, one must not forget an instant the drift of things in the later sixties. Lee had surrendered, Lincoln was dead, and Johnson and Congress were at loggerheads; the Thirteenth Amendment was adopted, the Fourteenth pending, and the Fifteenth declared in force in 1870.[29] Guerrilla raiding, the ever-present flickering after-flame of war, was spending its forces against the Negroes, and all the Southern land was awakening as from some wild dream to poverty and social revolution. In a time of perfect calm, amid willing neighbors and streaming wealth, the social uplifting of four million slaves to an assured and self-sustaining place in the body politic and economic would have been a herculean task; but when to the inherent difficulties of so delicate and nice a social operation were added the spite and hate of conflict, the hell of war; when suspicion and cruelty were rife, and gaunt Hunger wept beside Bereavement,—in such a case, the work of any instrument of social regeneration was in large part foredoomed to failure. The very name of the Bureau stood for a thing in the South which for two centuries and better men had refused even to argue,—that life amid free Negroes was simply unthinkable, the maddest of experiments.

The agents that the Bureau could command varied all the way from unselfish philanthropists to narrow-minded busy-bodies and thieves; and even though it be true that the average was far better than the worst, it was the occasional fly that helped spoil the ointment.

Then amid all crouched the freed slave, bewildered between friend and foe. He had emerged from slavery,—not the worst slavery in the world, not a slavery that made all life unbearable, rather a slavery that had here and there something of kindliness, fidelity, and happiness,—but withal slavery, which, so far as human aspiration and desert were concerned, classed the black man and the ox together. And the Negro knew full well that, whatever their deeper convictions may have been, Southern men had fought with desperate energy to perpetuate this slavery under which the black masses, with half-articulate thought, had writhed and shivered. They welcomed freedom with a cry. They shrank from the master who still strove for their chains; they fled to the friends that had freed them, even though those friends stood ready to use them as a club for driving the recalcitrant South back into loyalty. So the cleft between the white and black South grew. Idle to say it never should have been; it was as inevitable as its results were pitiable. Curiously incongruous elements were left arrayed against each other,—the North, the government, the carpet-bagger, and the slave, here; and there, all the

---

[29] The Fourteenth Amendment, ratified on July 28, 1868, guaranteed the civil rights of African-Americans, The Fifteenth Amendment, ratified March 30, 1870, guaranteed African-Americans the right to vote.

South that was white, whether gentleman or vagabond, honest man or rascal, lawless murderer or martyr to duty.

Thus it is doubly difficult to write of this period calmly, so intense was the feeling, so mighty the human passions that swayed and blinded men. Amid it all, two figures ever stand to typify that day to coming ages,—the one, a gray-haired gentleman, whose fathers had quit themselves like men, whose sons lay in nameless graves; who bowed to the evil of slavery because its abolition threatened untold ill to all; who stood at last, in the evening of life, a blighted, ruined form, with hate in his eyes;—and the other, a form hovering dark and mother-like, her awful face black with the mists of centuries, had aforetime quailed at that white master's command, had bent in love over the cradles of his sons and daughters, and closed in death the sunken eyes of his wife,—aye, too, at his behest had laid herself low to his lust, and borne a tawny man-child to the world, only to see her dark boy's limbs scattered to the winds by midnight marauders riding after "damned Niggers." These were the saddest sights of that woful day; and no man clasped the hands of these two passing figures of the present-past; but, hating, they went to their long home, and, hating, their children's children live today.

Here, then, was the field of work for the Freedmen's Bureau; and since, with some hesitation, it was continued by the act of 1868 until 1869, let us look upon four years of its work as a whole. There were, in 1868, nine hundred Bureau officials scattered from Washington to Texas, ruling, directly and indirectly, many millions of men. The deeds of these rulers fall mainly under seven heads: the relief of physical suffering, the overseeing of the beginnings of free labor, the buying and selling of land, the establishment of schools, the paying of bounties, the administration of justice, and the financiering of all these activities.

Up to June 1869, over half a million patients had been treated by Bureau physicians and surgeons, and sixty hospitals and asylums had been in operation. In fifty months twenty-one million free rations were distributed at a cost of over four million dollars. Next came the difficult question of labor. First, thirty thousand black men were transported from the refuges and relief stations back to the farms, back to the critical trial of a new way of working. Plain instructions went out from Washington: the laborers must be free to choose their employers, no fixed rate of wages was prescribed, and there was to be no peonage or forced labor. So far, so good; but where local agents differed *toto caelo*[30] in capacity and character, where the *personnel* was continually changing, the outcome was necessarily varied. The largest element of success lay in the fact that the majority of the freedmen were willing, even eager, to work.

---

[30] Absolutely or totally.

The Fifteenth Amendment and its results. G.F. Kahl illustrator. Courtesy of the Library of Congress.

So labor contracts were written,—fifty thousand in a single State,—laborers advised, wages guaranteed, and employers supplied. In truth, the organization became a vast labor bureau,—not perfect, indeed, notably defective here and there, but on the whole successful beyond the dreams of thoughtful men. The two great obstacles which confronted the officials were the tyrant and the idler,—the slaveholder who was determined to perpetuate slavery under another name; and, the freedman who regarded freedom as perpetual rest,—the Devil and the Deep Sea.

In the work of establishing the Negroes as peasant proprietors, the Bureau was from the first handicapped and at last absolutely checked. Something was done, and larger things were planned; abandoned lands were leased so long as they remained in the hands of the Bureau, and a total revenue of nearly half a million dollars derived from black tenants. Some other lands to which the nation had gained title were sold on easy terms, and public lands were opened for settlement to the very few freedmen who had tools and capital. But the vision of "forty acres and a mule"—the righteous and reasonable ambition to become a landholder, which the nation had all but categorically promised the freedmen—was destined in most cases to bitter disappointment.[31] And those men of marvellous hindsight who are today seeking to preach the Negro back to the present peonage of the soil know well, or ought to know, that the opportunity of binding the Negro peasant willingly to the soil was lost on that day when the Commissioner of the Freedmen's Bureau had to go to South Carolina and tell the weeping freedmen, after their years of toil, that their land was not theirs, that there was a mistake—somewhere. If by 1874 the Georgia Negro alone owned three hundred and fifty thousand acres of land, it was by grace of his thrift rather than by bounty of the government.

The greatest success of the Freedmen's Bureau lay in the planting of the free school among Negroes, and the idea of free elementary education among all classes in the South. It not only called the schoolmistresses through the benevolent agencies and built them schoolhouses, but it helped discover and support such apostles of human culture as Edmund Ware,[32] Samuel Armstrong,[33] and Erastus Cravath.[34] The opposition to Negro education in the South was at first bitter, and showed itself in ashes, insult, and blood; for the South believed an educated Negro to be a dangerous Negro. And the South was not wholly wrong; for education among all kinds of men always has had, and always will have, an element of danger and revolution, of dissatisfaction and discontent. Nevertheless, men strive to know. Perhaps some inkling of this paradox, even in the unquiet days of the Bureau, helped the bayonets allay an opposition to human training which still to-day lies smouldering in the South, but not flaming. Fisk, Atlanta, Howard, and Hampton[35] were founded in these days, and six million dollars were expended for educational work, seven hundred and fifty thousand dollars of which the freedmen themselves gave of their poverty.

Such contributions, together with the buying of land and various other enterprises, showed that the ex-slave was handling some free capital

---

[31] "Forty Acres and a Mule," is a phrase that came about as a result of General William T. Sherman's Special Field Order Number 15 (January 16, 1865) providing that every former slave family receive 40 acres of farmland. Ex-slaves were later lent army mules as plow animals.

[32] Edmond Ware (1837–1885) was appointed superintendent of schools for the Freedman's Bureau in Georgia in 1867. He was one the founders and first president of Atlanta University.

[33] Samuel Armstrong (1839–1893) Union officer, who led a black regiment during the Civil War. Armstrong was the founder of Hampton Institute in Virginia and became the mentor of Booker T. Washington.

[34] Erastus Cravath (1833–1900), clergyman and educator, who was one of the founders of Fisk University.

[35] African-American colleges and universities founded following Emancipation.

Group of Children from the Model School, Fisk University, Nashville Tennessee. Photograph included in the Exhibit of American Negroes at the Paris Exposition of 1900. Courtesy of the Library of Congress.

already. The chief initial source of this was labor in the army, and his pay and bounty as a soldier. Payments to Negro soldiers were at first complicated by the ignorance of the recipients, and the fact that the quotas of colored regiments from Northern States were largely filled by recruits from the South, unknown to their fellow soldiers. Consequently, payments were accompanied by such frauds that Congress, by joint resolution in 1867, put the whole matter in the hands of the Freedmen's Bureau. In two years six million dollars was thus distributed to five thousand claimants, and in the end the sum exceeded eight million dollars. Even in this system fraud was frequent; but still the work put needed capital in the hands of practical paupers, and some, at least, was well spent.

The most perplexing and least successful part of the Bureau's work lay in the exercise of its judicial functions. The regular Bureau court consisted of one representative of the employer, one of the Negro, and one of the Bureau. If the Bureau could have maintained a perfectly judicial attitude, this arrangement would have been ideal, and must in time have gained confidence; but the nature of its other activities and the character of its *personnel* prejudiced the Bureau in favor of the black litigants, and led without doubt to much injustice and annoyance. On the other hand, to leave the Negro in the hands of Southern courts was

Nine African American women, full-length portrait, seated on steps of a building at Atlanta University, Georgia, c. 1900. Courtesy of the Library of Congress.

impossible. In a distracted land where slavery had hardly fallen, to keep the strong from wanton abuse of the weak, and the weak from gloating insolently over the half-shorn strength of the strong, was a thankless, hopeless task. The former masters of the land were peremptorily ordered about, seized, and imprisoned, and punished over and again, with scant courtesy from army officers. The former slaves were intimidated, beaten, raped, and butchered by angry and revengeful men. Bureau courts tended to become centres simply for punishing whites, while the regular civil courts tended to become solely institutions for perpetuating the slavery of blacks. Almost every law and method ingenuity could devise was employed by the legislatures to reduce the Negroes to serfdom,—to make them the slaves of the State, if not of individual owners; while the Bureau officials too often were found striving to put the "bottom rail on top," and gave the freedmen a power and independence which they could not yet use. It is all well enough for us of another generation to wax wise with advice to those who bore the burden in the heat of the day. It is full easy now to see that the man who lost home, fortune, and family at a stroke, and saw his land ruled by "mules and niggers," was really benefited by the passing of slavery. It is not difficult now to say to the young freedman, cheated and cuffed about who has seen his father's head beaten to a jelly and his own mother namelessly assaulted, that the meek shall inherit the earth. Above all, nothing is more convenient than to heap

50

on the Freedmen's Bureau all the evils of that evil day, and damn it utterly for every mistake and blunder that was made.

All this is easy, but it is neither sensible nor just. Someone had blundered, but that was long before Oliver Howard was born; there was criminal aggression and heedless neglect, but without some system of control there would have been far more than there was. Had that control been from within, the Negro would have been re-enslaved, to all intents and purposes. Coming as the control did from without, perfect men and methods would have bettered all things; and even with imperfect agents and questionable methods, the work accomplished was not undeserving of commendation.

Such was the dawn of Freedom; such was the work of the Freedmen's Bureau, which, summed up in brief, may be epitomized thus: for some fifteen million dollars, beside the sums spent before 1865, and the dole of benevolent societies, this Bureau set going a system of free labor, established a beginning of peasant proprietorship, secured the recognition of black freedmen before courts of law, and founded the free common school in the South. On the other hand, it failed to begin the establishment of good-will between ex-masters and freedmen, to guard its work wholly from paternalistic methods which discouraged self-reliance, and to carry out to any considerable extent its implied promises to furnish the freedmen with land. Its successes were the result of hard work, supplemented by the aid of philanthropists and the eager striving of black men. Its failures were the result of bad local agents, the inherent difficulties of the work, and national neglect.

Such an institution, from its wide powers, great responsibilities, large control of moneys, and generally conspicuous position, was naturally open to repeated and bitter attack. It sustained a searching Congressional investigation at the instance of Fernando Wood[36] in 1870. Its archives and few remaining functions were with blunt discourtesy transferred from Howard's control, in his absence, to the supervision of Secretary of War Belknap[37] in 1872, on the Secretary's recommendation. Finally, in consequence of grave intimations of wrong-doing made by the Secretary and his subordinates, General Howard was court-martialed in 1874. In both of these trials the Commissioner of the Freedmen's Bureau was officially exonerated from any wilful misdoing, and his work commended. Nevertheless, many unpleasant things were brought to light, —the methods of transacting the business of the Bureau were faulty;

---

[36] Fernando Wood (1812–1881), congressman and mayor of New York.

[37] William W. Belknap (1829–1890), secretary of war during the Grant administration, who was impeached in 1876 for accepting bribes.

several cases of defalcation[38] were proved, and other frauds strongly suspected; there were some business transactions which savored of dangerous speculation, if not dishonesty; and around it all lay the smirch of the Freedmen's Bank. ·

Morally and practically, the Freedmen's Bank[39] was part of the Freedmen's Bureau, although it had no legal connection with it. With the prestige of the government back of it, and a directing board of unusual respectability and national reputation, this banking institution had made a remarkable start in the development of that thrift among black folk which slavery had kept them from knowing. Then in one sad day came the crash,—all the hard-earned dollars of the freedmen disappeared; but that was the least of the loss,—all the faith in saving went too, and much of the faith in men; and that was a loss that a Nation which to-day sneers at Negro shiftlessness has never yet made good. Not even ten additional years of slavery could have done so much to throttle the thrift of the freedmen as the mismanagement and bankruptcy of the series of savings banks chartered by the Nation for their especial aid. Where all the blame should rest, it is hard to say; whether the Bureau and the Bank died chiefly by reason of the blows of its selfish friends or the dark machinations of its foes, perhaps even time will never reveal, for here lies unwritten history.

Of the foes without the Bureau, the bitterest were those who attacked not so much its conduct or policy under the law as the necessity for any such institution at all. Such attacks came primarily from the Border States[40] and the South; and they were summed up by Senator Davis,[41] of Kentucky, when he moved to entitle the act of 1866 a bill "to promote strife and conflict between the white and black races . . . by a grant of unconstitutional power." The argument gathered tremendous strength South and North; but its very strength was its weakness. For, argued the plain common-sense of the nation, if it is unconstitutional, unpractical, and futile for the nation to stand guardian over its helpless wards, then there is left but one alternative,—to make those wards their own guardians by arming them with the ballot. Moreover, the path of the practical politician pointed the same way; for, argued this opportunist, if

---

[38] An archaic term for embezzlement.

[39] The Freedman's Savings and Trust company was founded in 1865. It closed as a result of financial failure in 1874.

[40] The Border States included Kentucky, Missouri, West Virginia, and Maryland. Despite Southern sympathies among much of their populations, all of them remained in the Union throughout the Civil War.

[41] Garrett Davis (1815–1882), Democratic Senator from Kentucky, who opposed federal involvement with the Freedmen.

Hampton Institute campus. Frances Benjamin Johnston, photographer, 1899. Photograph included in the Exhibit of American Negroes at the Paris Exposition of 1900. Courtesy of the Library of Congress.

we cannot peacefully reconstruct the South with white votes, we certainly can with black votes. So justice and force joined hands.

The alternative thus offered the nation was not between full and restricted Negro suffrage; else every sensible man, black and white, would easily have chosen the latter. It was rather a choice between suffrage and slavery, after endless blood and gold had flowed to sweep human bondage away. Not a single Southern legislature stood ready to admit a Negro, under any conditions, to the polls; not a single Southern legislature believed free Negro labor was possible without a system of restrictions that took all its freedom away; there was scarcely a white man in the South who did not honestly regard Emancipation as a crime, and its practical nullification as a duty. In such a situation, the granting of the ballot to the black man was a necessity, the very least a guilty nation could grant a wronged race, and the only method of compelling the South to accept the results of the war. Thus Negro suffrage ended a civil war by beginning a race feud. And some felt gratitude toward the race thus sacrificed in its swaddling clothes on the altar of national integrity; and some felt and feel only indifference and contempt.

Had political exigencies been less pressing, the opposition to government guardianship of Negroes less bitter, and the attachment to the slave system less strong, the social seer can well imagine a far better policy,—a permanent Freedmen's Bureau, with a national system of

Negro schools; a carefully supervised employment and labor office; a system of impartial protection before the regular courts; and such institutions for social betterment as savings-banks, land and building associations, and social settlements. All this vast expenditure of money and brains might have formed a great school of prospective citizenship, and solved in a way we have not yet solved the most perplexing and persistent of the Negro problems.

That such an institution was unthinkable in 1870 was due in part to certain acts of the Freedmen's Bureau itself. It came to regard its work as merely temporary, and Negro suffrage as a final answer to all present perplexities. The political ambition of many of its agents and *proteges* led it far afield into questionable activities, until the South, nursing its own deep prejudices, came easily to ignore all the good deeds of the Bureau and hate its very name with perfect hatred. So the Freedmen's Bureau died, and its child was the Fifteenth Amendment.

The passing of a great human institution before its work is done, like the untimely passing of a single soul, but leaves a legacy of striving for other men. The legacy of the Freedmen's Bureau is the heavy heritage of this generation. To-day, when new and vaster problems are destined to strain every fibre of the national mind and soul, would it not be well to count this legacy honestly and carefully? For this much all men know: despite compromise, war, and struggle, the Negro is not free. In the backwoods of the Gulf States, for miles and miles, he may not leave the plantation of his birth; in well-nigh the whole rural South the black farmers are peons, bound by law and custom to an economic slavery, from which the only escape is death or the penitentiary. In the most cultured sections and cities of the South the Negroes are a segregated servile caste, with restricted rights and privileges. Before the courts, both in law and custom, they stand on a different and peculiar basis. Taxation without representation is the rule of their political life. And the result of all this is, and in nature must have been, lawlessness and crime. That is the large legacy of the Freedmen's Bureau, the work it did not do because it could not.

I have seen a land right merry with the sun, where children sing, and rolling hills lie like passioned women wanton with harvest. And there in the King's Highways[42] sat and sits a figure veiled and bowed, by which the traveller's footsteps hasten as they go. On the tainted air broods fear. Three centuries' thought has been the raising and unveiling of that bowed human heart, and now behold a century new for the duty and the deed. The problem of the Twentieth Century is the problem of the color-line.

---

[42] A reference to the Hebrew Scriptures, Numbers 20:17 and 21:22.

Document Number 3, Chapter II

On March 3, 1865, the United States Congress established a "bureau of refugees, freedmen and abandoned lands" to aid the approximately four million newly freed slaves. In 1866 Congress extended the bureau, placing it under the War Department. The purpose of the bureau was to provide relief for both black and white citizens—including the supervision of labor contracts to protect illiterate former slaves, setting up homesteading opportunities on public lands, establishing hospitals and schools, and protected civil rights of freedmen. The bureau ceased operation in 1872.

*   *   *

CHAP. XC.—An Act to establish a Bureau for the Relief of Freedmen and Refugees.[43]

Be it enacted by the Senate and House of Representatives of the United States of America in Congress assembled, That there is hereby established in the War Department, to continue during the present war of rebellion, and for one year thereafter, a bureau of refugees, freedmen, and abandoned lands, to which shall be committed, as hereinafter provided, the supervision and management of all abandoned lands, and the control of all subjects relating to refugees and freedmen from rebel states, or from any district of country within the territory embraced in the operations of the army, under such rules and regulations as may be prescribed by the head of the bureau and approved by the President. The said bureau shall be under the management and control of a commissioner to be appointed by the President, by and with the advice and consent of the Senate, whose compensation shall be three thousand dollars per annum, and such number of clerks as may be assigned to him by the Secretary of War, not exceeding one chief clerk, two of the fourth class, two of the third class, and five of the first class. And the commissioner and all persons appointed under this act, shall, before entering upon their duties, take the oath of office prescribed in an act entitled "An act to prescribe an oath of office, and for other purposes," approved July second, eighteen hundred and sixty-two, and the commissioner and the chief clerk shall, before entering upon their duties, give bonds to the treasurer of the United States, the former in the sum of fifty thousand dollars, and the latter in the sum of ten thousand dollars, conditioned for the faithful discharge of their duties respectively, with securities to be approved as sufficient by the Attorney-General, which bonds shall be filed in the office of the first comptroller of the treasury, to be by him put in suit for the benefit of any injured party upon any breach of the conditions thereof.

SEC. 2. And be it further enacted, That the Secretary of War may direct such issues of provisions, clothing, and fuel, as he may deem needful for the

---

[43] Source: *U.S., Statutes at Large, Treaties, and Proclamations of the United States of America*, vol. 13 (Boston, 1866), pp. 507–9.

immediate and temporary shelter and supply of destitute and suffering refugees and freedmen and their wives and children, under such rules and regulations as he may direct.

SEC. 3. And be it further enacted, That the President may, by and with the advice and consent of the Senate, appoint an assistant commissioner for each of the states declared to be in insurrection, not exceeding ten in number, who shall, under the direction of the commissioner, aid in the execution of the provisions of this act; and he shall give a bond to the Treasurer of the United States, in the sum of twenty thousand dollars, in the form and manner prescribed in the first section of this act. Each of said commissioners shall receive an annual salary of two thousand five hundred dollars in full compensation for all his services. And any military officer may be detailed and assigned to duty under this act without increase of pay or allowances. The commissioner shall, before the commencement of each regular session of congress, make full report of his proceedings with exhibits of the state of his accounts to the President, who shall communicate the same to congress, and shall also make special reports whenever required to do so by the President or either house of congress; and the assistant commissioners shall make quarterly reports of their proceedings to the commissioner, and also such other special reports as from time to time may be required.

SEC. 4. And be it further enacted, That the commissioner, under the direction of the President, shall have authority to set apart, for the use of loyal refugees and freedmen, such tracts of land within the insurrectionary states as shall have been abandoned, or to which the United States shall have acquired title by confiscation or sale, or otherwise, and to every male citizen, whether refugee or freedman, as aforesaid, there shall be assigned not more than forty acres of such land, and the person to whom it was so assigned shall be protected in the use and enjoyment of the land for the term of three years at an annual rent not exceeding six per centum upon the value of such land, as it was appraised by the state authorities in the year eighteen hundred and sixty, for the purpose of taxation, and in case no such appraisal can be found, then the rental shall be based upon the estimated value of the land in said year, to be ascertained in such manner as the commissioner may by regulation prescribe. At the end of said term, or at any time during said term, the occupants of any parcels so assigned may purchase the land and receive such title thereto as the United States can convey, upon paying therefor the value of the land, as ascertained and fixed for the purpose of determining the annual rent aforesaid.

SEC. 5. And be it further enacted, That all acts and parts of acts inconsistent with the provisions of this act, are hereby repealed.

APPROVED, March 3, 1865.

Booker Taliaferro Washington. Cheynes Studio. Photograph, ca. 1903.
Courtesy of the Library of Congress.

"A great Camp-meeting in de Promised Land," included in J. B. T. Marsh, *The Story of the Jubilee Singers* (Cleveland, Ohio: The Cleveland Printing and Publishing Company, 1892), p. 280.

III

Of Mr. Booker T. Washington and Others[1]

From birth till death enslaved; in word, in deed, unmanned!
Hereditary bondsmen! Know ye not
Who would be free themselves must strike the blow?

BYRON.[2]

asily the most striking thing in the history of the American Negro since 1876 is the ascendancy of Mr. Booker T. Washington.[3] It began at the time when war memories and ideals were rapidly passing; a day of astonishing commercial development was dawning; a sense of doubt and hesitation overtook the freedmen's sons,—then it was that his leading began. Mr. Washington came, with a single definite programme, at the psychological moment when the nation was a little ashamed of having bestowed so much sentiment on Negroes, and was concentrating its energies on Dollars. His programme of industrial education, conciliation of the South, and submission and silence as to civil and political rights, was not wholly original; the Free Negroes from 1830 up to wartime had striven to build industrial schools, and the American Missionary Association had from the first taught various

---

[1] This chapter is a revision of the article "The Evolution of Negro Leadership," *The Dial* (July 16, 1901), pp. 53–55.

[2] The three lines of poetry at the beginning of the chapter are from Lord Byron's 1812 poem "Childe Harold's Pilgrimmage."

[3] Booker T. Washington (1856–1915) founded the Tuskegee Institute in 1881. A graduate of Hampton Institute, his 1901 autobiography *Up from Slavery* recounts his personal life and of the founding of the Institute.

My Dear Mr Washington:
      Let me heartily congratulate you upon your phenomenal success at Atlanta — it was a word fitly spoken.

            Sincerely Yours,
                  W. E. B. Du Bois

Wilberforce, 24 Sept., '95

W. E. B. Du Bois to Booker T. Washington, September 24, 1895. Autograph letter. Booker T. Washington Papers, Manuscript Division, Library of Congress. Courtesy of the Library of Congress. While this Chapter of *The Souls of Black Folk* represents a major challenge to the work of Washington and the Hampton Model, at the time Washington gave the Atlanta Exposition Speech, Du Bois wrote Washington congratulating him on his "phenomenal success" with his presentation.

trades; and Price[4] and others had sought a way of honorable alliance with the best of the Southerners. But Mr. Washington first indissolubly linked these things; he put enthusiasm, unlimited energy, and perfect faith into his programme, and changed it from a by-path into a veritable Way of Life. And the tale of the methods by which he did this is a fascinating study of human life.

It startled the nation to hear a Negro advocating such a programme after many decades of bitter complaint; it startled and won the applause of the South, it interested and won the admiration of the North; and after a confused murmur of protest, it silenced if it did not convert the Negroes themselves.

---

[4] Joseph C. Price (1854–1893) was a minister of the African Methodist Episcopal Zion Church. A well-known orator, he founded several colleges and was an advocate for black higher education.

Carnegie Library, Tuskegee Institute, Alabama. Detroit Publishing Company, c. 1906. Courtesy of the Library of Congress.

To gain the sympathy and cooperation of the various elements comprising the white South was Mr. Washington's first task; and this, at the time Tuskegee was founded, seemed, for a black man, well-nigh impossible. And yet ten years later it was done in. the word spoken at Atlanta: "In all things purely social we can be as separate as the five fingers, and yet one as the hand in all things essential to mutual progress." This "Atlanta Compromise" is by all odds the most notable thing in Mr. Washington's career.[5] The South interpreted it in different ways: the radicals received it as a complete surrender of the demand for civil and political equality; the conservatives, as a generously conceived working basis for mutual understanding. So both approved it, and today its author is certainly the most distinguished Southerner since Jefferson

---

[5] On September 19, 1895, Washington delivered his most well-known speech at the Cotton States Exposition in Atlanta. In it, he emphasized the economic improvement of blacks, and also accepted the idea of the segregation of the races. At first many African-Americans, including Du Bois, viewed the speech positively. In time, it was seen as presenting a limiting set of opportunities for blacks—hence, it eventually came to be known as the Atlanta Compromise.

History class, Tuskegee Institute, Tuskegee, Alabama. Photographer Frances Benjamin Johnston, 1902. Courtesy of the Library of Congress.

Davis, and the one with the largest personal following.

Next to this achievement comes Mr. Washington's work in gaining place and consideration in the North. Others less shrewd and tactful had formerly essayed to sit on these two stools and had fallen between them; but as Mr. Washington knew the heart of the South from birth and training, so by singular insight he intuitively grasped the spirit of the age which was dominating the North. And so thoroughly did he learn the speech and thought of triumphant commercialism, and the ideals of material prosperity, that the picture of a lone black boy poring over a French grammar amid the weeds and dirt of a neglected home soon seemed to him the acme of absurdities. One wonders what Socrates[6] and St. Francis of Assisi[7] would say to this.

---

[6] Socrates (470–399 BCE), Ancient Greek philosopher, who was put to death by the citizens of Athens.

[7] St. Francis of Assisi (1182–1226), Medieval Catholic saint and monastic. He was the founder of the Franciscan Order and was known for the simplicity of his life and for his love of animals.

And yet this very singleness of vision and thorough oneness with his age is a mark of the successful man. It is as though Nature must needs make men narrow in order to give them force. So Mr. Washington's cult has gained unquestioning followers, his work has wonderfully prospered, his friends are legion, and his enemies are confounded. Today he stands as the one recognized spokesman of his ten million fellows, and one of the most notable figures in a nation of seventy millions. One hesitates, therefore, to criticise a life which, beginning with so little, has done so much. And yet the time is come when one may speak in all sincerity and utter courtesy of the mistakes and shortcomings of Mr. Washington's career, as well as of his triumphs, without being thought captious or envious, and without forgetting that it is easier to do ill than well in the world.

The criticism that has hitherto met Mr. Washington has not always been of this broad character. In the South especially has he had to walk warily to avoid the harshest judgments,—and naturally so, for he is

African American students in mattress-making class, Tuskegee Institute, Tuskegee, Alabama. Photographer Frances Benjamin Johnston, 1902. Johnston had also taken extensive photographs of Hampton Institute. Courtesy of the Library of Congress.

Tuskegee Institute faculty with Andrew Carnegie, Tuskegee, Alabama. Shown from left to right, seated in front row: R.C. Ogden; Mrs. Booker T. Washington; Booker T. Washington; Andrew Carnegie; and an unidentified person. Photographer, Frances Benjamin Johnston, 1906.

dealing with the one subject of deepest sensitiveness to that section. Twice—once when at the Chicago celebration of the Spanish-American War he alluded to the color-prejudice that is "eating away the vitals of the South," and once when he dined with President Roosevelt—has the resulting Southern criticism been violent enough to threaten seriously his popularity. In the North the feeling has several times forced itself into words, that Mr. Washington's counsels of submission overlooked certain elements of true manhood, and that his educational programme was unnecessarily narrow. Usually, however, such criticism has not found open expression, although, too, the spiritual sons of the Abolitionists have not been prepared to acknowledge that the schools founded before Tuskeegee, by men of broad ideals and self-sacrificing spirit, were wholly failures or worthy of ridicule. While, then, criticism has not failed to follow Mr. Washington, yet the prevailing public opinion of the land has been but too willing to deliver the solution of a wearisome problem into his hands, and say, "If that is all you and your race ask, take it."

Among his own people, however, Mr. Washington has encountered the strongest and most lasting opposition, amounting at times to bitterness, and even today continuing strong and insistent even though largely silenced in outward expression by the public opinion of the nation. Some of this opposition is, of course, mere envy; the disappointment of displaced demagogues and the spite of narrow minds. But aside from this, there is among educated and thoughtful colored men in all parts of the land a feeling of deep regret, sorrow, and apprehension at the wide currency and ascendancy which some of Mr. Washington's theories have gained. These same men admire his sincerity of purpose, and are willing to forgive much to honest endeavor which is doing something worth the doing. They cooperate with Mr. Washington as far as they conscientiously can; and, indeed, it is no ordinary tribute to this man's tact and power that, steering as he must between so many diverse interests and opinions, he so largely retains the respect of all.

But the hushing of the criticism of honest opponents is a dangerous thing. It leads some of the best of the critics to unfortunate silence and paralysis of effort, and others to burst into speech so passionately and intemperately as to lose listeners. Honest and earnest criticism from

Lithograph by C. H. Thomas and P. H. Lacey, 1903. Courtesy of the Smithsonian Institution.

those whose interests are most nearly touched,—criticism of writers by readers, of government by those governed, of leaders by those led,—this is the soul of democracy and the safeguard of modern society. If the best of the American Negroes receive by outer pressure a leader whom they had not recognized before, manifestly there is here a certain palpable gain. Yet there is also irreparable loss,—a loss of that peculiarly valuable education which a group receives when by search and criticism it finds and commissions its own leaders. The way in which this is done is at once the most elementary and the nicest problem of social growth. History is but the record of such group-leadership; and yet how infinitely changeful is its type and character! And of all types and kinds, what can be more instructive than the leadership of a group within a group?—that curious double movement where real progress may be negative and actual advance be relative retrogression. All this is the social student's inspiration and despair.

Now in the past the American Negro has had instructive experience in the choosing of group leaders, founding thus a peculiar dynasty which in the light of present conditions is worthwhile studying. When sticks and stones and beasts form the sole environment of a people, their attitude is largely one of determined opposition to and conquest of natural forces. But when to earth and brute is added an environment of men and ideas, then the attitude of the imprisoned group may take three main forms,—a feeling of revolt and revenge; an attempt to adjust all thought and action to the will of the greater group; or, finally, a determined effort at self-realization and self-development despite environing opinion. The influence of all of these attitudes at various times can be traced in the history of the American Negro, and in the evolution of his successive leaders.

Before 1750, while the fire of African freedom still burned in the veins of the slaves, there was in all leadership or attempted leadership but the one motive of revolt and revenge,—typified in the terrible Maroons, the Danish blacks, and Cato of Stono,[8] and veiling all the Americas in fear of insurrection. The liberalizing tendencies of the latter half of the eighteenth century brought, along with kindlier relations between black and white, thoughts of ultimate adjustment and assimilation. Such aspiration was especially voiced in the earnest songs of Phyllis,[9] in the martyrdom of Attucks,[10] the fighting of Salem and

---

[8] A rebellion of hundreds of slaves gathered along the banks of the Stono River in South Carolina that took place September 9, 1739.

[9] Phyllis Wheatley (1735?–1784), poetess who was brought from Africa as a slave in 1761.

[10] Crispus Attucks (1723–1770), was killed in the Boston Massacre in 1770.

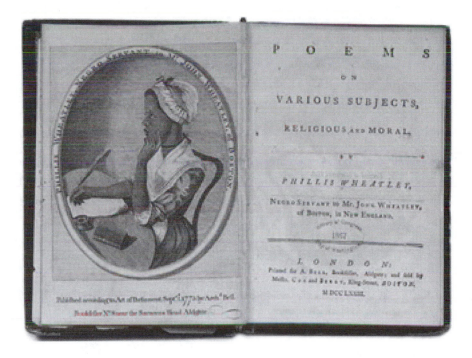

Phyllis Wheatley's *Poems on Various Subjects, Religious and Moral*, 1773. Courtesy of the Library of Congress.

Poor,[11] the intellectual accomplishments of Banneker[12] and Derham,[13] and the political demands of the Cuffes.[14]

Stern financial and social stress after the war cooled much of the previous humanitarian ardor. The disappointment and impatience of the Negroes at the persistence of slavery and serfdom voiced itself in two movements. The slaves in the South, aroused undoubtedly by vague rumors of the Haytian revolt, made three fierce attempts at insurrection,—in 1800 under Gabriel in Virginia, in 1822 under Vesey in Carolina, and in 1831 again in Virginia under the terrible Nat Turner.[15]

---

[11] Peter Salem (1750–1816) and Salem Poor (1747–?) both fought in the American Revolution.

[12] Benjamin Banneker (1731–1806), black mathematician, scientist and almanac writer. He helped survey and lay out Washington, D.C.

[13] James C. Durham (c. 1862–?) black slave who eventually earned his freedom and became a physician.

[14] Paul Cuffe (1759–1817), wealthy Massachusetts free black who had supported the return of African-Americans to Africa.

[15] The most important slave uprising in North American during the Nineteenth century was the Haitian uprising under Toussaint L'Ouverture in 1804. Du Bois

Portrayal of the March 5, 1770, skirmish between British soldiers and Boston citizens commonly known as the "Boston Massacre. " Among those listed as killed is the African-American Crispus Attucks. Created c. 1770. Courtesy of the Library of Congress.

In the Free States, on the other hand, a new and curious attempt at self-development was made. In Philadelphia and New York color-prescription led to a withdrawal of Negro communicants from white churches and the formation of a peculiar socio-religious institution among the Negroes known as the African Church,—an organization still living and controlling in its various branches over a million of men.[16]

Walker's wild appeal against the trend of the times showed how the

---

lists here the major slave uprisings that took place in the South prior to the Civil War, concluding with the Nat Turner Rebellion of 1832.

[16] Du Bois is referring to the African Methodist Episcopal Church.

world was changing after the coming of the cotton-gin.[17] By 1830 slavery seemed hopelessly fastened on the South, and the slaves thoroughly cowed into submission. The free Negroes of the North, inspired by the mulatto immigrants from the West Indies, began to change the basis of their demands; they recognized the slavery of slaves, but insisted that they themselves were freemen, and sought assimilation and amalgamation with the nation on the same terms with other men. Thus, Forten[18] and Purvis[19] of Philadelphia, Shad[20] of Wilmington, Du Bois[21] of New Haven, Barbadoes of Boston, and others, strove singly and

HORRID MASSACRE IN VIRGINIA

"Horrid Massacre in Virginia." Illustration in *Authentic and Impartial Narrative of the Tragical Scene Which Was Witnessed in Southampton County.* 1831. Courtesy of the Library of Congress.

---

[17] David Walker (1785–1830), African-American abolitionist who published *An Appeal to the Colored Citizens of the World* in 1829, which called for American slaves to revolt against their masters.

[18] James Forten (1766–1842), black revolutionary and co-founder of the American Anti-Slavery Society.

[19] Robert Purvis (1810–1898), abolitionist and civil rights leader following the Civil War.

[20] Abraham Shad (1801–1882), black leader from Deleware.

[21] Alexander Du Bois (1803–1888), W. E. B. Du Bois's paternal grandfather.

Patent for the Cotton Gin (1892). Courtesy of the National Archives and Records Administration.

together as men, they said, not as slaves; as "people of color," not as "Negroes." The trend of the times, however, refused them recognition save in individual and exceptional cases, considered them as one with all the despised blacks, and they soon found themselves striving to keep even the rights they formerly had of voting and working and moving as freemen. Schemes of migration and colonization arose among them; but these they refused to entertain, and they eventually turned to the Abolition movement as a final refuge.

Here, led by Redmond,[22] Nell,[23] Wells-Brown,[24] and Douglass,[25] a

---

[22] Charles Lenox Redmond (1810–1873), black abolitionist and civil rights leader from Boston.
[23] William Cooper Nell (1816–1874), historian and education leader.

Distinguished colored men (Head-and-shoulders portraits of Frederick Douglass, Robert Brown Elliott, Blanche K. Bruce, William Wells Brown, MD, Prof. R.T. Greener, Rt. Rev. Richard Allen, J.H. Rainey, E.D. Bassett, John Mercer Langston, P.B.S. Pinchback, and Henry Highland Garnet). Published by A. Muller & Co., c. 1883. Courtesy of the Library of Congress.

---

[24] William Wells Brown (1814–1884), ex-slave and novelist.
[25] Frederick Douglass (1818–1895), ex-slave, abolitionist and newspaper editor. Douglass was the author of the *Narrative Life of Frederick Douglass, and American Slave* (1845), probably the most famous and widely read personal narratives of living under slavery.

new period of self-assertion and self-development dawned. To be sure, ultimate freedom and assimilation was the ideal before the leaders, but the assertion of the manhood rights of the Negro by himself was the main reliance, and John Brown's raid was the extreme of its logic. After the war and Emancipation, the great form of Frederick Douglass, the greatest of American Negro leaders, still led the host. Self-assertion, especially in political lines, was the main programme, and behind Douglass came Elliot,[26] Bruce,[27] and Langston,[28] and the Reconstruction politicians, and, less conspicuous but of greater social significance, Alexander Crummell[29] and Bishop Daniel Payne.[30]

Then came the Revolution of 1876, the suppression of the Negro votes, the changing and shifting of ideals, and the seeking of new lights in the great night. Douglass, in his old age, still bravely stood for the ideals of his early manhood,—ultimate assimilation *through* self-assertion, and on no other terms. For a time Price arose as a new leader, destined, it seemed, not to give up, but to restate the old ideals in a form less repugnant to the white South. But he passed away in his prime. Then came the new leader. Nearly all the former ones had become leaders by the silent suffrage of their fellows, had sought to lead their own people alone, and were usually, save Douglass, little known outside their race. But Booker T. Washington arose as essentially the leader not of one race but of two,—a compromiser between the South, the North, and the Negro. Naturally the Negroes resented, at first bitterly, signs of compromise which surrendered their civil and political rights, even though this was to be exchanged for larger chances of economic development. The rich and dominating North, however, was not only weary of the race problem, but was investing largely in Southern enterprises, and welcomed any method of peaceful cooperation. Thus, by national opinion, the Negroes began to recognize Mr. Washington's leadership; and the voice of criticism was hushed.

---

[26] Robert Brown "Elliot" (1841–1884). Du Bois probably means Robert Brown Eliott whose name is spelled with two Ts and who was an African-American congressman during the Reconstruction period.

[27] Blanche K. Bruce (1841–1898), former slave and first African-American to serve a full term in the United States Senate.

[28] John Mercer Langston (1829–1897), who was educated at Oberlin College and was the first African-American elected to public office in the United States.

[29] Alexander Crummell (1819–1898), missionary to Liberia and one of the founders of the American Negro Academy. Chapter XII of *The Souls of Black Folk* is a biography of Crummell.

[30] Daniel Alexander Payne (1811–1893), bishop of the African Methodist Episcopal Chruch and the founder of Wilberforce University.

Atlanta, Georgia, Cotton States Exposition: "Looking North from Model Jail," 1995. Courtesy of the Library of Congress.

Mr. Washington represents in Negro thought the old attitude of adjustment and submission; but adjustment at such a peculiar time as to make his programme unique. This is an age of unusual economic development, and Mr. Washington's programme naturally takes an economic cast, becoming a gospel of Work and Money to such an extent as apparently almost completely to overshadow the higher aims of life. Moreover, this is an age when the more advanced races are coming in closer contact with the less developed races, and the race-feeling is therefore intensified; and Mr. Washington's programme practically accepts the alleged inferiority of the Negro races. Again, in our own land, the reaction from the sentiment of wartime has given impetus to race-prejudice against Negroes, and Mr. Washington withdraws many of the high demands of Negroes as men and American citizens. In other periods of intensified prejudice all the Negro's tendency to self-assertion has been called forth; at this period a policy of submission is advocated. In the history of nearly all other races and peoples the doctrine preached at such crises has been that manly self-respect is worth more than lands and houses, and that a people who voluntarily surrender such respect, or cease striving for it, are not worth civilizing.

In answer to this, it has been claimed that the Negro can survive only through submission. Mr. Washington distinctly asks that black people give up, at least for the present, three things,—

First, political power,

Second, insistence on civil rights,

Third, higher education of Negro youth,

—and concentrate all their energies on industrial education, the cumulation of wealth, and the conciliation of the South. This policy has been courageously and insistently advocated for over fifteen years, and has been triumphant for perhaps ten years. As a result of this tender of the palm-branch,[31] what has been the return? In the years there have occurred:

1. The disfranchisement of the Negro.

2. The legal creation of a distinct status of civil inferiority for the Negro.

3. The steady withdrawal of aid from institutions for the higher training of the Negro.

These movements are not, to be sure, direct results of Mr. Washington's teachings; but his propaganda has, without a shadow of doubt, helped their speedier accomplishment. The question then comes: Is it possible, and probable, that nine millions of men can make effective progress in economic lines if they are deprived of political rights, made a servile caste, and allowed only the most meagre chance for developing their exceptional men? If history and reason give any distinct answer to these questions, it is an emphatic *No*. And Mr. Washington thus faces the triple paradox of his career:

1. He is striving nobly to make Negro artisans businessmen and property-owners; but it is utterly impossible, under modern competitive methods, for workingmen and property-owners to defend their rights and exist without the right of suffrage.

2. He insists an thrift and self-respect, but at the same time counsels a silent submission to civic inferiority such as is bound to sap the manhood of any race in the long run.

3. He advocates common-school and industrial training, and depreciates institutions of higher learning; but neither the Negro common schools, nor Tuskegee itself, could remain open a day were it not for teachers trained in Negro colleges, or trained by their graduates.

---

[31] Du Bois is referring to Washington's compromise and his attempt to bring some type of peace between the races.

Tuskegee 25th anniversary—reviewing stand, Tuskegee Institute, Tuskegee, Alabama, 1906. Courtesy of the Library of Congress.

This triple paradox in Mr. Washington's position is the object of criticism by two classes of colored Americans. One class is spiritually descended from Toussaint the Savior, through Gabriel, Vesey, and Turner, and they represent the attitude of revolt and revenge; they hate the white South blindly and distrust the white race generally, and so far as they agree on definite action, think that the Negro's only hope lies in emigration beyond the borders of the United States. And yet, by the irony of fate, nothing has more effectually made this programme seem hopeless than the recent course of the United States toward weaker and darker peoples in the West Indies, Hawaii, and the Philippines,—for where in the world may we go and be safe from lying and brute force?[32]

The other class of Negroes who cannot agree with Mr. Washington has hitherto said little aloud. They deprecate the sight of scattered counsels, of internal disagreement; and especially they dislike making their just criticism of a useful and earnest man an excuse for a general discharge of venom from small-minded opponents. Nevertheless, the questions involved are so fundamental and serious that it is difficult to

[32] This is a reference to the emergence of the United States as a Colonialist power in the period following the Spanish American War.

see how men like the Grimkes,[33] Kelly Miller,[34] J. W. E. Bowen,[35] and other representatives of this group, can much longer be silent. Such men feel in conscience bound to ask of this nation three things:

1. The right to vote.
2. Civic equality.
3. The education of youth according to ability.

They acknowledge Mr. Washington's invaluable service in counselling patience and courtesy in such demands; they do not ask that ignorant black men vote when ignorant whites are debarred, or that any reasonable restrictions in the suffrage should not be applied; they know that the low social level of the mass of the race is responsible for much discrimination against it, but they also know, and the nation knows, that relentless color-prejudice is more often a cause than a result of the Negro's degradation; they seek the abatement of this relic of barbarism, and not its systematic encouragement and pampering by all agencies of social power from the Associated Press to the Church of Christ. They advocate, with Mr. Washington, a broad system of Negro common schools supplemented by thorough industrial training; but they are surprised that a man of Mr. Washington's insight cannot see that no such educational system ever has rested or can rest on any other basis than that of the well-equipped college and university, and they insist that there is a demand for a few such institutions throughout the South to train the best of the Negro youth as teachers, professional men, and leaders.

This group of men honor Mr. Washington for his attitude of conciliation toward the white South; they accept the "Atlanta Compromise" in its broadest interpretation; they recognize, with him, many signs of promise, many men of high purpose and fair judgment, in this section; they know that no easy task has been laid upon a region already tottering under heavy burdens. But, nevertheless, they insist that the way to truth and right lies in straightforward honesty, not in indiscriminate flattery; in praising those of the South who do well and criticizing uncompromisingly those who do ill; in taking advantage of the opportunities at hand and urging their fellows to do the same, but at the same time in remembering that only a firm adherence to their higher ideals and aspirations will ever keep those ideals within the realm of possibility. They do not expect that the free right to vote, to enjoy civic

---

[33] Archibald H. Grimke (1849–1930), and his brother Francis J. Grimke (1850–1937), were early civil rights leaders.

[34] Kelly Miller (1863–1939) was a mathematician and sociologist who taught at Howard University.

[35] John Wesley Edward Bowen (1855–1933) was a Methodist minister and educator involved in civil rights issues.

rights, and to be educated, will come in a moment; they do not expect to see the bias and prejudices of years disappear at the blast of a trumpet;[36] but they are absolutely certain that the way for a people to gain their reasonable rights is not by voluntarily throwing them away and insisting that they do not want them; that the way for a people to gain respect is not by continually belittling and ridiculing themselves; that, on the contrary, Negroes must insist continually, in season and out of season, that voting is necessary to modern manhood, that color discrimination is barbarism, and that black boys need education as well as white boys.

In failing thus to state plainly and unequivocally the legitimate demands of their people, even at the cost of opposing an honored leader, the thinking classes of American Negroes would shirk a heavy responsibility,—a responsibility to themselves, a responsibility to the struggling masses, a responsibility to the darker races of men whose future depends so largely on this American experiment, but especially a responsibility to this nation,—this common Fatherland. It is wrong to encourage a man or a people in evil-doing; it is wrong to aid and abet a national crime simply because it is unpopular not to do so. The growing spirit of kindliness and reconciliation between the North and South after the frightful difference of a generation ago ought to be a source of deep congratulation to all, and especially to those whose mistreatment caused the war; but if that reconciliation is to be marked by the industrial slavery and civic death of those same black men, with permanent legislation into a position of inferiority, then those black men, if they are really men, are called upon by every consideration of patriotism and loyalty to oppose such a course by all civilized methods, even though such opposition involves disagreement with Mr. Booker T. Washington. We have no right to sit silently by while the inevitable seeds are sown for a harvest of disaster to our children, black and white.

First, it is the duty of black men to judge the South discriminatingly. The present generation of Southerners are not responsible for the past, and they should not be blindly hated or blamed for it. Furthermore, to no class is the indiscriminate endorsement of the recent course of the South toward Negroes more nauseating than to the best thought of the South. The South is not "solid"; it is a land in the ferment of social change, wherein forces of all kinds are fighting for supremacy; and to praise the ill the South is today perpetrating is just as wrong as to condemn the good. Discriminating and broad-minded criticism is what the South needs,—needs it for the sake of her own white sons and daughters, and for the insurance of robust, healthy mental and moral development.

---

[36] In Joshua 6:15-21, God commands the Israelites to blow trumpets and shout, which leads to the fall of the walls of Jerricho.

Students in workshop, Tuskegee Institute, Alabama. Photograph by Frances Benjamin Johnston, 1902. Courtesy of the Library of Congress.

Today even the attitude of the Southern whites toward the blacks is not, as so many assume, in all cases the same; the ignorant Southerner hates the Negro, the workingmen fear his competition, the money-makers wish to use him as a laborer, some of the educated see a menace in his upward development, while others—usually the sons of the masters—wish to help him to rise. National opinion has enabled this last class to maintain the Negro common schools, and to protect the Negro partially in property, life, and limb. Through the pressure of the money-makers, the Negro is in danger of being reduced to semi-slavery, especially in the country districts; the workingmen, and those of the educated who fear the Negro, have united to disfranchise him, and some have urged his deportation; while the passions of the ignorant are easily aroused to lynch and abuse any black man. To praise this intricate whirl of thought and prejudice is nonsense; to inveigh indiscriminately against "the South" is unjust; but to use the same breath in praising Governor Aycock,[37] exposing Senator Morgan,[38] arguing with Mr. Thomas Nelson

---

[37] Charles Aycock (1859–1912), governor of North Carolina.

Page,[39] and denouncing Senator Ben Tillman,[40] is not only sane, but the imperative duty of thinking black men.

It would be unjust to Mr. Washington not to acknowledge that in several instances he has opposed movements in the South which were unjust to the Negro; he sent memorials to the Louisiana and Alabama constitutional conventions, he has spoken against lynching, and in other ways has openly or silently set his influence against sinister schemes and unfortunate happenings. Notwithstanding this, it is equally true to assert that on the whole the distinct impression left by Mr. Washington's propaganda is, first, that the South is justified in its present attitude toward the Negro because of the Negro's degradation; secondly, that the prime cause of the Negro's failure to rise more quickly is his wrong education in the past; and, thirdly, that his future rise depends primarily on his own efforts. Each of these propositions is a dangerous half-truth. The supplementary truths must never be lost sight of: first, slavery and race-prejudice are potent if not sufficient causes of the Negro's position; second, industrial and common-school training were necessarily slow in planting because they had to await the black teachers trained by higher institutions,—it being extremely doubtful if any essentially different development was possible, and certainly a Tuskegee was unthinkable before 1880; and, third, while it is a great truth to say that the Negro must strive and strive mightily to help himself, it is equally true that unless his striving be not simply seconded, but rather aroused and encouraged, by the initiative of the richer and wiser environing group, he cannot hope for great success.

In his failure to realize and impress this last point, Mr. Washington is especially to be criticised. His doctrine has tended to make the whites, North and South, shift the burden of the Negro problem to the Negro's shoulders and stand aside as critical and rather pessimistic spectators; when in fact the burden belongs to the nation, and the hands of none of us are clean if we bend not our energies to righting these great wrongs.

The South ought to be led, by candid and honest criticism, to assert her better self and do her full duty to the race she has cruelly wronged and is still wronging. The North—her co-partner in guilt—cannot salve her conscience by plastering it with gold. We cannot settle this problem by diplomacy and suaveness, by "policy" alone. If worse come to worst,

---

[38] John Tyler Morgan (1824–1907), senator and white supremacist from Alabama.
[39] Thomas Nelson Page (1853–1922), white supremacist.
[40] Benjamin R. Tilman (1847–1919), governor and white supremacist from South Carolina.

can the moral fibre of this country survive the slow throttling and murder of nine millions of men?

The black men of America have a duty to perform, a duty stern and delicate,—a forward movement to oppose a part of the work of their greatest leader. So far as Mr. Washington preaches Thrift, Patience, and Industrial Training for the masses, we must hold up his hands and strive with him, rejoicing in his honors and glorying in the strength of this Joshua[41] called of God and of man to lead the headless host. But so far as Mr. Washington apologizes for injustice, North or South, does not rightly value the privilege and duty of voting, belittles the emasculating effects of caste distinctions, and opposes the higher training and ambition of our brighter minds,—so far as he, the South, or the Nation, does this,—we must unceasingly and firmly oppose them. By every civilized and peaceful method we must strive for the rights which the world accords to men, clinging unwaveringly to those great words which the sons of the Fathers would fain forget: "We hold these truths to be self-evident: That all men are created equal; that they are endowed by their Creator with certain unalienable rights; that among these are life, liberty, and the pursuit of happiness."[42]

---

[41] Joshua led the Israelites into Israel after the death of Moses.

[42] Quote taken from the Preamble to the Declaration of Independence (1776).

Document Number 4, Chapter III

Booker T. Washington's Atlanta Exposition speech was delivered on September 18, 1895, at the Cotton States and International Exposition held in Atlanta, Georgia. Black participation had been extremely limited two years earlier at the 1893 Worlds Columbian Exposition in Chicago. Therefore, Washington's prominent involvement in the Atlanta Exposition was particularly noteworthy. Known as the Atlanta Compromise, Washington's speech set the tone for racial politics in the United States for the next twenty years.

*   *   *

Address of Booker T. Washington Principal of the Tuskegee Normal And Industrial Institute, Tusekegee, Alabama. Delivered at the Opening of the Cotton States And International Exposition, at Atlanta, GA. September 18, 1895, with a Letter Of Congratulation from the President of the United States.

Gray Gables, Buzzard's Bay, Mass.,
October 6, 1895.
Booker T. Washington, Esq.

My Dear Sir :

I thank you for sending me a copy of your address delivered at the Atlanta Exposition.

I thank you with much enthusiasm for making the address. I have read it with intense interest, and I think the Exposition would be fully justified if it did not do more than furnish the opportunity for its delivery. Your words cannot fail to delight and encourage all who wish well for your race; and if our colored fellow citizens do not from your utterances gather new hope and form new deterinations to gain every valuable advantage offered them by their citizenship, it will be strange indeed.

Yours very truly,

Grover Cleveland.

MR. WASHINGTON'S ADDRESS.

Mr. President and Gentlemen of the Board of Directors and Citizens:

One third of the population of the South is of the Negro race. No enterprise seeking the material, civil, or moral welfare of this section can disregard this element of our population and reach the highest success. I but convey to you, Mr. President and Directors, the sentiment of the masses of my race when I say that in no way have the value and manhood of the American Negro been more fittingly and generously recognized than by the managers of this magnificent Exposition at every stage of its progress. It is a recognition that will do more to cement the friendship of the two races than any occurrence since the dawn of our freedom.

Not only this, but the opportunity here afforded will awaken among us a new era of industrial progress. Ignorant and inexperienced, it is not strange that in the first years of our new life we began at the top instead of at the bottom; that a seat in Congress or the State Legislature was more sought than real estate or industrial skill; that the political convention or stump speaking had more attractions than starting a dairy farm or truck garden.

A ship lost at sea for many days suddenly sighted a friendly vessel. From the mast of the unfortunate vessel was seen a signal: "Water, water; we die of thirst!" The answer from the friendly vessel at once came back: "Cast down your bucket where you are." A second time the signal, "Water, water; send us water!" ran up from the distressed vessel, and was answered: "Cast down your bucket where you are." And a third and fourth signal for water was answered: "Cast down your bucket where you are." The captain of the distressed vessel, at last heeding the injunction, cast down his bucket, and it came up full of fresh, sparkling water from the mouth of the Amazon River. To those of my race who depend on bettering their condition in a foreign land, or who underestimate the importance of cultivating friendly relations with the Southern white man, who is their next door neighbor, I would say: "Cast down your bucket where you are"— cast it down in making friends in every manly way of the people of all races by whom we are surrounded.

Cast it down in agriculture, mechanics, in commerce, in domestic service, and in the professions. And in this connection it is well to bear in mind that whatever other sins the South may be called to bear, when it comes to business, pure and simple, it is in the South that the Negro is given a man's chance in the commercial world, and in nothing is this Exposition more eloquent than in emphasizing this chance. Our greatest danger is, that in the great leap from slavery to freedom we may overlook the fact that the masses of us are to live by the productions of our hands, and fail to keep in mind that we shall prosper in proportion as we learn to dignify and glorify common labor and put brains and skill into the common occupations of life; shall prosper in proportion as we learn to draw the line between the superficial and the substantial, the ornamental gewgaws of life and the useful. No race can prosper till it learns that there is as much dignity in tilling a field as in writing a poem. It is at the bottom of life we must begin, and not at the top. Nor should we permit our grievances to overshadow our opportunities.

To those of the white race who look to the incoming of those of foreign birth and strange tongue and habits for the prosperity of the South, were I permitted I would repeat what I say to my own race, "Cast down your bucket where you are." Cast it down among the 8,000,000 Negroes whose habits you know, whose fidelity and love you have tested in days when to have proved treacherous meant the ruin of your firesides. Cast down your bucket among these people who have, without strikes and labor wars, tilled your fields, cleared your forests, built your railroads and cities, and brought forth treasures from the bowels of the earth, and helped make possible this magnificent representation of the progress of the South. Casting down your bucket among my people, helping and encouraging them as you are doing on these grounds, and to education of head, hand, and heart, you will find that they will buy your surplus land, make blossom the waste places in your fields, and run your factories. While doing this, you can be sure in the future, as in the past, that you and your families will be surrounded by the most patient, faithful, law-abiding, and unresentful people that the world has seen. As we have proved our loyalty to you in the past, in nursing your children, watching by the sick bed of your mothers and fathers, and often following them with tear-dimmed eyes to their graves, so in the future, in our humble way, we shall stand by you with a devotion that no foreigner can approach, ready to lay down our lives, if need be, in defense of yours, interlacing our industrial, commercial, civil, and religious life with yours in a way that shall make the interests of both races one. In all things that are purely social we can be as separate as the fingers, yet one as the hand in all things essential to mutual progress.

There is no defense or security for any of us except in the highest intelligence and development of all. If anywhere there are efforts tending to curtail the fullest growth of the Negro, let these efforts be turned into stimulating, encouraging, and making him the most useful and intelligent citizen. Effort or means so invested will pay a thousand per cent interest. These efforts will be twice blessed—"blessing him that gives and him that takes."

There is no escape through law of man or God from the inevitable: The laws of changeless justice bind Oppressor with oppressed; And close as sin and suffering joined We march to fate abreast. Nearly sixteen millions of hands will aid you in pulling the load upwards, or they will pull you against the load downwards. We shall constitute one third and more of the ignorance and crime of the South, or one third its intelligence and progress; we shall contribute one third to the business and industrial prosperity of the South, or we shall prove a veritable body of death, stagnating, depressing, retarding every effort to advance the body politic. Gentlemen of the Exposition, as we present to you our humble effort at an exhibition of our progress, you must not expect overmuch. Starting thirty years ago with ownership here and there in a few quilts and pumpkins and chickens (gathered from miscellaneous sources), remember the path that has led from these to the inventions and production of agricultural implements, buggies, steam engines, newspapers, book, statuary, carving, paintings, the management of drug stores and banks has not been trodden without contact with thorns and thistles. While we take pride in what we exhibit as a result of our independent efforts, we do not for a moment forget that our part in this exhibition would fall far short of your expectations but for the constant help that has come to our educational life, not only from the Southern States, but especially from Northern philanthropists, who have made their gifts a constant stream of blessing and encouragement. The wisest among my race understand that the agitation of questions of social equality is the extremist folly, and that progress in the enjoyment of all the privileges that will come to us must be the result of severe and constant struggle rather than of artificial forcing. No race that has anything to contribute to the markets of the world is long in any degree ostracized. It is important and right that all privileges of the law be ours, but it is vastly more important that we be prepared for the exercises of these privileges. The opportunity to earn a dollar in a factory just now is worth infinitely more than the opportunity to spend a dollar in an opera house.

In conclusion, may I repeat that nothing in thirty years has given us more hope and encouragement, and drawn us so near to you of the white race, as this opportunity offered by the Exposition; and here bending, as it were, over the altar that represents the results of the struggles of your race and mine, both starting practically empty-handed three decades ago, I pledge that in your effort to work out the great and intricate problem which God has laid at the doors of the South you shall have at all times the patient, sympathetic help of my race; only let this be constantly in mind that, while from representations in these buildings of the product of field, of forest, of mine, of factory, letters, and art, much good will come, yet far above and beyond material benefits will be that higher good, that let us pray God will come, in a blotting out of sectional differences and racial animosities and suspicions, in a determination to administer absolute justice, in a willing obedience among all classes to the mandates of law. This, this, coupled with our material prosperity, will bring into our beloved South a new heaven and a new earth.

W. E. B. Du Bois _____ Teacher.

(Teacher's Cert.)

CONTRACT WITH THE DIRECTORS OF SCHOOL DISTRICT No. 13 _____

State of Tennessee, County of _W. E. B. Du Bois_. This Contract, entered into this __6th__ day of _July_ 1886, between the School Directors of the _13th_ District of said County of _Wilson,_ and _State of Tennessee_ Witnesseth: That the said Directors have engaged the said _W. E. B. Du Bois_ as a teacher of School No. _5_ in said District from the _19th_ day of _July_ 1886, and agree to pay _him_ the sum of _28_ dollars per month for _his_ services. The said _W. E. B. Du Bois_ agrees to give instruction in the studies required to be taught in said School and prescribed by the School Law, to such pupils as may attend the said school during the said term; to faithfully discharge the duties required by law of said school teachers, and at the close of the term, or of the period of _his_ service, to furnish the Clerk of said District with the Register of the school, said Register having been kept according to law.

R. M. Johnson Clerk
H. C. Barry } Directors.

W. E. B. Du Bois _____ Teacher.

Teaching certificate of W. E. B. Du Bois. Courtesy of the Special Collections and Archives, W .E. B. Du Bois Library, University of Massachusetts, Amherst.

My Way's Cloudy.*

Oh! breth-er-en, my way, my way's cloud-y, my way, Go send them an-gels down, Oh! breth-er-en, my way, my way's cloud-y, my way, Go send them an-gels down.

1. There's fire in the east and fire in the west, Send them angels down, And
2. Old Sa-tan's mad, and I am glad, Send them angels down, He
3. I'll tell you now as I told you be-fore, Send them angels down, To
4. This is the year of Ju-bi-lee, Send them angels down, The

D. C.

fire a-mong the Meth-o-dist, O send them an-gels down.
missed the soul he thought he had, O send them an-gels down.
the promised land I'm bound to go, O send them an-gels down.
Lord has come to set us free, O send them an-gels down.

* Fisk Jubilee Collection, by permission.

"My Way's Cloudy," included in J. B. T. Marsh, *The Story of the Jubilee Singers* (Cleveland, Ohio: The Cleveland Printing and Publishing Company, 1892), p. 201.

IV

Of the Meaning of Progress[1]

Villst Du Deine Macht verkünden,
Wähle sie die frei von Sünden,
Steh'n in Deinem ew'gen Haus !
Deine Geister sende aus!
Die Unsterblichen, die Reinen,
Die nicht fuhlen, die nicht weinen!
Nicht die zarte Jungfrau wahle,
Nicht der Hirtin weiche Seele !

SCHILLER.[2]

Once upon a time I taught school in the hills of Tennessee, where the broad dark vale of the Mississippi begins to roll and crumple to greet the Alleghenies. I was a Fisk student then, and all Fisk men thought that Tennessee—beyond the Veil—was theirs alone, and in vacation time they sallied forth in lusty bands to meet the county school-commissioners. Young and happy, I too went, and I shall not soon forget that summer, seventeen years ago.[3]

First, there was a Teachers' Institute at the county seat; and there distinguished guests of the superintendent taught the teachers fractions and spelling and other mysteries,—white teachers in the morning, Negroes at night. A picnic now and then, and a supper, and the rough world was softened by laughter and song. I remember how—But I wander.

---

[1] This chapter was revised from "A Negro Schoolmaster in the New South," *Atlantic Monthly*, January 1899, pp. 90–104.

[2] The line of verse is from Frederich von Schiller's 1801 work, "The Maid of Orleans."

[3] Du Bois taught outside of Alexander, Tennessee, for two summers in 1886 and 1887.

Fisk University, Nashville, Tennessee, Theological Hall, 1900. Photograph included in the American Negro exhibit at the Paris Exposition of 1900. Courtesy of the Library of Congress.

There came a day when all the teachers left the Institute and began the hunt for schools. I learn from hearsay (for my mother was mortally afraid of firearms) that the hunting of ducks and bears and men is wonderfully interesting, but I am sure that the man who has never hunted a country school has something to learn of the pleasures of the chase. I see now the white, hot roads lazily rise and fall and wind before me under the burning July sun; I feel the deep weariness of heart and limb as ten, eight, six miles stretch relentlessly ahead; I feel my heart sink heavily as I hear again and again, "Got a teacher? Yes." So I walked on and on—horses were too expensive—until I had wandered beyond railways, beyond stage lines, to a land of "varmints" and rattlesnakes, where the coming of a stranger was an event, and men lived and died in the shadow of one blue hill.

Sprinkled over hill and dale lay cabins and farmhouses, shut out from the world by the forests and the rolling hills toward the east. There I found at last a little school. Josie told me of it; she was a thin, homely girl of twenty, with a dark-brown face and thick, hard hair. I had crossed the stream at Watertown, and rested under the great willows; then I had gone to the little cabin in the lot where Josie was resting on her way to town. The gaunt farmer made me welcome, and Josie, hearing my errand, told me anxiously that they wanted a school over the hill; that but once since the war had a teacher been there; that she herself longed to learn,—and thus she ran on, talking fast and loud, with much earnestness and energy.

Next morning I crossed the tall round hill, lingered to look at the blue and yellow mountains stretching toward the Carolinas,[4] then plunged into the wood, and came out at Josie's home. It was a dull frame cottage with four rooms, perched just below the brow of the hill, amid peach-trees. The father was a quiet, simple soul, calmly ignorant, with no touch of vulgarity. The mother was different,—strong, bustling, and energetic, with a quick, restless tongue, and an ambition to live "like folks." There was a crowd of children. Two boys had gone away. There remained two growing girls; a shy midget of eight; John, tall, awkward, and eighteen; Jim, younger, quicker, and better looking; and two babies

Group of Children from the Model School, Fisk University, Nashville Tennessee. Photograph included in the American Negro exhibit at the Paris Exposition of 1900. Courtesy of the Library of Congress.

---

[4] This is the lower part of the Appalachian chain.

Old Aunt Julia Ann Jackson, age 102, and the corn crib where she lived in rural Arkansas, taken c. 1937. Included in the United States Works Progress Administration, Federal Writers' Project slave narratives collections. Courtesy of the Library of Congress. The building is probably similar to the type of space Du Bois used to teach class in during his two summers in rural Tennessee.

of indefinite age. Then there was Josie herself. She seemed to be the centre of the family: always busy at service, or at home, or berry-picking; a little nervous and inclined to scold, like her mother, yet faithful, too, like her father. She had about her a certain fineness, the shadow of an unconscious moral heroism that would willingly give all of life to make life broader, deeper, and fuller for her and hers. I saw much of this family afterwards, and grew to love them for their honest efforts to be decent and comfortable and for their knowledge of their own ignorance. There was with them no affectation. The mother would scold the father for being so "easy"; Josie would roundly berate the boys for carelessness; and all knew that it was a hard thing to dig a living out of a rocky side-hill.

I secured the school. I remember the day I rode horseback out to the commissioner's house with a pleasant young white fellow who wanted the white school. The road ran down the bed of a stream; the sun laughed and the water jingled, and we rode on.

"Come in," said the commissioner,—"come in. Have a seat. Yes, that certificate will do. Stay to dinner. What do you want a month?" "Oh," thought I, "this is lucky"; but even then fell the awful shadow of the Veil, for they ate first, then I—alone.

The schoolhouse was a log hut, where Colonel Wheeler used to shelter his corn. It sat in a lot behind a rail fence and thorn bushes, near the sweetest of springs. There was an entrance where a door once was, and within, a massive rickety fireplace; great chinks between the logs served as windows. Furniture was scarce. A pale blackboard crouched in the corner. My desk was made of three boards, reinforced at critical points, and my chair, borrowed from the landlady, had to be returned every night. Seats for the children—these puzzled me much. I was haunted by a New England vision of neat little desks and chairs, but, alas! the reality was rough plank benches without backs, and at times without legs. They had the one virtue of making naps dangerous,—possibly fatal, for the floor was not to be trusted.

It was a hot morning late in July when the school opened. I trembled when I heard the patter of little feet down the dusty road, and saw the growing row of dark solemn faces and bright eager eyes facing me. First came Josie and her brothers and sisters. The longing to know, to be a student in the great school at Nashville, hovered like a star above this child-woman amid her work and worry, and she studied doggedly. There were the Dowells from their farm over toward Alexandria,—Fanny with her smooth black face and wondering eyes; Martha, brown and dull; the pretty girl-wife of a brother, and the younger brood.

There were the Burkes,—two brown and yellow lads, and a tiny haughty-eyed girl. Fat Reuben's little chubby girl came, with golden face and old-gold hair, faithful and solemn. 'Thenie was on hand early,—a jolly, ugly, good-hearted girl, who slyly dipped snuff and looked after her little bow-legged brother. When her mother could spare her, 'Tildy came,—a midnight beauty, with starry eyes and tapering limbs; and her brother, correspondingly homely. And then the big boys,—the hulking Lawrences; the lazy Neills, unfathered sons of mother and daughter; Hickman, with a stoop in his shoulders; and the rest.

There they sat, nearly thirty of them, on the rough benches, their faces shading from a pale cream to a deep brown, the little feet bare and swinging, the eyes full of expectation, with here and there a twinkle of mischief, and the hands grasping Webster's blue-back spellingbook. I loved my school, and the fine faith the children had in the wisdom of their teacher was truly marvellous. We read and spelled together, wrote a little, picked flowers, sang, and listened to stories of the world beyond the hill. At times the school would dwindle away, and I would start out. I would visit Mun Eddings, who lived in two very dirty rooms, and ask why little Lugene, whose flaming face seemed ever ablaze with the dark-red hair uncombed, was absent all last week, or why I missed so often the inimitable rags of Mack and Ed. Then the father, who worked Colonel Wheeler's farm on shares, would tell me how the crops needed the boys;

Negro mother teaching children numbers and alphabet in the home of a sharecropper. Transylvania, Louisiana. Photographer Russell Lee, 1939. Courtesy of the Library of Congress.

and the thin, slovenly mother, whose face was pretty when washed, assured me that Lugene must mind the baby.[5] "But we'll start them again next week." When the Lawrences stopped, I knew that the doubts of the old folks about book-learning had conquered again, and so, toiling up the hill, and getting as far into the cabin as possible, I put Cicero "pro Archia Poeta" into the simplest English with local applications, and usually convinced them—for a week or so.

On Friday nights I often went home with some of the children,— sometimes to Doc Burke's farm. He was a great, loud, thin Black, ever working, and trying to buy the seventy-five acres of hill and dale where he lived; but people said that he would surely fail, and the "white folks would get it all." His wife was a magnificent Amazon,[6] with saffron face and shining hair, uncorseted and barefooted, and the children were strong

---

[5] The family is working the farm as sharecroppers. Under the sharecropping system, landlords would advance seed, equipment, and groceries against the production of future crops. The system was subject to considerable abuse and kept many poor black and white farmers in what was essentially a state of serfdom and peonage.

[6] In Greek mythology the Amazons were a tribe of female warriors.

and beautiful. They lived in a one-and-a-half-room cabin in the hollow of the farm, near the spring. The front room was full of great fat white beds, scrupulously neat; and there were bad chromos on the walls, and a tired centre-table. In the tiny back kitchen I was often invited to "take out and help" myself to fried chicken and wheat biscuit, "meat" and corn pone, string-beans and berries.[7] At first I used to be a little alarmed at the approach of bedtime in the one lone bedroom, but embarrassment was very deftly avoided. First, all the children nodded and slept, and were stowed away in one great pile of goose feathers; next, the mother and the father discreetly slipped away to the kitchen while I went to bed; then, blowing out the dim light, they retired in the dark. In the morning all were up and away before I thought of awaking. Across the road, where fat Reuben lived, they all went outdoors while the teacher retired, because they did not boast the luxury of a kitchen.

I liked to stay with the Dowells, for they had four rooms and plenty of good country fare. Uncle Bird had a small, rough farm, all woods and hills, miles from the big road; but he was full of tales,—he preached now and then,—and with his children, berries, horses, and wheat he was happy and prosperous. Often, to keep the peace, I must go where life was less lovely; for instance, 'Tildy's mother was incorrigibly dirty, Reuben's larder was limited seriously, and herds of untamed insects wandered over the Eddingses' beds. Best of all I loved to go to Josie's, and sit on the porch, eating peaches, while the mother bustled and talked: how Josie had bought the sewing-machine; how Josie worked at service in winter, but that four dollars a month was "mighty little" wages; how Josie longed to go away to school, but that it "looked like" they never could get far enough ahead to let her; how the crops failed and the well was yet unfinished; and, finally, how "mean" some of the white folks were.

For two summers I lived in this little world; it was dull and humdrum. The girls looked at the hill in wistful longing, and the boys fretted and haunted Alexandria. Alexandria was "town,"—a straggling, lazy village of houses, churches, and shops, and an aristocracy of Toms, Dicks, and Captains. Cuddled on the hill to the north was the village of the colored folks, who lived in three- or four-room unpainted cottages, some neat and homelike, and some dirty. The dwellings were scattered rather aimlessly, but they centred about the twin temples of the hamlet, the Methodist, and the Hard-Shell Baptist churches.[8] These, in turn, leaned gingerly on a sad-colored schoolhouse. Hither my little world wended its crooked way on Sunday to meet other worlds, and gossip, and wonder, and make the weekly sacrifice with frenzied priest at the altar of

---

[7] A type of cornbread made without eggs or milk.
[8] Fundamentalist, or religiously conservative Baptists.

the "old-time religion." Then the soft melody and mighty cadences of Negro song fluttered and thundered.

I have called my tiny community a world, and so its isolation made it; and yet there was among us but a half-awakened common consciousness, sprung from common joy and grief, at burial, birth, or wedding; from a common hardship in poverty, poor land, and low wages; and, above all, from the sight of the Veil that hung between us and Opportunity. All this caused us to think some thoughts together; but these, when ripe for speech, were spoken in various languages. Those whose eyes twenty-five and more years before had seen "the glory of the coming of the Lord," saw in every present hindrance or help a dark fatalism bound to bring all things right in His own good time. The mass of those to whom slavery was a dim recollection of childhood found the world a puzzling thing: it asked little of them, and they answered with little, and yet it ridiculed their offering. Such a paradox they could not understand, and therefore sank into listless indifference, or shiftlessness, or reckless bravado. There were, however, some—such as Josie, Jim, and Ben—to whom War, Hell, and Slavery were but childhood tales, whose

Cedar house at Wilson Cedar Forest project. Near Lebanon, Tennessee, approximately ten miles from Alexandria, Tennessee, where Du Bois taught summer school. Carl Mydans Photographer, March 1936. Courtesy of the Library of Congress.

young appetites had been whetted to an edge by school and story and half-awakened thought. Ill could they be content, born without and beyond the World. And their weak wings beat against their barriers,—barriers of caste, of youth, of life; at last, in dangerous moments, against everything that opposed even a whim.

The ten years that follow youth, the years when first the realization comes that life is leading somewhere,—these were the years that passed after I left my little school. When they were past, I came by chance once more to the walls of Fisk University, to the halls of the chapel of melody. As I lingered there in the joy and pain of meeting old school-friends, there swept over me a sudden longing to pass again beyond the blue hill, and to see the homes and the school of other days, and to learn how life had gone with my school-children; and I went.

Josie was dead, and the gray-haired mother said simply, "We've had a heap of trouble since you've been away." I had feared for Jim. With a cultured parentage and a social caste to uphold him, he might have made a venturesome merchant or a West Point cadet. But here he was, angry with life and reckless; and when Farmer Durham charged him with stealing wheat, the old man had to ride fast to escape the stones which the furious fool hurled after him. They told Jim to run away; but he would not run, and the constable came that afternoon. It grieved Josie, and great awkward John walked nine miles every day to see his little brother through the bars of Lebanon jail. At last the two came back together in the dark night. The mother cooked supper, and Josie emptied her purse, and the boys stole away. Josie grew thin and silent, yet worked the more. The hill became steep for the quiet old father, and with the boys away there was little to do in the valley. Josie helped them to sell the old farm, and they moved nearer town. Brother Dennis, the carpenter, built a new house with six rooms; Josie toiled a year in Nashville, and brought back ninety dollars to furnish the house and change it to a home.

When the spring came, and the birds twittered, and the stream ran proud and full, little sister Lizzie, bold and thoughtless, flushed with the passion of youth, bestowed herself on the tempter, and brought home a nameless child. Josie shivered and worked on, with the vision of schooldays all fled, with a face wan and tired,—worked until, on a summer's day, some one married another; then Josie crept to her mother like a hurt child, and slept—and sleeps.

I paused to scent the breeze as I entered the valley. The Lawrences have gone, —father and son forever, —and the other son lazily digs in the earth to live. A new young widow rents out their cabin to fat Reuben. Reuben is a Baptist preacher now, but I fear as lazy as ever, though his

Fisk University Class of 1888. W. E. B. Du Bois is seated on the right. Courtesy of Special Collections and Archives, W. E. B. Du Bois Library, University of Massachusetts, Amherst.

cabin has three rooms; and little Ella has grown into a bouncing woman and is ploughing corn on the hot hillside. There are babies a-plenty, and one half-witted girl. Across the valley is a house I did not know before, and there I found, rocking one baby and expecting another, one of my schoolgirls, a daughter of Uncle Bird Dowell. She looked somewhat worried with her new duties, but soon bristled into pride over her neat cabin and the tale of her thrifty husband, and the horse and cow, and the farm they were planning to buy.

My log schoolhouse was gone. In its place stood Progress; and Progress, I understand, is necessarily ugly. The crazy foundation stones still marked the former site of my poor little cabin, and not far away, on six weary boulders, perched a jaunty board house, perhaps twenty by thirty feet, with three windows and a door that locked. Some of the window-glass was broken, and part of an old iron stove lay mournfully under the house. I peeped through the window half reverently, and found things that were more familiar. The blackboard had grown by about two feet, and the seats were still without backs. The county owns the lot now, I hear, and every year there is a session of school. As I sat by the spring and looked on the Old and the New I felt glad, very glad, and yet—

After two long drinks I started on. There was the great double log-house on the corner. I remembered the broken, blighted family that used to live there. The strong, hard face of the mother, with its wilderness of hair, rose before me. She had driven her husband away, and while I taught school a strange man lived there, big and jovial, and people talked. I felt sure that Ben and 'Tildy would come to naught from such a home. But this is an odd world; for Ben is a busy farmer in County, "doing well, too," they say, and he had cared for little 'Tildy until last spring, when a lover married her. A hard life the lad had led, toiling for meat, and laughed at because he was homely and crooked. There was Sam Carlon, an impudent old skinflint, who had definite notions about "niggers," and hired Ben a summer and would not pay him. Then the hungry boy gathered his sacks together, and in broad daylight went into Carlon's corn; and when the hard-fisted farmer set upon him, the angry boy flew at him like a beast. Doc Burke saved a murder and a lynching that day.

The story reminded me again of the Burkes, and an impatience seized me to know who won in the battle, Doc or the seventy-five acres. For it is a hard thing to make a farm out of nothing, even in fifteen years. So I hurried on, thinking of the Burkes. They used to have a certain magnificent barbarism about them that I liked. They were never vulgar, never immoral, but rather rough and primitive, with an unconventionality that spent itself in loud guffaws, slaps on the back, and naps in the corner. I hurried by the cottage of the misborn Neill boys. It was empty, and they were grown into fat, lazy farm-hands. I saw the home of the Hickmans, but Albert, with his stooping shoulders, had passed from the world. Then I came to the Burkes' gate and peered through; the inclosure looked rough and untrimmed, and yet there were the same fences around the old farm save to the left, where lay twenty-five other acres. And lo! the cabin in the hollow had climbed the hill and swollen to a half-finished six-room cottage.

The Burkes held a hundred acres, but they were still in debt. Indeed, the gaunt father who toiled night and day would scarcely be happy out of debt, being so used to it. Some day he must stop, for his massive frame is showing decline. The mother wore shoes, but the lion-like physique of other days was broken. The children had grown up. Rob, the image of his father, was loud and rough with laughter. Birdie, my school baby of six, had grown to a picture of maiden beauty, tall and tawny. "Edgar is gone," said the mother, with head half-bowed,—"gone to work in Nashville; he and his father couldn't agree."

Little Doc, the boy born since the time of my school, took me horseback down the creek next morning toward Farmer Dowell's. The road and the stream were battling for mastery, and the stream had the better of it. We splashed and waded, and the merry boy, perched behind me, chattered and laughed. He showed me where Simon Thompson had bought a bit of ground and a home; but his daughter Lana, a plump, brown, slow girl, was not there. She had married a man and a farm twenty miles away. We wound on down the stream till we came to a gate that I did not recognize, but the boy insisted that it was "Uncle Bird's." The farm was fat with the growing crop. In that little valley was a strange stillness as I rode up; for death and marriage had stolen youth and left age and childhood there. We sat and talked that night after the chores were done. Uncle Bird was grayer, and his eyes did not see so well, but he was still jovial. We talked of the acres bought,—one hundred and twenty-five,—of the new guest-chamber added, of Martha's marrying. Then we talked of death: Fanny and Fred were gone; a shadow hung over the other daughter, and when it lifted she was to go to Nashville to school. At last we spoke of the neighbors, and as night fell, Uncle Bird told me how, on a night like that, 'Thenie came wandering back to her home over yonder, to escape the blows of her husband. And next morning she died in the home that her little bow-legged brother, working and saving, had bought for their widowed mother.

My journey was done, and behind me lay hill and dale, and Life and Death. How shall man measure Progress there where the dark-faced Josie lies? How many heartfuls of sorrow shall balance a bushel of wheat? How hard a thing is life to the lowly, and yet how human and real! And all this life and love and strife and failure,—is it the twilight of nightfall or the flush of some faint-dawning day?

Thus sadly musing, I rode to Nashville in the Jim Crow car.

Document Number 5, Chapter IV

In his 1940 autobiography *Dusk of Dawn*, Du Bois recalled how: "I believed in the higher education of the Talented tenth who through their knowledge of modern culture could guide the American Negro into a higher civilization. I knew that without this the Negro would have to accept white leadership, and that such leadership could not always be trusted to guide this group into self-realization and to its highest cultural possibilities." Du Bois had developed his ideas concerning the Talented Tenth nearly fifty years earlier in the second chapter of the 1903 publication *The Negro Problem*. While Du Bois objected to the white domination of black people, he does not seem to have considered the possibility that a black elite or "Talented Tenth" could have had their own class and social biases that did not necessarily conform with the needs and interests of the black "masses." Yet despite this fact, the idea of the Talented Tenth represents an important conceptualization of the need for leadership and autonomy among African-Americans.

*　　*　　*

The Talented Tenth[9]

The Negro race, like all races, is going to be saved by its exceptional men. The problem of education, then, among Negroes must first of all deal with the Talented Tenth; it is the problem of developing the Best of this race that they may guide the Mass away from the contamination and death of the Worst, in their own and other races. Now the training of men is a difficult and intricate task. Its technique is a matter for educational experts, but its object is for the vision of seers. If we make money the object of man-training, we shall develop money-makers but not necessarily men; if we make technical skill the object of education, we may possess artisans but not, in nature, men. Men we shall have only as we make manhood the object of the work of the schools—intelligence, broad sympathy, knowledge of the world that was and is, and of the relation of men to it—this is the curriculum of that Higher Education which must underlie true life. On this foundation we may build bread winning, skill of hand and quickness of brain, with never a fear lest the child and man mistake the means of living for the object of life.

---

[9] Source: W. E. B. Du Bois, 1903, included in "The Talented Tenth." *The Negro Problem: A Series of Articles by Representative American Negroes of Today. Contributions by Booker T. Washington, W. E. Burghardt Du Bois, Paul Laurence Dunbar, Charles W. Chesnutt and others* (New York: James Pott), pp. 33–75.

If this be true—and who can deny it—three tasks lay before me; first to show from the past that the Talented Tenth as they have risen among American Negroes have been worthy of leadership; secondly to show how these men may be educated and developed; and thirdly to show their relation to the Negro problem.

You misjudge us because you do not know us. From the very first it has been the educated and intelligent of the Negro people that have led and elevated the mass, and the sole obstacles that nullified and retarded their efforts were slavery and race prejudice; for what is slavery but the legalized survival of the unfit and the nullification of the work of natural internal leadership? Negro leadership therefore sought from the first to rid the race of this awful incubus that it might make way for natural selection and the survival of the fittest. In colonial days came Phillis Wheatley and Paul Cuffe striving against the bars of prejudice; and Benjamin Banneker, the almanac maker, voiced their longings when he said to Thomas Jefferson, "I freely and cheerfully acknowledge that I am of the African race and in colour which is natural to them, of the deepest dye; and it is under a sense of the most profound gratitude to the Supreme Ruler of the Universe, that I now confess to you that I am not under that state of tyrannical thraldom and inhuman captivity to which too many of my brethren are doomed, but that I have abundantly tasted of the fruition of those blessings which proceed from that free and unequalled liberty with which you are favored, and which I hope you will willingly allow, you have mercifully received from the immediate hand of that Being from whom proceedeth every good and perfect gift.

"Suffer me to recall to your mind that time, in which the arms of the British crown were exerted with every powerful effort, in order to reduce you to a state of servitude; look back, I entreat you, on the variety of dangers to which you were exposed; reflect on that period in which every human aid appeared unavailable, and in which even hope and fortitude wore the aspect of inability to the conflict, and you cannot but be led to a serious and grateful sense of your miraculous and providential preservation, you cannot but acknowledge, that the present freedom and tranquility which you enjoy, you have mercifully received, and that a peculiar blessing of heaven.

"This, sir, was a time when you clearly saw into the injustice of a state of Slavery, and in which you had just apprehensions of the horrors of its condition. It was then that your abhorrence thereof was so excited, that you publicly held forth this true and invaluable doctrine, which is worthy to be recorded and remembered in all succeeding ages: 'We hold these truths to be self evident, that all men are created equal; that they are endowed with certain inalienable rights, and that among these are life, liberty and the pursuit of happiness.'"

Then came Dr. James Derham, who could tell even the learned Dr. Rush something of medicine, and Lemuel Haynes, to whom Middlebury College gave an honorary A.M. in 1804. These and others we may call the Revolutionary group of distinguished Negroes—they were persons of marked ability, leaders of a Talented Tenth, standing conspicuously among the best of their time. They strove by word and deed to save the color line from becoming the line between the bond and free, but all they could do was nullified by Eli Whitney and the Curse of Gold. So they passed into forgetfulness.

But their spirit did not wholly die; here and there in the early part of the century came other exceptional men. Some were natural sons of unnatural fathers and were given often a liberal training and thus a race of educated mulattoes sprang up to plead for black men's rights. There was Ira Aldridge, whom all Europe loved to honor; there was that Voice crying in the Wilderness, David Walker, and saying:

"I declare it does appear to me as though some nations think God is asleep, or that he made the Africans for nothing else but to dig their mines and work their farms, or they cannot believe history sacred or profane. I ask every man who has a heart, and is blessed with the privilege of believing—Is not God a God of justice to all his creatures? Do you say he is? Then if he gives peace and tranquility to tyrants and permits them to keep our fathers, our mothers, ourselves and our children in eternal ignorance and wretchedness to support them and their families, would he be to us a God of Justice? I ask, O, ye Christians, who hold us and our children in the most abject ignorance and degradation that ever a people were afflicted with since the world began—I say if God gives you peace and tranquility, and suffers you thus to go on afflicting us, and our children, who have never given you the least provocation—would He be to us a God of Justice? If you will allow that we are men, who feel for each other, does not the blood of our fathers and of us, their children, cry aloud to the Lord of Sabaoth against you for the cruelties and murders with which you have and do continue to afflict us?"

This was the wild voice that first aroused Southern legislators in 1829 to the terrors of abolitionism. In 1831 there met that first Negro convention in Philadelphia, at which the world gaped curiously but which bravely attacked the problems of race and slavery, crying out against persecution and declaring that "Laws as cruel in themselves as they were unconstitutional and unjust, have in many places been enacted against our poor, unfriended and unoffending brethren (without a shadow of provocation on our part), at whose bare recital the very savage draws himself up for fear of contagion—looks noble and prides himself because he bears not the name of Christian." Side by side this free Negro movement, and the movement for abolition, strove until they merged in to one strong stream. Too little notice has been taken of the work which the Talented Tenth among Negroes took in the great abolition crusade. From the very day that a Philadelphia colored man became the first subscriber to Garrison's "Liberator," to the day when Negro soldiers made the Emancipation Proclamation possible, black leaders worked shoulder to shoulder with white men in a movement, the success of which would have been impossible without them. There was Purvis and Remond, Pennington and Highland Garnett, Sojourner Truth and Alexander Crummell, and above all, Frederick Douglass—what would the abolition movement have been without them? They stood as living examples of the possibilities of the Negro race, their own hard experiences and well wrought culture said silently more than all the drawn periods of orators—they were the men who made American slavery impossible. As Maria Weston Chapman once said, from the school of anti-slavery agitation, "a throng of authors, editors, lawyers, orators and accomplished gentlemen of color have taken their degree! It has equally implanted hopes and aspirations, noble thoughts, and sublime purposes, in the hearts of both races. It has prepared the white man for the freedom of the black man, and it has made the black man scorn the thought of enslavement, as does a white man, as far as its influence has extended. Strengthen that noble influence! Before its organization, the country only saw here and there in slavery some faithful Cudjoe or Dinah, whose strong natures blossomed even in bondage, like a fine plant beneath a heavy stone. Now, under the elevating and cherishing influence of the American Anti-Slavery Society, the colored race, like the white, furnishes Corinthian capitals for the noblest temples."

Where were these black abolitionists trained? Some, like Frederick Douglass, were self-trained, but yet trained liberally; others, like Alexander Crummell and McCune Smith, graduated from famous foreign universities. Most of them rose up through the colored schools of New York and Philadelphia and Boston, taught by college-bred men like Russworm, of Dartmouth, and college-bred white men like Neau and Benezet.

After emancipation came a new group of educated and gifted leaders: Langston, Bruce and Elliot, Greener, Williams and Payne. Through political organization, historical and polemic writing and moral regeneration, these men strove to uplift their people. It is the fashion of today to sneer at them and to say that with freedom Negro leadership should have begun at the plow and not in the Senate—a foolish and mischievous lie; two hundred and fifty years that black serf toiled at the plow and yet that toiling was in vain till the Senate passed the war amendments; and two hundred and fifty years more the half-free serf of today may toil at his plow, but unless he have political rights and righteously guarded civic status, he will still remain the poverty-stricken and ignorant plaything of rascals, that he now is. This all sane men know even if they dare not say it.

And so we come to the present—a day of cowardice and vacillation, of strident wide-voiced wrong and faint-hearted compromise; of double-faced dallying with Truth and Right. Who are today guiding the work of the Negro people? The "exceptions" of course. And yet so sure as this Talented Tenth is pointed out, the blind worshippers of the Average cry out in alarm: "These are exceptions, look here at death, disease and crime—these are the happy rule." Of course they are the rule, because a silly nation made them the rule: Because for three long centuries this people lynched Negroes who dared to be brave, raped black women who dared to be virtuous, crushed dark-hued youth who dared to be ambitious, and encouraged and made to flourish servility and lewdness and apathy. But not even this was able to crush all manhood and chastity and aspiration from black folk. A saving remnant continually survives and persists, continually aspires, continually shows itself in thrift and ability and character. Exceptional it is to be sure, but this is its chiefest promise; it shows the capability of Negro blood, the promise of black men. Do Americans ever stop to reflect that there are in this land a million men of Negro blood, well-educated, owners of homes, against the honor of whose womanhood no breath was ever raised, whose men occupy positions of trust and usefulness, and who, judged by any standard, have reached the full measure of the best type of modern European culture? Is it fair, is it decent, is it Christian to ignore these facts of the Negro problem, to belittle such aspiration, to nullify such leadership and seek to crush these people back into the mass out of which by toil and travail, they and their fathers have raised themselves?

Can the masses of the Negro people be in any possible way more quickly raised than by the effort and example of this aristocracy of talent and character? Was there ever a nation on God's fair earth civilized from the bottom upward? Never; it is, ever was and ever will be from the top downward that culture filters. The Talented Tenth rises and pulls all that are worth the saving up to their vantage ground. This is the history of human progress; and the two historic mistakes which have hindered that progress were the thinking first that no more could ever rise save the few already risen; or second, that it would better the uprisen to pull the risen down.

How then shall the leaders of a struggling people be trained and the hands of the risen few strengthened? There can be but one answer: The best and most capable of their youth must be schooled in the colleges and universities of the land. We will not quarrel as to just what the university of the Negro should teach or how it should teach it—I willingly admit that each soul and each race-soul needs its own peculiar curriculum. But this is true: A university is a human invention for the transmission of knowledge and culture from generation to generation, through the training of quick minds and pure hearts, and for this work no other human invention will suffice, not even trade and industrial schools.

All men cannot go to college but some men must; every isolated group or nation must have its yeast, must have for the talented few centers of training where men are not so mystified and befuddled by the hard and necessary toil of earning a living, as to have no aims higher than their bellies, and no God greater than Gold. This is true training, and thus in the beginning were the favored sons of the freedmen trained. Out of the colleges of the North came, after the blood of war, Ware, Cravath, Chase, Andrews, Bumstead and Spence to build the foundations of knowledge and civilization in the black South. Where ought they to have begun to build? At the bottom, of course, quibbles the mole with his eyes in the earth. Aye! truly at the bottom, at the very bottom; at the bottom of knowledge, down in the very depths of knowledge there where the roots of justice strike into the lowest soil of Truth. And so they did begin; they founded colleges, and up from the colleges shot normal schools, and out from the normal schools went teachers, and around the normal teachers clustered other teachers to teach the public schools; the college trained in Greek and Latin and mathematics, 2,000 men; and these men trained full 50,000 others in morals and manners, and they in turn taught thrift and the alphabet to nine millions of men, who today hold $300,000,000 of property. It was a miracle—the most wonderful peace-battle of the 19th century, and yet today men smile at it, and in fine superiority tell us that it was all a strange mistake; that a proper way to found a system of education is first to gather the children and buy them spelling books and hoes; afterward men may look about for teachers, if haply they may find them; or again they would teach men Work, but as for Life—why, what has Work to do with Life, they ask vacantly.

Was the work of these college founders successful; did it stand the test of time? Did the college graduates, with all their fine theories of life, really live? Are they useful men helping to civilize and elevate their less fortunate fellows? Let us see. Omitting all institutions which have not actually graduated students from a college course, there are today in the United States thirty-four institutions giving something above high school training to Negroes and designed especially for this race.

Three of these were established in border States before the War; thirteen were planted by the Freedmen's Bureau in the years 1864–1869; nine were established between 1870 and 1880 by various church bodies; five were established after 1881 by Negro churches, and four are state institutions supported by United States' agricultural funds. In most cases the college departments are small adjuncts to high and common schoolwork. As a matter of fact six institutions—Atlanta, Fisk, Howard, Shaw, Wilberforce and Leland,—are the important Negro colleges so far as actual work and number of students are concerned. In all these institutions, seven hundred and fifty Negro college students are enrolled. In grade the best of these colleges are about a year behind the smaller New England colleges and a typical curriculum is that of Atlanta University. Here students from the grammar grades, after a three years' high school course, take a college course of 136 weeks. One-fourth of this time is given to Latin and Greek; one-fifth, to English and modern languages; one-sixth, to history and social science; one-seventh, to natural science; one-eighth to mathematics, and one-eighth to philosophy and pedagogy.

In addition to these students in the South, Negroes have attended Northern colleges for many years. As early as 1826 one was graduated from Bowdoin College, and from that time till today nearly every year has seen elsewhere, other such graduates. They have, of course, met much color prejudice. Fifty years ago very few colleges would admit them at all. Even today no Negro has ever been admitted to Princeton, and at some other leading institutions they are rather endured than encouraged. Oberlin was the great pioneer in the work of blotting out the color line in colleges, and has more Negro graduates by far than any other Northern college.

The total number of Negro college graduates up to 1899 (several of the graduates of that year not being reported) was as follows:

		Negro Colleges	White Colleges
Before	1876	137	75
	1875–80	143	22
	1880–85	250	31
	1885–90	413	43
	1890–95	465	66
	1895–99	475	88
	Class Unknown	57	64
	Total	1,914	390

Of these graduates 2,079, were men and 252 were women; 50 per cent. of Northern-born college men come South to work among the masses of their people, at a sacrifice which few people realize; nearly 90 per cent. of the Southern-born graduates instead of seeking that personal freedom and broader intellectual atmosphere which their training has led them, in some degree, to conceive, stay and labor and wait in the midst of their black neighbors and relatives.

The most interesting question, and in many respects the crucial question, to be asked concerning college-bred Negroes, is: Do they earn a living? It has been intimated more than once that the higher training of Negroes has resulted in sending into the world of work, men who could find nothing to do suitable to their talents. Now and then there comes a rumor of a colored college man working at menial service, etc. Fortunately, returns as to occupations of college-bred Negroes, gathered by the Atlanta conference, are quite full—nearly sixty per cent of the total number of graduates.

This enables us to reach fairly certain conclusions as to the occupations of all college-bred Negroes. Of 1,312 persons reported, there were:

Teachers, 53.4%
Clergymen, 16.8%
Physicians, etc., 6.3%
Students, 5.6%
Lawyers, 4.7%
In Govt. Service, 4.0%
In Business, 3.6%
Farmers and Artisans, 2.7%
Editors, Secretaries and Clerks, 2.4%
Miscellaneous, .5%

Over half are teachers, a sixth are preachers, another sixth are students and professional men; over 6 per cent. are farmers, artisans and merchants, and 4 per cent. are in government service. In detail the occupations are as follows:

Occupations of College-Bred Men.

701 Teachers:
    Presidents and Deans, 19
    Teacher of Music, 7
    Professors, Principals and Teachers, 675
221 Clergymen:
    Bishop, 1
    Chaplains U.S. Army, 2
    Missionaries, 9
    Presiding Elders, 12
    Preachers, 197

83 Physicians:
    Doctors of Medicine, 76
    Druggists, 4
    Dentists, 3
74 Students
62 Lawyers
53 in Civil Service:
    U.S. Minister Plenipotentiary, 1
    U.S. Consul, 1
    U.S. Deputy Collector, 1
    U.S. Gauger, 1
    U.S. Postmasters, 2
    U.S. Clerks, 44
    State Civil Service, 2
    City Civil Service, 1
47 Business Men:
    Merchants, etc., 30
    Managers, 13
    Real Estate Dealers, 4
26 Farmers
22 Clerks and Secretaries:
    Secretary of National Societies, 7
    Clerks, etc., 15
9 Artisans
9 Editors
5 Miscellaneous

These figures illustrate vividly the function of the college-bred Negro. He is, as he ought to be, the group leader, the man who sets the ideals of the community where he lives, directs its thoughts and heads its social movements. It need hardly be argued that the Negro people need social leadership more than most groups; that they have no traditions to fall back upon, no long-established customs, no strong family ties, no well-defined social classes. All these things must be slowly and painfully evolved. The preacher was, even before the war, the group leader of the Negroes, and the church their greatest social institution. Naturally this preacher was ignorant and often immoral, and the problem of replacing the older type by better-educated men has been a difficult one. Both by direct work and by direct influence on other preachers, and on congregations, the college-bred preacher has an opportunity for reformatory work and moral inspiration, the value of which cannot be overestimated.

It has, however, been in the furnishing of teachers that the Negro college has found its peculiar function. Few persons realize how vast a work, how mighty a revolution has been thus accomplished. To furnish five millions and more of ignorant people with teachers of their own race and blood, in one generation, was not only a very difficult undertaking, but a very important one, in that it placed before the eyes of almost every Negro child an attainable ideal.

Of the Meaning of Progress

It brought the masses of the blacks in contact with modern civilization, made black men the leaders of their communities and trainers of the new generation. In this work college-bred Negroes were first teachers, and then teachers of teachers. And here it is that the broad culture of college work has been of peculiar value. Knowledge of life and its wider meaning, has been the point of the Negro's deepest ignorance, and the sending out of teachers whose training has not been simply for bread winning, but also for human culture, has been of inestimable value in the training of these men.

In earlier years the two occupations of preacher and teacher were practically the only ones open to the black college graduate. Of later years a larger diversity of life among his people, has opened new avenues of employment. Nor have these college men been paupers and spendthrifts; 557 college-bred Negroes owned in 1899, $1,342,862.50 worth of real estate (assessed value), or $2,411 per family. The real value of the total accumulations of the whole group is perhaps about $10,000,000, or $5,000 a piece. Pitiful is it not beside the fortunes of oil kings and steel trusts, but after all is the fortune of the millionaire the only stamp of true and successful living? Alas! it is, with many and there's the rub.

The problem of training the Negro is today immensely complicated by the fact that the whole question of the efficiency and appropriateness of our present systems of education, for any kind of child, is a matter of active debate, in which final settlement seems still afar off. Consequently it often happens that persons arguing for or against certain systems of education for Negroes, have these controversies in mind and miss the real question at issue. The main question, so far as the Southern Negro is concerned, is: What under the present circumstance, must a system of education do in order to raise the Negro as quickly as possible in the scale of civilization? The answer to this question seems to me clear: It must strengthen the Negro's character, increase his knowledge and teach him to earn a living. Now it goes without saying that it is hard to do all these things simultaneously or suddenly and that at the same time it will not do to give all the attention to one and neglect the others; we could give black boys trades, but that alone will not civilize a race of ex-slaves; we might simply increase their knowledge of the world, but this would not necessarily make them wish to use this knowledge honestly; we might seek to strengthen character and purpose, but to what end if this people have nothing to eat or to wear? A system of education is not one thing, nor does it have a single definite object, nor is it a mere matter of schools. Education is that whole system of human training within and without the school house walls, which molds and develops men. If then we start out to train an ignorant and unskilled people with a heritage of bad habits, our system of training must set before itself two great aims—the one dealing with knowledge and character, the other part seeking to give the child the technical knowledge necessary for him to earn a living under the present circumstances. These objects are accomplished in part by the opening of the common schools on the one, and of the industrial schools on the other. But only in part, for there must also be trained those who are to teach these schools—men and women of knowledge and culture and technical skill who understand modern civilization, and have the training and aptitude to impart it to the children under them. There must be teachers, and teachers of teachers, and to attempt to establish any sort of a system of common and industrial school training, without *first* (and I say *first* advisedly) without *first* providing for the higher training of the very best teachers, is simply throwing your money to the winds. School houses do not teach themselves—piles of brick and mortar and machinery do not send out *men*. It is the trained, living human soul, cultivated and strengthened by long study and thought, that breathes the real breath of life into boys and girls and makes them human, whether they be black or white, Greek, Russian or American. Nothing, in these latter days, has so dampened the faith of thinking Negroes in recent educational movements, as the fact that such movements have been accompanied by ridicule and denouncement and decrying of those very institutions of higher training which made the Negro public school possible, and make Negro industrial schools thinkable. It was: Fisk, Atlanta, Howard and Straight, those colleges born of the faith and sacrifice of the abolitionists, that placed in the black schools of the South the 30,000 teachers and more, which some, who depreciate the work of these higher schools, are using to teach their own new experiments. If Hampton, Tuskegee and the hundred other industrial schools prove in the future to be as successful as they deserve to be, then their success in training black artisans for the South, will be due primarily to the white colleges of the North and the black colleges of the South, which trained the teachers who today conduct these institutions. There was a time when the American people believed pretty devoutly that a log of wood with a boy at one end and Mark Hopkins at the other, represented the highest ideal of human training. But in these eager days it would seem that we have changed all that and think it necessary to add a couple of saw-mills and a hammer to this outfit, and, at a pinch, to dispense with the services of Mark Hopkins. I would not deny, or for a moment seem to deny, the paramount necessity of teaching the Negro to work, and to work steadily and skillfully; or seem to depreciate in the slightest degree the important part industrial schools must play in the accomplishment of these ends, but I *do* say, and insist upon it, that it is industrialism drunk with its vision of success, to imagine that its own work can be accomplished without providing for the training of broadly cultured men and women to teach its own teachers, and to teach the teachers of the public schools.

But I have already said that human education is not simply a matter of schools; it is much more a matter of family and group life—the training of one's home, of one's daily companions, of one's social class. Now the black boy of the South moves in a black world—a world with its own leaders, its own thoughts, its own ideals. In this world he gets by far the larger part of his life training, and through the eyes of this dark world he peers into the veiled world beyond. Who guides and determines the education which he receives in his world? His teachers here are the group-leaders of the Negro people—the physicians and clergymen, the trained fathers and mothers, the influential and forceful men about him of all kinds; here it is, if at all, that the culture of the surrounding world trickles through and is handed on by the graduates of the higher schools. Can such culture training of group leaders be neglected? Can we afford to ignore it? Do you think that if the leaders of thought among Negroes are not trained and educated thinkers, that they will have no leaders? On the contrary a hundred half-trained demagogues will still hold the places they so largely occupy now, and hundreds of vociferous busy-bodies will multiply. You have no choice; either you must help furnish this race from within its own ranks with thoughtful men of trained leadership, or you must suffer the evil consequences of a headless misguided rabble.

I am an earnest advocate of manual training and trade teaching for black boys, and for white boys, too. I believe that next to the founding of Negro colleges the most valuable addition to Negro education since the war has been industrial training for black boys. Nevertheless, I insist that the object of all true education is not to make men carpenters, it is to make carpenters men; there are two means of making the carpenter a man, each equally important: the first is to give the group and community in which he works, liberally trained teachers and leaders to teach him and his family what life means; the second is to give him sufficient intelligence and technical skill to make him an efficient workman; the first object demands the Negro college and college-bred men—not a quantity of such colleges, but a few of excellent quality; not too many college-bred men, but enough to leaven the lump, to inspire the masses, to raise the Talented Tenth to leadership; the second object demands a good system of common schools, well-taught, conveniently located and properly equipped.

The Sixth Atlanta Conference truly said in 1901:

"We call the attention of the Nation to the fact that less than one million of the three million Negro children of school age, are at present regularly attending school, and these attend a session which lasts only a few months.

"We are today deliberately rearing millions of our citizens in ignorance, and at the same time limiting the rights of citizenship by educational qualifications. This is unjust. Half the black youth of the land have no opportunities open to them for learning to read, write and cipher. In the discussion as to the proper training of Negro children after they leave the public schools, we have forgotten that they are not yet decently provided with public schools.

"Propositions are beginning to be made in the South to reduce the already meagre school facilities of Negroes. We congratulate the South on resisting, as much as it has, this pressure, and on the many millions it has spent on Negro education. But it is only fair to point out that Negro taxes and the Negroes' share of the income from indirect taxes and endowments have fully repaid this expenditure, so that the Negro public school system has not in all probability cost the white taxpayers a single cent since the war.

"This is not fair. Negro schools should be a public burden, since they are a public benefit. The Negro has a right to demand good common school training at the hands of the States and the Nation since by their fault he is not in position to pay for this himself."

What is the chief need for the building up of the Negro public school in the South? The Negro race in the South needs teachers today above all else. This is the concurrent testimony of all who know the situation. For the supply of this great demand two things are needed—institutions of higher education and money for school houses and salaries. It is usually assumed that a hundred or more institutions for Negro training are today turning out so many teachers and college-bred men that the race is threatened with an over-supply. This is sheer nonsense. There are today less than 3,000 living Negro college graduates in the

United States, and less than 1,000 Negroes in college. Moreover, in the 164 schools for Negroes, 95 per cent. of their students are doing elementary and secondary work, work which should be done in the public schools. Over half the remaining 2,157 students are taking high school studies. The mass of so-called "normal" schools for the Negro, are simply doing elementary common schoolwork, or, at most, high school work, with a little instruction in methods. The Negro colleges and the post-graduate courses at other institutions are the only agencies for the broader and more careful training of teachers. The work of these institutions is hampered for lack of funds. It is getting increasingly difficult to get funds for training teachers in the best modern methods, and yet all over the South, from State Superintendents, county officials, city boards and school principals comes the wail, "We need TEACHERS!" and teachers must be trained. As the fairest minded of all white Southerners, Atticus G. Haygood, once said: "The defects of colored teachers are so great as to create an urgent necessity for training better ones. Their excellencies and their successes are sufficient to justify the best hopes of success in the effort, and to vindicate the judgment of those who make large investments of money and service, to give to colored students opportunity for thoroughly preparing themselves for the work of teaching children of their people."

The truth of this has been strikingly shown in the marked improvement of white teachers in the South. Twenty years ago the rank and file of white public school teachers were not as good as the Negro teachers. But they, by scholarships and good salaries, have been encouraged to thorough normal and collegiate preparation, while the Negro teachers have been discouraged by starvation wages and the idea that any training will do for a black teacher. If carpenters are needed it is well and good to train men as carpenters. But to train men as carpenters, and then set them to teaching is wasteful and criminal; and to train men as teachers and then refuse them living wages, unless they become carpenters, is rank nonsense.

The United States Commissioner of Education says in his report for 1900: "For comparison between the white and colored enrollment in secondary and higher education, I have added together the enrollment in high schools and secondary schools, with the attendance on colleges and universities, not being sure of the actual grade of work done in the colleges and universities. The work done in the secondary schools is reported in such detail in this office, that there can be no doubt of its grade."

He then makes the following comparisons of persons in every million enrolled in secondary and higher education:

	Whole Country	*Negroes*
1880	4,362	1,289
1900	10,743	2,061

And he concludes: "While the number in colored high schools and colleges had increased somewhat faster than the population, it had not kept pace with the average of the whole country, for it had fallen from 30 per cent. to 24 per cent. of the average quota. Of all colored pupils, one (1) in one hundred was engaged in secondary and higher work, and that ratio has continued substantially for the past twenty years. If the ratio of colored population in secondary and higher education is to be equal to the average for the whole country, it must be increased to five times its present average." And if this be true of the secondary and higher education, it is safe to say that the Negro has not one-tenth his quota in college studies. How baseless, therefore, is the charge of too much training! We need Negro teachers for the Negro common schools, and we need first-class normal schools and colleges to train them. This is the work of higher Negro education and it must be done.

Further than this, after being provided with group leaders of civilization, and a foundation of intelligence in the public schools, the carpenter, in order to be a man, needs technical skill. This calls for trade schools. Now trade schools are not nearly such simple things as people once thought. The original idea was that the "Industrial" school was to furnish education, practically free, to those willing to work for it; it was to "do" things—i.e.: become a center of productive industry, it was to be partially, if not wholly, self-supporting, and it was to teach trades. Admirable as were some of the ideas underlying this scheme, the whole thing simply would not work in practice; it was found that if you were to use time and material to teach trades thoroughly, you could not at the same time keep the industries on a commercial basis and make them pay. Many schools started out to do this on a large scale and went into virtual bankruptcy. Moreover, it was found also that it was possible to teach a boy a trade mechanically, without giving him the full educative benefit of the process, and, vice versa, that there was a distinctive educative value in teaching a boy to use his hands and eyes in carrying out certain physical processes, even though he did not actually learn a trade. It has happened, therefore, in the last decade, that a noticeable change has come over the industrial schools. In the first place the idea of commercially remunerative industry in a school is being pushed rapidly to the background. There are still schools with shops and farms that bring an income, and schools that use student labor partially for the erection of their buildings and the furnishing of equipment. It is coming to be seen, however, in the education of the Negro, as clearly as it has been seen in the education of the youths the world over, that it is the *boy* and not the material product, that is the true object of education. Consequently the object of the industrial school came to be the thorough training of boys regardless of the cost of the training, so long as it was thoroughly well done.

Even at this point, however, the difficulties were not surmounted. In the first place modern industry has taken great strides since the war, and the teaching of trades is no longer a simple matter. Machinery and long processes of work have greatly changed the work of the carpenter, the ironworker and the shoemaker. A really efficient workman must be today an intelligent man who has had good technical training in addition to thorough common school, and perhaps even higher training. To meet this situation the industrial schools began a further development; they established distinct Trade Schools for the thorough training of better-class artisans, and at the same time they sought to preserve for the purposes of general education, such of the simpler processes of elementary trade learning as were best suited therefor. In this differentiation of the Trade School and manual training, the best of the industrial schools simply followed the plain trend of the present educational epoch. A prominent educator tells us that, in Sweden, "In the beginning the economic conception was generally adopted, and everywhere manual training was looked upon as a means of preparing the children of the common people to earn their living. But gradually it came to be recognized that manual training has a more elevated purpose, and one, indeed, more useful in the deeper meaning of the term. It came to be considered as an educative process for the complete moral, physical and intellectual development of the child."

Thus, again, in the manning of trade schools and manual training schools we are thrown back upon the higher training as its source and chief support. There was a time when any aged and worn-out carpenter could teach in a trade school. But not so today. Indeed the demand for college-bred men by a school like Tuskegee, ought to make Mr. Booker T. Washington the firmest friend of higher training. Here he has as helpers the son of a Negro senator, trained in Greek and the humanities, and graduated at Harvard; the son of a Negro congressman and lawyer, trained in Latin and mathematics, and graduated at Oberlin; he has as his wife, a woman who read Virgil and Homer in the same class room with me; he has as college chaplain, a classical graduate of Atlanta University; as teacher of science, a graduate of Fisk; as teacher of history, a graduate of Smith,—indeed some thirty of his chief teachers are college graduates, and instead of studying French grammars in the midst of weeds, or buying pianos for dirty cabins, they are at Mr. Washington's right hand helping him in a noble work. And yet one of the effects of Mr. Washington's propaganda has been to throw doubt upon the expediency of such training for Negroes, as these persons have had.

Men of America, the problem is plain before you. Here is a race transplanted through the criminal foolishness of your fathers. Whether you like it or not the millions are here, and here they will remain. If you do not lift them up, they will pull you down. Education and work are the levers to uplift a people. Work alone will not do it unless inspired by the right ideals and guided by intelligence. Education must not simply teach work—it must teach Life. The Talented Tenth of the Negro race must be made leaders of thought and missionaries of culture among their people. No others can do this work and Negro colleges must train men for it. The Negro race, like all other races, is going to be saved by its exceptional men.

An early French illustration depicting the race between Atalanta and Hippomenös.

March On.

1. Way over in the E-gypt land, You shall gain the vic-to-ry, Way over in the E-gypt land, You shall gain the day. March on, and you shall gain the vic-to-ry, March on, and you shall gain the day.

2 When Peter was preaching at the Pentecost,
  You shall gain the victory;
He was endowed with the Holy Ghost,
  You shall gain the day.
    Cho.—March on, &c.

3 When Peter was fishing in the sea,
  You shall gain the victory;
He dropped his net and followed me,
  You shall gain the day.
    Cho.—March on, &c.

4 King Jesus on the mountain top,
  You shall gain the victory:
King Jesus speaks and the chaf.ot stops,
  You shall gain the day.
    Cho.—March on, &c.

"March On," included in J. B. T. Marsh, *The Story of the Jubilee Singers* (Cleveland, Ohio: The Cleveland Printing and Publishing Company, 1892), p. 280.

V

Of the Wings of Atalanta

O black boy of Atlanta!
  But half was spoken;
The slave's chains and the master's
  Alike are broken;
The one curse of the races
  Held both in tether;
They are rising—all are rising—
  The black and white together.

WHITTIER.[1]

South of the North, yet north of the South, lies the City of a Hundred Hills,[2] peering out from the shadows of the past into the promise of the future. I have seen her in the morning, when the first flush of day had half-roused her; she lay gray and still on the crimson soil of Georgia; then the blue smoke began to curl from her chimneys, the tinkle of bell and scream of whistle broke the silence, the rattle and roar of busy life slowly gathered and swelled, until the seething whirl of the city seemed a strange thing in a sleepy land.

Once, they say, even Atlanta slept dull and drowsy at the foot-hills of the Alleghenies, until the iron baptism of war awakened her with its sullen waters, aroused and maddened her, and left her listening to the sea. And the sea cried to the hills and the hills answered the sea, till the city rose like a widow and cast away her weeds, and toiled for her daily bread; toiled steadily, toiled cunningly,—perhaps with some bitterness, with a touch of reclame,[3]—and yet with real earnestness, and real sweat.

It is a hard thing to live haunted by the ghost of an untrue dream; to see the wide vision of empire fade into real ashes and dirt; to feel the pang of the conquered, and yet know that with all the Bad that fell on one black day, something was vanquished that deserved to live, something

---

[1] The selection of verse is taken from John Greenleaf Whittier's poem, "Howard at Atlanta," (1869).

[2] The mythic or poetic name given to the city of Atlanta.

[3] A sense of public acclaim.

115

"Atlanta before being burnt: by order of General Sherman, from the cupola of the Female Seminary." Courtesy of the Library of Congress.

killed that in justice had not dared to die; to know that with the Right that triumphed, triumphed something of Wrong, something sordid and mean, something less than the broadest and best. All this is bitter hard, and many a man and city and people have found in it excuse for sulking, and brooding, and listless waiting.[4]

Such are not men of the sturdier make; they of Atlanta turned resolutely toward the future; and that future held aloft vistas of purple and gold:—Atlanta, Queen of the cotton kingdom; Atlanta, Gateway to the Land of the Sun; Atlanta, the new Lachesis,[5] spinner of web and woof for the world. So the city crowned her hundred hills with factories, and stored her shops with cunning handiwork, and stretched long iron ways to greet the busy Mercury[6] in his coming. And the Nation talked of her striving.

Perhaps Atlanta was not christened for the winged maiden of dull Boeotia;[7] you know the tale,—how swarthy Atalanta, tall and wild, would marry only him who out-raced her; and how the wily Hippomenes laid three apples of gold in the way.[8] She fled like a shadow, paused startled over the first apple, but even as he stretched his hand, fled again; hovered over the second, then, slipping from his hot grasp, flew over river, vale, and hill; but as she lingered over the third, his arms fell round her, and looking on each other, the blazing passion of their love profaned the sanc-

---

[4] Du Bois, of course, is referring to the Civil War and also almost certainly the burning of Atlanta by Union forces under William Tecumsah Sherman.

[5] Lachesis was one of the three Fates in Ancient Greek Mythology.

[6] Roman god of commerce and travel, commonly known as the messenger of the gods.

[7] Province in Greece.

[8] Atalanta was a swift-footed Greek woman who agreed to marry any man who could defeat her in a race. Hippomenes defeated her by throwing golden apples in her path which she stopped to pick up, thus slowing her down.

Atlanta, Ga. Ruins of depot, blown up on Sherman's departure. George Barnard photographer, 1864. Courtesy of the Library of Congress.

tuary of Love, and they were cursed. If Atlanta be not named for Atalanta, she ought to have been.

Atalanta is not the first or the last maiden whom greed of gold has led to defile the temple of Love; and not maid alone, but men in the race of life, sink from the high and generous ideals of youth to the gambler's code of the Bourse; and in all our Nation's striving is not the Gospel of Work befouled by the Gospel of Pay? So common is this that one-half think it normal; so unquestioned, that we almost fear to question if the

"A Georgia cotton plantation," 1917. Courtesy of the Library of Congress.

end of racing is not gold, if the aim of man is not rightly to be rich. And this is the fault of America, how dire a danger lies before a new land and a new city, lest Atlanta, stooping for mere gold, shall find that gold accursed!

It was no maiden's idle whim that started this hard racing; a fearful wilderness lay about the feet of that city after the War,—feudalism, poverty, the rise of the Third Estate,[9] serfdom, the rebirth of Law and Order, and above and between all, the Veil of Race. How heavy a journey for weary feet! What wings must Atalanta have to flit over all this hollow and hill, through sour wood and sullen water, and by the red waste of sun-baked clay! How fleet must Atalanta be if she will not be tempted by gold to profane the Sanctuary!

The Sanctuary of our fathers has, to be sure, few Gods,—some sneer, "all too few." There is the thrifty Mercury of New England, Pluto[10] of the North, and Ceres[11] of the West; and there, too, is the half-forgotten Apollo[12] of the South, under whose aegis the maiden ran,—and as she ran she forgot him, even as there in Boeotia Venus[13] was forgot. She forgot the old ideal of the Southern gentleman,—that new-world heir of the grace and courtliness of patrician, knight, and noble; forgot his honor with his foibles, his kindliness with his carelessness, and stooped to apples of gold,—to men busier and sharper, thriftier and more unscrupulous. Golden apples are beautiful—I remember the lawless days of boyhood, when orchards in crimson and gold tempted me over fence and field—and, too, the merchant who has dethroned the planter is no despicable *parvenu*.[14] Work and wealth are the mighty levers to lift this old new land; thrift and toil and saving are the highways to new hopes and new possibilities; and yet the warning is needed lest the wily

---

[9] The lowest level in the Feudal order—the peasantry or serfdom. The First Estate was the clergy and the Second Estate the nobility.

[10] Greek and Roman god of death and the underworld.

[11] Goddess of the Earth, also known as Demeter.

[12] Greek and Roman god of the sun.

[13] Roman goddess of love.

[14] Newly arrived.

Hippomenes tempt Atalanta to thinking that golden apples are the goal of racing, and not mere incidents by the way.

Atlanta must not lead the South to dream of material prosperity as the touchstone of all success; already the fatal might of this idea is beginning to spread; it is replacing the finer type of Southerner with vulgar money-getters; it is burying the sweeter beauties of Southern life beneath pretence and ostentation. For every social ill the panacea of Wealth has been urged,—wealth to overthrow the remains of the slave feudalism; wealth to raise the "cracker"[15] Third Estate; wealth to employ the black serfs, and the prospect of wealth to keep them working; wealth as the end and aim of politics, and as the legal tender for law and order; and, finally, instead of Truth, Beauty, and Goodness, wealth as the ideal of the Public School. Not only is this true in the world which Atlanta typifies, but it is threatening to be true of a world beneath and beyond that world,—the Black World beyond the Veil. Today it makes little difference to Atlanta, to the South, what the Negro thinks or dreams or wills. In the soul-life of the land he is today, and naturally will long remain, unthought of, half forgotten; and yet when he does come to think and will and do for himself,—and let no man dream that day will never come,—then the part he plays will not be one of sudden learning, but words and thoughts he has been taught to lisp in his race-childhood. Today the ferment of his striving toward self-realization is to the strife of the white world like a wheel within a wheel: beyond the Veil are smaller but like problems of ideals, of leaders and the led, of serfdom, of poverty, of order and subordination, and, through all, the Veil of Race. Few know of these problems, few who know notice them; and yet there they are, awaiting student, artist, and seer,—a field for somebody sometime to discover. Hither has the temptation of Hippomenes penetrated; already in this smaller world, which now indirectly and anon directly must influence the larger for good or ill, the habit is forming of interpreting the world in dollars. The old leaders of Negro opinion, in the little groups where there is a Negro social consciousness, are being replaced by new; neither the black preacher nor the black teacher leads as he did two decades ago. Into their places are pushing the farmers and gardeners, the well-paid porters and artisans, the businessmen,—all those with property and money. And with all this change, so curiously parallel to that of the Other-world, goes too the same inevitable change in ideals. The South laments today the slow, steady disappearance of a certain type of Negro,—the faithful, courteous slave of other days, with his incorruptible honesty and dignified humility. He is passing away just as

---

[15] A poor rural Southerner.

surely as the old type of Southern gentleman is passing, and from Not dissimilar causes,—the sudden transformation of a fair far-off ideal of Freedom into the hard reality of bread-winning and the consequent deification of Bread.

In the Black World, the Preacher and Teacher embodied once the ideals of this people,—the strife for another and a juster world, the vague dream of righteousness, the mystery of knowing; but today the danger is that these ideals, with their simple beauty and weird inspiration, will suddenly sink to a question of cash and a lust for gold. Here stands this black young Atalanta, girding herself for the race that must be run; and if her eyes be still toward the hills and sky as in the days of old, then we may look for noble running; but what if some ruthless or wily or even thoughtless Hippomenes lay golden apples before her? What if the Negro people be wooed from a strife for righteousness, from a love of knowing, to regard dollars as the be-all and end-all of life? What if to the Mammonism[16] of America be added the rising Mammonism of the reborn South, and the Mammonism of this South be reinforced by the budding Mammonism of its half-wakened black millions? Whither, then, is the new-world quest of Goodness and Beauty and Truth gone glimmering? Must this, and that fair flower of Freedom which, despite the jeers of latter-day striplings, sprung from our fathers' blood, must that too degenerate into a dusty quest of gold,—into lawless lust with Hippomenes?

The hundred hills of Atlanta are not all crowned with factories. On one, toward the west, the setting sun throws three buildings in bold relief against the sky. The beauty of the group lies in its simple unity:—a broad lawn of green rising from the red street with mingled roses and peaches; north and south, two plain and stately halls; and in the midst, half hidden in ivy, a larger building, boldly graceful, sparingly decorated, and with one low spire. It is a restful group,—one never looks for more; it is all here, all intelligible. There I live, and there I hear from day to day the low hum of restful life. In winter's twilight, when the red sun glows, I can see the dark figures pass between the halls to the music of the night-bell. In the morning, when the sun is golden, the clang of the day-bell brings the hurry and laughter of three hundred young hearts from hall and street, and from the busy city below,—children all dark and heavy-haired,—to join their clear young voices in the music of the morning sacrifice. In a half dozen classrooms they gather then,—here to follow the love-song of Dido,[17] here to listen to the tale of Troy divine;

---

[16] Devotion to the pursuit of wealth.
[17] The Queen of Carthage in *The Aneid*.

there to wander among the stars, there to wander among men and nations,—and elsewhere other well-worn ways of knowing this queer world. Nothing new, no time-saving devices,—simply old time-glorified methods of delving for Truth, and searching out the hidden beauties of life, and learning the good of living. The riddle of existence is the college curriculum that was laid before the Pharaohs,[18] that was taught in the groves by Plato,[19] that formed the *trivium* and *quadrivium*,[20] and is today laid before the freedmen's sons by Atlanta University.[21] And this course of study will not change; its methods will grow more deft and effectual, its content richer by toil of scholar and sight of seer; but the true college will ever have one goal,—not to earn meat, but to know the end and aim of that life which meat nourishes.

Young men training in blacksmithing at Hampton Institute, Hampton, Virginia, c. 1900. Courtesy of the Library of Congress.

---

[18] The rulers of Ancient Egypt.

[19] Plato (427–347 B.C.E.) Greek philosopher.

[20] The seven liberal arts of the Medieval period. *Trivium* (grammar, logic, and rhetoric), and *Quadrivium* (Arithmetic, music, geometry, and astronomy).

[21] Atlanta University was founded in 1865 by members of the Freedmen's Bureau.

The vision of life that rises before these dark eyes has in it nothing mean or selfish. Not at Oxford or at Leipzig, not at Yale or Columbia,[22] is there an air of higher resolve or more unfettered striving; the determination to realize for men, both black and white, the broadest possibilities of life, to seek the better and the best, to spread with their own hands the Gospel of Sacrifice,—all this is the burden of their talk and dream. Here, amid a wide desert of caste and proscription, amid the heart-hurting slights and jars and vagaries of a deep race-dislike, lies this green oasis, where hot anger cools, and the bitterness of disappointment is sweetened by the springs and breezes of Parnassus;[23] and here men may lie and listen, and learn of a future fuller than the past, and hear the voice of Time:

"Entbehren sollst du, sollst entbehren."[24]

They made their mistakes, those who planted Fisk and Howard and Atlanta before the smoke of battle had lifted; they made their mistakes, but those mistakes were not the things at which we lately laughed somewhat uproariously. They were right when they sought to found a new educational system upon the University: where, forsooth, shall we ground knowledge save on the broadest and deepest knowledge? The roots of the tree, rather than the leaves, are the sources of its life; and from the dawn of history, from Academus[25] to Cambridge,[26] the culture of the University has been the broad foundation-stone on which is built the kindergarten's ABCs.

But these builders did make a mistake in minimizing the gravity of the problem before them; in thinking it a matter of years and decades; in therefore building quickly and laying their foundation carelessly, and lowering the standard of knowing, until they had scattered haphazard through the South some dozen poorly equipped high schools and miscalled them universities. They forgot, too, just as their successors are forgetting, the rule of inequality:—that of the million black youth, some were fitted to know and some to dig; that some had the talent and capacity of university men, and some the talent and capacity of blacksmiths; and that true training meant neither that all should be college men nor all artisans, but that the one should be made a

---

[22] Great European and American universities.

[23] Mountain in Greece located near Delphi, which was the home of the oracle of the god Apollo.

[24] A quote from Goethe's 1808 *Faust*: "Renounce will thee, thee will renounce."

[25] The sacred area Northwest of Athens where Plato founded his school. Hence, the term for his students "academics."

[26] One of England's most famous and oldest universities.

missionary of culture to an untaught people, and the other a free workman among serfs. And to seek to make the blacksmith a scholar is almost as silly as the more modern scheme of making the scholar a blacksmith; almost, but not quite.

The function of the university is not simply to teach bread-winning, or to furnish teachers for the public schools or to be a centre of polite society; it is, above all, to be the organ of that fine adjustment between real life and the growing knowledge of life, an adjustment which forms the secret of civilization. Such an institution the South of today sorely needs. She has religion, earnest, bigoted:—religion that on both sides the Veil often omits the sixth, seventh, and eighth commandments, but substitutes a dozen supplementary ones. She has, as Atlanta shows, growing thrift and love of toil; but she lacks that broad knowledge of what the world knows and knew of human living and doing, which she may apply to the thousand problems of real life today confronting her. The need of the South is knowledge and culture,—not in dainty limited quantity, as before the war, but in broad busy abundance in the world of work; and until she has this, not all the Apples of Hesperides, be they golden and bejewelled, can save her from the curse of the Boeotian lovers.

The Wings of Atalanta are the coming universities of the South. They alone can bear the maiden past the temptation of golden fruit. They will not guide her flying feet away from the cotton and gold; for—ah, thoughtful Hippomenes!—do not the apples lie in the very Way of Life? But they will guide her over and beyond them, and leave her kneeling in the Sanctuary of Truth and Freedom and broad Humanity, virgin and undefiled. Sadly did the Old South err in human education, despising the education of the masses, and niggardly in the support of colleges. Her ancient university foundations dwindled and withered under the foul breath of slavery; and even since the war they have fought a failing fight for life in the tainted air of social unrest and commercial selfishness, stunted by the death of criticism, and starving for lack of broadly cultured men. And if this is the white South's need and danger, how much heavier the danger and need of the freedmen's sons! How pressing here the need of broad ideals and true culture, the conservation of soul from sordid aims and petty passions! Let us build the Southern university—William and Mary, Trinity, Georgia, Texas, Tulane, Vanderbilt, and the others—fit to live; let us build, too, the Negro universities:—Fisk, whose foundation was ever broad; Howard, at the heart of the Nation; Atlanta at Atlanta, whose ideal of scholarship has been held above the temptation of numbers. Why not here, and perhaps

Pharmaceutical laboratory at Howard University, Washington, D.C. Photograph included in the Exhibit of American Negroes at the Paris Exposition of 1900. Courtesy of the Library of Congress.

elsewhere, plant deeply and for all time centres of learning and living, colleges that yearly would send into the life of the South a few white men and a few black men of broad culture, catholic tolerance, and trained ability, joining their hands to other hands, and giving to this squabble of the Races a decent and dignified peace?

Patience, Humility, Manners, and Taste, common schools and kindergartens, industrial and technical schools, literature and tolerance,—all these spring from knowledge and culture, the children of the university. So must men and nations build, not otherwise, not upside down.

Teach workers to work,—a wise saying; wise when applied to German boys and American girls; wiser when said of Negro boys, for they have less knowledge of working and none to teach them. Teach thinkers to think,—a needed knowledge in a day of loose and careless logic; and they whose lot is gravest must have the carefulest training to think aright. If these things are so, how foolish to ask what is the best education for one or seven or sixty million souls! Shall we teach them trades, or train them in liberal arts? Neither and both: teach the workers to work and the thinkers to think; make carpenters of carpenters, and philosophers of philosophers, and fops of fools. Nor can we pause here. We are training not isolated men but a living group of men,—nay, a group within a group. And the final product of our training must be neither a psychologist nor a brickmason, but a man. And to make men, we must have ideals, broad, pure, and inspiring ends of living,—not sordid money-getting, not apples of gold. The worker must work for the glory of his handiwork, not simply for pay; the thinker must think for truth, not for fame. And all this is gained only by human strife and longing; by ceaseless training and education; by founding Right on righteousness and Truth on the unhampered search for Truth; by founding the common school on the university, and the industrial school on the common school; and weaving thus a system, not a distortion, and bringing a birth, not an abortion.

When night falls on the City of a Hundred Hills, a wind gathers itself from the seas and comes murmuring westward. And at its bidding, the smoke of the drowsy factories sweeps down upon the mighty city and covers it like a pall, while yonder at the University the stars twinkle above Stone Hall. And they say that yon gray mist is the tunic of Atalanta pausing over her golden apples. Fly, my maiden, fly, for yonder comes Hippomenes!

Advertisement for Atlanta University. Source: *The Crisis*, 1:4 (February 1911), p. 33.

Document Number 6, Chapter V

Originally published as a book review of Booker T. Washington's autobiography *Up From Slavery* in the July 1901 issue of *The Dial* magazine, this essay would eventually become the basis of Chapter Three of *The Souls of Black Folk*: "Of Mr. Booker T. Washington and Others." It is an important document for observing the increasing breach between Du Bois and the founder of Tuskegee Institute.

*   *   *

The Evolution of Negro Leadership[27]

In every generation of our national life, from Phillis Wheatley to Booker Washington, the Negro race in America has succeeded in bringing forth men whom the country, at times spontaneously, at times in spite of itself, has been impelled to honor and respect. Mr. Washington is one of the most striking of these cases, and his autobiography is a partial history of the steps which made him a group leader, and the one man who in the eyes of the nation typified at present more nearly than all others the work and worth of his nine million fellows.

The way in which groups of human beings are led to choose certain of their number as their spokesmen and leaders is at once the most elementary and the nicest problem of social growth. History is but the record of this group leadership; and yet how infinitely changeful is its type and history! And of all types and kinds, what can be more instructive than the leadership of a group within a group—that curious double movement where real progress may be negative and actual advance be relative retrogression? All this is the social student's inspiration and despair.

When sticks and stones and beasts form the sole environment of a people, their attitude is ever one of determined opposition to, and conquest of, natural forces. But when to earth and brute is added an environment of men and ideas, then the attitude of the imprisoned group may take three main forms: a feeling of revolt and revenge; an attempt to adjust all thought and action to the will of the greater group; or, finally, a determined attempt at self-development, self-realization, in spite of environing discouragements and prejudice. The influence of all three of these attitudes is plainly to be traced in the evolution of race leaders among American negroes. Before 1750 there was but the one motive of revolt and revenge which animated the terrible Maroons and veiled all the Americas in fear of insurrection. But the liberalizing tendencies of the latter half of the eighteenth century brought the first thought of adjustment and assimilation in the crude and earnest songs of Phillis and the martyrdom of Attucks and Salem.

---

[27] Originally published in *The Dial*, 31 (July 16, 1901), pp. 53–55.

The cotton-gin changed all this, and men then, as the Lyman Abbotts of to-day, found a new meaning in human blackness. A season of hesitation and stress settled on the black world as the hope of emancipation receded. Forten and the free Negroes of the North still hoped for eventual assimilation with the nation; Allen, the founder of the great African Methodist Church, strove for unbending self-development, and the Southern freedmen followed him; while among the black slaves at the South arose the avenging Nat Turner, fired by the memory of Toussaint the Savior. So far, Negro leadership had been local and spasmodic; but now, about 1840, arose a national leadership—a dynasty not to be broken. Frederick Douglass and the moral revolt against slavery dominated Negro thought and effort until after the war. Then, with the sole weapon of self-defense in perilous times, the ballot, which the nation gave the freedmen, men like Langston and Bruce sought to guide the political fortunes of the blacks, while Payne and Price still clung to the old ideal of self-development.

Then came the reaction. War memories and ideals rapidly passed, and a period of astonishing commercial development and expansion ensued. A time of doubt and hesitation, of storm and stress, overtook the freedmen's sons; and then it was that Booker Washington's leadership began. Mr. Washington came with a clear simple programme, at the psychological moment; at a time when the nation was a little ashamed of having bestowed so much sentiment on Negroes and was concentrating its energies on Dollars. The industrial training of Negro youth was not an idea originating with Mr. Washington, nor was the policy of conciliating the white South wholly his. But he first put life, unlimited energy, and perfect faith into this programme; he changed it from an article of belief into a whole creed; he broadened it from a by-path into a veritable Way of Life. And the method by which he accomplished this is an interesting study of human life.

Mr. Washington's narrative gives but glimpses of the real struggle which he has had for leadership. First of all, he strove to gain the sympathy and cooperation of the white South, and gained it after that epoch-making sentence spoken at Atlanta: "In all things that are purely social we can be as separate as the fingers, yet one as the hand in all things essential to mutual progress " (p. 221). This conquest of the South is by all odds the most notable thing in Mr. Washington's career. Next to this comes his achievement in gaining place and consideration in the North. Many others less shrewd and tactful would have fallen between these two stools; but as Mr. Washington knew the heart of the South from birth and training, so by singular insight he intuitively grasped the spirit of the age that was dominating the North. He learned so thoroughly the speech and thought of triumphant commercialism and the ideals of material prosperity that he pictures as the height of absurdity a black boy studying a French grammar in the midst of weeds and dirt. One wonders how Socrates or St. Francis of Assissi would receive this!

And yet this very singleness of vision and thorough oneness with his age is a mark of the successful man. It is as though Nature must needs make men a little narrow to give them force. At the same time, Mr. Washington's success, North and South, with his gospel of Work and Money, raised opposition to him from widely divergent sources. The spiritual sons of the Abolitionists were not prepared to acknowledge that the schools founded before Tuskegee, by men of broad ideals and self-sacrificing souls, were wholly failures, or worthy of ridicule. On the other hand, among his own people Mr. Washington found deep suspicion and dislike for a man on such good terms with Southern whites.

Such opposition has only been silenced by Mr. Washington's very evident sincerity of purpose. We forgive much to honest purpose which is accomplishing something. We may not agree with the man at all points, but we admire him and cooperate with him so far as we conscientiously can. It is no ordinary tribute to this man's tact and power, that, steering as he must amid so many diverse interests and opinions, he to-day commands not simply the applause of those who believe in his theories, but also the respect of those who do not.

Among the Negroes, Mr. Washington is still far from a popular leader. Educated and thoughtful Negroes everywhere are glad to honor him and aid him, but all cannot agree with him. He represents in Negro thought the old attitude of adjustment to environment, emphasizing the economic phase; but the two other strong currents of feeling, descended from the past, still oppose him. One is the thought of a small but not unimportant group, unfortunate in their choice of spokesman, but nevertheless of much weight, who represent the old ideas of revolt and revenge, and see in migration alone an outlet for the Negro people. The second attitude is that of the large and important group represented by Dunbar, Tanner, Chesnutt, Miller, and the Grimkes, who, without any single definite programme, and with complex aims, seek nevertheless that self-development and self-realization in all lines of human endeavor which they believe will eventually place the Negro beside the other races. While these men respect the Hampton-Tuskegee idea to a degree, they believe it falls far short of a complete programme. They believe, therefore, also in the higher education of Fisk and Atlanta Universities; they believe in self-assertion and ambition; and they believe in the right of suffrage for blacks on the same terms with whites.

Such is the complicated world of thought and action in which Mr. Booker Washington has been called of God and man to lead, and in which he has gained so rare a meed of success.

W. E. Burghardt Du Bois.
Atlanta University, Atlanta, Ga.

"The Slave Deck of the Bark Wildfire," published in the June 2, 1860, issue of *Harper's Weekly*, p. 129.

No. 44. March On.

1. Way o-ver in the E-gypt land, You shall gain the vic-to-ry, Way o-ver in the E-gypt land, You shall gain the day. March on, and you shall gain the vic-to-ry, March on, and you shall gain the day.

Repeat. pp

2 When Peter was preaching at the Pentecost,
   You shall gain the victory;
   He was endowed with the Holy Ghost,
   You shall gain the day.
   Cho.—March on, &c.

3 When Peter was fishing in the sea,
   You shall gain the victory;
   He dropped his net and followed me,
   You shall gain the day.
   Cho.—March on, &c.

4 King Jesus on the mountain top,
   You shall gain the victory;
   King Jesus speaks and the char.ot stops,
   You shall gain the day.
   Cho.—March on, &c.

"March On," included in J. B. T. Marsh, *The Story of the Jubilee Singers* (Cleveland, Ohio: The Cleveland Printing and Publishing Company, 1892), p. 280.

VI

Of the Training of Black Men[1]

Why, if the Soul can fling the Dust aside,
And naked on the Air of Heaven ride,
    Were't not a Shame—were't not a Shame for him
In this clay carcase crippled to abide?

OMAR KHAYYAM (FITZGERALD).

From the shimmering swirl of waters where many, many thoughts ago the slave-ship first saw the square tower of Jamestown,[2] have flowed down to our day three streams of thinking: one swollen from the larger world here and overseas, saying, the multiplying of human wants in culture-lands calls for the worldwide cooperation of men in satisfying them. Hence arises a new human unity, pulling the ends of earth nearer, and all men, black, yellow, and white. The larger humanity strives to feel in this contact of living Nations and sleeping hordes a thrill of new life in the world, crying, "If the contact of Life and Sleep be Death, shame on such Life." To be sure, behind this thought lurks the afterthought of force and dominion,—the making of brown men to delve when the temptation of beads and red calico cloys.

The second thought streaming from the death-ship[3] and the curving river is the thought of the older South,—the sincere and passionate belief that somewhere between men and cattle, God created a *tertium quid*,[4] and called it a Negro,—a clownish, simple creature, at times even lovable within its limitations, but straitly foreordained to walk within the Veil.

---

[1] This chapter is a revised version of an article of the same name published in the *Atlantic Monthly*, September 1902, pp. 287–297.
[2] The first slaves brought to the North American Colonies were brought through Jamestown in 1619.
[3] A slave ship.
[4] In Latin, an ambiguous state or condition.

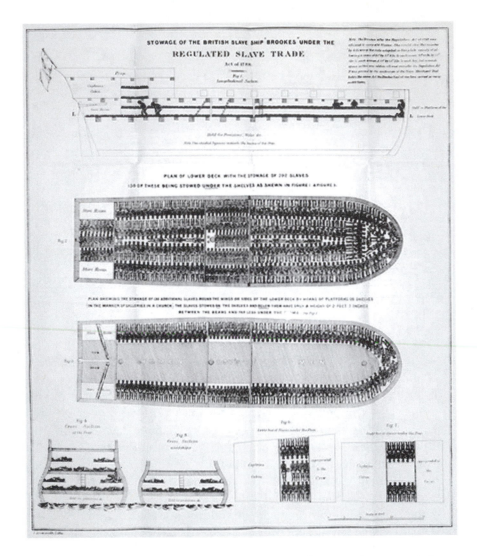

"Stowage of the British Slave Ship Brookes." Source: Regulated Slave Trade: From the Evidence of Robert Stokes, Esq., given before the Select Committee of the House of Lords. London: J. Ridgway, 1851. Courtesy of the Library of Congress.

To be sure, behind the thought lurks the afterthought,—some of them with favoring chance might become men, but in sheer self-defence we dare not let them, and we build about them walls so high, and hang between them and the light a veil so thick, that they shall not even think of breaking through.

And last of all there trickles down that third and darker thought,— the thought of the things themselves, the confused, half-conscious mutter of men who are black and whitened, crying "Liberty, Freedom, Opportunity—vouchsafe to us, 0 boastful World, the chance of living men!" To be sure, behind the thought lurks the afterthought,—suppose, after all, the World is right and we are less than men? Suppose this mad impulse within is all wrong, some mock mirage from the untrue?

So here we stand among thoughts of human unity, even through conquest and slavery; the inferiority of black men, even if forced by fraud; a shriek in the night for the freedom of men who themselves are not yet sure of their right to demand it. This is the tangle of thought and afterthought wherein we are called to solve the problem of training men for life.

Behind all its curiousness, so attractive alike to sage and *dilettante*,[5] lie its dim dangers, throwing across us shadows at once grotesque and awful. Plain it is to us that what the world seeks through desert and wild we have within our threshold,—a stalwart laboring force, suited to the semi-tropics; if, deaf to the voice of the Zeitgeist,[6] we refuse to use and develop these men, we risk poverty and loss. If, on the other hand, seized by the brutal afterthought, we debauch the race thus caught in our talons, selfishly sucking their blood and brains in the future as in the past, what shall save us from national decadence? Only that saner selfishness, which Education teaches, can find the rights of all in the whirl of work.

Again, we may decry the color-prejudice of the South, yet it remains a heavy fact. Such curious kinks of the human mind exist and must be reckoned with soberly. They cannot be laughed away, nor always successfully stormed at, nor easily abolished by act of legislature. And yet they must not be encouraged by being let alone. They must be recognized as facts, but unpleasant facts; things that stand in the way of civilization and religion and common decency. They can be met in but one way,—by the breadth and broadening of human reason, by catholicity of taste and culture. And so, too, the native ambition and aspiration of men, even though they be black, backward, and ungraceful, must not lightly be dealt with. To stimulate wildly weak and untrained minds is to play with mighty fires; to flout their striving idly is to welcome a harvest of brutish crime and shameless lethargy in our very laps. The guiding of thought and the deft coordination of deed is at once the path of honor and humanity.

And so, in this great question of reconciling three vast and partially contradictory streams of thought, the one panacea of Education leaps to the lips of all:—such human training as will best use the labor of all men

---

[5] An amateur.
[6] German meaning the spirit of a time or era.

133

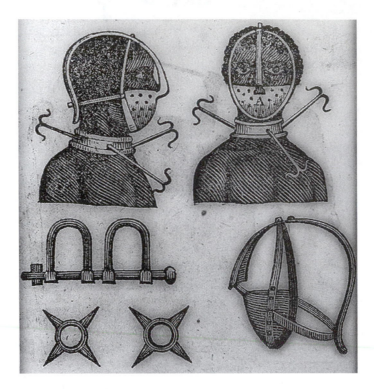

Iron mask, collar, leg shackles and spurs used to restrict slaves. Engraving created by Samuel Wood, 1807. Courtesy of the Library of Congress.

without enslaving or brutalizing; such training as will give us poise to encourage the prejudices that bulwark society, and to stamp out those that in sheer barbarity deafen us to the wail of prisoned souls within the Veil, and the mounting fury of shackled men.

But when we have vaguely said that Education will set this tangle straight, what have we uttered but a truism? Training for life teaches living; but what training for the profitable living together of black men and white? A hundred and fifty years ago our task would have seemed easier. Then Dr. Johnson[7] blandly assured us that education was needful solely for the embellishments of life, and was useless for ordinary vermin. Today we have climbed to heights where we would open at least the outer courts of knowledge to all, display its treasures to many, and select the few to whom its mystery of Truth is revealed, not wholly by birth or the accidents of the stock market, but at least in part according to deftness and aim, talent and character. This programme, however, we are

---

[7] Samuel Johnson (1709–1784), English dictionary writer, poet and essayist.

sorely puzzled in carrying out through that part of the land where the blight of slavery fell hardest, and where we are dealing with two backward peoples. To make here in human education that ever necessary combination of the permanent and the contingent—of the ideal and the practical in workable equilibrium—has been there, as it ever must be in every age and place, a matter of infinite experiment and frequent mistakes.

In rough approximation we may point out four varying decades of work in Southern education since the Civil War. From the close of the war until 1876, was the period of uncertain groping and temporary relief.[8] There were army schools, mission schools, and schools of the Freedmen's Bureau in chaotic disarrangement seeking system and cooperation. Then followed ten years of constructive definite effort toward the building of complete school systems in the South. Normal schools and colleges were founded for the freedmen, and teachers trained there to man the public schools. There was the inevitable tendency of war to underestimate the prejudices of the master and the ignorance of the slave, and all seemed clear sailing out of the wreckage of the storm. Meantime, starting in this decade yet especially developing from 1885 to 1895, began the industrial revolution of the South. The land saw glimpses of a new destiny and the stirring of new ideals. The educational system striving to complete itself saw new obstacles and a field of work ever broader and deeper. The Negro colleges, hurriedly founded, were inadequately equipped, illogically distributed, and of varying efficiency and grade; the normal and high schools were doing little more than common-school work, and the common schools were training but a third of the children who ought to be in them, and training these too often poorly. At the same time the white South, by reason of its sudden conversion from the slavery ideal, by so much the more became set and strengthened in its racial prejudice, and crystallized it into harsh law and harsher custom; while the marvellous pushing forward of the poor white daily threatened to take even bread and butter from the mouths of the heavily handicapped sons of the freedmen. In the midst, then, of the larger problem of Negro education sprang up the more practical question of work, the inevitable economic quandary that faces a people in the transition from slavery to freedom, and especially those who make that change amid hate and prejudice, lawlessness and ruthless competition.

The industrial school springing to notice in this decade, but coming to full recognition in the decade beginning with 1895, was the proffered answer to this combined educational and economic crisis, and an answer of singular wisdom and timeliness. From the very first in nearly all the

---

[8] The Reconstruction Period.

schools some attention had been given to training in handiwork, but now was this training first raised to a dignity that brought it in direct touch with the South's magnificent industrial development, and given an emphasis which reminded black folk that before the Temple of Knowledge swing the Gates of Toil.

Yet after all they are but gates, and when turning our eyes from the temporary and the contingent in the Negro problem to the broader question of the permanent uplifting and civilization of black men in America, we have a right to inquire, as this enthusiasm for material advancement mounts to its height, if after all the industrial school is the final and sufficient answer in the training of the Negro race; and to ask gently, but in all sincerity, the ever-recurring query of the ages, Is not life more than meat, and the body more than raiment?[9] And men ask this today all the more eagerly because of sinister signs in recent educational movements. The tendency is here, born of slavery and quickened to renewed life by the crazy imperialism of the day, to regard human beings as among the material resources of a land to be trained with an eye single to future dividends. Race-prejudices, which keep brown and black men in their "places," we are coming to regard as useful allies with such a theory, no matter how much they may dull the ambition and sicken the hearts of struggling human beings. And above all, we daily hear that an education that encourages aspiration, that sets the loftiest of ideals and seeks as an end culture and character rather than bread-winning, is the privilege of white men and the danger and delusion of black.

Especially has criticism been directed against the former educational efforts to aid the Negro. In the four periods I have entioned, we find first, boundless, planless enthusiasm and sacrifice; then the preparation of teachers for a vast public-school system; then the launching and expansion of that school system amid increasing difficulties; and finally the training of workmen for the new and growing industries. This development has been sharply ridiculed as a logical anomaly and flat reversal of nature. Soothly we have been told that first industrial and manual training should have taught the Negro to work, then simple schools should have taught him to read and write, and finally, after years, high and normal schools could have completed the system, as intelligence and wealth demanded.

That a system logically so complete was historically impossible, it needs but a little thought to prove. Progress in human affairs is more often a pull than a push, a surging forward of the exceptional man, and the lifting of his duller brethren slowly and painfully to his vantage-ground. Thus it was no accident that gave birth to universities centuries

---

[9] A reference to Matthew 6:25.

before the common schools, that made fair Harvard the first flower of our wilderness. So in the South: the mass of the freedmen at the end of the war lacked the intelligence so necessary to modern workingmen. They must first have the common school to teach them to read, write, and cipher; and they must have higher schools to teach teachers for the common schools. The white teachers who flocked South went to establish such a common-school system. Few held the idea of founding colleges; most of them at first would have laughed at the idea. But they faced, as all men since them have faced, that central paradox of the South,—the social separation of the races. At that time it was the sudden volcanic rupture of nearly all relations between black and white, in work and government and family life. Since then a new adjustment of relations in economic and political affairs has grown up,—an adjustment subtle and difficult to grasp, yet singularly ingenious, which leaves still that frightful chasm at the color-line across which men pass at their peril. Thus, then and now, there stand in the South two separate worlds; and separate not simply in the higher realms of social intercourse, but also in church and school, on railway and street-car, in hotels and theatres, in streets and city sections, in books and newspapers, in asylums and jails, in hospitals and graveyards. There is still enough of contact for large economic and group cooperation, but the separation is so thorough and deep that it absolutely precludes for the present between the races anything like that sympathetic and effective group-training and leadership of the one by the other, such as the American Negro and all backward peoples must have for effectual progress.

This the missionaries of '68[10] soon saw; and if effective industrial and trade schools were impracticable before the establishment of a common-school system, just as certainly no adequate common schools could be founded until there were teachers to teach them. Southern whites would not teach them; Northern whites in sufficient numbers could not be had. If the Negro was to learn, he must teach himself, and the most effective help that could be given him was the establishment of schools to train Negro teachers. This conclusion was slowly but surely reached by every student of the situation until simultaneously, in widely separated regions, without consultation or systematic plan, there arose a series of institutions designed to furnish teachers for the untaught. Above defects of this procedure must ever stand its one crushing rejoinder: in a single generation they put thirty thousand black teachers in the South; they wiped out illiteracy of the majority of the black people of the land, and they made Tuskegee possible.

---

[10] Members of the Freedmen's Bureau.

"Louis Firetail (Sioux, Crow Creek), wearing tribal clothing, in American history class, Hampton Institute, Hampton, Virginia." The inclusion of Native Americans at Hampton was part of its efforts to Americanize "less" civilized populations. Photograph included in Exhibit of American Negroes, Paris Exposition, 1900. Courtesy of the Library of Congress.

Such higher training-schools tended naturally to deepen broader development: at first they were common and grammar schools, then some became high schools. And finally, by 1900, some thirty-four had one year or more of studies of college grade. This development was reached with different degrees of speed in different institutions: Hampton[11] is still a high school, while Fisk University started her college in 1871,[12] and Spelman Seminary about 1896.[13] In all cases the aim was identical,—to maintain the standards of the lower training by giving

---

[11] Hampton Normal and Agricultural Institute was opened in April 1868 by the American Missionary Association of New York, as a school to provide education for Freedmen. Native Americans were accepted at the school beginning in 1878. By the turn of the century, nearly 1,000 African and Native Americans were attending the school.

[12] Du Bois's first undergraduate college in Nashville, Tennessee.

[13] Spelman Seminary became the modern Spelman College in Atlanta.

teachers and leaders the best practicable training; and above all, to furnish the black world with adequate standards of human culture and lofty ideals of life. It was not enough that the teachers of teachers should be trained in technical normal methods; they must also, so far as possible, be broadminded, cultured men and women, to scatter civilization among a people whose ignorance was not simply of letters, but of life itself. It can thus be seen that the work of education in the South began with higher institutions of training, which threw off as their foliage common schools, and later industrial schools, and at the same time strove to shoot their roots ever deeper toward college and university training. That this was an inevitable and necessary development, sooner or later, goes without saying; but there has been, and still is, a question in many minds if the natural growth was not forced, and if the higher training was not either overdone or done with cheap and unsound methods. Among white Southerners this feeling is widespread and positive. A prominent Southern journal voiced this in a recent editorial.

"The experiment that has been made to give the colored students classical training has not been satisfactory. Even though many were able to pursue the course, most of them did so in a parrot-like way, learning what was taught, but not seeming to appropriate the truth and import of their instruction, and graduating without sensible aim or valuable occupation for their future. The whole scheme has proved a waste of time, efforts, and the money of the state."

While most fair-minded men would recognize this as extreme and overdrawn, still without doubt many are asking, Are there a sufficient number of Negroes ready for college training to warrant the undertaking? Are not too many students prematurely forced into this work? Does it not have the effect of dissatisfying the young Negro with his environment? And do these graduates succeed in real life? Such natural questions cannot be evaded, nor on the other hand must a Nation naturally skeptical as to Negro ability assume an unfavorable answer without careful inquiry and patient openness to conviction. We must not forget that most Americans answer all queries regarding the Negro *a priori*, and that the least that human courtesy can do is to listen to evidence.

The advocates of the higher education of the Negro would be the last to deny the incompleteness and glaring defects of the present system: too many institutions have attempted to do college work, the work in some cases has not been thoroughly done, and quantity rather than quality has sometimes been sought. But all this can be said of higher education throughout the land; it is the almost inevitable incident of educational growth, and leaves the deeper question of the legitimate demand for the higher training of Negroes untouched. And this latter question can be settled in but one way,—by a first-hand study of the facts. If we leave out of view all institutions which have not actually graduated students from a course higher than that of a New England high school, even though they be called colleges; if then we take the thirty-four remaining institutions, we may clear up many misapprehensions by asking searchingly, What kind of institutions are they? What do they teach? And what sort of men do they graduate?

And first we may say that this type of college, including Atlanta, Fisk, and Howard, Wilberforce[14] and Claflin,[15] Shaw,[16] and the rest, is peculiar, almost unique. Through the shining trees that whisper before me as I write, I catch glimpses of a boulder of New England granite, covering a grave, which graduates of Atlanta University have placed there,—

GRATEFUL MEMORY OF THEIR FORMER TEACHER AND FRIEND AND OF THE UNSELFISH LIFE HE LIVED, AND THE NOBLE WORK HE WROUGHT; THAT THEY, THEIR CHILDREN, AND THEIR CHILDREN'S CHILDREN MIGHT BE BLESSED.

This was the gift of New England to the freed Negro: not alms, but a friend; not cash, but character. It was not and is not money these seething millions want, but love and sympathy, the pulse of hearts beating with red blood;—a gift which today only their own kindred and race can bring to the masses, but which once saintly souls brought to their favored children in the crusade of the sixties, that finest thing in American history, and one of the few things untainted by sordid greed and cheap vainglory. The teachers in these institutions came not to keep the Negroes in their place, but to raise them out of the defilement of the places where slavery had allowed them. The colleges they founded were social settlements; homes where the best of the sons of the freedmen came in close and sympathetic touch with the best traditions of New England. They lived and ate together, studied and worked, hoped and harkened in the dawning light. In actual formal content their curriculum

---

[14] Founded in 1856, and named after the eighteenth century English abolitionist William Wilberforce, Wilberforce University, located in Wilberforce, Ohio, was the first institution of higher education in the United States to be owned and operated by African Americans.

[15] Located in Orangeburg, South Carolina, Claflin University was opened in 1869.

[16] Located in Raleigh, North Carolina, Shaw University, founded in 1865, is the oldest historically black college in the South.

Library at Claflin University, Orangeburg, South Carolina. Photograph included in Exhibit of American Negroes, Paris Exposition, 1900. Courtesy of the Library of Congress.

was doubtless old-fashioned, but in educational power it was supreme, for it was the contact of living souls.

From such schools about two thousand Negroes have gone forth with the bachelor's degree. The number in itself is enough to put at rest the argument that too large a proportion of Negroes are receiving higher training. If the ratio to population of all Negro students throughout the land, in both college and secondary training, be counted, Commissioner Harris[17] assures us "it must be increased to five times its present average" to equal the average of the land.

Fifty years ago the ability of Negro students in any appreciable numbers to master a modern college course would have been difficult to prove. Today it is proved by the fact that four hundred Negroes, many of whom have been reported as brilliant students, have received the bachelor's degree from Harvard, Yale, Oberlin, and seventy other leading colleges.

Here we have, then, nearly twenty-five hundred Negro graduates, of whom the crucial query must be made, How far did their training fit them

---

[17] William Torrey Harris (1835-1909), American educator and philosopher.

for life? It is of course extremely difficult to collect satisfactory data on such a point,—difficult to reach the men, to get trustworthy testimony, to study these graduates, and published the results.[18] First they sought to know what these graduates were doing, and succeeded in getting answers from nearly two-thirds of the living. The direct testimony was in almost all cases corroborated by the reports of the colleges where they graduated, so that in the main the reports were worthy of credence. Fifty-three per cent of these graduates were teachers,—presidents of institutions, heads of normal schools, principals of city school-systems, and the like. Seventeen per cent were clergymen; another seventeen per cent were in the professions, chiefly as physicians. Over six per cent were merchants, farmers, and artisans, and four per cent were in the government civil service. Granting even that a considerable proportion of the third unheard from are unsuccessful, this is a record of usefulness. Personally I know many hundreds of these graduates, and have corresponded with more than a thousand; through others I have followed carefully the life-work of scores; I have taught some of them and some of the pupils whom they have taught, lived in homes which they have builded, and looked at life through their eyes. Comparing them as a class with my fellow students in New England and in Europe, I cannot hesitate in saying that nowhere have I met men and women with a broader spirit of helpfulness, with deeper devotion to their life-work, or with more consecrated determination to succeed in the face of bitter difficulties than among Negro college-bred men. They have, to be sure, their proportion of ne'er-do-wells, their pedants and lettered fools, but they have a surprisingly small proportion of them; they have not that culture of manner which we instinctively associate with university men, forgetting that in reality it is the heritage from cultured homes, and that no people a generation removed from slavery can escape a certain unpleasant rawness and *gaucherie*,[19] despite the best of training.

With all their larger vision and deeper sensibility, these men have usually been conservative, careful leaders. They have seldom been agitators, have withstood the temptation to head the mob, and have worked steadily and faithfully in a thousand communities in the South. As teachers, they have given the South a commendable system of city schools and large numbers of private normal schools and academies. Colored college-bred men have worked side by side with white college graduates at Hampton; almost from the beginning the backbone of Tuskegee's teaching force has been formed of graduates from Fisk and

---

[18] W. E. B. Du Bois, editor, *The College-Bred Negro* (Atlanta: Atlanta University Press, 1900).

[19] Rudeness or lack of manners.

Atlanta. And today the institute is filled with college graduates, from the energetic wife of the principal[20] down to the teacher of agriculture, including nearly half of the executive council and a majority of the heads of departments. In the professions, college men are slowly but surely leavening the Negro church, are healing and preventing the devastations of disease, and beginning to furnish legal protection for the liberty and property of the toiling masses. All this is needful work. Who would do it if Negroes did not? How could Negroes do it if they were not trained carefully for it? If white people need colleges to furnish teachers, ministers, lawyers, and doctors, do black people–need nothing of the sort?

If it is true that there are an appreciable number of Negro youth in the land capable by character and talent to receive that higher training, the end of which is culture, and if the two and a half thousand who have

Howard University, Washington, D.C., c. 1900 class picture. Photograph included in Exhibit of American Negroes, Paris Exposition, 1900. Courtesy of the Library of Congress.

---

[20] A reference to Margaret ("Maggie") James Murray Washington (1865?–1925) a classmate of W. E. B. Du Bois's at Fisk and the third wife of Booker T. Washington, the "principal" of Tuskegee.

had something of this training in the past have in the main proved themselves useful to their race and generation, the question then comes, What place in the future development of the South ought the Negro college and college-bred man to occupy? That the present social separation and acute race-sensitiveness must eventually yield to the influences of culture, as the South grows civilized, is clear. But such transformation calls for singular wisdom and patience. If, while the healing of this vast sore is progressing, the races are to live for many years side by side, united in economic effort, obeying a common government, sensitive to mutual thought and feeling, yet subtly and silently separate in many matters of deeper human intimacy,—if this unusual and dangerous development is to progress amid peace and order, mutual respect and growing intelligence, it will call for social surgery at once the delicatest and nicest in modem history. It will demand broad-minded, upright men, both white and black, and in its final accomplishment American civilization will triumph. So far as white men are concerned, this fact is today being recognized in the South, and a happy renaissance of university education seems imminent. But the very voices that cry hail to this good work are, strange to relate, largely silent or antagonistic to the higher education of the Negro.

Strange to relate! for this is certain, no secure civilization can be built in the South with the Negro as an ignorant, turbulent proletariat. Suppose we seek to remedy this by making them laborers and nothing more: they are not fools, they have tasted of the Tree of Life, and they will not cease to think, will not cease attempting to read the riddle of the world. By taking away their best equipped teachers and leaders, by slamming the door of opportunity in the faces of their bolder and brighter minds, will you make them satisfied with their lot? Or will you not rather transfer their leading from the hands of men taught to think to the hands of untrained demagogues? We ought not to forget that despite the pressure of poverty, and despite the active discouragement and even ridicule of friends, the demand for higher training steadily increases among Negro youth: there were, in the years from 1875 to 1880, 22 Negro graduates from Northern colleges; from 1885 to 1890 there were 43, and from 1895 to 1900, nearly 100 graduates. From Southern Negro colleges there were, in the same three periods, 143, 413, and over 500 graduates. Here, then, is the plain thirst for training; by refusing to give this Talented Tenth[21] the key to knowledge, can any sane man imagine

---

[21] Du Bois's name for the educated black elite who would provide leadership to the African-American people. See: Document Number 4, Chapter 4, pages 74–90 of this work.

that they will lightly lay aside their yearning and contentedly become hewers of wood and drawers of water?

No. The dangerously clear logic of the Negro's position will more and more loudly assert itself in that day when increasing wealth and more intricate social organization preclude the South from being, as it so largely is, simply an armed camp for intimidating black folk. Such waste of energy cannot be spared if the South is to catch up with civilization. And as the black third of the land grows in thrift and skill, unless skilfully guided in its larger philosophy, it must more and more brood over the red past and the creeping, crooked present, until it grasps a gospel of revolt and revenge and throws its new-found energies athwart the current of advance. Even today the masses of the Negroes see all too clearly the anomalies of their position and the moral crookedness of yours. You may marshal strong indictments against them, but their counter-cries, lacking though they be in formal logic, have burning truths within them which you may not wholly ignore, O Southern Gentlemen! If you deplore their presence here, they ask, Who brought us? When you cry, Deliver us from the vision of intermarriage, they answer that legal marriage is infinitely better than systematic concubinage and prostitution. And if in just fury you accuse their vagabonds of violating women, they also in fury quite as just may reply: The rape which your gentlemen have done against helpless black women in defiance of your own laws is written on the foreheads of two millions of mulattoes, and written in ineffaceable blood. And finally, when you fasten crime uponthis race as its peculiar trait, they answer that slavery was the arch-crime, and lynching and lawlessness its twin abortion; that color and race are not crimes, and yet it is they which in this land receive most unceasing condemnation, North, East, South, and West.

I will not say such arguments are wholly justified,—I will not insist that there is no other side to the shield; but I do say that of the nine millions of Negroes in this nation, there is scarcely one out of the cradle to whom these arguments do not daily present themselves in the guise of terrible truth. I insist that the question of the future is how best to keep these millions from brooding over the wrongs of the past and the difficulties of the present, so that all their energies may be bent toward a cheerful striving and cooperation with their white neighbors toward a larger, juster, and fuller future. That one wise method of doing this lies in the closer knitting of the Negro to the great industrial possibilities of the South is a great truth. And this the common schools and the manual training and trade schools are working to accomplish. But these alone are not enough. The foundations of knowledge in this race, as in others, must be sunk deep in the college and university if we would build a solid, permanent structure. Internal problems of social advance must inevitably

Wood work shop of Claflin University, Orangeburg, South Carolina. Photograph included in Exhibit of American Negroes, Paris Exposition, 1900. Courtesy of the Library of Congress.

come,—problems of work and wages, of families and homes, of morals and the true valuing of the things of life; and all these and other Inevitable problems of civilization the Negro must meet and solve largely for himself, by reason of his isolation; and can there be any possible solution than by study and thought and an appeal to the rich experience of the past? Is there not, with such a group and in such a crisis, infinitely more danger to be apprehended from half-trained minds and shallow thinking than from over-education and over-refinement? Surely we have wit enough to found a Negro college so manned and equipped as to steer successfully between the *dilettante* and the fool. We shall hardly induce black men to believe that if their stomachs be full, it matters little about their brains. They already dimly perceive that the paths of peace winding between honest toil and dignified manhood call for the guidance of skilled thinkers, the loving, reverent comradeship between the black lowly and the black men emancipated by training and culture.

The function of the Negro college, then, is clear: it must maintain the standards of popular education, it must seek the social regeneration of the Negro, and it must help in the solution of problems of race contact and cooperation. And finally, beyond all this, it must develop men. Above our modem socialism, and out of the worship of the mass, must persist and evolve that higher individualism which the centres of culture protect; there must come a loftier respect for the sovereign human soul that seeks to know itself and the world about it; that seeks a freedom for expansion and self-development; that will love and hate and labor in its own way, untrammeled alike by old and new. Such souls aforetime have inspired and guided worlds, and if we be not wholly bewitched by our Rhinegold,[22] they shall again. Herein the longing of black men must have respect: the rich and bitter depth of their experience, the unknown treasures of their inner life, the strange rendings of nature they have seen, may give the world new points of view and make their loving, living, and doing precious to all human hearts. And to themselves in these the days that try their souls, the chance to soar in the dim blue air above the smoke is to their inner spirits boon and guerdon for what they lose on earth by being black.

I sit with Shakespeare[23] and he winces not. Across the color-line I move arm in arm with Balzac[24] and Dumas,[25] where smiling men and welcoming women glide in gilded halls. From out the caves of evening that swing between the strong-limbed earth and the tracery of the stars, I summon Aristotle[26] and Aurelius[27] and what soul I will, and they come all graciously with no scorn nor condescension. So, wed with Truth, I dwell above the Veil. Is this the life you grudge us, O knightly America? Is this the life you long to change into the dull red hideousness of Georgia? Are you so fraid lest peering from this high Pisgah,[28] between Philistine and Amalekite,[29] we sight the Promised Land?

---

[22] In German mythology the gold treasure guarded by the Rhine maidens. It is the title of one of the German composer Richard Wagner's most famous operas, *Das Rheingold.*

[23] William Shakespeare (1564–1616), English playwright.

[24] Honoré de Balzac (1799–1850), French novelist.

[25] Alexandre Dumas (1802–1870), French novelist and playwright.

[26] Aristotle (384–322 B.C.E.), Greek philosopher.

[27] Marcus Aurelius (121–180), Roman emperor and philosopher.

[28] The mountain from which Moses viewed the promised land.

[29] Enemies of the Israelites.

Document Number 7, Chapter VI

Hampton and Tuskegee Institutes set the model for African-American higher education until the beginning of the First World War. Du Bois's opposition to the "Hampton" curriculum as the exclusive model of higher education for African-Americans is clear throughout *The Souls of Black Folk*. One can get a clear idea of how Industrial Education worked for African-Americans by carefully reading the annual reports of a school such as Tuskegee Institute—one of which is included below.

* * *

Nineteenth Annual Report of The Principal of the Tuskegee Normal and Industrial Institute, Tuskegee, Alabama. For the Year Ending May 31, 1900.

To the Trustees of the Tuskegee Normal and Industrial Institute:

Gentlemen.—there has not been a year since freedom came to the Negro, that has witnessed such widespread discussion, both North and South, of all phases of his condition, as the present one. I cannot rid myself of the feeling that much, if not all this discussion, is going to prove most helpful to the Negro's education and general development. I am of the opinion that there is more thoughtful interest in the Negro at the present time, than has ever existed. The mere spasmodic and sentimental interest in him has been, in a large degree, replaced by the more substantial, thoughtful kind, based upon a comprehension of the facts.

The Value and Purpose of Industrial Education

One is often surprised at the misleading and unfounded statements made regarding the progress of the Negro, but these very exaggerations serve a good purpose in causing individuals to seek facts for themselves. For example, I have recently seen a statement going the rounds of the press, to the effect that out of 1,200 students educated at industrial schools, only twelve were farming, and three working at the trades for which they were educated. Whether the Tuskegee Institute was included in this list, I do not know. It is to be regretted that those who presume to speak with authority on the advancement of the Negro, do not in more cases actually visit him, where they can see his better life. Few of the people who make discouraging statements regarding him, have ever taken the trouble to inspect his home life, his school life, his church life, or his business or industrial life. It is always misleading to judge any race or community by its worst. The Negro race should, like other races, be judged by its best types, rather than by its worst.

Any one who judges of the value of industrial education by the mere number who actually follow the industry or trade learned at a school, makes a mistake. One might as well judge of the value of arithmetic by the number of people who spend their time after leaving school, in working out problems in arithmetic.

The chief value of industrial education is to give to the students habits of industry, thrift, economy and an idea of the dignity of labour. But in addition to this, in the present economic condition of the colored people, it is most important that a very large proportion of those trained in such institutions as this, actually spend their time at industrial occupations. Let us value the work of Tuskegee by this test: On January 10th of this school year, we dedicated the Slater-Armstrong Memorial Trades' Building. This building is in the form of a double Greek cross and, in its main dimension, is 283 x 315 feet, and is two stories high. The plans of this building were drawn by our instructor in mechanical drawing, a colored man. Eight hundred thousand bricks were required to construct it, and every one of them was manufactured by our students, while learning the trade of brickmaking. All the bricks were laid into the building by students who were being taught the trade of brickmasonry. The plastering, carpentry work, painting and tin-roofing, were done by students while learning these trades. The whole number of students who received training on this building alone was about one hundred and ninety-six. It is to be lighted by electricity and all the electric fixtures are being put in by students who are learning electrical engineering. The power to operate the machinery in this building comes from a one hundred and twenty-five horse-power engine and a seventy-five horse-power boiler. All this machinery is not only operated by students who are learning the trade of steam engineering, but was installed by students under the guidance of their instructor.

Let us take another example, that of agriculture: Our students actually cultivate every day, seven hundred acres of land, while studying agriculture. The students studying dairying, actually milk and care for seventy-five milch cows daily. Besides, they, of course, take care of all the dairy products. All of this is done while learning the industry of dairying. The whole number of students receiving instruction in the divisions of Agriculture and Dairying the past year, is one hundred and forty-two.

The students who are receiving training in farming, have cared for six hundred and nineteen head of hogs this year, and so, I could go on and give not theory, nor hearsay, but actual facts, gleaned from all the departments of the school.

Tuskegee Graduates Work at Their Trades

It does not look reasonable that, of all the large number of students engaged upon the farms and in the diary, that only about one per cent, should make any practical use of their knowledge after leaving Tuskegee. But this is not the fact. The best place to get a true estimate of an individual is at his home. The same is true of an institution. Let us take for example, Macon County, Alabama, in which the Tuskegee Institute is located. By a careful investigation, it is found that there are not less than thirty-five graduates and former students in Macon County and the town of Tuskegee alone who are working at trades or industries which they learned at this institution. At the present time, a large, two-story brick building is going up in the town of Tuskegee that is to be used as a store. In the first place, the store is owned by a graduate of this institution. From the making of the brick to the completion of all the details of this building, the work is being done by graduates or former students of this school; and so the examples could be multiplied. Following the graduates and former students into the outer world. The record is as follows: A careful examination shows that at least three-fourths of them are actually using during the whole time, or a part of the time, the industrial knowledge which they gained here. Even those who do not use this knowledge in making a living, use it as housekeepers in their private homes, and those who teach in the public schools, either directly or indirectly, use it in helping their pupils.

Aside from all that I have said, it must be kept in mind that the whole subject of industrial training on any large and systematic scale is new, and besides, is confined to a very few institutions in the South. Industrial training could not be expected to revolutionize the progress of a race within ten or fifteen years. At the present time the call for graduates from this institution to take positions as instructors of industries in other smaller institutions, as well as in city schools, is so urgent and constant that many of our graduates who would work independently at their trades, are not permitted to do so. In fact, one of the most regretful things in connection with our whole work, is that the calls for our graduates are so many more than we can supply. As the demand for instructors in industrial branches of various schools becomes supplied, a still larger percentage of graduates will use their knowledge of the trades in independent occupations.

The Masses Should Remain in Rural Districts

One thing which every Negro institution should seek to do, is the giving of such training as will result in creating an influence that will keep the masses of the colored people in the rural districts. This should be done both in the interest of the white man and in the interest of the Negro, himself. Every land-owner needs every laborer he can secure. The Negro is not so much in demand in cities as in the country. The colored man is at his best in the rural districts, where he is kept away from the demoralizing influences of city life, and besides, in most cases, the competition in the cities is too severe for him. The only way to keep the colored man in the rural districts and away from the cities, is to give him first-class agricultural training, to the extent that he will not consider farming a drudgery and a degradation, but will see in farm life dignity and beauty. It should, then, be borne in mind that any agitation which makes the Negro feel that he is likely to be deprived of school privileges in the country for the cities.

The Introduction of Industrial Training into the Public Schools

The demand for the introduction of industrial or manual training into the public schools of both the cities and the country, has become so wide-spread throughout the South, that this institution is constantly appealed to for information and help. Besides numerous letters from school officials, we are having visits from school superintendents and boards of education, seeking such information as will enable them to introduce our methods into their schools. In connection with this subject, however, I wish it thoroughly understood that I do not advocate the lowering of the mental standard as I understand is proposed by the public school boards of one, or two of our Southern cities. No race can be elevated till its mind is awakened and strengthened. In order that we may meet these demands in the best manner, we ought to have an addition to our present industrial department for the older students, a model primary school that will serve as an object lesson to those who want to get information as to the manner of introducing manual and industrial training into the public schools. The present primary school of 176 pupils, which is taught upon the grounds, will serve as a foundation. To carry out the plan that I have mentioned, we should have a new and larger building and the location should be where there is plenty of land that can be used for their purpose of teaching, among other things, simple lessons in gardening, to the small children. In addition to the usual class rooms, such a building should contain space for teaching kindergarten, mechanical drawing, carpentry, sewing, cooking and laundering. There should also be a place for bathing. Such a building, well equipped, would cost about $2,000. I urge this as one of our most pressing needs. Few things would so much extend the influence for good in all parts of the South as the securing of this building.

Attendance and Growth of the School

The average attendance for the school year has been 1,083; 321 young women, and 762 young men. The total enrollment has been 1,231; 359 young women and 872 young men. Nine-tenths of the number have boarded and slept on the school grounds.

In all the departments, including officers, clerks and instructors, 103 persons are in the employ of the school. Counting students, officers and teachers, together with their families, the total number of persons constantly upon the school grounds, is about 1,200. Students have come to us from 27 States and territories, from Africa, Porto Rico, Cuba, Jamaica and Barbadoes. There are 12 students from Cuba alone.

During the present school year students have been trained in the following 28 industries, in addition to the religious and academic training: Agriculture, Dairying, Horticulture, Stock raising, Blacksmithing, Brickmasonry, Carpentry, Carriage Trimming, Cooking, Architectural, Freehand and Mechanical Drawing, Plain Sewing, Plastering, Plumbing, Printing, Sawmilling, Founding, Housekeeping, Harnessmaking, Electrical Engineering, Laundering, Machinery,

Mattress-making, Millinery, Nurse Training, Painting, Shoemaking, Tailoring, Tinning and Wheelwrighting.

This year we have made progress in the matter of training young women in outdoor occupations. Beginning with this school year, we are now giving a number of girls training in poultry raising, bee culture, dairying, gardening, fruit growing, etc....

Notwithstanding the stress put upon industrial training, we are not in any degree neglecting normal training for those who are to teach in the public schools. The number of graduates this year from all the departments is 51. In addition to religious and academic training, each one of these graduates has had training at some trade or industry.... Our graduates and former students are now scattered all over the South, and wherever they can, they not only help the colored people, but use their influence in cultivating friendly relations between the races....

Respectfully Submitted: ....BOOKER T. WASHINGTON

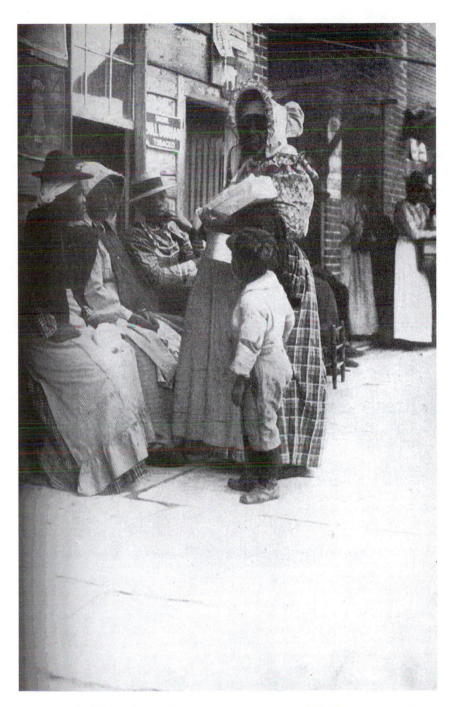

"Her Week's Marketing," Photograph by A. Radcliffe Dugmore included in W. E. B. Du Bois's "The Negro as He Really Is," *The World's Work*, June 1901, p. 855.

"Bright Sparkles in de Churchyard," included in J. B. T. Marsh, *The Story of the Jubilee Singers* (Cleveland, Ohio: The Cleveland Printing and Publishing Company, 1892), p. 280.

VII

Of the Black Belt[1]

I am black but comely, O ye daughters of Jerusalem,
As the tents of Kedar, as the curtains of Solomon.
Look not upon me, because I am black,
Because the sun hath looked upon me:
My mother's children were angry with me;
They made me the keeper of the vineyards;
But mine own vineyard have I not kept.

THE SONG OF SOLOMON.

Out of the North the train thundered, and we woke to see the crimson soil of Georgia stretching away bare and monotonous right and left. Here and there lay straggling, unlovely villages, and lean men loafed leisurely at the depots; then again came the stretch of pines and clay. Yet we did not nod, nor weary of the scene; for this is historic ground. Right across our track, three hundred and sixty years ago, wandered the cavalcade of Hernando de Soto,[2] looking for gold and the Great Sea;[3] and he and his foot-sore captives disappeared yonder in the grim forests to the west. Here sits Atlanta, the city of a hundred hills,

---

[1] This chapter and the one that follows are revisions of Du Bois's article "The Negro as He really Is," *The World's Work* (June 1901), pp. 848–846. The German photographer Major A. Radcliffe Dugmore accompanied Du Bois in his travels through Dougherty County, Georgia.
[2] Spanish conquistador (1496?–1542) and the European discoverer of the Mississippi.
[3] The Pacific Ocean.

Title page from the article "The Negro as He Really Is," *The World's Work*, June 1901, p. 848.

with something Western, something Southern, and something quite its own, in its busy life. Just this side of Atlanta is the land of the Cherokees[4] and to the southwest, not far from where Sam Hose[5] was crucified, you may stand on a spot which is today the centre of the Negro problem,—the centre of those nine million men who are America's dark heritage from slavery and the slave-trade.

Not only is Georgia thus the geographical focus of our Negro population, but in many other respects, both now and yesterday, the Negro problems have seemed to be centered in this State. No other State in the Union can count a million Negroes among its citizens,—a population as large as the slave population of the whole Union in 1800; no other State fought so long and strenuously to gather this host of Africans. Oglethorpe[6] thought slavery against law and gospel; but the

---

[4] The Cherokee people are a branch of the Iroquois nation. At the time of the European contact, their lands covered a large part of what is now the southeastern United States.

[5] Sam Hose was a black farm worker from Palmetto, Georgia, who in 1899 fled from his home after murdering his employer. On his capture, he was also accused of raping his owner's wife. Hose admitted to the murder, but not the rape. He was lynched by a crowd of approximately 2,000 people, who burned and dismembered his body.

[6] James E. Ogelthorpe (1696–1785) founded Georgia as a British colony in 1733.

circumstances which gave Georgia its first inhabitants were not calculated to furnish citizens over-nice in their ideas about rum and slaves. Despite the prohibitions of the trustees, these Georgians, like some of their descendants, proceeded to take the law into their own hands; and so pliant were the judges, and so flagrant the smuggling, and so earnest were the prayers of Whitefield,[7] that by the middle of the eighteenth century all restrictions were swept away, and the slave-trade went merrily on for fifty years and more.

Down in Darien, where the Delegal riots took place some summers ago,[8] there used to come a strong protest against slavery from the Scotch Highlanders; and the Moravians of Ebenezer did not like the system.[9] But not till the Haytian Terror of Toussaint[10] was the trade in men even

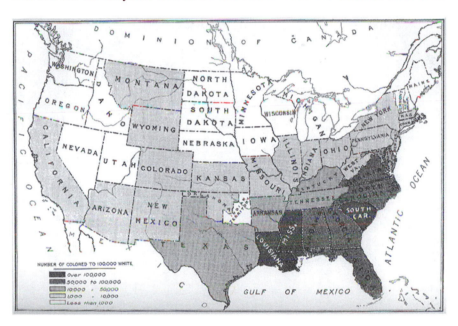

"The Distribution of the Negro Population in the United States," from "The Negro as He Really Is," *The World's Work* (June 1901), p. 862.

---

[7] George Whitefield (1714–1770), English evangelist who conducted missionary work in the Georgia Colony. A supporter of slavery, he also called for the more humane treatment of slaves.
[8] The Delegal riot took place on August 23, 1899, when hundreds of blacks removed a black man from jail in Darien, Georgia, because they feared that he would be lynched.
[9] The Scotch Highlanders were among the most important settlers of Colonial Georgia.
[10] Francois Toussaint L'Ouverture (1744?–1803), Haitian revolutionary.

TABLE XVIII.—*Negro population and number and per cent of increase by ten and twenty year periods: 1790 to 1900.*

CENSUS.	Negro population.	INCREASE OF NEGRO POPULATION DURING—				PER CENT OF INCREASE OF WHITE POPULATION DURING—	
		Preceding ten years.		Preceding twenty years.		Preceding ten years.	Preceding twenty years.
		Number.	Per cent.	Number.	Per cent.		
Continental U.S.:							
1900	8,833,994	1,345,318	18.0	2,253,201	34.2	21.2	53.9
1890[1]	7,488,676	....	......	....	......	......	......
1890[2]	7,470,040	889,247	13.5	....	......	26.7	......
1880	6,580,793	1,700,784	34.9	2,138,963	48.2	29.2	61.2
1870	4,880,009	438,179	9.9	....	......	24.8	......
1860	4,441,830	803,022	22.1	1,568,182	54.6	37.7	89.7
1850	3,638,808	765,160	26.6	....	......	37.7	......
1840	2,873,648	545,006	23.4	1,101,992	62.2	34.7	80.5
1830	2,328,642	556,986	31.4	....	......	33.9	......
1820	1,771,656	393,848	28.6	769,619	76.8	34.2	82.7
1810	1,377,808	375,771	37.5	....	......	36.1	......
1800	1,002,037	244,829	32.3	....	......	35.8	......
1790	757,208	....	......	....	......	......	......

[1] Includes population of Indian Territory and Indian reservations.
[2] Excludes population of Indian Territory and Indian reservations.

Black population in the United States, 1790–1900. Source: Department of Commerce and Labor, Bureau of the Census, Bulletin No. 8, *Negroes in the United States* (Washington, D.C.: U. S. Government Printing Office), p. 29.

checked; while the national statute of 1808[11] did not suffice to stop it How the Africans poured in!—fifty thousand between 1790 and 1810,and then, from Virginia and from smugglers, two thousand a year for many years more. So the thirty thousand Negroes of Georgia in 1790 doubled in a decade,—were over a hundred thousand in 1810, had reached two hundred thousand in 1820, and half a million at the time of the war. Thus like a snake the black population writhed upward.

But we must hasten on our journey. This that we pass as we near Atlanta is the ancient land of the Cherokees,—that brave Indian nation which strove so long for its fatherland, until Fate and the United States

---

[11] On March 2, 1807, President Thomas Jefferson signed a bill abolishing the slave trade, which took effect on January 1, 1808.

Government drove them beyond the Mississippi. If you wish to ride with me you must come into the "Jim Crow car."[12] There will be no objection,—already four other white men, and a little white girl with her nurse, are in there. Usually the races are mixed in there; but the white coach is all white. Of course this car is not so good as the other, but it is fairly clean and comfortable. The discomfort lies chiefly in the hearts of those four black men yonder—and in mine.

Portrait of Toussaint L'Ouverture in Marcus Rainsford's *An Historical Account of the Black Empire in Hayti*, published in 1805.

---

[12] The term "Jim Crow car" refers to the segregated railroad car provided to black passengers throughout both the North and the South. During the 1890s, the term "Jim Crow" became associated with an expanded, legally enforced, segregation of blacks, particularly in the South—one that was successfully maintained until the middle of the twentieth century.

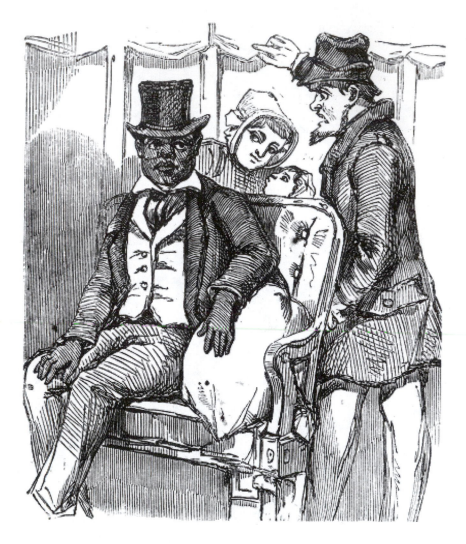

Negro expulsion from a railway car. Wood engraving in the *Illustrated London News*, September 27, 1856. Courtesy of the Library of Congress.

We rumble south in quite a business-like way. The bare red clay and pines of Northern Georgia begin to disappear, and in their place appears a rich rolling land, luxuriant, and here and there well-tilled. This is the land of the Creek Indians; and a hard time the Georgians had to seize it. The towns grow more frequent and more interesting, and brand-new cotton mills rise on every side. Below Macon the world grows darker; for now we approach the Black Belt,—that strange land of shadows, at which even slaves paled in the past, and whence come now only faint and half-intelligible murmurs to the world beyond.[13] The "Jim Crow car" grows larger and a shade better; three rough field-hands and two or three white loafers accompany us, and the newsboy still spreads his wares at one end. The sun is setting, but we can see the great cotton country as we enter it,—the soil now dark and fertile, now thin and gray, with fruit-trees and dilapidated buildings,—all the way to Albany.

At Albany, in the heart of the Black Belt, we stop. Two hundred miles south of Atlanta, two hundred miles west of the Atlantic, and one hundred miles north of the Great Gulf lies Dougherty County, with ten thousand Negroes and two thousand whites. The Flint River winds down from Andersonville, and, turning suddenly at Albany, the county seat, hurries on to join the Chattahoochee and the sea. Andrew Jackson knew the Flint well, and marched across it once to avenge the Indian Massacre at Fort Mims. That was in 1814, not long before the battle of New Orleans; and by the Creek treaty that followed this campaign, all Dougherty County, and much other rich land, was ceded to Georgia. Still, settlers fought shy of this land, for the Indians were all about, and they were unpleasant neighbors in those days. The panic of 1837, which Jackson bequeathed to Van Buren, turned the planters from the impoverished lands of Virginia, the Carolinas, and east Georgia, toward the West. The Indians were removed to Indian Territory, and settlers poured into these coveted lands to retrieve their broken fortunes. For a radius of a hundred miles about Albany, stretched a great fertile land,

"Big House" and Negro Quarters (The House is no longer in use although the Negro quarters are)," in "The Negro as He Really Is," *The World's Work*, June 1901, p. 850.

---

[13] "Black Belt" refers to that section of Georgia and Alabama where the black population is greater than the white population.

"'Women from the Country' (A Saturday group in Albany Georgia)," in "The Negro as He Really Is," *The World's Work*, June 1901, p. 854.

luxuriant with forests of pine, oak, ash, hickory, and poplar; hot with the sun and damp with the rich black swamp-land; and here the corner-stone of the Cotton Kingdom was laid.

Albany is today a wide-streeted, placid, Southern town, with a broad sweep of stores and saloons, and flanking rows of homes,—whites usually to the north, and blacks to the south. Six days in the week the town looks decidedly too small for itself, and takes frequent and prolonged naps. But on Saturday suddenly the whole county disgorges itself upon the place, and a perfect flood of black peasantry pours through the streets, fills the stores, blocks the sidewalks, chokes the thoroughfares, and takes full possession of the town. They are black, sturdy, uncouth country folk, good-natured and simple, talkative to a degree, and yet far more silent and brooding than the crowds of the Rhine-pfalz, or Naples, or Cracow. They drink considerable quantities of whiskey, but do not get very drunk; they talk and laugh loudly at times, but seldom quarrel or fight. They walk up and down the streets, meet and gossip with friends, stare at the shop windows, buy coffee, cheap candy, and clothes, and at dusk drive home—happy? Well no, not exactly happy, but much happier than as though they had not come.

Thus Albany is a real capital,—a typical Southern county town, the centre of the life of ten thousand souls; their point of contact with the outer world, their centre of news and gossip, their market for buying and selling, borrowing and lending, their fountain of justice and law. Once upon a time we knew country life so well and city life so little, that we illustrated city life as that of a closely crowded country district. Now the world has well-nigh forgotten what the country is, and we must imagine a little city of black people scattered far and wide over three hundred lonesome square miles of land, without train or trolley, in the midst of cotton and corn, and wide patches of sand and gloomy soil.

It gets pretty hot in Southern Georgia in July,—a sort of dull, determined heat that seems quite independent of the sun; so it took us some days to muster courage enough to leave the porch and venture out on the long country roads, that we might see this unknown world. Finally we started. It was about ten in the morning, bright with a faint breeze, and we jogged leisurely southward in the valley of the Flint. We passed the scattered box-like cabins of the brick-yard hands, and the long tenement-row facetiously called "The Ark," and were soon in the open country, and on the confines of the great plantations of other days. There is the "Joe Fields place"; a rough old fellow was he, and had killed many a "nigger" in his day. Twelve miles his plantation used to run,—a regular barony. It is nearly all gone now; only straggling bits belong to the family, and the rest has passed to Jews and Negroes. Even the bits which are left are heavily mortgaged, and, like the rest of the land, tilled by tenants. Here is one of them now,—a tall brown man, a hard worker and a hard drinker, illiterate, but versed in farmlore, as his nodding crops

"Negro Cottages," in "The Negro as He Really Is," *The World's Work,* June 1901, p. 850.

"A parson and part of his flock," "The Negro as He Really Is," "*The World's Work*, June 1901, p. 854.

declare. This distressingly new board house is his, and he has just moved out of yonder moss-grown cabin with its one square room.

From the curtains in Benton's house, down the road, a dark comely face is staring at the strangers; for passing carriages are not everyday occurrences here. Benton is an intelligent yellow man with a good-sized family, and manages a plantation blasted by the war and now the broken staff of the widow. He might be well-to-do, they say; but he carouses too much in Albany. And the half-desolate spirit of neglect born of the very soil seems to have settled on these acres. In times past there were cotton-gins and machinery here; but they have rotted away.

The whole land seems forlorn and forsaken. Here are the remnants of the vast plantations of the Sheldons, the Pellots, and the Rensons; but the souls of them are passed. The houses lie in half ruin, or have wholly disappeared; the fences have flown, and the families are wandering in the world. Strange vicissitudes have met these whilom masters. Yonder stretch the wide acres of Bildad Reasor; he died in wartime, but the upstart overseer hastened to wed the widow. Then he went, and his neighbors too, and now only the black tenant remains; but the shadow-hand of the master's grand-nephew or cousin or creditor stretches out of the gray distance to collect the rack-rent remorselessly, and so the land is uncared-for and poor. Only black tenants can stand such a system, and they only because they must. Ten miles we have ridden today and have seen no white face.

A resistless feeling of depression falls slowly upon us, despite the gaudy sunshine and the green cottonfields. This, then, is the Cotton Kingdom,—the shadow of a marvellous dream. And where is the King? Perhaps this is he,—the sweating ploughman, tilling his eighty acres with two lean mules, and fighting a hard battle with debt. So we sit musing, until, as we turn a corner on the sandy road, there comes a fairer scene suddenly in view,—a neat cottage snugly ensconced by the road, and near it a little store. A tall bronzed man rises from the porch as we hail him, and comes out to our carriage. He is six feet in height, with a sober face that smiles gravely. He walks too straight to be a tenant,—yes, he owns two hundred and forty acres. "The land is run down since the boom-days of eighteen hundred and fifty," he explains, and cotton is low. Three black tenants live on his place, and in his little store he keeps a

"A Typical Negro Store," in "The Negro as He Really Is," *The World's Work*, June 1901, p. 858.

"A Negro School Near Albany Georgia (Where children go after 'crops are laid by')," in "The Negro as He Really Is," *The World's Work*, June 1901, p. 851.

small stock of tobacco, snuff, soap, and soda, for the neighborhood. Here is his gin-house with new machinery just installed. Three hundred bales of cotton went through it last year. Two children he has sent away to school. Yes, he says sadly, he is getting on, but cotton is down to four cents; I know how debt sits staring at him.

Wherever the King may be, the parks and palaces of the Cotton Kingdom have not wholly disappeared. We plunge even now into great groves of oak and towering pine, with an undergrowth of myrtle and shrubbery. This was the "home-house" of the Thompsons,—slave-barons who drove their coach and four in the merry past. All is silence now, and ashes, and tangled weeds. The owner put his whole fortune into the rising cotton industry of the fifties, and with the falling prices of the eighties he packed up and stole away. Yonder is another grove, with unkempt lawn, great magnolias, and grass-grown paths. The Big House stands in half-ruin, its great front door staring blankly at the street, and the back part grotesquely restored for its black tenant. A shabby, well-built Negro he is, unlucky and irresolute. He digs hard to pay rent to the white girl who owns the remnant of the place. She married a policeman, and lives in Savannah.

Now and again we come to churches. Here is one now,—Shepherd's, they call it,—a great whitewashed barn of a thing, perched on stilts of stone, and looking for all the world as though it were just resting here a moment and might be expected to waddle off down the road at almost any time. And yet it is the centre of a hundred cabin homes; and sometimes, of a Sunday, five hundred persons from far and near gather here and talk and eat and sing. There is a schoolhouse near,—a very airy, empty shed: but even this is an improvement, for usually the school is held in the church. The churches vary from log-huts to those like Shepherd's, and the schools from nothing to this little house that sits demurely on the county line. It is a tiny plank-house, perhaps ten by twenty, and has within a double row of rough unplaned benches, resting mostly on legs, sometimes on boxes. Opposite the door is a square home-made desk. In one corner are the ruins of a stove, and in the other a dim blackboard. It is the cheerfulest schoolhouse I have seen in Dougherty, save in town. Back of the schoolhouse is a lodgehouse two stories high and not quite finished. Societies meet there,—societies "to care for the sick and bury the dead"; and these societies grow and flourish.

We had come to the boundaries of Dougherty, and were about to turn west along the county line, when all these sights were pointed out to us by a kindly old man, black, white-haired, and seventy. Forty-five years he had lived here, and now supports himself and his old wife by the help of the steer tethered yonder and the charity of his black neighbors. He shows us the farm of the Hills just across the county line in Baker,—a widow and two strapping sons, who raised ten bales (one need not add "cotton" down here) last year. There are fences and pigs and cows, and the soft-voiced, velvet-skinned young Memnon,[14] who sauntered half-bashfully over to greet the strangers, is proud of his home. We turn now to the west along the county line. Great dismantled trunks of pines tower above the green cotton-fields, cracking their naked gnarled fingers toward the border of living forest beyond. There is little beauty in this region, only a sort of crude abandon that suggests power,—a naked grandeur, as it were. The houses are bare and straight; there are no hammocks or easy-chairs, and few flowers. So when, as here at Rawdon's, one sees a vine clinging to a little porch, and home-like windows peeping over the fences, one takes a long breath. I think I never before quite realized the place of the Fence in civilization. This is the Land of the Unfenced, where crouch on either hand scores of ugly one-

---

[14] A king of Ethiopia mentioned in Ancient Greek mythology.

"Huts Near Albany, Georgia (Showing old mud and wood chimney)," in "The Negro as He Really Is," *The World's Work*, June 1901, p. 857.

room cabins, cheerless and dirty. Here lies the Negro problem in its naked dirt and penury. And here are no fences. But now and then the criss-cross rails or straight palings break into view, and then we know a touch of culture is near. Of course Harrison Gohagen,—a quiet yellow man, young, smooth-faced, and diligent,—of course he is lord of some hundred acres, and we expect to see a vision of well-kept rooms and fat beds and laughing children. For has he not fine fences? And those over yonder, why should they build fences on the rack-rented land? It will only increase their rent.

On we wind, through sand and pines and glimpses of old plantations, till there creeps into sight a cluster of buildings,—wood and brick, mills and houses, and scattered cabins. It seemed quite a village. As it came nearer and nearer, however, the aspect changed: the buildings were rotten, the bricks were falling out, the mills were silent, and the store was closed. Only in the cabins appeared now and then a bit of lazy life. I could imagine the place under some weird spell, and was half-minded to search out the princess. An old ragged black man, honest, simple, and improvident, told us the tale. The Wizard of the North—the Capitalist— had rushed down in the seventies to woo this coy dark soil. He bought a square mile or more, and for a time the field-hands sang, the gins groaned, and the mills buzzed. Then came a change. The agent's son embezzled the funds and ran off with them. Then the agent himself disappeared. Finally the new agent stole even the books, and the company in wrath closed its business and its houses, refused to sell, and let houses and furniture and machinery rust and rot. So the Waters-Loring plantation was stilled by the spell of dishonesty, and stands like some gaunt rebuke to a scarred land.

Somehow that plantation ended our day's journey; for I could not shake off the influence of that silent scene. Back toward town we glided, past the straight and thread-like pines, past a dark tree-dotted pond where the air was heavy with a dead sweet perfume. White slender-legged curlews flitted by us, and the garnet blooms of the cotton looked gay against the green and purple stalks. A peasant girl was hoeing in the field, white-turbaned and black-limbed. All this we saw, but the spell still lay upon us.

How curious a land is this,—how full of untold story, of tragedy and laughter, and the rich legacy of human life; shadowed with a tragic past, and big with future promise! This is the Black Belt of Georgia. Dougherty County is the west end of the Black Belt, and men once called it the Egypt of the Confederacy.[15] It is full of historic interest. First there is the Swamp, to the west, where the Chickasawhatchee flows sullenly southward. The shadow of an old plantation lies at its edge, forlorn and dark. Then comes the pool; pendent gray moss and brackish waters appear, and forests filled with wildfowl. In one place the wood is on fire, smouldering in dull red anger; but nobody minds. Then the swamp grows beautiful; a raised road, built by chained Negro convicts, dips down into it, and forms a way walled and almost covered in living green. Spreading trees spring from a prodigal luxuriance of undergrowth; great dark green shadows fade into the black background, until all is one mass of tangled semi-tropical foliage, marvellous in its weird savage splendor. Once we crossed a black silent stream, where the sad trees and writhing creepers, all glinting fiery yellow and green, seemed like some vast cathedral,— some green Milan[16] builded of wildwood. And as I crossed, I seemed to

---

[15] Historically, Egypt has also been a great producer of cotton—hence the reference.

[16] City in Northern Italy with a famous cathedral.

"Women 'Sowing' Guano," in "The Negro as He Really Is, "*The World's Work*, June 1901, p. 860.

see again that fierce tragedy of seventy years ago. Osceola,[17] the Indian-Negro chieftain, had risen in the swamps of Florida, vowing vengeance. His war-cry reached the red Creeks of Dougherty, and their war-cry rang from the Chattahoochee to the sea. Men and women and children fled and fell before them as they swept into Dougherty. In yonder shadows a dark and hideously painted warrior glided stealthily on,—another and another, until three hundred had crept into the treacherous swamp. Then the false slime closing about them called the white men from the east. Waist-deep, they fought beneath the tall trees, until the war-cry was hushed and the Indians glided back into the west. Small wonder the wood is red.

---

[17] Osceola (c. 1804–1838), Seminole tribal leader.

Then came the black slaves. Day after day the clank of chained feet marching from Virginia and Carolina to Georgia was heard in these rich swamp lands. Day after day the songs of the callous, the wail of the motherless, and the muttered curses of the wretched echoed from the Flint to the Chickasawhatchee, until by 1860 there had risen in West Dougherty perhaps the richest slave kingdom the modern world ever knew. A hundred and fifty barons commanded the labor of nearly six thousand Negroes, held sway over farms with ninety thousand acres tilled land, valued even in times of cheap soil at three millions of dollars. Twenty thousand bales of ginned cotton went yearly to England, New and Old; and men that came there bankrupt made money and grew rich. In a single decade the cotton output increased four-fold and the value of lands was tripled. It was the heyday of the *nouveau riche*, and a life a careless extravagance among the masters. Four and six bob-tailed thoroughbreds rolled their coaches to town; open hospitality and gay entertainment were the rule. Parks and groves were laid out, rich with flower and vine, and in the midst stood the low wide-halled "Big House," with its porch and columns and great fireplaces.

And yet with all this there was something sordid, something forced,—a certain feverish unrest and recklessness; for was not all this show and tinsel built upon a groan? "This land was a little Hell," said a ragged, brown, and grave-faced man to me. We were seated near a roadside blacksmith shop, and behind was the bare ruin of some master's home. "I've seen niggers drop dead in the furrow, but they were kicked aside, and the plough never stopped. Down in the guard-house, there's where the blood ran."

With such foundations a kingdom must in time sway and fall. The masters moved to Macon and Augusta, and left only the irresponsible overseers on the land. And the result is such ruin as this, the Lloyd "home-place":—great waving oaks, a spread of lawn, myrtles and chestnuts, all ragged and wild; a solitary gate-post standing where once was a castle entrance; an old rusty anvil lying mid rotting bellows and wood in the ruins of a blacksmith shop; a wide rambling old mansion, brown and dingy, filled now with the grandchildren of the slaves who once waited on its tables; while the family of the master has dwindled to two lone women, who live in Macon and feed hungrily off the remnants of an earldom. So we ride on, past phantom gates and failing homes,— past the once flourishing farms of the Smiths, the Gandys, and the Lagores,—and find all dilapidated and half-ruined, even there where a solitary white woman, a relic of other days, sits alone in state among miles of Negroes and rides to town in her ancient coach each day.

This was indeed the Egypt of the Confederacy,—the rich granary whence potatoes and corn and cotton poured out to the famished and ragged Confederate troops as they battled for a cause lost long before 1861. Sheltered and secure, it became the place of refuge for families, wealth and slaves. Yet even then the hard ruthless rape of the land began to tell. The red-clay sub-soil already had begun to peer above the loam. The harder the slaves were driven the more careless and fatal was their farming. Then came the revolution of war and Emancipation, the bewilderment of Reconstruction,—and now, what is the Egypt of the Confederacy, and what meaning has it for the nation's weal or woe?

It is a land of rapid contrasts and of curiously mingled hope and pain. Here sits a pretty blue-eyed quadroon hiding her bare feet; she was married only last week, and yonder in the field is her dark young husband, hoeing to support her, at thirty cents a day without board. Across the way is Gatesby, brown and tall, lord of two thousand acres shrewdly won and held. There is a store conducted by his black son, a blacksmith shop, and a ginnery. Five miles below here is a town owned and controlled by one white New Englander. He owns almost a Rhode Island county, with thousands of acres and hundreds of black laborers. Their cabins look better than most, and the farm, with machinery and fertilizers, is much more business-like than any in the county, although the manager drives hard bargains in wages. When now we turn and look five miles above, there on the edge of town are five houses of prostitutes,—two of blacks and three of whites; and in one of the houses of the whites a worthless black boy was harbored too openly two years ago; so he was hanged for rape. And here, too, is the high whitewashed fence of the "stockade," as the county prison is called; the white folks say it is ever full of black criminals,—the black folks say that only colored boys are sent to jail, and they not because they are guilty, but because the State needs criminals to eke out its income by their forced labor.

Immigrants are heirs of the slave baron in Dougherty; and as we ride westward, by wide stretching cornfields and stubby orchards of peach and pear, we see on all sides within the circle of dark forest a Land of Canaan. Here and there are tales of projects for money-getting, born in the swift days of Reconstruction,—"improvement" companies, wine companies, mills and factories; most failed, and foreigners fell heir. It is a beautiful land, this Dougherty, west of the Flint. The forests are wonderful, the solemn pines have disappeared, and this is the "Oakey Woods," with its wealth of hickories, beeches, oaks and palmettos. But a pall of debt hangs over the beautiful land; the merchants are in debt to the wholesalers, the planters are in debt to the merchants, the tenants owe the planters, and laborers bow and bend beneath the burden of it all. Here and there a man has raised his head above these murky waters. We passed one fenced stock-farm with grass and grazing cattle, that looked very homelike after endless corn and cotton. Here and there are black free-holders: there is the gaunt dull-black Jackson, with his hundred acres. "I says, 'Look up! If you don't look up you can't get up,'" remarks Jackson, philosophically. And he's gotten up. Dark Carter's neat barns would do credit to New England. His master helped him to get a start, but when the black man died last fall the master's sons immediately laid claim to the estate. "And them white folks will get it, too," said my yellow gossip.

I turn from these well-tended acres with a comfortable feeling that the Negro is rising. Even then, however, the fields, as we proceed, begin to redden and the trees disappear. Rows of old cabins appear filled with renters and laborers,—cheerless, bare, and dirty, for the most part, although here and there the very age and decay makes the scene picturesque. A young black fellow greets us. He is twenty-two, and just married. Until last year he had good luck renting; then cotton fell, and the sheriff seized and sold all he had. So he moved here, where the rent is higher, the land poorer, and the owner inflexible; he rents a forty-dollar mule for twenty dollars a year. Poor lad!—a slave at twenty-two. This plantation, owned now by a foreigner, was a part of the famous Bolton estate. After the war it was for many years worked by gangs of Negro convicts,—and black convicts then were even more plentiful than now; it was a way of making Negroes work, and the question of guilt was a minor one. Hard tales of cruelty and mistreatment of the chained freemen are told, but the county authorities were deaf until the free-labor market was nearly ruined by wholesale migration. Then they took the convicts from the plantations, but not until one of the fairest regions of the "Oakey Woods" had been ruined and ravished into a red waste, out of which only a Yankee or an immigrant could squeeze more blood from debt-cursed tenants.

No wonder that Luke Black, slow, dull, and discouraged, shuffles to our carriage and talks hopelessly. Why should he strive? Every year finds him deeper in debt. How strange that Georgia, the world-heralded refuge of poor debtors, should bind her own to sloth and misfortune as ruthlessly as ever England did! The poor land groans with its birth-pains, and brings forth scarcely a hundred pounds of cotton to the acre, where fifty years ago it yielded eight times as much. Of this meagre yield the tenant pays from a quarter to a third in rent, and most of the rest in interest on food and supplies bought on credit. Twenty years yonder sunken-cheeked, old black man has labored under that system, and now, turned day-laborer, is supporting his wife and boarding himself on his wages of a dollar and a half a week, received only part of the year.

The Bolton convict farm formerly included the neighboring plantation. Here it was that the convicts were lodged in the great log prison still standing. A dismal place it still remains, with rows of ugly huts filled with surly ignorant tenants. "What rent do you pay here?" I inquired. "I don't know,—what is it, Sam?" "All we make," answered Sam. It is a depressing place,—bare, unshaded, with no charm of past association, only a memory of forced human toil,—now, then, and before the war. They are not happy, these black men whom we meet throughout this region. There is little of the joyous abandon and playfulness which we are wont to associate with the plantation Negro. At best, the natural good nature is edged with complaint or has changed into sullenness and gloom. And now and then it blazes forth in veiled but hot anger. I remember one big red-eyed black whom we met by the roadside. Forty-five years he had labored on this farm, beginning with nothing, and still having nothing. To be sure, he had given four children a common-school training, and perhaps if the new fence law had not allowed unfenced crops in West Dougherty he. might have raised a little stock and kept ahead. As it is, he is hopelessly in debt, disappointed, and embittered. He stopped us to inquire after the black boy in Albany, whom it was said a policeman had shot and killed for loud talking on the sidewalk. And then he said slowly: "Let a white man touch me, and he dies; I don't boast this,—I don't say it around loud, or before the children,—but I mean it. I've seen them whip my father and my old mother in them cotton-rows till the blood ran; by—" and we passed on.

Now Sears, whom we met next lolling under the chubby oak-trees, was of quite different fibre. Happy?—Well, yes; he laughed and flipped pebbles, and thought the world was as it was. He had worked here twelve years and has nothing but a mortgaged mule. Children? Yes, seven; but they hadn't been to school this year,—couldn't afford books and clothes, and couldn't spare their work. There I go part of them to the fields now,—three big boys astride mules, and a strapping girl with bare brown legs. Careless ignorance and laziness here, fierce hate and vindictiveness there;—these are the extremes of the Negro problem which we met that day, and we scarce knew which we preferred.

Here and there we meet distinct characters quite out of the ordinary. One came out of a piece of newly cleared ground, making a wide detour to avoid the snakes. He was an old, hollow-cheeked man, with a drawn and characterful brown face. He had a sort of self-contained quaintness and rough humor impossible to describe; a certain cynical earnestness that puzzled one. "The niggers were jealous of me over on the other place," he said, "and so me and the old woman begged this piece of woods, and I cleared it up myself. Made nothing for two years, but I reckon I've got a crop now." The cotton looked tall and rich, and we praised it. He curtsied low, and then bowed almost to the ground, with an imperturbable gravity that seemed almost suspicious. Then he continued, "My mule died last week,"—a calamity in this land equal to a devastating fire in town,—"but a white man loaned me another." Then he added, eyeing us, "Oh, I gets along with white folks." We turned the conversation. "Bears? deer?" he answered, "well, I should say there were," and he let fly a string of brave oaths, as he told hunting-tales of the swamp. We left him standing still in the middle of the road looking after us, and yet apparently not noticing us.

The Whistle place, which includes his bit of land, was bought soon after the war by an English syndicate, the "Dixie Cotton and Corn Company." A marvellous deal of style their factor put on, with his servants and coach-and-six; so much so that the concern soon landed in inextricable bankruptcy. Nobody lives in the old house now, but a man comes each winter out of the North and collects his high rents. I know not which are the more touching,—such old empty homes, or the homes of the masters' sons. Sad and bitter tales lie hidden back of those white doors,—tales of poverty, of struggle, of disappointment. A revolution such as that of '63 is a terrible thing; they that rose rich in the morning often slept in paupers' beds. Beggars and vulgar speculators rose to rule over them, and their children went astray. See yonder sad-colored house, with its cabins and fences and glad crops! It is not glad within; last month the prodigal son of the struggling father wrote home from the city for money. Money! Where was it to come from? And so the son rose in the night and killed his baby, and killed his wife, and shot himself dead. And the world passed on.

I remember wheeling around a bend in the road beside a graceful bit of forest and a singing brook. A long low house faced us, with porch and flying pillars, great oaken door, and a broad lawn shining in the evening sun. But the window-panes were gone, the pillars were worm-eaten, and the moss-grown roof was falling in. Half curiously I peered through the unhinged door, and saw where, on the wall across the hall, was written in once gay letters a faded "Welcome."

Quite a contrast to the southwestern part of Dougherty County is the northwest. Soberly timbered in oak and pine, it has none of that half-tropical luxuriance of the southwest. Then, too, there are fewer signs of a romantic past, and more of systematic modern land-grabbing and money-getting. White people are more in evidence here, and farmer and hired labor replace to some extent the absentee landlord and rack-rented tenant. The crops have neither the luxuriance of the richer land nor the signs of neglect so often seen, and there were fences and meadows here and there. Most of this land was poor, and beneath the notice of the slave-baron, before the war. Since then his poor relations and foreign immigrants have seized it. The returns of the farmer are too small to allow much for wages, and yet he will not sell off small farms. There is the Negro Sanford; he has worked fourteen years as overseer on the

Ladson place, and "paid out enough for fertilizers to have bought a farm," but the owner will not sell off a few acres.

Two children—a boy and a girl—are hoeing sturdily in the fields on the farm where Corliss works. He is smooth-faced and brown, and is fencing up his pigs. He used to run a successful cotton-gin, but the Cotton Seed Oil Trust has forced the price of ginning so low that he says it hardly pays him. He points out a stately old house over the way as the home of "Pa Willis."   We eagerly ride over, for "Pa Willis" was the tall and powerful black Moses who led the Negroes for a generation, and led them well. He was a Baptist preacher, and when he died, two thousand black people followed him to the grave; and now they preach his funeral sermon each year. His widow lives here,—a weazened, sharp-featured little woman, who curtsied quaintly as we greeted her. Further on lives Jack Delson, the most prosperous Negro farmer in the county. It is a joy to meet bim,—a great broad-shouldered, handsome black man, intelligent and jovial. Six hundred and fifty acres he owns, and has eleven black tenants. A neat and tidy home nestles in a flower-garden, and a little store stands beside it.

We pass the Munson Place, where a plucky white widow is renting and struggling; and the eleven hundred acres of the Sennet plantation, with its Negro overseer. Then the character of the farms begins to change. Nearly all the lands belong to Russian Jews; the overseers are white, and the cabins are bare board houses scattered here and there. The rents are high, and day-laborers and "contract" hands abound. It is a keen, hard struggle for living here, and few have time to talk. Tired with the long ride, we gladly drive into Gillonsville. It is a silent cluster of farmhouses standing on the crossroads, with one of its stores closed and the other kept by a Negro preacher. They tell great tales of busy times at Gillonsville before all the railroads came to Albany; now it is chiefly memory. Riding down the street, we stop at the preacher's and seat ourselves before the door. It was one of those scenes one cannot soon forget:—a wide, low, little house, whose motherly roof reached over and sheltered a snug little porch. There we sat, after the long hot drive, drinking cool water,—the talkative little store-keeper who is my daily companion; the silent old black woman patching pantaloons and saying never a word; the ragged picture of helpless misfortune who called in just to see the preacher; and finally the neat matronly preacher's wife, plump, yellow, and intelligent. "Own land?" said the wife; "well, only this house." Then she added quietly, "We did buy seven hundred acres up yonder, and paid for it; but they cheated us out of it. Sells was the owner."

"Sells!" echoed the ragged misfortune, who was leaning against the balustrade and listening, "he's a regular cheat. I worked for him thirty-seven days this spring, and he paid me in cardboard checks which were to be cashed at the end of the month. But he never cashed them,— kept putting me off. Then the sheriff came and took my mule and corn and furniture—" "Furniture? But furniture is exempt from seizure by law." "Well, he took it just the same," said the hard-faced man.

"A sign at the Greyhound bus station." Rome, Georgia. September 1943, Esther Bubley, photographer. Courtesy of the Library of Congress.

Document 8, Chapter VII

Ida Wells-Barnett (1862–1931) achieved nationwide attention early in her career as a vocal opponent of lynching. First a teacher, and then a journalist, she eventually became an owner of the Memphis newspaper *Free Speech*. In May 1892, a mob ransacked her offices and threatened her life because of an article she wrote protesting a local lynching. Wells-Barnett moved to Chicago and in 1895 published *The Red Record*, the first documented statistical report on lynching in the United States.

* * *

Tortured and Burned Alive[18]
by
Ida B. Wells-Barnett

The burning of Samuel Hose, or, to give his right name, Samuel Wilkes, gave to the United States the distinction of having burned alive seven human beings during the past ten years. The details of this deed of unspeakable barbarism have shocked the civilized world, for it is conceded universally that no other nation on earth, civilized or savage, has put to death any human being with such atrocious cruelty as that inflicted upon Samuel Hose by the Christian white people of Georgia.

The charge is generally made that lynch law is condemned by the best white people of the South, and that lynching is the work of the lowest and lawless class. Those who seek the truth know the fact to be, that all classes are equally guilty, for what the one class does the other encourages, excuses and condones.

This was clearly shown in the burning of Hose. This awful deed was suggested, encouraged and made possible by the daily press of Atlanta, Georgia, until the burning actually occurred, and then it immediately condoned the burning by a hysterical plea to "consider the facts."

Samuel Hose killed Alfred Cranford Wednesday afternoon, April 12, 1899, in a dispute over the wages due Hose. The dispatch which announced the killing of Cranford stated that Hose had assaulted Mrs. Cranford and that bloodhounds had been put on his track.

The next day the *Atlanta Constitution*, in glaring double headlines, predicted a lynching and suggested burning at the stake. This it repeated in the body of the dispatch in the following language:

"When Hose is caught he will either be lynched and his body riddled with bullets or he will be burned at the stake." And further in the same issue the *Constitution* suggests torture in these words: "There have been whisperings of

---

[18] Chapter 2 of *Lynch Law in Georgia*, included *in A Six-Weeks' Record in the Center of Southern Civilization, As Faithfully Chronicled by the "Atlanta Journal" and the "Atlanta Constitution,"* pp. 7–10.

burning at the stake and of torturing the fellow low, and so great is the excitement, and so high the indignation, that this is among the possibilities."

In the issue of the 15th, in another double-column display heading, the *Constitution* announces: "Negro will probably be burned," and in the body of the dispatch burning and torture is confidently predicted in these words:

"Several modes of death have been suggested for him, but it seems to be the universal opinion that he will be burned at the stake and probably tortured before burned."

The next day, April 16th, the double-column head still does its inflammatory work. Never a word for law and order, but daily encouragement for burning. The headline reads: "Excitement still continues intense, and it is openly declared that if Sam Hose is brought in alive he will be burned," and in the dispatch it is said:

"The residents have shown no disposition to abandon the search in the immediate neighborhood of Palmetto; their ardor has in no degree cooled, and if Sam Hose is brought here by his captors he will be publicly burned at the stake as an example to members of his race who are said to have been causing the residents of this vicinity trouble for some time."

On the 19th the *Constitution* assures the public that interest in the pursuit of Hose does not lag, and in proof of the zeal of the pursuers said: "'If Hose is on earth I'll never rest easy until he's caught and burned alive. And that's the way all of us feel,' said one of them last night."

Clark Howell, editor, and W. A. Hemphill, business manager, of the *Constitution*, had offered through their paper a reward of five hundred dollars for the arrest of the fugitive. This reward, together with the persistent suggestion that the Negro be burned as soon as caught, make it plain as day that the purpose to burn Hose at the stake was formed by the leading citizens of Georgia. The *Constitution* offered the reward to capture him, and then day after day suggested and predicted that he be burned when caught. The Chicago anarchists were hanged, not because they threw the bomb, but because they incited to that act the unknown man who did throw it. Pity that the same law cannot be carried into force in Georgia!

Hose was caught Saturday night, April 23, and let the *Constitution* tell the story of his torture and death. From the issue of April 24th the following account is condensed: "Newman, Ga., April 23.—(Special.)—Sam Hose, the Negro murderer of Alfred Cranford and the assailant of Cranford's wife, was burned at the stake one mile and a quarter from this place this afternoon at 2:30 o'clock. Fully 2,000 people surrounded the small sapling to which he was fastened and watched the flames eat away his flesh, saw his body mutilated by knives and witnessed the contortions of his body in his extreme agony.

"Such suffering has seldom been witnessed, and through it all the Negro uttered hardly a cry. During the contortions of his body several blood vessels bursted. The spot selected was an ideal one for such an affair, and the stake was in full view of those who stood about and with unfeigned satisfaction saw the Negro meet his death and saw him tortured before the flames killed him.

"A few smoldering ashes scattered about the place, a blackened stake, are all that is left to tell the story. Not even the bones of the Negro were left in the place, but were eagerly snatched by a crowd of people drawn here from all directions, who almost fought over the burning body of the man, carving it with knives and seeking souvenirs of the occurrence.

"Preparations for the execution were not necessarily elaborate, and it required only a few minutes to arrange to make Sam Hose pay the penalty of his crime. To the sapling Sam Hose was tied, and he watched the cool, determined men who went about arranging to burn him.

"First he was made to remove his clothing, and when the flames began to eat into his body it was almost nude. Before the fire was lighted his left ear was severed from his body. Then his right ear was cut away. During this proceeding he uttered not a groan. Other portions of his body were mutilated by the knives of those who gathered about him, but he was not wounded to such an extent that he was not fully conscious and could feel the excruciating pain. Oil was poured over the wood that was placed about him and this was ignited.

"The scene that followed is one that never will be forgotten by those who saw it, and while Sam Hose writhed and performed contortions in his agony, many of those present turned away from the sickening sight, and others could hardly look at it. Not a sound but the crackling of the flames broke the stillness of the place, and the situation grew more sickening as it proceeded.

"The stake bent under the strains of the Negro in his agony and his sufferings cannot be described, although he uttered not a sound. After his ears had been cut off he was asked about the crime, and then it was he made a full confession. At one juncture, before the flames had begun to get in their work well, the fastenings that held him to the stake broke and he fell forward partially out of the fire.

"He writhed in agony and his sufferings can be imagined when it is said that several blood vessels burst during the contortions of his body. When he fell from the stake he was kicked back and the flames renewed. Then it was that the flames consumed his body and in a few minutes only a few bones and a small part of the body was all that was left of Sam Hose.

"One of the most sickening sights of the day was the eagerness with which the people grabbed after souvenirs, and they almost fought over the ashes of the dead criminal. Large pieces of his flesh were carried away, and persons were seen walking through the streets carrying bones in their hands.

"When all the larger bones, together with the flesh, had been carried away by the early comers, others scraped in the ashes, and for a great length of time a crowd was about the place scraping in the ashes. Not even the stake to which the Negro was tied when burned was left, but it was promptly chopped down and carried away as the largest souvenir of the burning.

"The real purpose of these savage demonstrations is to teach the Negro that in the South he has no rights that the law will enforce. Samuel Hose was burned to teach the Negroes that no matter what a white man does to them, they must not resist."

"In the Cobbler's Shop," included in "The Negro as He Really Is," *The World's Work*, June 1901, p. 849.

No. 16. **Children, you'll be called on.**

1. Chil-dren, you'll be called on   To march in   the field, of
2. Preachers, you'll be called on   To march in   the field, &c.
3. Sinners you'll be called on   To march in   the field, &c.
4. Seek-ers, you'll be called on   To march in   the field, &c.
5. Christians, you'll be called on   To march in   the field, &c.

bat - tle, When this war-fare'll be   end-ed, Hal-le - lu.

CHORUS.

When this war-fare'll be end-ed, I'm a sol-dier of the

D. C.

ju - bi-lee, This warfare'll be ended, I'm a soldier of the cross.

"Children, You'll Be Called On," included in J. B. T. Marsh, *The Story of the Jubilee Singers* (Cleveland, Ohio: The Cleveland Printing and Publishing Company, 1892), p. 174.

VIII

Of the Quest of the Golden Fleece

But the Brute said in his breast, "Till the mills I grind have ceased,
The riches shall be dust of dust, dry ashes be the feast!

　"On the strong and cunning few
　Cynic favors I will strew;
I will stuff their maw with overplus until their spirit dies;
　From the patient and the low
　I will take the joys they know:
　They shall hunger after vanities and still an-hungered go.
Madness shall be on the people, ghastly jealousies arise;
Brother's blood shall cry on brother up the dead and empty skies."

WILLIAM VAUGHN MOODY.[1]

Have you ever seen a cotton-field white with the harvest,—its golden fleece hovering above the black earth like a silvery cloud edged with dark green, its bold white signals waving like the foam of billows from Carolina to Texas across that Black and human Sea? I have, sometimes half suspected that here the winged ram Chrysomallus left that Fleece after which Jason and his Argonauts went vaguely wandering into the shadowy East three thousand years ago; and certainly one might frame a pretty and not far-fetched analogy of witchery and dragon's teeth, and blood and armed men, between the

---

[1] This chapter is revised, in part, from Du Bois's article "The Negro as He Really Is," *The World's Work* (June 1901), pp. 846-848. As in the previous chapter the photographs included are from the same magazine article and were taken by the German photographer Major A. Radcliffe Dugmore.

Cotton Gin at Dahomey, Mississippi, circa 1885--1898. Courtesy of the Library of Congress.

Ancient and the modern quest of the Golden Fleece in the Black Sea.[2]

And now the golden fleece is found; not only found, but, in its birthplace, woven. For the hum of the cotton-mills is the newest and most significant thing in the New South today. All through the Carolinas and Georgia, away down to Mexico, rise these gaunt red buildings, bare and homely, and yet so busy and noisy withal that they scarce seem to belong to the slow and sleepy land. Perhaps they sprang from dragons' teeth. So the Cotton Kingdom still lives; the world still bows beneath her sceptre. Even the markets that once defied the *parvenu*[3] have crept one by one across the seas, and then slowly and reluctantly, but surely, have started toward the Black Belt.

To be sure, there are those who wag their heads knowingly and tell us that the capital of the Cotton Kingdom has moved from the Black to the White Belt,—that the Negro of today raises not more than half of the cotton crop. Such men forget that the cotton crop has doubled, and more than doubled, since the era of slavery, and that, even granting their

---

[2] Du Bois is referring to the Greek myth of Jason and the Argonauts, which involves a quest for a golden fleece. In this case, the golden fleece is cotton.
[3] A social climber or one who has risen above his or her social class.

contention, the Negro is still supreme in a Cotton Kingdom larger than that on which the Confederacy builded its hopes. So the Negro forms today one of the chief figures in a great world-industry; and this, for its own sake, and in the light of historic interest, makes the field-hands of the cotton country worth studying.

We seldom study the condition of the Negro today honestly and carefully. It is so much easier to assume that we know it all. Or perhaps, having already reached conclusions in our own minds, we are loth to have them disturbed by facts. And yet how little we really know of these millions,—of their daily lives and longings, of their homely joys and sorrows, of their real shortcomings and the meaning of their crimes! All this we can only learn by intimate contact with the masses, and not by wholesale arguments covering millions separate in time, and space, and differing widely in training and culture, Today, then, my reader, let us turn our faces to the Black Belt of Georgia and seek simply to know the condition of the black farm-laborers of one county there.

Here in 1890 lived ten thousand Negroes and two thousand whites. The country is rich, yet the people are poor. The keynote of the Black Belt is debt; not commercial credit, but debt in the sense of continued inability on the part of the mass of the population to make income cover expense. This is the direct heritage of the South from the wasteful economies of the slave *regime*; but it was emphasized and brought to a crisis by the Emancipation of the slaves. In 1860, Dougherty County had six thousand slaves, worth at least two and a half millions of dollars; its farms were estimated at three millions,—making five and a half millions of property, the value of which depended largely on the slave system, and on the speculative demand for land once marvelously rich but already partially devitalized by careless and exhaustive culture. The war then meant a financial crash; in place of the five and a half millions of 1860, there remained in 1870 only farms valued at less than two millions. With this came increased competition in cotton culture from the rich lands of Texas; a steady fall in the normal price of cotton followed, from about fourteen cents a pound in 1860 until it reached four cents in 1898. Such a financial revolution was it that involved the owners of the cotton-belt in debt. And if things went ill with the master, how fared it with the man?

The plantations of Dougherty County in slavery days were not as imposing and aristocratic as those of Virginia. the Big House[4] was smaller and usually one-storied, and sat very near the slave cabins. Sometimes these cabins stretched off on either side like wings;

---

[4] The slave owner's residence.

"King Cotton," (panoramic photograph, c. 1907. Courtesy of the Library of Congress.

sometimes only on one side, forming a double row, or edging the road that turned into the plantation from the main thoroughfare. The form and disposition of the laborers' cabins throughout the Black Belt is today the same as in slavery days. Some live in the self-same cabins, others in cabins rebuilt on the sites of the old. All are sprinkled in little groups over the face of the land, centering about some dilapidated Big House where the head-tenant or agent lives. The general character and arrangement of these dwellings remains on the whole unaltered. There were in the county, outside the corporate town of Albany, about fifteen hundred Negro families in 1898. Out of all these, only a single family occupied a house with seven rooms; only fourteen have five rooms or more. The mass live in one- and two-room homes.

The size and arrangements of a people's homes are no unfair index of their condition. If, then, we inquire more carefully into these Negro homes, we find much that is unsatisfactory. All over the face of the land is the one-room cabin,—now standing in the shadow of the Big House, now staring at the dusty road, now rising dark and sombre amid the green of the cotton-fields. It is nearly always old and bare, built of rough boards, and neither plastered nor ceiled. Light and ventilation are supplied by the single door and by the square hole in the wall with its wooden shutter. There is no glass, porch, or ornamentation without. Within is a fireplace, black and smoky, and usually unsteady with age. A bed or two, a table, a wooden chest, and a few chairs compose the furniture; while a stray show-bill or a newspaper makes up the decorations for the walls. Now and then one may find such a cabin kept scrupulously neat, with merry steaming fireplace and hospitable door; but the majority are dirty and dilapidated, smelling of eating and sleeping, poorly ventilated, and anything but homes.

Above all, the cabins are crowded. We have come to associate crowding with homes in cities almost exclusively. This is primarily because we have so little accurate knowledge of country life. Here in Dougherty County one may find families of eight and ten occupying one or two rooms, and for every ten rooms of house accommodation for the Negroes there are twenty-five persons. The worst tenement abominations of New York do not have above twenty-two persons for every ten rooms. Of course, one small, close room in a city, without a yard, is in many respects worse than the larger single country room. In other respects it is better; it has glass windows, a decent chimney, and a trustworthy floor. The single great advantage of the Negro peasant is that he may spend most of his life outside his hovel, in the open fields.

There are four chief causes of these wretched homes: First, long custom born of slavery has assigned such homes to Negroes; white laborers would be offered better accommodations, and might, for that and similar reasons, give better work. Secondly, the Negroes, used to such accommodations, do not as a rule demand better; they do not know what better houses mean. Thirdly, the landlords as a class have not yet come to realize that it is a good business investment to raise the standard of living among labor by slow and judicious methods; that a Negro laborer who demands three rooms and fifty cents a day would give more efficient work and leave a larger profit than a discouraged toiler herding his family in one room. and working for thirty cents. Lastly, among such conditions of life there are few incentives to make the laborer become a better farmer. If he is ambitious, he moves to town or tries other labor; as a tenant-farmer his outlook is almost hopeless, and following it as a makeshift, he takes the house that is given him without protest.

"Log Cabin Home," included in "The Negro as He Really Is," *The World's Work,* June 1901, p. 849.

"A Friend of George Washington (He believes that he was with Washington when the cherry tree was cut down and allowed his photograph to be taken only on condition that a copy would be sent to his friend), included in "The Negro as He Really Is," *The World's Work,* June 1901, p. 860.

In such homes, then, these Negro peasants live. The families are both small and large; there are many single tenants,—widows and bachelors, and remnants of broken groups. The system of labor and the size of the houses both tend to the breaking up of family groups: the grown children go away as contract hands or migrate to town, the sister goes into service; and so one finds many families with hosts of babies, and many newly married couples, but comparatively few families with half-grown and grown sons and daughters. The average size of Negro families has undoubtedly decreased since the war, primarily from economic stress. In Russia over a third of the bridegrooms and over half the brides are under twenty; the same was true of the ante-bellum Negroes. Today, however, very few of the boys and less than a fifth of the Negro girls under twenty are married. The young men marry between the ages of twenty-five and thirty-five; the young women between twenty and thirty. Such postponement is due to the difficulty of earning sufficient to rear and support a family; and it undoubtedly leads, in the country districts, to sexual immorality. The form of this immorality, however, is very seldom that of prostitution, and less frequently that of illegitimacy than one would imagine. Rather, it takes the form of separation and desertion after a family group has been formed. The number of separated persons is thirty-five to the thousand,—a very large number. It would of course be unfair to compare this number with divorce statistics, for many of these separated women are in reality widowed, were the truth known, and in other cases the separation is not permanent. Nevertheless, here lies the seat of greatest moral danger. There is little or no prostitution among these Negroes, and over three-fourths of the families, as found by house-to-house investigation, deserve to be classed as decent people with considerable regard for female chastity. To be sure, the ideas of the mass would not suit New England, and there are many loose habits and notions. Yet the rate of illegitimacy is undoubtedly lower than in Austria or Italy, and the women as a class are modest. The plague-spot in sexual relations is easy marriage and easy separation. This is no sudden development, nor the fruit of Emancipation. It is the plain heritage from slavery. In those days Sam, with his master's consent, "took up" with Mary. No ceremony was necessary, and in the busy life of the great plantations of the Black Belt it was usually dispensed with. If now the master needed Sam's work in another plantation or in another part of the same plantation, or if he took a notion to sell the slave, Sam's married life with Mary was usually unceremoniously broken, and then it was clearly to the master's interest to have both of them take new mates. This widespread custom of two centuries has not been eradicated in thirty years. Today Sam's grandson "takes up" with a woman without license or ceremony; they live together decently and honestly, and are, to all intents and purposes, man and wife. Sometimes these unions are never broken until death; but in too many cases family quarrels, a roving spirit, a rival suitor, or perhaps more frequently the hopeless battle to support a family, lead to separation, and a broken household is the result. The Negro church has done much to stop this practice, and now most marriage ceremonies are performed by the pastors. Nevertheless, the evil is still deep-seated, and only a general raising of the standard of living will finally cure it.

Looking now at the county black population as a whole, it is fair to characterize it as poor and ignorant. Perhaps ten per cent compose the well-to-do and the best of laborers, while at least nine per cent are thoroughly lewd and vicious. The rest, over eighty per cent, are poor and ignorant, fairly honest and well-meaning, plodding, and to a degree shiftless, with some but not great sexual looseness. Such class lines are cotton. The degree of ignorance cannot easily be expressed. We may say, for instance, that nearly two-thirds of them cannot read or write. This but partially expresses the fact. They are ignorant of the world about them, of modern economic organization, of the function of government, of individual worth and possibilities,—of nearly all those things which slavery in self-defence had to keep them from learning. Much that the white boy imbibes from his earliest social atmosphere forms the puzzling problems of the black boy's mature years. America is not another world for Opportunity to *all* her sons.

It is easy for us to lose ourselves in details in endeavoring to grasp and comprehend the real condition of a mass of human beings. We often forget that each unit in the mass is a throbbing human soul. Ignorant it may be, and poverty-stricken, black and curious in limb and ways and thought; and yet it loves and hates, it toils and tires, it laughs and weeps its bitter tears, and looks in vague and awful longing at the grim horizon of its life,—all this, even as you and I. These black thousands are not in reality lazy; they are improvident and careless; they insist on breaking the monotony of toil with a glimpse at the great town-world on Saturday; they have their loafers and their rascals; but the great mass of them work

"Learning to Shuffle Early," included in "The Negro as He Really Is," *The World's Work,* June 1901, p. 860. Note: The racist caption almost certainly is not Du Bois's, but probably written by an editor.

"A Pickaninny Cake Walk," included in "The Negro as He Really Is," *The World's Work,* June 1901, p. 856. See the previous caption's note

continuously and faithfully for a return, and under circumstances that would call forth equal voluntary effort from few if any other modern laboring class. Over eighty-eight per cent of them—men, women, and children—are farmers. Indeed, this is almost the only industry. Most of the children get their schooling after the "crops are laid by," and very few there are that stay in school after the spring work has begun. Child labor is to be found here in some of its worst phases, as fostering ignorance and stunting physical development. With the grown men of the county there is little variety in work: thirteen hundred are farmers, and two hundred are laborers, teamsters, etc., including twenty-four artisans, ten merchants, twenty-one preachers, and four teachers. This narrowness of life reaches its maximum among the women: thirteen hundred and fifty of these are farm laborers, one hundred are servants and washerwomen, leaving sixty-five housewives, eight teachers, and six seamstresses.

Among this people there is no leisure class. We often forget that in the United States over half the youth and adults are not in the world earning incomes, but are making homes, learning of the world, or resting after the heat of the strife. But here ninety-six per cent are toiling; no one with leisure to turn the bare and cheerless cabin into a home, no old folks to sit beside the fire and hand down traditions daily toil is broken only by the gayety of the thoughtless and the Saturday trip to town. The toil, like all farm toil, is monotonous, and here there are little machinery and few tools to relieve its burdensome drudgery. But with all this, it is

"At Work Making Brooms," included in "The Negro as He Really Is," *The World's Work,* June 1901, p. 859.

work in the pure open air and this is something in a day when fresh air is scarce.

The land on the whole is still fertile, despite long abuse. For nine or ten months in succession the crops will come if asked: garden vegetables in April, grain in May, melons in June and July, hay in August, sweet potatoes in September, and cotton from then to Christmas. And yet on two-thirds of the land there is but one crop, and that leaves the toilers in debt. Why is this?

Away down the Baysan road, where the broad flat fields are flanked by great oak forests, is a plantation; many thousands of acres it used to run, here and there, and beyond the great wood. Thirteen hundred human beings here obeyed the call of one,—were his in body, and largely in soul. One of them lives there yet, —a short, stocky man, his dull-brown face seamed and drawn, and his tightly curled hair gray-white. The crops? Just tolerable, he said; just tolerable. Getting on? No—he wasn't getting on at all. Smith of Albany "furnishes" him, and his rent is eight hundred pounds of cotton. Can't make anything at that. Why didn't he buy land! Humph! Takes money to buy land. And he turns away. Free! The most piteous thing amid all the black ruin of wartime, amid the broken fortunes of the masters, the blighted hopes of mothers and maidens, and the fall of an empire,—the most piteous thing amid all this was the black freedman who threw down his hoe because the world called him free. What did such a mockery of freedom mean? Not a cent of money, not an inch of land, not a mouthful of victuals,—not even ownership of the rags on his back. Free! On Saturday, once or twice a month, the old master, before the war, used to dole out bacon and meal to his Negroes. And after the first flush of freedom wore off, and his true helplessness dawned on the freedman, he came back and picked up his hoe, and old master still doled out his bacon and meal. The legal form of service was theoretically far different; in practice, task-work or "cropping" was substituted for daily toil in gangs; and the slave

"On the Street, (They meet and gossip with their friends.)," included in "The Negro as He Really Is," *The World's Work*, June 1901, p. 859.

gradually became a metayer,[5] or tenant on shares, in name, but a laborer with indeterminate wages in fact.

Still the price of cotton fell, and gradually the landlords deserted their plantations, and the reign of the merchant began. The merchant of the Black Belt is a contractor, and part despot. His store, which used most frequently to stand at the cross-roads and become the centre of a weekly village, has now moved to town; and thither the Negro tenant follows him. The merchant keeps everything,—clothes and shoes, coffee and sugar, pork and meal, canned and dried goods, wagons and ploughs, seed and fertilizer,—and what he has not in stock he can give you an order for at the store across the way. Here, then, comes the tenant, Sam Scott, after he has contracted with some absent landlord's agent for hiring forty acres of land; he fingers his hat nervously until the merchant finishes his morning chat with Colonel Saunders, and calls out, "Well, Sam, what do you want?" Sam wants him to "furnish" him,—i.e., to advance him food and clothing for the year, and perhaps seed and tools, until his crop is raised and sold. If Sam seems a favorable subject, he and the merchant go to a lawyer, and Sam executes a chattel mortgage on his mule and wagon in return for seed and a week's rations. As soon as the green cotton-leaves appear above the ground, another mortgage is given on the "crop." Every Saturday, or at longer intervals, Sam calls upon the merchant for his "rations"; a family of five usually gets about thirty pounds of fat side-pork and a couple of bushels of commeal a month. Besides this, clothing and shoes must be furnished; if Sam or his family is sick, there are orders on the druggist and doctor; if the mule wants shoeing, an order on the blacksmith, etc. If Sam is a hard worker and crops promise well, he is often encouraged to buy more,—sugar, extra clothes, perhaps a buggy. But he is seldom encouraged to save. When cotton rose to ten cents last fall, the shrewd merchants of Dougherty County sold a thousand buggies in one season, mostly to black men.

The security offered for such transactions—a crop and chattel mortgage—may at first seem slight. And, indeed, the merchants tell many a true tale of shiftlessness and cheating; of cotton picked at night, mules disappearing, and tenants absconding But on the whole the merchant of the Black Belt is the most prosperous man in the section. So skillfully and so closely has he drawn the bonds of the law about the tenant, that the black man has often simply to choose between pauperism and crime; he "waives" all homestead exemptions in his contract; he cannot touch his own mortgaged crop, which the laws put almost in the full control of the landowner and of the merchant. When the crop is

---

[5] French term for one who cultivates land owned by others for a share of the crop—usually one half.

growing the merchant watches it like a hawk; as soon as it is ready for market he takes possession of it, sells it, pays the landowner his rent, subtracts his bill for supplies, and if, as sometimes happens, there is anything left, he hands it over to the black serf for his Christmas celebration.

The direct result of this system is an all-cotton scheme of agriculture and the continued bankruptcy of the tenant. The currency of the Black Belt is cotton. It is a crop always salable for ready money, not usually subject to great yearly fluctuations in price, and one which the Negroes know how to raise. The landlord therefore demands his rent in cotton, and the merchant will accept mortgages on no other crop. There is no use asking the black tenant, then, to diversify his crops,—he cannot under this system. Moreover, the system is bound to bankrupt the tenant. I remember once meeting a little one-mule wagon on the River road. A young black fellow sat in it driving listlessly, his elbows on his knees. His dark-faced wife sat beside him, stolid, silent.

"Hello!" cried my driver,—he has a most impudent way of addressing these people, though they seem used to it,—"what have you got there?"

"Meat and meal," answered the man, stopping. The meat lay uncovered in the bottom of the wagon,—a great thin side of fat pork covered with salt; the meal was in a white bushel bag.

"What did you pay for that meat?"

"Ten cents a pound." It could have been bought for six or seven cents cash.

"And the meal?"

"Two dollars." One dollar and ten cents is the cash price in town. Here was a man paying five dollars for goods which he could have bought for three dollars cash, and raised for one dollar or one dollar and a half.

Yet is is not wholly his fault. The Negro farmer started behind,—started in debt. This was not his choosing, but the crime of this happy-go-lucky nation which goes blundering along with its Reconstruction tragedies, its Spanish war interludes and Philippine matinees, just as though God really were dead. Once in debt, it is no easy matter for a whole race to emerge.

In the year of low-priced cotton, 1898, out of three hundred tenant families one hundred and seventy-five ended their year's work in debt to the extent of fourteen thousand dollars; fifty cleared nothing, and the remaining seventy-five made a total profit of sixteen hundred dollars. The net indebtedness of the black tenant families of the whole county must have been at least sixty thousand dollars. In a more prosperous year the situation is far better; but on the average the majority of tenants end the year even, or in debt, which means that they work for board and clothes. Such an economic organization is radically wrong. Whose is the blame?

The underlying causes of this situation are complicated but discernible. And one of the chief, outside the carelessness of the nation in letting the slave start with nothing, is the widespread opinion among the merchants and employers of the Black Belt that only by the slavery of debt can the Negro be kept at work. Without doubt, some pressure was necessary at the beginning of the free-labor system to keep the listless and lazy at work; and even today the mass of the Negro laborers need stricter guardianship than most Northern laborers. Behind this honest and widespread opinion dishonesty and cheating of the ignorant laborers have a good chance to take refuge. And to all this must be added the obvious fact that a slave ancestry and a system of unrequited toil has not improved the efficiency or temper of the mass of black laborers. Nor is this peculiar to Sambo;[6] it has in history been just as true of John and Hans, of Jacques and Pat, of all ground-down peasantries. Such is the situation of the mass of the Negroes in the Black Belt today; and they are thinking about it. Crime, and a cheap and dangerous socialism, are the inevitable results of this pondering. I see now that ragged black man sitting on a log, aimlessly whittling a stick. He muttered to me with the murmur of many ages, when he said: "White man sit down whole year; Nigger work day and night and make crop; Nigger hardly gits bread and meat; white man sittin' down gits all. *It's wrong.*" And what do the better classes of Negroes do to improve their situation? One of two things: if any way is possible, they buy land; if not, they migrate to town. Just as centuries ago it was no easy thing for the serf to escape into the freedom of town life, even so today there are hindrances laid in the way of country laborers. In considerable parts of all the Gulf States, and especially in Mississippi, Louisana, and Arkansas, the Negroes on the plantations in the back-country districts are still held at forced labor practically without wages. Especially is this true in districts where the farmers are composed of the more ignorant class of poor whites, and the Negroes are beyond the reach of schools and intercourse with their advancing fellows. If such a peon should run away, the sheriff, elected by white suffrage, can usually be depended on to catch the fugitive, return him, and ask no questions. If he escape to another county, a charge of petty thieving, easily true, can be depended upon to secure his return. Even if some unduly officious person insist upon a trial, neighborly comity will probably make his conviction sure, and then the labor due the county can easily be bought by the master. Such a system is

---

[6] Derogatory term for a black—particularly used with men.

impossible in the more civilized parts of the South, or near the large towns and cities; but in those vast stretches of land beyond the telegraph and the newspaper the spirit of the Thirteenth Amendment[7] is sadly broken. This represents the lowest economic depths of the black American peasant; and in a study of the rise and condition of the Negro freeholder we must trace his economic progress from the modern serfdom.

Even in the better-ordered country districts of the South the free movement of agricultural laborers is hindered by the migration-agent laws.[8] The "Associated Press" recently informed the world of the arrest of a young white man in Southern Georgia who represented the "Atlantic Naval Supplies Company," and who "was caught in the act of enticing hands from the turpentine farm of Mr. John Greer." The crime for which this young man was arrested is taxed five hundred dollars for each county in which the employment agent proposes to gather laborers for work outside the State. Thus the Negroes' ignorance of the labor-market outside his own vicinity is increased rather than diminished by the laws of nearly every Southern State.

Similar to such measures is the unwritten law of the back districts and small towns of the South, that the character of all Negroes unknown to the mass of the community must be vouched for by some white man. This is really a revival of the old Roman idea of the patron under whose protection the new-made freedman was put. In many instances this system has been of great good to the Negro, and very often under the protection and guidance of the former master's family, or other white friends, the freedman progressed in wealth and morality. But the same system has in other cases resulted in the refusal of whole communities to recognize the right of a Negro to change his habitation and to be master of his own fortunes. A black stranger in Baker County, Georgia, for instance, is liable to be stopped anywhere on the public highway and made to state his business to the satisfaction of any white interrogator. If he fails to give a suitable answer, or seems too independent or "sassy," he may be arrested or summarily driven away.

Thus it is that in the country districts of the South, by written or unwritten law, peonage,[9] hindrances to the migration of labor, and a system of white patronage exists over large areas. Besides this, the chance for lawless oppression and illegal exactions is vastly greater in

---

[7] The Amendment to the Constitution that abolished slavery.

[8] Laws that were passed in the South that kept agricultural workers from moving to other parts of the region to compete for better wages.

[9] A system in which debtors are bound in servitude to the person to whom they owe money until the debt is paid.

the country than in the city, and nearly all the more serious race disturbances of the last decade have arisen from disputes in the country between master and man,—as, for instance, the Sam Hose affair. As a result of such a situation, there arose, first, the Black Belt; and, second, the Migration to Town. The Black Belt was not, as many assumed, a movement toward fields of labor under more genial climatic conditions; it was primarily, a huddling for self-protection,—a massing of the black population for mutual defence in order to secure the peace and tranquillity necessary to economic advance. This movement took place between Emancipation and 1880, and only partially accomplished the desired results. The rush to town since 1880 is the counter-movement of men disappointed in the economic opportunities of the Black Belt.

In Dougherty County, Georgia, one can see easily the results of this experiment in huddling for protection. Only ten per cent of the adult population was born in the county, and yet the blacks outnumber the whites four or five to one. There is undoubtedly a security to the blacks in their very numbers,—a personal freedom from arbitrary treatment, which makes hundreds of laborers cling to Dougherty in spite of low wages and economic distress. But a change is coming, and slowly but surely even here the agricultural laborers are drifting to town and leaving the broad acres behind. Why is this? Why do not the Negroes become landowners, and build up the black landed peasantry which has for a generation and more been the dream of philanthropist and statesman?

To the car-window sociologist, to the man who seeks to understand and know the South by devoting the few leisure hours of a holiday trip to unravelling the snarl of centuries,—to such men very often the whole trouble with the black field-hand may be summed up by Aunt Ophelia's word, "Shiftless!" They have noted repeatedly scenes like one I saw last summer. We were riding along the highroad to town at the close of a long hot day. A couple of young black fellows passed us in a muleteam, with several bushels of loose corn in the ear. One was driving, listlessly bent forward, his elbows on knees,—a happy-go-lucky, careless picture of irresponsibility. The other was fast asleep in the bottom of the wagon. As we passed we noticed an ear of corn fall from the wagon. They never saw it,—not they. A rod farther on we noted another ear on the ground; and between that creeping mule and town we counted twenty-six ears of corn. Shiftless? Yes, the personification of shiftlessness. And yet follow those boys: they are not lazy; tomorrow morning they'll be up with the sun; they work hard when they do work, and they work willingly. They have no sordid, selfish, money-getting ways, but rather a fine disdain for mere cash. They'll loaf before your face and work behind your back with good-natured honesty. They'll steal a watermelon and hand you back your lost purse intact. Their great defect as laborers lies in their lack of incentive to work beyond the mere pleasure of physical exertion. They are careless because they have not found that it pays to be careful; they are improvident because the improvident ones of their acquaintance get on about as well as the provident. Above all, they cannot see why they should take unusual pains to make the white man's land better, or to fatten his mule, or save his corn. On the other hand, the white landowner argues that any attempt to improve these laborers by increased responsibility, or higher wages, or better homes, or land of their own, would be sure to result in failure. He shows his Northern visitor the scarred and wretched land; the ruined mansions, the worn-out soil and mortgaged acres, and says, This is Negro freedom!

Now it happens that both master and man have just enough argument on their respective sides to make it difficult for them to understand each other. The Negro dimly personifies in the white man all his ills and misfortunes; if he is poor, it is becasuse the white man seizes the fruit of his toil; if he is ignorant, it is because the white man gives him neither time nor facilities to learn; and, indeed, if any misfortune happens to him, it is because of some hidden machinations of "white folks." On the other hand, the masters and the masters' sons have never been able to see why the Negro, instead of settling down to be day-laborers for bread and clothes, are infected with a silly desire to rise in the world, and why they are sulky, dissatisfied, and careless, where their fathers were happy and dumb and faithful. "Why, you niggers have an easier time than I do," said a puzzled Albany merchant to his black customer. "Yes," he replied, "and so does yo' hogs."

Taking, then, the dissatisfied and shiftless field-hand as a starting-point, let us inquire how the black thousands of Dougherty have struggled from him up toward their ideal, and what that ideal is. All social struggle is evidenced by the rise, first of economic, then of social classes, among a homogeneous population. Today the following economic classes are plainly differentiated among these Negroes.

A "submerged tenth" of croppers, with a few paupers; forty per cent who are metayers and thirty-nine per cent of semi-metayers and wage-Laborers. There are left five per cent of money renters and six per cent of freeholders,—the "Upper Ten" of the land. The croppers are entirely without capital, even in the limited sense of food or money to keep them from seed-time to harvest. All they furnish is their labor; the landowner furnishes land, stock, tools, seed, and house; and at the end of the year the laborer gets from a third to a half of the crop. Out of his share, however, comes pay and interest for food and clothing advanced him during the year. Thus we have a laborer without capital and without wages, and an employer whose capital is largely his employees' wages. It is an unsatisfactory arrangement, both for hirer and hired, and is usually in vogue on poor land with hard-pressed owners.

Above the croppers come the great mass of the black population who work the land on their own responsibility, paying rent in cotton and supported by the crop-mortgage system. After the war this system was attractive to the freedmen on account of its larger freedom and its possibility for making a surplus. But with the carrying out of the crop-lien system, the deterioration of the land, and the slavery of debt, the position of the metayers has sunk to a dead level of practically unrewarded toil. Formerly all tenants had some capital, and often considerable; but absentee landlordism, rising rack-rent, and falling cotton have stripped them well-nigh of all, and probably not over half of them today own their mules. The change from cropper to tenant was accomplished by fixing the rent. If, now, the rent fixed was reasonable, this was an incentive to the tenant to strive. On the other hand, if the rent was too high, or if the land deteriorated, the result was to discourage and check the efforts of the black peasantry. There is no doubt that the latter case is true; that in Dougherty County every economic advantage of the price of cotton in market and of the strivings of the tenant has been taken advantage of by the landlords and merchants, and swallowed up in rent and interest. If cotton rose in price, the rent rose even higher; if cotton fell, the rent remained or followed reluctantly. If the tenant worked hard and raised a large crop, his rent was raised the next year; if that year the crop failed, his corn was confiscated and his mule sold for debt. There were of course, exceptions to this,—cases of personal kindness and forbearance; but in the vast majority of cases the rule was to extract the uttermost farthing from the mass of the black farm laborers.

The average metayer pays from twenty to thirty per cent of his crop in rent. The result of such rack-rent can only be evil,—abuse and neglect of the soil, deterioration in the character of the laborers, and a widespread sense of injustice. "Wherever the country is poor," cried Arthur Young,[10] "it is in the hands of metayers," and "their condition is more wretched than that of day-laborers." He was talking of Italy a century ago; but he might have been talking of Dougherty County today. And especially is that true today which he declares was true in France before the Revolution: "The metayers are considered as little better than menial servants, removable at pleasure, and obliged to conform in all things to the will of the landlords." On this low plane half the black

---

[10]Arthur Young (1741–1820), agriculturalist, traveler and writer most well-known for his book *Travels in France During the Years 1787, 1788, and 1789* (1792).

population of Dougherty County—perhaps more than half the black millions of this land—are today struggling.

A degree above these we may place those laborers who receive money wages for their work. Some receive a house with perhaps a garden-spot; then supplies of food and clothing are advanced, and certain fixed wages are given at the end of the year, varying from thirty to sixty dollars, out of which the supplies must be paid for, with interest. About eighteen per cent of the population belong to this class of semi-metayers, while twenty-two per cent are laborers paid by the month or year, and are either "furnished" by their own savings or perhaps more usually by some merchant who takes his chances of payment. Such laborers receive from thirty-five to fifty cents a day during the working season. They are usually young unmarried persons, some being women; and when they marry they sink to the class of metayers, or, more seldom, become renters.

The renters for fixed money rentals are the first of the emerging classes, and form five per cent of the families, The sole advantage of this small class is their freedom to choose their crops, and the increased responsibility which comes through having money transactions. While some of the renters differ little in condition from the metayers, yet on the whole they are more intelligent and responsible persons, and are the ones who eventually become landowners. Their better character and greater shrewdness enable them to gain, perhaps to demand, better terms in rents; rented farms, varying from forty to a hundred acres, bear an average rental of about fifty-four dollars a year. The men who conduct such farms do not long remain renters; either they sink to metayers, or with a successful series of harvests rise to be landowners.

In 1870 the tax-books of Dougherty report no Negroes as landholders. If there were any such at that time,—and there may have been a few,—their land was probably held in the name of some white patron,—a method not uncommon during slavery. In 1875 ownership of land had begun with seven hundred and fifty acres; ten years later this had increased to over sixty-five hundred acres, to nine thousand acres in 1890 and ten thousand in 1900. The total assessed property has in this same period risen from eighty thousand dollars in 1875 to two hundred and forty thousand dollars in 1900.

Two circumstances complicate this development and make it in some respects difficult to be sure of the real tendencies; they are the panic of 1893, and the low price of cotton in 1898. Besides this, the system of assessing property in the country districts of Georgia is somewhat antiquated and of uncertain statistical value; there are no assessors, and each man makes a sworn return to a tax-receiver. Thus public opinion plays a large part, and the returns vary strangely from year to year. Certainly these figures show the small amount of accumulated capital among the Negroes, and the consequent large dependence of their property on temporary prosperity. They have little to tide over a few years of economic depression, and are at the mercy of the cotton-market far more than the whites. And thus the landowners, despite their marvellous efforts, are really a transient class, continually being depleted by those who fall back into the class of renters or metayers, and augmented by newcomers from the masses. Of the one hundred landowners in 1898, half had bought their land since 1893, a fourth between 1890 and 1893, a fifth between 1884 and 1890, and the rest between 1870 and 1884. In all, one hundred and eighty-five Negroes have owned land in this county since 1875.

If all the black landowners who had ever held land here had kept it or left it in the hands of black men, the Negroes would have owned nearer thirty thousand acres than the fifteen thousand they now hold. And yet these fifteen thousand acres are a creditable showing,—a proof of no little weight of the worth and ability of the Negro people. If they had been given an economic start at Emancipation, if they had been in an enlightened and rich community which really desired their best good, then we might perhaps call such a result small or even insignificant. But for a few thousand poor ignorant field-hands, in the face of poverty, a falling market, and social stress, to save and capitalize two hundred thousand dollars in a generation has meant a tremendous effort. The rise of a nation, the pressing forward of a social class, means a bitter struggle, a hard and soul-sickening battle with the world such as few of the more favored classes know or appreciate.

Out of the hard economic conditions of this portion of the Black Belt, only six per cent of the population have succeeded in emerging into peasant proprietorship; and these are not all firmly fixed, but grow and shrink in number with the wavering of the cotton-market. Fully ninety-four per cent have struggled for land and failed, and half of them sit in hopeless serfdom. For these there is one other avenue of escape toward which they have turned in increasing numbers, namely, migration to town. A glance at the distribution of land among the black owners curiously reveals this fact. In 1898 the holdings were as follows: Under forty acres, forty-nine families; forty to two hundred and fifty acres, seventeen families; two hundred and fifty to one thousand acres, thirteen families; one thousand or more acres, two families. Now in 1890 there were forty-four holdings, but only nine of these were under forty acres. The great increase of holdings, then, has come in the buying of small homesteads near town, where their owners really share in the town life; this is a part of the rush to town. And for every landowner who has thus hurried away from the narrow and hard conditions of country life, how many field-hands, how many tenants, how many ruined renters, have joined that long procession? Is it not strange compensation?

The sin of the country districts is visited on the town, and the social sores of city life today may, here in Dougherty County, and perhaps in many places near and far, look for their final healing without the city walls.

"Triumph," M. H. Traubel. Copyrighted 1861. Allegory predicting the triumph of the Union over the dark forces of the Confederacy and "King Cotton." Courtesy of the Library of Congress.

Document Number 9, Chapter VIII

Du Bois early in his career undertook a number of studies for the Federal government. They represent the first systematic sociological studies of rural Black communities undertaken in the United States. The following is an excerpt from a study on Georgia Blacks whose data was collected by his students at Atlanta University. It includes the analysis of Blacks in De Kalb County, close to Atlanta, and provides for an interesting comparison with his reflections on Dougherty County, Georgia, included in *The Souls of Black Folk*.

*   *   *

The Negro in The Black Belt: Some Social Sketches[11]

W. E. Burghardt Du Bois, Ph. D.

The studies of Negro economic development here presented are based mainly on seminary notes made by members of the senior class of Atlanta University. These young persons, born and bred under the conditions which they describe, have unusual facilities for first-hand knowledge of a difficult and intricate subject. They are also somewhat more experienced in life than corresponding classes in Northern institutions being in school for the most part through their own exertions and teaching in various communities in vacation time.

Six small groups, containing a total of 920 Negroes, have been studied, all but one of which are situated in Georgia. The groups, however, differ greatly from each other and are designed to represent the development of the Negro from country to city life, from semi-barbarism to a fair degree of culture. The first sketch, for instance, is of 11 families in a small country district of Georgia, and the second of 16 families in a small village of the same State. Here we get a glimpse of the real Negro problem; of the poverty and degradation of the country Negro, which means the mass of Negroes in the United States. Next our attention is called to two towns, both county seats and centers of trade. To such towns both the energetic and listless class of country Negroes are migrating. In these towns are taken up the condition of 83 families, which are mostly, though not entirely, families of the better class and represent the possibilities of the town Negroes. Finally we consider two groups of 85 families, in two small cities, who represent distinctly the better class of Negroes—the class that sends its children to Atlanta, Fisk, and Tuskegee.

Thus it will be seen that there is here no attempt at a complete study of the Negro in the Black Belt, but rather a series of sketches, whose chief value lies in their local color.

---

[11] Selection from W. E. B. Du Bois, "The Negro in the Black Belt: Some Social Sketches," Department of Labor, Vol. IV, May 1899 (Washington: Government Printing Office), pp. 401–417.

A COUNTRY DISTRICT IN DEKALB COUNTY, GEORGIA

Seventeen miles east of Atlanta is a small village of less than 500 persons called Doraville; 21 miles southeast is a bit of country without a special name. There are in these two localities between 60 and 75 Negro families, of whom 11 fairly representative ones have been chosen for this study.

In general these Negroes are a degraded set. Except in two families, whisky, tobacco, and snuff are used to excess, even when there is a scarcity of bread. In other respects also the low moral condition of these people is manifest, and in the main there is no attempt at social distinctions among them.

In these 11 families there are 131 individuals, an average of nearly 12 persons to a family. In size the families rank as shown in the following table:

NUMBER OF PERSONS IN 11 SELECTED FAMILIES OF A COUNTRY DISTRICT OF DEKALB COUNTY, GEORGIA, BY SIZE OF FAMILIES

	Number of families	Number Of individuals
Size of family		
7 persons	1	7
9 persons	1	9
10 persons	2	20
11 persons	1	11
12 persons	2	24
13 persons	3	39
21 persons	1	21
Total		131
Average		11.9

The fecundity of this population is astonishing. Here is one family with 19 children—14 girls and 5 boys, ranging in age from 6 to 25 years. Another family has one set of triplets, two sets of twins, and 4 single children. The girls of the present generation, however, are not marrying as early as their mothers did. Once in a while a girl of 12 or 13 runs off and marries, but this does not often happen. Probably the families of the next generation will be smaller.

Four of the 11 heads of families can read and write. Of their children, a majority, possibly two-thirds, can read and write a little. Five of the families own their homes. The farms vary from 1 to 11 acres in extent, and are worth from $100 to $400. Two of these farms are heavily mortgaged. Six families rent farms on shares, paying one-half the crop. They clear from $5 to $10 in cash at the end of a year's work. They usually own a mule or two and sometimes a cow.

Nearly all the workers are farm hands, women and girls as well as men being employed in the fields. Children as young as 6 are given light tasks, such as dropping seed and bringing water. The families rise early, often before daylight, working until breakfast time and returning again after the meal. One of the men is a stonecutter. He earns $1.50 a day, owns a neat little home, and lives comfortably. Most, of the houses are rudely constructed of logs or boards, with one large and one small room. There is usually no glass in the openings which serve as windows. They are closed by wooden shutters. The large room always contains several beds and homemade furniture, consisting of tables, chairs, and chests. A few homes had three rooms, and one or two families had sewing machines, which, however, were not yet paid for.

These families raise nearly all that they eat—corn, wheat, pork, and molasses. Chickens and eggs are used as currency at the country store to purchase cloth, tobacco, coffee, etc. The character of the home life varies with the different families. The family of 21 is a poverty-stricken, reckless, dirty set. The children are stupid and repulsive, and fight for their food at the table. They are poorly dressed, sickly, and cross. The table dishes stand from one meal to another unwashed, and the house is in perpetual disorder. Now and then the father and mother engage in a hand-to-hand fight.

In some respects this family is exceptionally bad, but several others are nearly as barbarous. A few were much better, and in the stonecutter's five-room house one can find clean, decent family life, with neatly dressed children and many signs of aspiration. The average of the communities, however, was nearer the condition of the family first described than that of the latter one.

In religion the people are sharply divided into Baptists and Methodists, who are in open antagonism, and have separate day schools. The Baptists are the more boisterous and superstitious, and their pastor is ignorant and loud-mouthed, preaching in his shirt sleeves and spitting tobacco juice on either side of the pulpit as he works his audience up to the frenzy of a "shouting." Outside the churches there is a small, women's beneficial society for sickness and death, under the presidency of the stonecutter's wife. Many of the members are in arrears with their payments. There is also a lodge of Odd Fellows. The schools run only 3 months in the year, the wretched schoolhouses and the system of child labor preventing a longer term.

On the whole, a stay in this community has a distinctly depressing effect. There are a few indications of progress, but those of listlessness and stagnation seem more powerful.

A SMALL VILLAGE: LITHONIA, DEKALB COUNTY, GA.

Lithonia is 24 miles east of Atlanta, and has a population of perhaps 800. There are in the town two dry goods stores, a drug store, three grocery stores, a barber shop, and a millinery shop conducted by white persons, and a blacksmith shop and a barber shop conducted by Negroes. Nearly all the workingmen of the town are employed in the three rock quarries, which furnish the chief business of the village. The Negro stonecutters here used to earn from $10 to $14 a week, but now they receive from $5 to $8.50 a week. There are many "scabbers" outside the union who work for still less. They now include the majority of the Negro laborers. Some Negroes are also employed in domestic service and at the large boarding house.

Less than a dozen homes are owned by the Negroes; they rent for the most part small, two-room tenements, at $4 a month. The whites have a private and a public school, giving them a term of 8 or 9 months. The Negro schools are divided into a Methodist and a Baptist school, each of which has a term of 3 months. The school buildings are old and dilapidated and scarcely fit to teach in; they will not accommodate nearly all the Negro children of school age.

Sixteen of these Negro families have been especially studied; they represent the average of the village. The families by size are shown in the following table:

NUMBER OF PERSONS IN 16 SELECTED FAMILIES OF LITHONIA, GA., BY SIZE OF FAMILIES

Size of family	Number of families	Number of individuals
2 persons	1	2
4 persons	1	4
5 persons	4	20
6 persons	4	24
7 persons	3	21
9 persons	1	9
10 persons	1	10
11 persons	1	11
Total	16	101
Average		6.3

The next table shows the number of persons in these families, by age and sex:

NUMBER OF PERSONS IN 16 SELECTED FAMILIES OF LITHONIA, GA., BY AGE AND SEX

Age	Males	Females	Total
Under 15 years	21	21	42
15 to 40 years	27	20	47
40 years or over	5	7	12
Total	53	48	101

Most of these persons were born in the State; 6 were born in Virginia, 6 in Alabama, and 3 in South Carolina. Of those 10 years of age or over, 8 out of 63, or 13 per cent, were illiterate.

Six of these families owned their homes. The following table shows the condition of each family:

CONDITION OF 6 SELECTED FAMILIES OWNING HOMES IN LITHONIA, GA.

Family number	Size of family	Rooms in house	Wage earners in family	Occupation of wage earners	Wages per week	Weeks employed per year	Yearly wages of wage earners	Yearly earnings of families
				{ Stonecutter	$8.50	48	$408 }	
1......	5	3	3	Stonecutter	5.00	48	240	$75 2
				Hotel waiter	(a) 2.00	52	104	
2......	11	4	5	{ 1 drayman	(b)	(b)	c 250 }	c 550
				4 farm hands	(b)	(b)	d 300	
3......	6	3	1	Stonecutter	e $15.00 to 20.00	(b)	200	200
4......	6	2	1	Stonecutter	f 5.00	(b)	200	200

....								
5......	6	2	1	Stonecutter	f 5.00	(b)	200	200
....								
6......	5	4	1	Stonecutter	6.50	48	312	312
...								

a And board.   c Approximate.   e Per month.
b Not Reported.   d Approximate total for 4 farm hands.   f Or less.

Besides a house of 3 rooms, family No. 1 owned 6 acres of farm land, and the hotel waiter earned his board in addition to $2 a week wages. Family No. 2 owned a four-room house with a lot 150 by 35 feet. In this family there were 5 daughters, who helped on the farm, besides the 4 male farm hands. Family No. 3 saved from $20 to $30 a year out of earnings of $200. They owned a three-room house and a lot 150 by 50 feet. Families Nos. 4 and 5 each owned a two-room house with lots, and family No. 6 owned a four-room house with a large lot.

The remaining 10 families investigated at Lithonia rented houses, and the size of such houses and the rent paid are shown in the following table:

RENT PAID BY 10 SELECTED FAMILIES RENTING HOUSES IN LITHONIA, GA. BY SIZE OF HOUSES

Size of house.	Rent paid Per month.	Families renting.
2 rooms	$4.00	5
2 rooms	(a)	1
3 rooms	4.00	1
3 rooms	4.50	1
3 rooms	5.00	1
4 rooms	5.00	1

In these 16 families there is an average of 2 3/4 rooms to a family and a little over 2 persons to a room. The following table presents the 16 families by size of family and classified income:

CLASSIFIED INCOME OF 16 SELECTED FAMILIES OF LITHONIA, GA.,
BY SIZE OF FAMILIES

Income per family.	Families of --								Total families.
	2 per-sons	4 per-sons	5 per-sons	6 per-sons	7 per-sons	9 per-sons	10 per-sons	11 per-sons	
Under $200...	1		1	1	1		1		5
$200 to $300			1	3					4
$300 to $400		1	1		1				3
$400 to $500					1	1			2
$500 or over			1					1	2
Total...........	1	1	4	4	3	1	1	1	16

The morals of the colored people in the town are decidedly low. They dress and live better than the country Negroes, however, and send their children more regularly to school. The union stonecutters are nearly all members of a local branch of the Odd Fellows. The women have a beneficial society. There are three churches—two Baptist and one Methodist—whose pastors are fairly intelligent.[a]

---

[a] The data on which the two studies on conditions in a country district in Dekalb County and in the small village of Lithonia, Ga., are based were furnished by Miss Aletha Howard, a graduate of Atlanta University, who has been the school-teacher in these communities.

Portrait Group of African American Bricklayers Union, Jacksonville, Florida. Photograph included in the American Negro exhibit at the 1900 Paris Exposition. Courtesy of the Library of Congress.

"I'm a Rolling," included in J. B. T. Marsh, *The Story of the Jubilee Singers* (Cleveland, Ohio: The Cleveland Printing and Publishing Company, 1892), p. 167.

IX

Of the Sons of Master and Man[1]

Life treads on life, and heart on heart;
We press too close in church and mart
To keep a dream or grave apart.[2]

MRS. BROWNING.

The world-old phenomenon of the contact of diverse races of men is to have new exemplification during the new century. Indeed, the characteristic of our age is the contact of European civilization with the world's undeveloped peoples. Whatever we may say of the results of such contact in the past, it certainly forms a chapter in human action not pleasant to look back upon. War, murder, slavery, extermination, and debauchery,—this has again and again been the result of carrying civilization and the blessed gospel to the isles of the sea and the heathen without the law. Nor does it altogether satisfy the conscience of the modern world to be told complacently that all this has been right and proper, the fated triumph of strength over weakness, of righteousness over evil, of superiors over inferiors. It would certainly be soothing if one could readily believe all this; and yet there are too many ugly facts for everything to be thus easily explained away. We feel and know that there are many delicate differences in race psychology, numberless changes that our crude social measurements are not yet able to follow minutely, which explain much of history and social development. At the

[1] This chapter is revised from the article "The Relation of the Negroes to the Whites in the South," which was first published in the *Annals of the American Academy of Political and Social Science* (July–December 1901), pp. 121–140.
[2] The verse is from Elizabeth Barrett Browning's 1844 poem "A Vision of Poets."

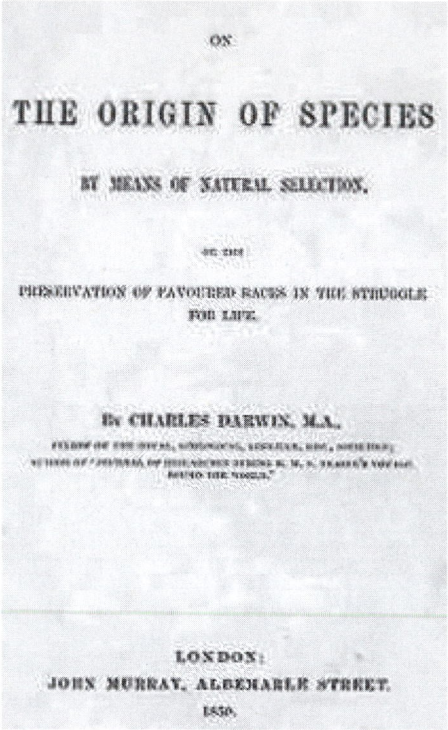

ON

THE ORIGIN OF SPECIES

BY MEANS OF NATURAL SELECTION,

OR THE

PRESERVATION OF FAVOURED RACES IN THE STRUGGLE
FOR LIFE.

By CHARLES DARWIN, M.A.,

LONDON:
JOHN MURRAY, ALBEMARLE STREET.
1859.

Title page from the first edition of Charles Darwin's *The Origin of Species*. Courtesy of the Library of Congress.

same time, too, we know that these considerations have never adequately explained or excused the triumph of brute force and cunning over weakness and innocence.

It is, then, the strife of all honorable men of the twentieth century to see that in the future competition of races the survival of the fittest shall mean the triumph of the good, the beautiful, and the true; that we may be able to preserve for future civilization all that is really fine and noble and strong, and not continue to put a premium on greed and impudence and cruelty.[3] To bring this hope to fruition, we are compelled daily to turn more and more to a conscientious study of the phenomena of race-contact,—to a study frank and fair, and not falsified and colored by our wishes or our fears. And we have in the South as fine a field for such a study as the world affords,—a field, to be sure, which the average American scientist deems somewhat beneath his dignity, and which the

---

[3] The phrase "survival of the fittest" is a reference to the British biologist Charles Darwin (1809-1882) and his theory of Evolution which was outlined in his 1859 book, *The Origin of Species*.

214

"Unpaved street or alley between houses in Georgia." Photograph included in the Exhibit of the American Negroes at the 1900 Paris Exposition. Courtesy of the Library of Congress.

average man who is not a scientist knows all about, but nevertheless a line of study which by reason of the enormous race complications with which God seems about to punish this nation must increasingly claim our sober attention, study, and thought. We must ask, what are the actual relations of whites and blacks in the South? And we must be answered, not by apology or fault-finding, but by a plain, unvarnished tale.

In the civilized life of today the contact of men and their relations to each other fall in a few main lines of action and communication: there is, first, the physical proximity of homes and dwelling-places, the way in which neighborhoods group themselves, and the contiguity of neighborhoods. Secondly, and in our age chiefest, there are the economic relations,—the methods by which individuals cooperate for earning a living, for the mutual satisfaction of wants, for the production of wealth. Next, there are the political relations, the cooperation in social control, in group government, in laying and paying the burden of taxation. In the fourth place there are the less tangible but highly important forms of intellectual contact and commerce, the interchange of ideas through conversation and conference, through periodicals and libraries; and, above all, the gradual formation for each community of that curious *tertium quid*[4] which we call public opinion. Closely allied with this come the various forms of social contact in everyday life, in travel, in theatres, in house gatherings, in marrying and giving in marriage. Finally, there are the varying forms of religious enterprise, of moral teaching and benevolent endeavor. These are the principal ways in which men living in the same communities are brought into contact with each other. It is my present task, therefore, to indicate, from my point of view, how the black race in the South meet and mingle with the whites in these matters of everyday life.

First, as to physical dwelling. It is usually possible to draw in nearly every Southern community a physical color-line on the map, on the one side of which whites dwell and on the other Negroes. The winding and intricacy of the geographical color line varies, of course, in different communities. I know some towns where a straight line drawn through the middle of the main street separates nine-tenths of the whites from nine-tenths of the blacks. In other towns the older settlement of whites has been encircled by a broad band of blacks; in still other cases little settlements or nuclei of blacks have sprung up amid surrounding whites. Usually in cities each street has its distinctive color, and only now and then do the colors meet in close proximity. Even in the country something of this segregation is manifest in the smaller areas, and of course in the larger phenomena of the Black Belt.

All this segregation by color is largely independent of that natural clustering by social grades common to all communities. A Negro slum may be in dangerous proximity to a white residence quarter, while it is quite common to find a white slum planted in the heart of a respectable Negro district. One thing, however, seldom occurs: the best of the whites and the best of the Negroes almost never live in anything like close proximity. It thus happens that in nearly every Southern town and city, both whites and blacks see commonly the worst of each other. This is a vast change from the situation in the past, when, through the close contact of master and house-servant in the patriarchal Big House, one found the best of both races in close contact and sympathy, while at the same time the squalor and dull round of toil among the field-hands was removed from the sight and hearing of the family. One can easily see how a person who saw slavery thus from his father's parlors, and sees freedom on the streets of a great city, fails to grasp or comprehend the whole of the new picture. On the other hand, the settled belief of the mass of the Negroes that the Southern white people do not have the black man's best interests at heart has been intensified in later years by this

---

[4] Latin, meaning an ambiguous state.

"Three African Americans on porch, in Georgia." Photograph included in the Exhibit of the American Negroes at the 1900 Paris Exposition. Courtesy of the Library of Congress.

continual daily contact of the better class of blacks with the worst representatives of the white race.

Coming now to the economic relations of the races, we are on ground made familiar by study, much discussion and no little philanthropic effort. And yet with all this there are many essential elements in the cooperation of Negroes and whites for work and wealth that are too readily overlooked or not thoroughly understood. The average American can easily conceive of a rich land awaiting development and filled with black laborers. To him the Southern problem is simply that of making efficient workingmen out of this

"'Lumpers' at the T. B. Williams Tobacco Co., Richmond, Virginia."
Photograph included in the Exhibit of the American Negroes at the 1900
Paris Exposition. Courtesy of the Library of Congress.

material, by giving them the requisite technical skill and the help of
invested capital. The problem, however, is by no means as simple as this,
from the obvious fact that these workingmen have been trained for
centuries as slaves. They exhibit, therefore, all the advantages and
defects of such training; they are willing and good-natured, but not
self-reliant, provident, or careful. If now the economic development of
the South is to be pushed to the verge of exploitation, as seems probable,
then we have a mass of workingmen thrown into relentless competition
with the workingmen of the world, but handicapped by a training the
very opposite to that of the modern self-reliant democratic laborer. What
the black laborer needs is careful personal guidance, group leadership of
men with hearts in their bosoms, to train them to foresight, carefulness,
and honesty. Nor does it require any fine-spun theories of racial
differences to prove the necessity of such group training after the brains
of the race have been knocked out by two hundred and fifty years of
assiduous education in submission, carelessness, and stealing. After
Emancipation, it was the plain duty of some one to assume this group
leadership and training of the Negro laborer. I will not stop here to

inquire whose duty it was,—whether that of the white ex-master who had profited by unpaid toil, or the Northern philanthropist whose persistence brought on the crisis, or the National Government whose edict freed the bondmen; I will not stop to ask whose duty it was, but I insist it was the duty of some one to see that these workingmen were not left alone and unguided, without capital, without land, without skill, without economic organization, without even the bald protection of law, order, and decency,—left in a great land, not to settle down to slow and careful internal development, but destined to be thrown almost immediately into relentless and sharp competition with the best of modern workingmen under an economic system where every participant is fighting for himself, and too often utterly regardless of the rights or welfare of his neighbor.

For we must never forget that the economic system of the South today which has succeeded the old regime[5] is not the same system as that of the old industrial North, of England, or of France, with their trade-unions, their restrictive laws, their written and unwritten commercial customs, and their long experience. It is, rather, a copy of that England of the early nineteenth century, before the factory acts,—the England that wrung pity from thinkers and fired the wrath of Carlyle. The rod of empire that passed from the hands of Southern gentlemen in 1865, partly by force, partly by their own petulance, has never returned to them. Rather it has passed to those men who have come to take charge of the industrial exploitation of the New South,—the sons of poor whites fired with a new thirst for wealth and power, thrifty and avaricious Yankees, and unscrupulous immigrants. Into the hands of these men the Southern laborers, white and black, have fallen; and this to their sorrow. For the laborers as such, there is in these new captains of industry neither love nor hate, neither sympathy nor romance; it is a cold question of dollars and dividends. Under such a system all labor is bound to suffer. Even the white laborers are not yet intelligent, thrifty, and well-trained enough to maintain themselves against the powerful inroads of organized capital. The results among them, even, are long hours of toil, low wages, child labor, and lack of protection against usury and cheating. But among the black laborers all this is aggravated, first, by a race prejudice which varies from a doubt and distrust among the best element of whites to a frenzied hatred among the worst; and, secondly, it is aggravated, as I have said before, by the wretched economic heritage of the freedmen from slavery. With this training it is difficult for the freedman to learn to grasp the opportunities already opened to him, and the new opportunities are seldom given him, but go by favor to the whites.

---

[5] French, meaning the group or government in power.

Left by the best elements of the South with little protection or oversight, he has been made in law and custom the victim of the worst and most unscrupulous men in each community. The crop-lien system which is depopulating the fields of the South is not simply the result of shiftlessness on the part of Negroes, but is also the result of cunningly devised laws as to mortgages, liens, and misdemeanors, which can be made by conscienceless men to entrap and snare the unwary until escape is impossible, further toil a farce, and protest a crime. I have seen, in the Black Belt of Georgia, an ignorant, honest Negro buy and pay for a farm in installments three separate times, and then in the face of law and decency the enterprising American who sold it to him pocketed money and deed and left the black man landless, to labor on his own land at thirty cents a day. I have seen a black farmer fall in debt to a white storekeeper, and that storekeeper go to his farm and strip it of every single marketable article,—mules, ploughs, stored crops, tools, furniture, bedding, clocks, looking-glass,—and all this without a sheriff or officer, in the face of the law for homestead exemptions, and without rendering to a single responsible person any account or reckoning. And such proceedings can happen, and will happen, in any community where a class of ignorant toilers are placed by custom and race-prejudice beyond the pale of sympathy and race-brotherhood. So long as the best elements of a community do not feel in duty bound to protect and train and care for the weaker members of their group, they leave them to be preyed upon by these swindlers and rascals.

This unfortunate economic situation does not mean the hindrance of all advance in the black South, or the absence of a class of black landlords and mechanics who, in spite of disadvantages, are accumulating property and making good citizens. But it does mean that this class is not nearly so large as a fairer economic system might easily make it, that those who survive in the competition are handicapped so as to accomplish much less than they deserve to, and that, above all, the *personnel* of the successful class is left to chance and accident, and not to any intelligent culling or reasonable methods of selection. As a remedy for this, there is but one possible procedure. We must accept some of the race prejudice in the South as a fact,—deplorable in its intensity, unfortunate in results, and dangerous for the future, but nevertheless a hard fact which only time can efface. We cannot hope, then, in this generation, or for several generations, that the mass of the whites can be brought to assume that close sympathetic and self-sacrificing leadership of the blacks which their present situation so eloquently demands. Such leadership, such social teaching and example, must come from the blacks themselves. For some time men doubted as to whether the Negro could develop such leaders; but today no one seriously disputes the capability of individual Negroes to assimilate the culture and common sense of modern civilization, and to pass it on, to some extent at least, to their fellows. If this is true, then here is the path out of the economic situation, and here is the imperative demand for trained Negro leaders of character and intelligence,—men of skill, men of light and leading, college-bred men, black captains of industry, and missionaries of culture; men who thoroughly comprehend and know modern civilization, and can take hold of Negro communities and raise and train them by force of precept and example, deep sympathy, and the inspiration of common blood and ideals. But if such men are to be effective they must have some power,— they must be backed by the best public opinion of these communities, and be able to wield for their objects and aims such weapons as the experience of the world has taught are indispensable to human progress.

Of such weapons the greatest, perhaps, in the modern world is the power of the ballot; and this brings me to a consideration of the third form of contact between whites and blacks in the South,—political activity.

In the attitude of the American mind toward Negro suffrage can be traced with unusual accuracy the prevalent conceptions of government. In the fifties we were near enough the echoes of the French Revolution to believe pretty thoroughly in universal suffrage. We argued, as we thought then rather logically, that no social class was so good, so true, and so disinterested as to be trusted wholly with the political destiny of its neighbors; that in every state the best arbiters of their own welfare are the persons directly affected; consequently that it is only by arming every hand with a ballot,—with the right to have a voice in the policy of the state,—that the greatest good to the greatest number could be attained. To be sure, there were objections to these arguments, but we thought we had answered them tersely and convincingly; if some one complained of the ignorance of voters, we answered, "Educate them." If another complained of their venality, we replied, "Disfranchise them or put them in jail." And, finally, to the men who feared demagogues and the natural perversity of some human beings we insisted that time and bitter experience would teach the most hardheaded. It was at this time that the question of Negro suffrage in the South was raised. Here was a defenceless people suddenly made free. How were they to be protected from those who did not believe in their freedom and were determined to thwart it? Not by force, said the North; not by government guardianship, said the South; then by the ballot, the sole and legitimate defence of a free people, said the Common Sense of the Nation. No one thought, at the time, that the ex-slaves could use the ballot intelligently or very effectively; but they did think that the possession of so great power by a great class in the nation would compel their fellows to educate this class

"The color line still exists—in this case." Cartoon in *Harper's Weekly*, January 18, 1879. Education and suffrage were ongoing issues from the Civil War and throughout Du Bois's life.

to its intelligent use.

Meantime, new thoughts came to the nation: the inevitable period of moral retrogression and political trickery that ever follows in the wake of war overtook us. So flagrant became the political scandals that reputable men began to leave politics alone, and politics consequently became disreputable. Men began to pride themselves on having nothing to do with their own government, and to agree tacitly with those who regarded public office as a private perquisite. In this state of mind it became easy to wink at the suppression of the Negro vote in the South, and to advise self-respecting Negroes to leave politics entirely alone. The decent and reputable citizens of the North who neglected their own civic duties grew hilarious over the exaggerated importance with which the Negro regarded the franchise. Thus it easily happened that more and more the better class of Negroes followed the advice from abroad and the pressure from home, and took no further interest in politics, leaving to the careless and the venal of their race the exercise of their rights as voters. The black vote that still remained was not trained and educated, but further debauched by open and unblushing bribery, or force and fraud; until the Negro voter was thoroughly inoculated with the idea that politics was a method of private gain by disreputable means.

And finally, now, today, when we are awakening to the fact that the perpetuity of republican institutions on this continent depends on the purification of the ballot, the civic training of voters, and the raising of voting to the plane of a solemn duty which a patriotic citizen neglects to his peril and to the peril of his children's children,—in this day, when we are striving for a renaissance of civic virtue, what are we going to say to the black voter of the South? Are we going to tell him still that politics is a disreputable and useless form of human activity? Are we going to induce the best class of Negroes to take less and less interest in government, and to give up their right to take such an interest, without a protest? I am not saying a word against all legitimate efforts to purge the ballot of ignorance, pauperism, and crime. But few have pretended that the present movement for disfranchisement in the South is for such a purpose; it has been plainly and frankly declared in nearly every case that the object of the disfranchising laws is the elimination of the black man from politics.

Now, is this a minor matter which has no influence on the main question of the industrial and intellectual development of the Negro? Can we establish a mass of black laborers and artisans and landholders in the South who, by law and public opinion, have absolutely no voice in shaping the laws under which they live and work? Can the modern organization of industry, assuming as it does free democratic government and the power and ability of the laboring classes to compel respect for their welfare,—can this system be carried out in the South when half its laboring force is voiceless in the public councils and powerless in its own defence? Today the black man of the South has almost nothing to say as to how much he shall be taxed, or how those taxes shall be expended; as to who shall execute the laws, and how they shall do it; as to who shall make the laws, and how they shall be made. It is pitiable that frantic efforts must be made at critical times to get law-makers in some States even to listen to the respectful presentation of the black man's side of a current controversy. Daily the Negro is coming more and more to look upon law and justice, not as protecting safeguards, but as sources of humiliation and oppression. The laws are made by men who have little interest in him; they are executed by men who have absolutely no motive for treating the black people with courtesy or consideration; and, finally, the accused law-breaker is tried, not by his peers, but too often by men who would rather punish ten innocent Negroes than let one guilty one escape.

I should be the last one to deny the patent weaknesses and shortcomings of the Negro people; I should be the last to withhold sympathy from the white South in its efforts to solve its intricate social problems. I freely acknowledged that it is possible, and sometimes best, that a partially undeveloped people should be ruled by the best of their stronger and better neighbors for their own good, until such time as they can start and fight the world's battles alone. I have already pointed out how sorely in need of such economic and spiritual guidance the emancipated Negro was, and I am quite willing to admit that if the representatives of the best white Southern public opinion were the ruling and guiding powers in the South today the conditions indicated would be fairly well fulfilled. But the point I have insisted upon, and now emphasize again, is that the best opinion of the South today is not the ruling opinion. That to leave the Negro helpless and without a ballot today is to leave him, not to the guidance of the best, but rather to the exploitation and debauchment of the worst; that this is no truer of the South than of the North,—of the North than of Europe: in any land, in any country under modern free competition, to lay any class of weak and despised people, be they white, black, or blue, at the political mercy of their stronger, richer, and more resourceful fellows, is a temptation which human nature seldom has withstood and seldom will withstand.

Moreover, the political status of the Negro in the South is closely connected with the question of Negro crime. There can be no doubt that crime among Negroes has sensibly increased in the last thirty years, and that there has appeared in the slums of great cities a distinct criminal class among the blacks. In explaining this unfortunate development, we must note two things: (1) that the inevitable result of Emancipation was to increase crime and criminals, and (2) that the police system of the South was primarily designed to control slaves. As to the first point, we must not forget that under a strict slave system there can scarcely be such a thing as crime. But when these variously constituted human particles are suddenly thrown broadcast on the sea of life, some swim, some sink, and some hang suspended, to be forced up or down by the chance currents of a busy hurrying world. So great an economic and social revolution as swept the South in '63 meant a weeding out among the Negroes of the incompetents and vicious, the beginning of a differentiation of social grades. Now a rising group of people are not lifted bodily from the ground like an inert solid mass, but rather stretch upward like a living plant with its roots still clinging in the mould. The appearance, therefore, of the Negro criminal was a phenomenon to be awaited; and while it causes anxiety, it should not occasion surprise.

"Houses in African-American community in Georgia." Photograph included in the Exhibit of the American Negroes at the 1900 Paris Exposition. Courtesy of the Library of Congress.

Here again the hope for the future depended peculiarly on careful and delicate dealing with these criminals. Their offences at first were those of laziness, carelessness, and impulse, rather than of malignity or ungoverned viciousness. Such misdemeanors needed discriminating treatment, firm but reformatory, with no hint of injustice, and full proof of guilt. For such dealing with criminals, white or black, the South had no machinery, no adequate jails or reformatories; its police system was arranged to deal with blacks alone, and tacitly assumed that every white man was *ipso facto*[6] a member of that police. Thus grew up a double system of justice, which erred on the white side by undue leniency and the practical immunity of red-handed criminals, and erred on the black side by undue severity, injustice, and lack of discrimination. For, as I have said, the police system of the South was originally designed to keep track of all Negroes, not simply of criminals; and when the Negroes were freed and the whole South was convinced of the impossibility of free Negro labor, the first and almost universal device was to use the courts as a means of re-enslaving the blacks. It was not then a question of crime, but rather one of color, that settled a man's conviction on almost any

---

[6] In Latin, by the fact itself or therefore.

charge. Thus Negroes came to look upon courts as instruments of injustice and oppression, and upon those convicted in them as martyrs and victims.

When, now, the real Negro criminal appeared, and instead of petty stealing and vagrancy we began to have highway robbery, burglary, murder, and rape, there was a curious effect on both sides of the color-line: the Negroes refused to believe the evidence of white witnesses or the fairness of white juries, so that the greatest deterrent to crime, the public opinion of one's own social caste, was lost, and the criminal was looked upon as crucified rather than hanged. On the other hand, the whites, used to being careless as to the guilt or innocence of accused Negroes, were swept in moments of passion beyond law, reason, and decency. Such a situation is bound to increase crime, and has increased it. To natural viciousness and vagrancy are being daily added motives of revolt and revenge which stir up all the latent savagery of both races and make peaceful attention to economic development often impossible.

But the chief problem in any community cursed with crime is not the punishment of the criminals, but the preventing of the young from being trained to crime. And here again the peculiar conditions of the South have prevented proper precautions. I have seen twelve-year-old boys working in chains on the public streets of Atlanta, directly in front of the schools, in company with old and hardened criminals; and this indiscriminate mingling of men and women and children makes the chain gangs perfect schools of crime and debauchery. The struggle for reformatories, which has gone on in Virginia, Georgia, and other States, is the one encouraging sign of the awakening of some communities to the suicidal results of this policy.

It is the public schools, however, which can be made, outside the homes, the greatest means of training decent self-respecting citizens. We have been so hotly engaged recently in discussing trade-schools and the higher education that the pitiable plight of the public-school system in the South has almost dropped from view. Of every five dollars spent for public education in the State of Georgia, the white schools get four dollars and the Negro one dollar; and even then the white public-school system, save in the cities, is bad and cries for reform. If this is true of the whites, what of the blacks? I am becoming more and more convinced, as I look upon the system of common-school training in the South, that the national government must soon step in and aid popular education in some way. Today it has been only by the most strenuous efforts on the part of the thinking men of the South that the Negro's share of the school fund has not been cut down to a pittance in some half-dozen States; and that movement not only is not dead, but in many communities is gaining strength. What in the name of reason does this nation expect of a people, poorly trained and hard pressed in severe economic competition, without political rights, and with ludicrously inadequate common-school facilities? What can it expect but crime and listlessness, offset here and there by the dogged struggles of the fortunate and more determined who are themselves buoyed by the hope that in due time the country will come to its senses?

I have thus far sought to make clear the physical, economic, and political relations of the Negroes and whites in the South, as I have conceived them, including, for the reasons set forth, crime and education. But after all that has been said on these more tangible matters of human contact, there still remains a part essential to a proper description of the South which it is difficult to describe or fix in terms easily understood by strangers. It is, in fine, the atmosphere of the land, the thought and feeling, the thousand and one little actions which go to make up life. In any community or nation it is these little things which are most elusive to the grasp and yet most essential to any clear conception of the group life taken as a whole. What is thus true of all communities is peculiarly true of the South, where, outside of written history and outside of printed law, there has been going on for a generation as deep a storm and stress of human souls, as intense a ferment of feeling, as intricate a writhing of spirit, as ever a people experienced. Within and without the sombre veil of color vast social forces have been at work,—efforts for human betterment, movements toward disintegration and despair, tragedies and comedies in social and economic life, and a swaying and lifting and sinking of human hearts which have made this land a land of mingled sorrow and joy, of change and excitement and unrest.

The centre of this spiritual turmoil has ever been the millions of black freedmen and their sons, whose destiny is so fatefully bound up with that of the nation. And yet the casual observer visiting the South sees at first little of this. He notes the growing frequency of dark faces as he rides along,—but otherwise the days slip lazily on, the sun shines, and this little world seems as happy and contented as other worlds he has visited. Indeed, on the question of questions—the Negro problem—he hears so little that there almost seems to be a conspiracy of silence; the morning papers seldom mention it, and then usually in a far-fetched academic way, and indeed almost every one seems to forget and ignore the darker half of the land, until the astonished visitor is inclined to ask if after all there *is* any problem here. But if he lingers long enough there comes the awakening: perhaps in a sudden whirl of passion which leaves him gasping at its bitter intensity; more likely in a gradually dawning sense of things he had not at first noticed. Slowly but surely his eyes begin to catch the shadows of the color-line: here he meets crowds of

Negroes and whites; then he is suddenly aware that he cannot discover a single dark face; or again at the close of a day's wandering he may find himself in some strange assembly, where all faces are tinged brown or black, and where he has the vague, uncomfortable feeling of the stranger. He realizes at last that silently, resistlessly, the world about flows by him in two great streams: they ripple on in the same sunshine, they approach and mingle their waters in seeming carelessness,—then they divide and flow wide apart. It is done quietly; no mistakes are made, or if one occurs, the swift arm of the law and of public opinion swings down for a moment, as when the other day a black man and a white woman were arrested for talking together on Whitehall Street in Atlanta.

Now if one notices carefully one will see that between these two worlds, despite much physical contact and daily intermingling, there is almost no community of intellectual life or point of transference where the thoughts and feelings of one race can come into direct contact and sympathy with the thoughts and feelings of the other. Before and directly after the war, when all the best of the Negroes were domestic servants in the best of the white families, there were bonds of intimacy, affection, and sometimes blood relationship, between the races. They lived in the same home, shared in the family life, often attended the same church, and talked and conversed with each other. But the increasing civilization of the Negro since then has naturally meant the development of higher classes: there are increasing numbers of ministers, teachers, physicians, merchants, mechanics, and independent farmers, who by nature and training are the aristocracy and leaders of the blacks. Between them, however, and the best element of the whites, there is little or no intellectual commerce. They go to separate churches, they live in separate sections, they are strictly separated in all public gatherings, they travel separately, and they are beginning to read different papers and books. To most libraries, lectures, concerts, and museums, Negroes are either not admitted at all, or on terms peculiarly galling to the pride of the very classes who might otherwise be attracted. The daily paper chronicles the doings of the black world from afar with no great regard for accuracy; and so on, throughout the category of means for intellectual communication,—schools, conferences, efforts for social betterment, and the like,—it is usually true that the very representatives of the two races, who for mutual benefit and the welfare of the land ought to be in complete understanding and sympathy, are so far strangers that one side thinks all whites are narrow and prejudiced, and the other thinks educated Negroes dangerous and insolent. Moreover, in a land where the tyranny of public opinion and the intolerance of criticism is for obvious historical reasons so strong as in the South, such a situation is extremely difficult to correct. The white man, as well as the Negro, is bound and

"Street scene in business district, possibly in Atlanta, Georgia." Photograph included in the Exhibit of the American Negroes at the 1900 Paris Exposition. Courtesy of the Library of Congress.

barred by the color-line, and many a scheme of friendliness and philanthropy, of broad-minded sympathy and generous fellowship between the two has dropped still-born because some busybody has forced the color-question to the front and brought the tremendous force of unwritten law against the innovators.

It is hardly necessary for me to add very much in regard to the social contact between the races. Nothing has come to replace that finer sympathy and love between some masters and house servants which the radical and more uncompromising drawing of the color-line in recent years has caused almost completely to disappear. In a world where it means so much to take a man by the hand and sit beside him, to look frankly into his eyes and feel his heart beating with red blood; in a world where a social cigar or a cup of tea together means more than legislative halls and magazine articles and speeches,—one can imagine the consequences of the almost utter absence of such social amenities between estranged races, whose separation extends even to parks and streetcars.

Here there can be none of that social going down to the people,—the opening of heart and hand of the best to the worst, in generous acknowl-edgment of a common humanity and a common destiny. On the other hand, in matters of simple almsgiving, where there can be no question of social contact, and in the succor of the aged and sick, the South, as if stirred by a feeling of its unfortunate limitations is generous to a fault. The black beggar is never turned away without a good deal more than a crust, and a call for help for the unfortunate meets quick response. I remember, one cold winter, in Atlanta, when I refrained from contributing to a public relief fund lest Negroes should be discriminated against, I afterward inquired of a friend: "Were any black people receiving aid?" "Why," said he, "they were *all* black."

And yet this does not touch the kernel of the problem. Human advancement is not a mere question of almsgiving, but rather of sympathy and cooperation among classes who would scorn charity. And here is a land where, in the higher walks of life, in all the higher striving for the good and noble and true, the color-line comes to separate natural friends and coworkers; while at the bottom of the social group, in the saloon, the gambling-hell, and the brothel, that same line wavers and disappears.

I have sought to paint an average picture of real relations between the sons of master and man in the South. I have not glossed over matters for policy's sake, for I fear we have already gone too far in that sort of thing. On the other hand, I have sincerely sought to let no unfair exaggerations creep in. I do not doubt that in some Southern communities conditions are better than those I have indicated; while I am no less certain that in other communities they are far worse.

Nor does the paradox and danger of this situation fail to interest and perplex the best conscience of the South. Deeply religious and intensely democratic as are the mass of the whites, they feel acutely the false position in which Negro problems place them. Such an essentially honest-hearted and generous people cannot cite the caste-levelling precepts of Christianity, or believe in equality of opportunity for all men, without coming to feel more and more with each generation that the present drawing of the color-line is a flat contradiction to their beliefs and professions. But just as often as they come to this point, the present social condition of the Negro stands as a menace and a portent before even the most open-minded: if there were nothing to charge against the Negro but his blackness or other physical peculiarities, they argue, the problem would be comparatively simple; but what can we say to his ignorance, shiftlessness, poverty, and crime? Can a self-respecting group hold anything but the least possible fellowship with such persons and survive? And shall we let a mawkish sentiment sweep away the culture of our fathers or the hope of our children? The argument so put is of great strength, but it is not a whit stronger than the argument of thinking Negroes: granted, they reply, that the condition of our masses is bad;

there is certainly on the one hand adequate historical cause for this, and unmistakable evidence that no small number have, in spite of tremendous disadvantages, risen to the level of American civilization. And when, by proscription and prejudice, these same Negroes are classed with and treated like the lowest of their people, simply *because* they are Negroes, such a policy not only discourages thrift and intelligence among black men, but puts a direct premium on the very things you complain of,— inefficiency and crime. Draw lines of crime, of incompetency, of vice, as tightly and uncompromisingly as you will, for these things must be proscribed; but a color-line not only does not accomplish this purpose, but thwarts it.

In the face of two such arguments, the future of the South depends on the ability of the representatives of these opposing views to see and appreciate and sympathize with each other's position,—for the Negro to realize more deeply than he does at present the need of uplifting the masses of his people, for the white people to realize more vividly than they have yet done the deadening and disastrous effect of a color-prejudice that classes Phillis Wheatley and Sam Hose in the same despised class.

It is not enough for the Negroes to declare that color-prejudice is the sole cause of their social condition, nor for the white South to reply that their social condition is the main cause of prejudice. They both act as reciprocal cause and effect, and a change in neither alone will bring the desired effect. Both must change, or neither can improve to any great extent. The Negro cannot stand the present reactionary tendencies and unreasoning drawing of the color-line indefinitely without discouragement and retrogression. And the condition of the Negro is ever the excuse for further discrimination. Only by a union of intelligence and sympathy across the color-line in this critical period of the Republic shall justice and right triumph,

"That mind and soul according well,
May make one music as before,
   But vaster."[7]

---

[7] From Alfred Lord Tennyson's *In Memoriam* (1850).

Document Number 10, Chapter IX

The lynching of African-Americans was increasingly used as a means of intimidation during the late nineteenth and early twentieth centuries in the United States. Du Bois compiled the following list in 1910 for the National Association of Colored People's magazine *The Crisis.*

* * *

Colored Men Lynched Without Trial[8]

Year	Count
1885	78
1886	71
1887	90
1888	95
1889	95
1890	90
1891	121
1892	155
1893	154
1894	134
1895	112
1896	80
1897	122
1899	102
1899	84
1900	107
1901	107
1902	86
1903	86
1904	83
1905*	60
1906*	60
1907*	60
1908*	80
1909	73
1910**	50
Total	2,425

*Estimated   **Estimated to date

[8] Source: *The Crisis*, December 1910, p. 26.

"Sisters of the Holy Family, New Orleans, Louisiana." Photograph included in the American Negro exhibit at the Paris Exposition of 1900. Courtesy of the Library of Congress.

"Steal Away," included in J. B. T. Marsh, *The Story of the Jubilee Singers* (Cleveland, Ohio: The Cleveland Printing and Publishing Company, 1892), p. 181.

X

Of the Faith of the Fathers[1]

Dim face of Beauty haunting all the world,
Fair face of Beauty all too fair to see,
Where the lost stars adown the heavens are hurled,—
There, there alone for thee
May white peace be.

Beauty, sad face of Beauty, Mystery, Wonder,
What are these dreams to foolish babbling men
Who cry with little noises 'neath the thunder
Of Ages ground to sand,
To a little sand.

                                        FIONA MACLEOD.[2]

It was out in the country, far from home, far from my foster home, on a dark Sunday night. The road wandered from our rambling log-house up the stony bed of a creek, past wheat and corn, until we could hear dimly across the fields a rhythmic cadence of song,—soft, thrilling, powerful, that swelled and died sorrowfully in our ears. I was a country school-teacher then, fresh from the East, and had never seen a Southern Negro revival. To be sure, we in Berkshire[3] were not perhaps as stiff and formal as they in Suffolk of olden time; yet we were very quiet and subdued, and I know not what would have happened those clear Sabbath mornings had some one punctuated the sermon with a wild scream, or interrupted the long prayer with a loud Amen! And so most striking to me, as I approached the village and the little plain church perched aloft, was the air of intense excitement that possessed that mass

---

[1] This chapter is a revision of Du Bois's article "The Religion of the American Negro," published in the December 1900 issue of *The New World: A Quarterly Review of Religious Ethics and Theology*, pp. 614–625.
[2] The selection of verse is from the poem "Dim Face of Beauty," by Fiona MacLeod, the pen name of Scottish poet and man of letters William Sharp (1855–1905).
[3] Du Bois was raised in the Berkshire region of western Massachusetts.

Meeting in the African Church, Cincinnati, *Illustrated London News*, 1870.

of black folk. A sort of suppressed terror hung in the air and seemed to seize us,—a pythian madness,[4] a demoniac possession, that lent terrible reality to song and word. The black and massive form of the preacher swayed and quivered as the words crowded to his lips and flew at us in singular eloquence. The people moaned and fluttered, and then the gaunt-cheeked brown woman beside me suddenly leaped straight into the air and shrieked like a lost soul, while round about came wail and groan and outcry, and a scene of human passion such as I had never conceived before.

Those who have not thus witnessed the frenzy of a Negro revival in the untouched backwoods of the South can but dimly realize the religious feeling of the slave; as described, such scenes appear grotesque and funny, but as seen they are awful. Three things characterized this religion of the slave,—the Preacher, the Music, and the Frenzy. The Preacher is the most unique personality developed by the Negro on American soil. A leader, a politician, an orator, a "boss," an intriguer, an idealist,—all these he is, and ever, too, the centre of a group of men, now twenty, now

---

[4] The Pythian priestess at Delphi in Ancient Greece would go into trances and deliver prophecies.

a thousand in number. The combination of a certain adroitness with deep-seated earnestness, of tact with consummate ability, gave him his preeminence, and helps him maintain it. The type, of course, varies according to time and place, from the West Indies in the sixteenth century to New England in the nineteenth, and from the Mississippi bottoms to cities like New Orleans or New York.

The Music of Negro religion is that plaintive rhythmic melody, with its touching minor cadences, which, despite caricature and defilement, still remains the most original and beautiful expression of human life and longing yet born on American soil. Sprung from the African forests, where its counterpart can still be heard, it was adapted, changed, and intensified by the tragic soul-life of the slave, until, under the stress of law and whip, it became the one true expression of a people's sorrow, despair, and hope.

Finally the Frenzy or "Shouting," when the Spirit of the Lord passed by, and, seizing the devotee, made him mad with supernatural joy, was the last essential of Negro religion and the one more devoutly believed in

"Exterior View of Church" (probably taken in Georgia). Photograph included in the American Negro exhibit at the 1900 Paris Exposition. Courtesy of the Library of Congress.

than all the rest. It varied in expression from the silent rapt countenance or the low murmur and moan to the mad abandon of physical fervor,—the stamping, shrieking, and shouting, the rushing to and fro and wild waving of arms, the weeping and laughing, the vision and the trance. All this is nothing new in the world, but old as religion, as Delphi and Endor.[5] And so firm a hold did it have on the Negro, that many generations firmly believed that without this visible manifestation of the God there could be no true communion with the Invisible.

These were the characteristics of Negro religious life as developed up to the time of Emancipation. Since under the peculiar circumstances of the black man's environment they were the one expression of his higher life, they are of deep interest to the student of his development, both socially and psychologically. Numerous are the attractive lines of inquiry that here group themselves. What did slavery mean to the African savage? What was his attitude toward the World and Life? What seemed to him good and evil,—God and Devil? Whither went his longings and strivings, and wherefore were his heart-burnings and disappointments? Answers to such questions can come only from a study of Negro religion as a development, through its gradual changes from the heathenism of the Gold Coast to the institutional Negro church of Chicago.

Moreover, the religious growth of millions of men, even though they be slaves, cannot be without potent influence upon their contemporaries. The Methodists and Baptists of America owe much of their condition to the silent but potent influence of their millions of Negro converts. Especially is this noticeable in the South, where theology and religious philosophy are on this account a long way behind the North, and where the religion of the poor whites is a plain copy of Negro thought and methods. The mass of "gospel" hymns which has swept through American churches and well-nigh ruined our sense of song consists largely of debased imitations of Negro melodies made by ears that caught the jingle but not the music, the body but not the soul, of the Jubilee songs.[6] It is thus clear that the study of Negro religion is not only a vital part of the history of the Negro in America, but no uninteresting part of American history.

The Negro church of today is the social centre of Negro life in the United States, and the most characteristic expression of African character. Take a typical church in a small Virginia town: it is the "First Baptist"—a roomy brick edifice seating five hundred or more persons, tastefully finished in Georgia pine, with a carpet, a small organ, and

---

[5] In 1 Samuel 28:7-14 Endor summoned the ghost of King Saul.
[6] Du Bois is referring to the genuine Black spirituals and not the corrupted versions that had come into widespread use in both Black and White churches.

stained-glass windows. Underneath is a large assembly room with benches. This building is the central club-house of a community of a thousand or more Negroes. Various organizations meet here,—the church proper, the Sunday-school, two or three insurance societies, women's societies, secret societies, and mass meetings of various kinds. Entertainments, suppers, and lectures are held beside the five or six regular weekly religious services. Considerable sums of money are collected and expended here, employment is found for the idle, strangers are introduced, news is disseminated and charity distributed. At the same time this social, intellectual, and economic centre is a religious centre of great power. Depravity, Sin, Redemption, Heaven, Hell, and Damnation are preached twice a Sunday with much fervor, and revivals take place every year after the crops are laid by; and few indeed of the community have the hardihood to withstand conversion. Back of this more formal religion, the Church often stands as a real conserver of morals, a strengthener of family life, and the final authority on what is Good and Right.

Thus one can see in the Negro church today, reproduced in microcosm, all that great world from which the Negro is cut off by color-prejudice and social condition. In the great city churches the same tendency is noticeable and in many respects emphasized. A great church like the Bethel of Philadelphia[7] has over eleven hundred members, an edifice seating fifteen hundred persons and valued at one hundred thousand dollars, an annual budget of five thousand dollars, and a government consisting of a pastor with several assisting local preachers, an executive and legislative board, financial boards and tax collectors; general church meetings for making laws; subdivided groups led by class leaders, a company of militia, and twenty-four auxiliary societies. The activity of a church like this is immense and far-reaching, and the bishops who preside over these organizations throughout the land are among the most powerful Negro rulers in the world.

Such churches are really governments of men, and consequently a little investigation reveals the curious fact that, in the South, at least, practically every American Negro is a church member. Some, to be sure, are not regularly enrolled, and a few do not habitually attend services; but, practically, a proscribed people must have a social centre, and that centre for this people is the Negro church. The census of 1890 showed nearly twenty-four thousand Negro churches in the country, with a total enrolled membership of over two and a half millions, or ten actual

---

[7] The Mother Bethel Church in Philadelphia was founded in 1794 by Richard Allen and was the first founding church of the African Methodist Episcopal denomination in the States.

church members to every twenty-eight persons, and in some Southern States one in every two persons. Besides these there is the large number who, while not enrolled as members, attend and take part in many of the activities of the church. There is an organized Negro church for every sixty black families in the nation, and in some States for every forty families, owning, on an average, a thousand dollars' worth of property each, or nearly twenty-six million dollars in all.

Such, then, is the large development of the Negro church since Emancipation. The question now is, What have been the successive steps of this social history and what are the present tendencies? First, we must realize that no such institution as the Negro church could rear itself without definite historical foundations. These foundations we can find if we remember that the social history of the Negro did not start in America. He was brought from a definite social environment,—the polygamous clan life under the headship of the chief and the potent influence of the priest. His religion was nature-worship, with profound belief in invisible surrounding influences, good and bad, and his worship was through incantation and sacrifice. The first rude change in this life was the slave ship and the West Indian sugar-fields. The plantation organization replaced the clan and tribe, and the white master replaced the chief with far greater and more despotic powers. Forced and long-continued toil became the rule of life, the old ties of blood relationship and kinship disappeared, and instead of the family appeared a new polygamy and polyandry,[8] which, in some cases, almost reached promiscuity. It was a terrific social revolution, and yet some traces were retained of the former group life, and the chief remaining institution was the Priest or Medicine-man. He early appeared on the plantation and found his function as the healer of the sick, the interpreter of the Unknown, the comforter of the sorrowing, the supernatural avenger of wrong, and the one who rudely but picturesquely expressed the longing, disappointment, and resentment of a stolen and oppressed people. Thus, as bard, physician, judge, and priest, within the narrow limits allowed by the slave system, rose the Negro preacher, and under him the first Afro-American institution, the Negro church. This church was not at first by any means Christian nor definitely organized; rather it was an adaptation and mingling of heathen rites among the members of each plantation, and roughly designated as Voodooism.[9] Association with the masters, missionary effort and motives of expediency gave these rites an

---

[8] Social and cultural systems allowing multiple marriages to more than one spouse at a time.

[9] A syncretic religion practiced in the Caribbean that combines elements of Catholicism with West African traditions of animism and magic.

African Americans standing outside of a church, probably in rural Georgia. Photograph included in the American Negro exhibit at the 1900 Paris Exposition. Courtesy of the Library of Congress.

early veneer of Christianity, and after the lapse of many generations the Negro church became Christian.

Two characteristic things must be noticed in regard to this church. First, it became almost entirely Baptist and Methodist in faith; secondly, as a social institution it antedated by many decades the monogamic[10] Negro home. From the very circumstances of its beginning, the church was confined to the plantation, and consisted primarily of a series of disconnected units; although, later on, some freedom of movement was allowed, still this geographical limitation was always important and was one cause of the spread of the decentralized and democratic Baptist faith among the slaves. At the same time, the visible rite of baptism appealed strongly to their mystic temperament. Today the Baptist Church is still largest in membership among Negroes, and has a million and a half communicants. Next in popularity came the churches organized in connection with the white neighboring churches, chiefly Baptist and Methodist, with a few Episcopalian and others. The Methodists still form

[10] Pertaining to monogamy or single spouse marriage.

the second greatest denomination, with nearly a million members. The faith of these two leading denominations was more suited to the slave church from the prominence they gave to religious feeling and fervor.The Negro membership in other denominations has always been small and relatively unimportant, although the Episcopalians and Presbyterians are gaining among the more intelligent classes today, and the Catholic Church is making headway in certain sections. After Emancipation, and still earlier in the North, the Negro churches largely severed such affiliations as they had had with the white churches, either by choice or by compulsion. The Baptist churches became independent, but the Methodists were compelled early to unite for purposes of episcopal government. This gave rise to the great African Methodist Church, the greatest Negro organization in the world, to the Zion Church and the Colored Methodist, and to the black conferences and churches in this and other denominations. [11]

The second fact noted, namely, that the Negro church antedates the Negro home, leads to an explanation of much that is paradoxical in this communistic institution and in the morals of its members. But especially it leads us to regard this institution as peculiarly the expression of the inner ethical life of a people in a sense seldom true elsewhere. Let us turn, then, from the outer physical development of the church to the more important inner ethical life of the people who compose it. The Negro has already been pointed out many times as a religious animal,—a being of that deep emotional nature which turns instinctively toward the supernatural. Endowed with a rich tropical imagination and a keen, delicate appreciation of Nature, the transplanted African lived in a world animate with gods and devils, elves and witches; full of strange influences,—of Good to be implored, of Evil to be propitiated. Slavery, then, was to him the dark triumph of Evil over him. All the hateful powers of the Under-world were striving against him, and a spirit of revolt and revenge filled his heart. He called up all the resources of heathenism to aid,—exorcism and witchcraft, the mysterious Obi[12] worship with its barbarous rites, spells, and blood-sacrifice even, now and then, of human victims. Weird midnight orgies and mystic conjurations were invoked, the witch-woman and the voodoo-priest became the centre of Negro group life, and that vein of vague superstition which characterizes the unlettered Negro even today was deepened and strengthened.

---

[11] The African Methodist Episcopal Church was founded in 1787 in Philadelphia by Richard Allen. The Zion Church broke off from the African Methodist Episcopal Church. It is less traditional in its orientation.

[12] A West Indian religion based around magic and sorcery.

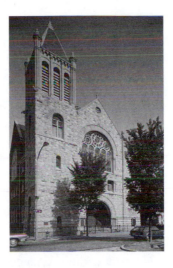

"Bethel African Methodist Episcopal Church." Jack Boucher photographer, Historic American Buildings Survey, July 1973. Courtesy of the Library of Congress.

In spite, however, of such success as that of the fierce Maroons,[13] the Danish[14] blacks, and others, the spirit of revolt gradually died away under the untiring energy and superior strength of the slave masters. By the middle of the eighteenth century the black slave had sunk, with hushed murmurs, to his place at the bottom of a new economic system, and was unconsciously ripe for a new philosophy of life. Nothing suited his condition then better than the doctrines of passive submission embodied in the newly learned Christianity. Slave masters early realized this, and cheerfully aided religious propaganda within certain bounds. The long system of repression and degradation of the Negro tended to emphasize the elements in his character which made him a valuable chattel: courtesy became humility, moral strength degenerated into submission, and the exquisite native appreciation of the beautiful became an infinite capacity for dumb suffering. The Negro, losing the joy of this world, eagerly seized upon the offered conceptions of the next; the avenging Spirit of the Lord enjoining patience in this world, under sorrow and tribulation until the Great Day when He should lead His dark children home,—this became his comforting dream. His preacher repeated the prophecy, and his bards sang,—

---

[13] Fugitive Black slaves from the West Indies during the seventeenth and eighteenth centuries.

[14] Danish blacks were slaves who took control of the Dutch West Indies (the modern Virgin Islands) in 1723.

"Children, we all shall be free
When the Lord shall appear!"

This deep religious fatalism, painted so beautifully in "Uncle Tom,"[15] came soon to breed, as all fatalistic faiths will, the sensualist side by side with the martyr. Under the lax moral life of the plantation, where marriage was a farce, laziness a virtue, and property a theft, a religion of resignation and submission degenerated easily, in less strenuous minds, into a philosophy of indulgence and crime. Many of the worst characteristics of the Negro masses of today had their seed in this period of the slave's ethical growth. Here it was that the Home was ruined under the very shadow of the Church, white and black; here habits of shiftlessness took root, and sullen hopelessness replaced hopeful strife.

With the beginning of the Abolition Movement and the gradual growth of a class of free Negroes came a change. We often neglect the influence of the freedman before the war, because of the paucity of his numbers and the small weight he had in the history of the nation. But we must not forget that his chief influence was internal,—was exerted on the black world; and that there he was the ethical and social leader. Huddled as he was in a few centres like Philadelphia, New York, and New Orleans, the masses of the freedmen sank into poverty and listlessness; but not all of them. The free Negro leader early arose and his chief characteristic was intense earnestness and deep feeling on the slavery question. Freedom became to him a real thing and not a dream. His religion became darker and more intense, and into his ethics crept a note of revenge, into his songs a day of reckoning close at hand. The "Coming of the Lord" swept this side of Death, and came to be a thing to be hoped for in this day. Through fugitive slaves and irrepressible discussion this desire for freedom seized the black millions still in bondage, and became their one ideal of life. The black bards caught new notes, and sometimes even dared to sing,—

0 Freedom, 0 Freedom, 0 Freedom over me!
Before I'll be a slave
I'll be buried in my grave,
And go home to my Lord
And be free.[16]

---

[15] The deeply religious slave who is martyred in Harriet Beecher Stowe's 1852 novel *Uncle Tom's Cabin.*

[16] Verse from the Black spiritual "O Freedom."

Baptist Preacher, Alma Plantation, False River, La., July, 1934." Alan Lomax photographer. Courtesy of the Library of Congress.

For fifty years Negro religion thus transformed itself and identified itself with the dream of Abolition, until that which was a radical fad in the white North and an anarchistic plot in the white South had become a religion to the black world. Thus, when Emancipation finally came, it seemed to the freedman a literal Coming of the Lord. His fervid imagination was stirred as never before, by the tramp of armies, the blood and dust of battle, and the wail and whirl of social upheaval. He stood dumb and motionless before the whirlwind: what had he to do with it? Was it not the Lord's doing, and marvellous in his eyes? Joyed and bewildered with what came, he stood awaiting new wonders till the inevitable Age of Reaction swept over the nation and brought the crisis of today.

It is difficult to explain clearly the present critical stage of Negro religion. First, we must remember that living as the blacks do in close contact with a great modern nation, and sharing, although imperfectly, the soul-life of that nation, they must necessarily be affected more or less directly by all the religious and ethical forces that are today moving the United States. These questions and movements are, however, overshadowed and dwarfed by the (to them) all-important question of their civil, political, and economic status. They must perpetually discuss the "Negro Problem,"—must live, move, and have their being in it, and interpret all else in its light or darkness. With this comes, too, peculiar problems of their inner life,—of the status of women, the maintenance of Home, the training of children, the accumulation of wealth, and the prevention of crime. All this must mean a time of intense ethical ferment, of religious heart-searching and intellectual unrest. From the double life every American Negro must live, as a Negro and as an American, as swept on by the current of the nineteenth while yet struggling in the eddies of the fifteenth century,—from this must arise a painful self-consciousness, an almost morbid sense of personality and a moral hesitancy which is fatal to self-confidence. The worlds within and without the Veil of Color are changing, and changing rapidly, but not at the same rate, not in the same way; and this must produce a peculiar wrenching of the soul, a peculiar sense of doubt and bewilderment. Such a double life, with double thoughts, double duties, and double social classes, must give rise to double words and double ideals, and tempt the mind to pretence or revolt, to hypocrisy or radicalism.

In some such doubtful words and phrases can one perhaps most clearly picture the peculiar ethical paradox that faces the Negro of today and is tingeing and changing his religious life. Feeling that his rights and his dearest ideals are being trampled upon, that the public conscience is ever more deaf to his righteous appeal, and that all the reactionary forces of prejudice, greed, and revenge are daily gaining new strength and fresh allies, the Negro faces no enviable dilemma. Conscious of his impotence, and pessimistic; he often becomes bitter and vindictive; and his religion, instead of a worship, is a complaint and a curse, a wail rather than a hope, a sneer rather than a faith. On the other hand, another type of mind, shrewder and keener and more tortuous too, sees in the very strength of the anti-Negro movement its patent weaknesses, and with Jesuitic casuistry[17] is deterred by no ethical considerations in the endeavor to turn this weakness to the black man's strength. Thus we have two great and hardly reconcilable streams of thought and ethical strivings; the danger of the one lies in anarchy, that of the other in hypocrisy. The one type of Negro stands almost ready to curse God and die, and the other is too often found a traitor to right and a coward before force; the one is wedded to ideals remote, whimsical, perhaps impossible of realization; the other forgets that life is more than meat and the body more than raiment. But, after all, is not this simply the writhing of the aged translated into black,—the triumph of the Lie which today, with its false

---

[17] A negative reference to the Catholic religious order of the Jesuits and their use of excessively subtle reasoning intended to rationalize and mislead.

"American Sketches: A Negro Congregation in Washington," *Illustrated London News*, November 18, 1876. Courtesy of the Library of Congress.

culture, faces the hideousness of the anarchist assassin?

Today the two groups of Negroes, the one in the North, the other in the South, represent these divergent ethical tendencies, the first tending toward radicalism, the other toward hypocritical compromise. It is no idle regret with which the white South mourns the loss of the old-time Negro,—the frank, honest, simple old servant who stood for the earlier religious age of submission and humility. With all his laziness and lack of many elements of true manhood, he was at least open-hearted, faithful, and sincere. Today he is gone, but who is to blame for his going? Is it not those very persons who mourn for him? Is it not the tendency, born of Reconstruction and Reaction, to found a society on lawlessness and deception, to tamper with the moral fibre of a naturally honest and straightforward people until the whites threaten to become ungovernable tyrants and the blacks criminals and hypocrites? Deception is the natural defence of the weak against the strong, and the South used it for many years against its conquerors; today it must be prepared to see its black proletariat turn that same two-edged weapon against itself. And how natural this is! The death of Denmark Vesey and Nat Turner proved long since to the Negro the present hopelessness of physical defence. Political defence is becoming less and less available, and economic defence is still only partially effective. But there is a patent defence at hand,—the defence of deception and flattery, of cajoling and lying. It is the same defence which peasants of the Middle Age used and which left its stamp on their character for centuries. Today the young Negro of the South who would succeed cannot be frank and outspoken, honest and self-assertive, but rather he is daily tempted to be silent and wary, politic and sly; he must flatter and be pleasant, endure petty insults with a smile, shut his eyes to wrong; in too many cases he sees positive personal advantage in deception and lying. His real thoughts, his real aspirations, must be guarded in whispers; he must not criticise, he must not complain. Patience, humility, and adroitness must, in these growing black youth, replace impulse, manliness, and courage. With this sacrifice there is an economic opening, and perhaps peace and some prosperity. Without this there is riot, migration, or crime. Nor is this situation peculiar to the Southern United States, is it not rather the only method by which undeveloped races have gained the right to share modern culture? The price of culture is a Lie.

On the other hand, in the North the tendency is to emphasize the radicalism of the Negro. Driven from his birthright in the South by a situation at which every fibre of his more outspoken and assertive nature revolts, he finds himself in a land where he can scarcely earn a decent living amid the harsh competition and the color discrimination. At the same time, through schools and periodicals, discussions and lectures, he is intellectually quickened and awakened. The soul, long pent up and dwarfed, suddenly expands in new-found freedom. What wonder that every tendency is to excess,—radical complaint, radical remedies, bitter denunciation or angry silence. Some sink, some rise. The criminal and the sensualist leave the church for the gambling-hell and the brothel, and fill the slums of Chicago and Baltimore; the better classes segregate themselves from the group-life of both white and black, and form an aristocracy, cultured but pessimistic, whose bitter criticism stings while it points out no way of escape. They despise the submission and subserviency of the Southern Negroes, but offer no other means by which a poor and oppressed minority can exist side by side with its masters. Feeling deeply and keenly the tendencies and opportunities of the age in which they live, their souls are bitter at the fate which drops the Veil between; and the very fact that this bitterness is natural and justifiable only serves to intensify it and make it more maddening.

Between the two extreme types of ethical attitude which I have thus sought to make clear wavers the mass of the millions of Negroes, North and South; and their religious life and activity partake of this social conflict within their ranks. Their churches are differentiating,—now into groups of cold, fashionable devotees, in no way distinguishable from similar white groups save in color of skin; now into large social and business institutions catering to the desire for information and amusement of their members, warily avoiding unpleasant questions both within and without the black world, and preaching in effect if not in word: *Dum vivimus, vivamus.*[18]

But back of this still broods silently the deep religious feeling of the real Negro heart, the stirring, unguided might of powerful human souls who have lost the guiding star of the past and seek in the great night a new religious ideal. Some day the Awakening will come, when the pent-up vigor of ten million souls shall sweep irresistibly toward the Goal, out of the Valley of the Shadow of Death, where all that makes life worth living—Liberty, Justice, and Right—is marked "For White People Only."

"Sign on a restaurant, ('We Cater to White Trade Only')," Lancaster, Ohio. August 1938. Photograph by Ben Shahn, photographer. Courtesy of the Library of Congress.

---

[18] In Latin meaning "while we live, let us live."

Document Number 11, Chapter X

W. E. B. Du Bois's *The Philadelphia Negro* was first published in 1899 by the University of Pennsylvania Press. It is a pioneering work in urban Sociology and African-American Studies, and provides what is the first large-scale systematic study of African-Americans in an urban setting. The selection included below is from Chapter XVI and addresses the issue of Color Prejudice.

*   *   *

Color Prejudice[19]

Incidentally throughout this study the prejudice against the Negro has been again and again mentioned. It is time now to reduce this somewhat indefinite term to something tangible. Everybody speaks of the matter, everybody knows that it exists, but in just what form it shows itself or how influential it is few agree. In the Negro's mind, color prejudice in Philadelphia is that widespread feeling of dislike for his blood, which keeps him and his children out of decent employment, from certain public conveniences and amusements, from hiring houses in many sections, and in general, from being recognized as a man. Negroes regard this prejudice as the chief cause of their present unfortunate condition. On the other hand most white people are quite unconscious of any such powerful and vindictive feeling; they regard color prejudice as the easily explicable feeling that intimate social intercourse with a lower race is not only undesirable but impracticable if our present standards of culture are to be maintained; and although they are aware that some people feel the aversion more intensely than others, they cannot see how such a feeling has much influence on the real situation or alters the social condition of the mass of Negroes.

As a matter of fact, color prejudice in this city is something between these two extreme views: it is not today responsible for all, or perhaps the greater part of the Negro problems, or of the disabilities under which the race labors; on the other hand it is a far more powerful social force than most Philadelphians realize. The practical results of the attitude of most of the inhabitants of Philadelphia toward persons of Negro descent are as follows:

1. As to getting work:

No matter how well trained a Negro may be, or how fitted for work of any kind, he cannot in the ordinary course of competition hope to be much more than a menial servant.

He cannot get clerical or supervisory work to do save in exceptional cases.

He cannot teach save in a few of the remaining Negro schools.

---

[19] W. E. B. DuBois, "The Contact of the Race" selection from Chapter XVI, The Contact of the Race," included in *The Philadelphia Negro* (New York: Lippincott, 1899), pp. 322–367.

He cannot become a mechanic except for small transient jobs, and cannot join a trades union.

A Negro woman has but three careers open to her in this city: domestic service, sewing, or married life.

2. As to keeping work:

The Negro suffers in competition more severely than white men. Change in fashion is causing him to be replaced by whites in the better paid positions of domestic service.

Whim and accident will cause him to lose a hard-earned place more quickly than the same things would affect a white man.

Being few in number compared with the whites the crime or carelessness of a few of his race is easily imputed to all, and the reputation of the good, industrious and reliable suffer thereby.

Because Negro workmen may not often work side by side with white workmen, the individual black workman is rated not by his own efficiency, but by the efficiency of a whole group of black fellow workmen which may often be low.

Because of these difficulties which virtually increase competition in his case, he is forced to take lower wages for the same work than white workmen.

3. As to entering new lines of work:

Men are used to seeing Negroes in inferior positions; when, therefore, by any chance a Negro gets in a better position, most men immediately conclude that he is not fitted for it, even before he has a chance to show his fitness.

If, therefore, he set up a store, men will not patronize him.

If he is put into public position men will complain.

If he gain a position in the commercial world, men will quietly secure his dismissal or see that a white man succeeds him.

4. As to his expenditure:

The comparative smallness of the patronage of the Negro, and the dislike of other customers makes it usual to increase the charges or difficulties in certain directions in which a Negro must spend money.

He must pay more house-rent for worse houses than most white people pay.

He is sometimes liable to insult or reluctant service in some restaurants, hotels and stores, at public resorts, theatres and places of recreation; and at nearly all barber shops.

5. As to his children:

The Negro finds it extremely difficult to rear children in such an atmosphere and not have them either cringing or impudent: if he impresses upon them patience with their lot, they may grow up satisfied with their condition; if he inspires them with ambition to rise, they may grow to despise their own people, hate the whites and become embittered with the world.

His children are discriminated against, often in public schools.

They are advised when seeking employment to become waiters and maids.

They are liable to species of insult and temptation peculiarly trying to children.

6. As to social intercourse:

In all walks of life the Negro is liable to meet some objection to his presence or some discourteous treatment; and the ties of friendship or memory seldom are strong enough to hold across the color line.

If an invitation is issued to the public for any occasion, the Negro can never know whether he would be welcomed or not; if he goes he is liable to have his feelings hurt and get into unpleasant altercation; if he stays away, he is blamed for indifference.

If he meet a lifelong white friend on the street, he is in a dilemma; if he does not greet the friend he is put down as boorish and impolite; if he does greet the friend he is liable to be flatly snubbed.

If by chance he is introduced to a white woman or man, he expects to be ignored on the next meeting, and usually is.

White friends may call on him, but he is scarcely expected to call on them, save for strictly business matters.

If he gain the affections of a white woman and marry her he may invariably expect that slurs will be thrown on her reputation and on his, and that both his and her race will shun their company.

When he dies he cannot be buried beside white corpses.

7. The result:

Any one of these things happening now and then would not be remarkable or call for especial comment; but when one group of people suffer all these little differences of treatment and discriminations and insults continually, the result is either discouragement, or bitterness, or over-sensitiveness, or recklessness. And a people feeling thus cannot do their best.

Presumably the first impulse of the average Philadelphian would be emphatically to deny any such marked and blighting discrimination as the above against a group of citizens in this metropolis. Every one knows that in the past color prejudice in the city was deep and passionate; living men can remember when a Negro could not sit in a street car or walk many streets in peace. These times have passed, however, and many imagine that active discrimination against the Negro has passed with them. Careful inquiry will convince any such one of his error. To be sure a colored man today can walk the streets of Philadelphia without personal insult; he can go to theatres, parks and some places of amusement without meeting rmore than stares and discourtesy; he can be accommodated at most hotels and restaurants, although his treatment in some would not be pleasant. All this is a vast advance and augurs much for the future. And yet all that has been said of the remaining discrimination is but too true.

During the investigation of 1896 there was collected a number of actual cases, which may illustrate the discriminations spoken of. So far as possible these have been sifted and only those which seem undoubtedly true have been selected.

1. As to getting work.

It is hardly necessary to dwell upon the situation of the Negro in regard to work in the higher walks of life: the white boy may start in the lawyer's office and work himself into a lucrative practice; he may serve a physician as office boy or enter a hospital in a minor position, and have his talent alone between him and affluence and fame; if he is bright in school, he may make his mark in a university, become a tutor with some time and much inspiration for study, and eventually fill a professor's chair. All these careers are at the very outset closed to the Negro on account of his color; what lawyer would give even a minor case to a Negro assistant? or what university would appoint a promising young Negro as tutor? Thus the young white man starts in life knowing that within some limits and barring accidents, talent and application will tell. The young Negro starts knowing that on all sides his advance is made doubly difficult if not wholly shut off by his color. Let us come, however, to ordinary occupations which concern more nearly the mass of Negroes. Philadelphia is a great industrial and business centre, with thousands of foremen, managers and clerks—the lieutenants of industry who direct its progress. They are paid for thinking and for skill to direct, and naturally such positions are coveted because they are well paid, well thought-of and carry some authority. To such positions Negro boys and girls may not aspire no matter what their qualifications. Even as teachers and ordinary clerks and stenographers they find almost no openings. Let us note some actual instances:

A young woman who graduated with credit from the Girls' Normal School in 1892, has taught in the kindergarten, acted as substitute, and waited in vain for a permanent position. Once she was allowed to substitute in a school with white teachers; the principal commended her work, but when the permanent appointment was made a white woman got it.

A girl who graduated from a Pennsylvania high school and from a business college sought work in the city as a stenographer and typewriter. A prominent lawyer undertook to find her a position; he went to friends and said, "Here is a girl that does excellent work and is of good character; can you not give her work?" Several immediately answered yes. "But," said the lawyer, "I will be perfectly frank with you and tell you she is colored"; and not in the whole city could he find a man willing to employ her. It happened, however, that the girl was so light in complexion that few not knowing would have suspected her descent. The lawyer therefore gave her temporary work in his own office until she found a position outside the city. "But," said he, "to this day I have not dared to tell my clerks that they worked beside a Negress." Another woman graduated from the high school and the Palmer College of Shorthand, but all over the city has met with nothing but refusal of work.

Several graduates in pharmacy have sought to get their three years required apprenticeship in the city and in only one case did one succeed, although they offered to work for nothing. One young pharmacist came from Massachusetts and for weeks sought in vain for work here at any price; "I wouldn't have a darky to clean out my store, much less to stand behind the counter," answered one druggist. A colored man answered an advertisement for a clerk in the suburbs. "What do you suppose we'd want of a nigger?" was the plain answer. A graduate of the University of Pennsylvania in mechanical engineering, well recommended, obtained work in the city, through an advertisement, on account of his excellent record. He worked a few hours and then was discharged because he was found to be colored. He is now a waiter at the University Club, where his white fellow graduates dine. Another young man attended Spring Garden Institute and studied drawing for lithography. He had good references from the institute and elsewhere, but application at the five largest establishments in the city could secure him no work. A telegraph operator has hunted in vain for an opening, and two graduates of the Central High School have sunk to menial labor. "What's the use of an education?" asked one. Mr. A—has elsewhere been employed as a traveling salesman. He applied for a position here by letter and was told he could have one. When they saw him they had no work for him.

Such cases could be multiplied indefinitely. But that is not necessary; one has but to note that, notwithstanding the acknowledged ability of many colored men, the Negro is conspicuously absent from all places of honor, trust or emolument, as well as from those of respectable grade in commerce and industry.

Even in the world of skilled labor the Negro is largely excluded. Many would explain the absence of Negroes from higher vocations by saying that while a few may now and then be found competent, the great mass are not fitted for that sort of work and are destined for some time to form a laboring class. In the matter of the trades, however, there can be raised no serious question of ability; for years the Negroes filled satisfactorily the trades of the city, and to-day in many parts of the South they are still prominent. And yet in Philadelphia a determined prejudice, aided by public opinion, has succeeded nearly in driving them from the field:

A---- who works at a bookbinding establishment on Front street, has learned to bind books and often does so for his friends. He is not allowed to work at the trade in the shop, however, but must remain a porter at a porter's wages.

B---- is a brushmaker; he has applied at several establishments, but they would not even examine his testimonials. They simply said: "We do not employ colored people."

C---- is a shoemaker; he tried to get work in some of the large department stores. They "had no place" for him.

D---- was a bricklayer, but experienced so much trouble in getting work that he is now a messenger.

E---- is a painter, but has found it impossible to get work because he is colored.

F---- is a telegraph line man, who formerly worked in Richmond, Va. When he applied here he was told that Negroes were not employed.

G---- is an iron puddler, who belonged to a Pittsburg union. Here he was not recognized as a uniou man and could not get work except as a stevedore.

H---- was a cooper, but could get no work after repeated trials, and is now a common laborer.

I---- is a candy-maker, but has never been able to find employment in the city; he is always told that the white help will not work with him.

J---- is a carpenter; he can only secure odd jobs or work where only Negroes are employed.

K---- was an upholsterer, but could get no work save in the few colored shops, which had workmen; he is now a waiter on a dining car.

L---- was a first-class baker; he applied for work some time ago near Green street and was told shortly, "We don't work no niggers here."

M---- is a good typesetter; he has not been allowed to join the union and has been refused work at eight different places in the city.

N---- is a printer by trade, but can only find work as a porter.

O---- is a sign-painter, but can get but little work.

P---- is a painter and gets considerable work, but never with white workmen.

Q---- is a good stationary engineer, but can find no employment; is at present a waiter in a private family.

R---- was born in Jamaica; he went to England and worked fifteen years in the Sir Edward Green Economizing Works in Wakefield, Yorkshire. During dull times he emigrated to America, bringing excellent references. He applied for a place as mechanic in nearly all the large iron working establishments in the city. A locomotive works assured him that his letters were all right, but that their men would not work with Negroes. At a manufactory of railway switches they told him they had no vacancy and he could call again; he called and finally was frankly told that they could not employ Negroes. He applied twice to a foundry company: they told him: "We have use for only one Negro—a porter," and refusing either further conversation or even to look at his letters showed him out. He then applied for work on a new building; the man told him he could leave an application, then added: "To tell the truth, it's no use, for we don't employ Negroes." Thus the man has searched for work two years and has not yet found a permanent position. He can only support his family by odd jobs as a common laborer.

S---- is a stone-cutter; he was refused work repeatedly on account of color. At last he got a job during a strike and was found to be so good a workman that his employer refused to dismiss him.

T---- was a boy, who, together with a white boy came to the city to hunt work. The colored boy was very light in complexion, and consequently both were taken in as apprentices at a large locomotive works; they worked there some months, but it was finally disclosed that the boy was colored; he was dismissed and the white boy retained.

These all seem typical and reliable cases. There are, of course, some exceptions to the general rule, but even these seem to confirm the fact that exclusion is a matter of prejudice and thoughtlessness which sometimes yields to determination and good sense. The most notable case in point is that of the Midvale Steel Works, where a large number of Negro workmen are regularly employed as mechanics and work alongside whites. If another foreman should take charge there, or if friction should arise, it would be easy for all this to receive a serious set-back, for ultimate success in such matters demands many experiments and a widespread public sympathy.

There are several cases where strong personal influence has secured colored boys positions; in one cabinet-making factory, a porter who had served the firm thirty years, asked to have his son learn the trade and work in the shop. The workmen objected strenuously at first, but the employer was firm and the young man has been at work there now seven years. The S. S. White Dental Company has a colored chemist who has worked up to his place and gives satisfaction. A jeweler allowed his colored fellow-soldier in the late war to learn the gold beaters' trade and work in his shop. A few other cases follow:

A----was intimately acquainted with a merchant and secured his son a position as a typewriter in the merchant's office.

B----, a stationary engineer, came with his employer from Washington and still works with him.

C----, a plasterer, learned his trade with a Finn in Virginia who especially recommended him to the firm where he now works.

D---- is a boy whose mother's friend got him work as cutter in a bag and rope factory; the hands objected but the friend's influence was strong enough to keep him there.

All these exceptions prove the rule, viz., that without strong effort and special influence it is next to impossible for a Negro in Philadelphia to get regular employment in most of the trades, except he work as an independent workman and take small transient jobs.

The chief agency that brings about this state of affairs is public opinion; if they were not intrenched, and strongly intrenched, back of an active prejudice or at least passive acquiescence in this effort to deprive Negroes of a decent livelihood, both trades unions and arbitrary bosses would be powerless to do the harm they now do; where, however, a large section of the public more or less openly applaud the stamina of a man who refuses to work with a "Nigger," the results are inevitable. The object of the trades union is purely business-like; it aims to restrict the labor market, just as the manufacturer aims to raise the price of his goods. Here is a chance to keep out of the market a vast number of workmen, and the unions seize the chance save in cases where they dare not as in the case of the cigar-makers and coal-miners. If they could keep out the foreign workmen in the same way they would; but here public opinion within and without their ranks forbids hostile action. Of course, most unions do not flatly declare their discriminations; a few plainly put the word "white" into their constitutions; most of them do not and will say that they consider each case on its merits. Then they quietly blackball the Negro applicant. Others delay and temporize and put off action until the Negro withdraws; still others discriminate against the Negro in initiation fees and dues, making a Negro pay $100, where the whites pay $25. On the other hand in times of strikes or other disturbances cordial invitations to join are often sent to Negro workmen.

At a time when women are engaged in bread-winning to a larger degree than ever before, the field open to Negro women is unusually narrow. This is, of course, due largely to the more intense prejudices of females on all subjects, and especially to the fact that women who work dislike to be in any way mistaken for menials, and they regard Negro women as menials *par excellence*.

A----, a dressmaker and seamstress of proven ability, sought work in the large department stores. They all commended her work, but could not employ her on account of her color.

B---- is a typewriter, but has applied at stores and offices in vain for work; "very sorry" they all say, but they can give her no work. She has answered many advertisements without result.

C---- has attended the Girls High School for two years, and has been unable to find any work; she is washing and sewing for a living now.

Of the Faith of the Fathers

D---- is a dressmaker and milliner, and does bead work. "Your work is very good," they say to her, "but if we hired you all of our ladies would leave."

E----, a seamstress, was given work from a store once, to do at home. It was commended as satisfactory, but they gave her no more.

F---- had two daughters who tried to get work as stenographers, but got only one small job.

G---- is a graduate of the Girls High School, with, excellent record; both teachers and influential friends have been seeking work for her but have not been able to find any.

H---- a girl, applied at seven stores for some work not menial; they had none.

I---- started at the Schuylkill, on Market street, and applied at almost every store nearly to the Delaware for work; she was only offered scrubbing.

2. So much for the difficulty of getting work. In addition to this the Negro is meeting difficulties in keeping the work he has, or at least the better part of it. Outside of all dissatisfaction with Negro work there are whims and fashions that affect his economic position; today general European travel has made the trained English servant popular and consequently well-shaven white men-servants, whether English or not, find it easy to replace Negro butlers and coachmen at higher wages. Again, though a man ordinarily does not dismiss all his white mill-hands because some turn out badly, yet it repeatedly happens that men dismiss all their colored servants and condemn their race because one or two in their employ have proven untrustworthy. Finally, the antipathies of lower classes are so great that it is often impracticable to mix races among the servants. A young colored girl went to work temporarily in Germantown; "I should like so much to keep you permanently," said the mistress, "but all my other servants are white." She was discharged. Usually now advertisements for help state whether white or Negro servants are wanted, and the Negro who applies at the wrong place must not be surprised to have the door slammed in his face.

The difficulties encountered by the Negro on account of sweeping conclusions made about him are manifold; a large building, for instance, has several poorly paid Negro janitors, without facilities for their work or guidance in its prosecution. Finally the building is thoroughly overhauled or rebuilt, elevators and electricity installed and a well paid set of white uniformed janitors put to work under a responsible salaried chief. Immediately the public concludes that the improvement in the service is due to the change of color. In some cases, of course, the change is due to a widening of the field of choice in selecting servants; for assuredly one cannot expect that one twenty-fifth of the population can furnish as many good workmen or as uniformly good ones as the other twenty-four twenty-fifths. One actual case illustrates this tendency to exclude the Negro without proper consideration from even menial employment:

A great church which has a number of members among the most respectable Negro families in the city has recently erected a large new building for its offices, etc., in the city. As the building was nearing completion a colored clergyman of that sect was surprised to hear that no Negroes were to be employed in the building; he thought that a peculiar stand for a Christian church to take and so he went to the manager of the building; the manager blandly assured him that the rumor was true; and that there was not the shadow of a chance for a Negro to get employment under him, except one woman to clean the water-closet. The reason for this, he said, was that the janitors and help were all to be uniformed and the whites would not wear uniforms with Negroes. The clergyman thereupon went to a prominent rnember of the church who was serving on the building committee; he denied that the committee had made any such decision, but sent him to another member of the committee; this member said the same thing and referred to the third, a blunt business man. The business man said: "That building is called the --------- Church House, but it is more than that, it is a business enterprise, to be run on business principles. We hired a man to run it so as to get the most out of it. We found such a man in the present manager, and put all power in his hands." He acknowledged then, that while the committee had made no decision, the question of hiring Negroes had come up and it was left solely to the manager's decision. The manager thought most Negroes were dishonest and untrustworthy, etc. And thus the Christian church joins hands with trades unions and a large public opinion to force Negroes into idleness and crime.

Sometimes Negroes, by special influence, as has been pointed out before, secure good positions; then there are other cases where colored men have by sheer merit and pluck secured positions. In all these cases, however, they are liable to lose their places through no fault of their own and primarily on account of their Negro blood. It may be that at first their Negro descent is not known, or other causes may operate; in all cases the Negro's tenure of office is insecure:

A---- worked in a large tailor's establishment on Third Street for three weeks. His work was acceptable. Then it became known he was colored and he was discharged as the other tailors refused to work with him.

B----, a pressman, was employed on Twelfth Street, but a week later was discharged when they knew he was colored; he then worked as a door-boy for five years, and finally got another job in a Jewish shop as pressman.

C---- was nine years a painter in Stewart's Furniture Factory, until Stewart failed four years ago. Has applied repeatedly, but could get no work on account of color. He now works as a night watchman on the streets for the city.

D---- was a stationary engineer; his employer died, and he has never been able to find another.

E---- was light in complexion and got a job as driver; he "kept his cap on," but when they found he was colored they discharged him.

F---- was one of many colored laborers at an ink factory. The heads of the firm died, and now whenever a Negro leaves a white man is put in his place.

G---- worked for a long time as a typesetter on Taggart's *Times*; when the paper changed hands he was discharged and has never been able to get another job; he is now a janitor.

H---- was a brickmason, but his employers finally refused to let him lay brick longer as his fellow workmen were all white; he is now a waiter.

L---- learned the trade of range-setting from his employer; the employer then refused him work and he went into business for himself; he has taught four apprentices.

M---- is a woman whose husband was janitor for a firm twenty years; when they moved to the new Betz Building they discharged him as all the janitors there were white; after his death they could find no work for his boy.

N---- was a porter in a book store and rose to be head postmaster of a sub-station in Philadelphia which handles $250,000, it is said, a year; he was also at the head of a very efficient Bureau of Information in a large department store. Recently attempts have been made to displace him for no specified fault but because "we want his place for another [white] man."

O---- is a well-known instance; an observer in 1898 wrote: "If any Philadelphian who is anxious to study the matter with his own eyes, will walk along South Eleventh Street, from Chestnut down, and will note the most tasteful and enterprising stationery and periodical store along the way, it will pay him to enter it. On entering he will, according to his way of thinking, be pleased or grieved to see that it is conducted by Negroes. If the proprietor happens to be in he may know that this keen-looking pleasant young man was once assistant business manager of a large white religious newspaper in the city. A change of management led to his dismissal. No fault was found, his work was commended, but a white man was put into his place, and profuse apologies made.

"The clerk behind the counter is his sister; a neat lady-like woman, educated, and trained in stenography and typewriting. She could not find in the city of Philadelphia, any one who had the slightest use for such a colored woman.

"The result of this situation is this little store, which is remarkably successful. The proprietor owns the stock, the store and the building. This is one tale of its sort with a pleasant ending. Other tales are far less pleasing."

Much discouragement results from the persistent refusal to promote a colored employee. The humblest white employee knows that the better he does his work the more chance there is for him to rise in the business. The black employee knows that the better he does his work the longer he may do it; he cannot often hope for promotion. This makes much of the criticism aimed against Negroes, because some of them want to refuse menial labor, lose something of its point. If the better class of Negro boys could look on such labor as a stepping-stone to something higher it would be different; if they must view it as a lifework we cannot wonder at their hesitation:

A---- has been a porter at a great locomotive works for ten years. He is a carpenter by trade and has picked up considerable knowledge of machinery; he was formerly allowed to work a little as a machinist; now that is stopped and he has never been promoted and probably never will be.

B---- has worked in a shop eight years and never been promoted from his porter's position, although he is a capable man.

C---- is a porter; he has been in a hardware store six years; he is bright and has repeatedly been promised advancement but has never got it.

D---- was for seven years in a gang of porters in a department store, and part of the time acted as foreman. He had a white boy under him who disliked him; eventually the boy was promoted but he remained a porter. Finally the boy became his boss and discharged him.

E----, a woman, worked long in a family of lawyers; a white lad went into their office as office-boy and came to be a member of the firm; she had a smart, ambitious son and asked for any sort of office work for him—anything in which he could hope for promotion. "Why don't you make him a waiter ?" they asked.

F---- has for twenty-one years driven for a lumber firm; speaks German and is very useful to them, but they have never promoted him.

G---- was a porter; he begged for a chance to work up; offering to do clerical work for nothing, but was refused. White companions were repeatedly promoted over his head. He has been a porter seventeen years.

H---- was a servant in the family of one of the members of a large dry goods firm; he was so capable that the employer sent him down to the store for a place which the manager very reluctantly gave him. He rose to be registering clerk in the delivering department where he worked fourteen years and his work was commended. Recently without notice or complaint he was changed to run an elevator at the same wages. He thinks that pressure from other members of the firm made him lose his work.

Once in a while there are exceptions to this rule. The Pennsylvania Railroad has promoted one bright and persistent porter to a clerkship, which he has held for years. He had, however, spent his life hunting chances for promotion and had been told "You have ability enough, George, if you were not colored...."

There is much discrimination against Negroes in wages.

The Negroes have fewer chances for work, have been used to low wages, and consequently the first thought that occurs to the average employer is to give a Negro less than he would offer a white man for the same work. This is not universal, but it is widespread. In domestic service of the ordinary sort there is no difference, because the wages are a matter of custom. When it comes to waiters, butlers and coachmen, however, there is considerable difference made; while white coachmen receive from $50-$75, the Negroes do not get usually more than $30-$60. Negro hotel waiters get from $18-$20, while whites receive $20-$30. Naturally when a hotel manager replaces $20 men with $30 men he may expect, outside any question of color, better service.

In ordinary work the competition forces down the wages outside mere race reasons, though the Negro is the greatest sufferer; this is especially the case in laundry work. "I've counted as high as seven dozen pieces in that washing," said a weary black woman," and she pays me only $1.25 a week for it." Persons who throw away $5 a week on gew-gaws will often haggle over twenty-five cents with a washerwoman. There are, however, notable exceptions to these cases, where good wages are paid to persons who have long worked for the same family.

Very often if a Negro is given a chance to work at a trade his wages are cut down for the privilege. This gives the workingman's prejudice additional intensity:

A---- got a job formerly held by a white porter; the wages were reduced from $12 to $8.

B---- worked for a firm as china packer, and they said he was the best packer they had. He, however, received but $6 a week while the white packers received $12.

C---- has been porter and assistant shipping clerk in an Arch Street store for five years. He receives $6 a week and whites get $8 for the same work.

D---- is a stationary engineer; he learned his trade with this firm and has been with them ten years. Formerly he received $9 a week, now $10.50; whites get $12 for the same work.

E---- is a stationary engineer and has been in his place three years. He receives but $9 a week.

F---- works with several other Negroes with a firm of electrical engineers. The white laborers receive $2 a day: "We've got to be glad to get $1.75."

G---- was a carpenter, but could get neither sufficient work nor satisfactory wages. For a job on which he received $15 a week, his white successor got $18.

H---- , a cementer, receives $1.75 a day; white workmen get $2-$3. He has been promised more next fall.

I----, a plasterer, has worked for one boss twenty-seven years. Regular plasterers get $4 or more a day; he does the same work, but cannot join the union and is paid as a laborer--$2.50 a day.

J---- works as a porter in a department store; is married, and receives $8 a week. "They pay the same to white unmarried shop girls, who stand a chance to be promoted."

3. If a Negro enters some line of employment in which people are not used to seeing him, he suffers from an assumption that he is unfit for the work. It is reported that a Chestnut Street firm once took a Negro shop girl, but the protests of their customers were such that they had to dismiss her. A great many merchants hesitate to advance Negroes lest they should lose custom. Negro merchants who have attempted to start business in the city at first encounter much difficulty from this prejudice:

A---- has a bakery; white people sometimes enter and finding Negroes in charge abruptly leave.

B---- is a baker and had a shop some years on Vine Street, but prejudice against him barred him from gaining much custom.

C---- is a successful expressman with a large business; he is sometimes told by persons that they prefer to patronize white expressmen.

D---- is a woman and keeps a hair store on South street. Customers sometimes enter, look at her, and leave.

E---- is a music teacher on Lombard Street. Several white people have entered and seeing him, said: "Oh! I thought you were white—excuse me! " or "I'll call again!"

Even among the colored people themselves some prejudice of this sort is met. Once a Negro physician could not get the patronage of Negroes because they were not used to the innovation. Now they have a large part of the Negro patronage. The Negro merchant, however, still lacks the full confidence of his own people though this is slowly growing. It is one of the paradoxes of this question to see a people so discriminated against sometimes add to their misfortunes by discriminating against themselves. They themselves, however, are beginning to recognize this.

4. The chief discrimination against Negroes in expenditure is in the matter of rents. There can be no reasonable doubt but that Negroes pay excessive rents:

A---- paid $13 a month where the preceding white family had paid $10.

B---- paid $I6; "heard that former white family paid $12."

C---- paid $25; "heard that former white family paid $20."

D---- paid $12; neighbors say that former white family paid $9.

E---- paid $25, instead of $18.

F---- paid $12, instead of $10.

G---- the Negro inhabitants of the whole street pay $12 to $14 and the whites $9 and $10. The houses are all alike.

H---- whites on this street pay $15-$18; Negroes pay $18-$21.

Not only is there this pretty general discrimination in rent, but agents and owners will not usually repair the houses of the blacks willingly or improve them. In addition to this, agents and owners in many sections utterly refuse to rent to Negroes on any terms. Both these sorts of discrimination are easily defended from a merely business point of view; public opinion in the city is such that the presence of even a respectable colored family in a block will affect its value for renting or sale; increased rent to Negroes is therefore a sort of insurance, and refusal to rent a device for money-getting. The indefensible cruelty lies with those classes who refuse to recognize the right of respectable Negro citizens to respectable houses. Real estate agents also increase prejudice by refusing to discriminate between different classes of Negroes. A quiet Negro family moves into a street. The agent finds no great objection, and allows the next empty house to go to any Negro who applies. This family may disgrace and scandalize the neighborhood and make it harder for decent families to find homes.

In the last fifteen years, however, public opinion has so greatly changed in this matter that we may expect much in the future. Today the Negro population is more widely scattered over the city than ever before. At the same time it remains true that as a rule they must occupy the worst houses of the districts where they live. The advance made has been a battle for the better class of Negroes. An ex-Minister to Hayti moved to the northwestern part of the city and his white neighbors insulted him, barricaded their steps against him, and tried in every way to make him move; today he is honored and respected in the whole neighborhood. Many such cases have occurred; in others the result was different. An estimable young Negro, just married, moved with his bride into a little street. The neighborhood rose in arms and besieged the tenant and the landlord so relentlessly that the landlord leased the house and compelled the young couple to move within a month. One of the bishops of the A. M. E. Church recently moved into the newly purchased Episcopal residence on Belmont Avenue, and his neighbors have barricaded their porches against his view.

5. The chief discrimination against Negro children is in the matter of educational facilities. Prejudice here works to compel colored children to attend certain schools where most Negro children go, or to keep them out of private and higher schools.

A---- tried to get her little girl into the kindergarten nearest to her, at Fifteenth and Locust. The teachers wanted her to send it down across Broad to the kindergarten chiefly attended by colored children and much further away from its home. This journey was dangerous for the child, but the teachers refused to receive it for six months, until the authorities were appealed to.

In transfers from schools Negroes have difficulty in getting convenient accommodations; only within comparatively few years have Negroes been allowed to complete the course at the High and Normal Schools without difficulty. Earlier than that the University of Pennsylvania refused to let Negroes sit in the Auditorium and listen to lectures, much less to be students. Within two or three years a Negro student had to fight his way through a city dental school with his fists, and was treated with every indignity. Several times Negroes have been asked to leave schools of stenography, etc., on account of their fellow students. In 1893 a colored woman applied at Temple College, a church institution, for admission and was refused and advised to go elsewhere. The college then offered scholarships to churches, but would not admit applicants from colored churches. Two years later the same woman applied again. The faculty declared that they did not object, but that the students would; she persisted and was finally admitted with evident reluctance.

It goes without saying that most private schools, music schools, etc., will not admit Negroes and in some cases have insulted applicants.

Such is the tangible form of Negro prejudice in Philadelphia. Possibly some of the particular cases cited can be proven to have had extenuating circumstances unknown to the investigator; at the same time many not cited would be just as much in point. At any rate, no one who has with any diligence studied the situation of the Negro in the city can long doubt but that his opportunities are limited and his ambition circumscribed about as has been shown. There are of course numerous exceptions, but the mass of the Negroes have been so often refused openings and discouraged in efforts to better their condition that many of them say, as one said, "I never apply—I know it is useless." Beside these tangible and measurable forms there are deeper and less easily described results of the attitude of the white population toward the Negroes: a certain manifestation of a real or assumed aversion, a spirit of ridicule or patronage, a vindictive hatred in some, absolute indifference in others; all this of course does not make much difference to the mass of the race, but it deeply wounds the better classes, the very classes who are attaining to that to which we wish the mass to attain. Notwithstanding all this, most Negroes would patiently await the effect of time and commonsense on such prejudice did it not today touch them in matters of life and death; threaten their homes, their food, their children, their hopes. And the result of this is bound to be increased crime, inefficiency and bitterness.

It would, of course, be idle to assert that most of the Negro crime was caused by prejudice; the violent economic and social changes which the last fifty years have brought to the American Negro, the sad social history that preceded these changes, have all contributed to unsettle morals and pervert talents. Nevertheless it is certain that Negro prejudice in cities like Philadelphia has been a vast factor in aiding and abetting all other causes which impel a half-developed race to recklessness and excess. Certainly a great amount of crime can be without doubt traced to the discrimination against Negro boys and girls in the matter of employment. Or to put it differently, Negro prejudice costs the city something.

The connection of crime and prejudice is, on the other hand, neither simple nor direct. The boy who is refused promotion in his job as porter does not go out and snatch somebody's pocketbook. Conversely the loafers at Twelfth and Kater streets, and the thugs in the county prison are not usually graduates of high schools who have been refused work. The connections are much more subtle and dangerous; it is the atmosphere of rebellion and discontent that unrewarded merit and reasonable but unsatisfied ambition make. The social environment of excuse, listless despair, careless indulgence and lack of inspiration to work is the growing force that turns black boys and girls into gamblers, prostitutes and rascals. And this social environment has been built up slowly out of the disappointments of deserving men and the sloth of the unawakened. How long can a city say to a part of its citizens, "It is useless to work; it is fruitless to deserve well of men; education will gain you nothing but disappointment and humiliation?" How long can a city teach its black children that the road to success is to have a white face? How long can a city do this and escape the inevitable penalty?

For thirty years and more Philadelphia has said to its black children: "Honesty, efficiency and talent have little to do with your success; if you work hard spend little and are good you may earn your bread and butter at those sorts of work which we frankly confess we despise; if you are dishonest and lazy, the State will furnish your bread free." Thus the class of Negroes which the prejudices of the city have distinctly encouraged is that of the criminal, the lazy and the shiftless; for them the city teems with institutions and charities; for them there is succor and sympathy; for them Philadelphians are thinking and planning; but for the educated and industrious young colored man who wants work and not platitudes, wages and not alms, just rewards and not sermons—for such colored men Philadelphia apparently has no use.

What then do such men do? What becomes of the graduates of the many schools of the city? The answer is simple: most of those who amount to anything leave the city, the others take what they can get for a livelihood. Let us for a moment glance at the statistics of three colored schools:

1. The O. V. Catto Primary School.
2. The Robert Vaux Grammar School.
3. The Institute for Colored Youth.

There attended the Catto school, 1867–97, 5915 pupils. Of these there were promoted from the full course, 653. 129 of the latter are known to be in positions of higher grade; or taking out 93 who are still in school, there remain 36 as follows: 18 teachers, 10 clerks, 2 physicians, 2 engravers, 2 printers, 1 lawyer and 1 mechanic.

The other 524 are for the most part in service, laborers and housewives. Of the 36 more successful ones fully half are at work outside of the city.

Of the Vaux school there were, 1877–89, 76 graduates. Of these there are 16 unaccounted for; the rest are:

Teachers	27	Barbers	4
Musicians	5	Clerks	3

Merchants	3	Physicians	1
Mechanic	1	Deceased	8
Clergymen	3	Housewives	5
			47

From one-half to two-thirds of these have been compelled to leave the city in order to find work; one, the artist, Tanner, whom France recently honored, could not in his native land much less in his native city find room for his talents. He taught school in Georgia in order to earn money enough to go abroad.

The Institute of Colored Youth has had 340 graduates, 1856–97; 57 of these are dead. Of the 283 remaining 91 are unaccounted for. The rest are:

Teachers	117	Electrical Engineer	1
Lawyers	4	Professor	1
Physicians	4	Government clerks	5
Musicians	4	Merchants	7
Dentists	2	Mechanics	5
Clergymen	2	Clerks	23
Nurses	2	Teacher of cooking	1
Editor	1	Dressmakers	4
Civil Engineer	1	Students	7
			192

Here, again, nearly three-fourths of the graduates who have amounted to anything have had to leave the city for work. The civil engineer, for instance, tried in vain to get work here and finally had to go to New Jersey to teach.

There have been 9, possibly 11, colored graduates of the Central High School. These are engaged as follows:

Grocer	1	Porter	1
Clerks in service of city	2	Butler	1
Caterer	1	Unknown	3 or 5

It is high time that the best conscience of Philadelphia awakened to her duty; her Negro citizens are here to remain; they can be made good citizens or burdens to the community; if we want them to be sources of wealth and power and not of poverty and weakness then they must be given employment according to their ability and encouraged to train that ability and increase their talents by the hope of reasonable reward. To educate boys and girls and then refuse them work is to train loafers and rogues.[10]

From another point of view it could be argued with much cogency that the cause of economic stress, and consequently of crime, was the recent inconsiderate rush of Negroes into cities; and that the unpleasant results of this migration, while deplorable, will nevertheless serve to check the movement of Negroes to cities and keep them in the country where their chance for economic development is widest. This argument loses much of its point from the fact that it is the better class of educated Philadelphia-born Negroes who have the most difficulty in obtaining employment. The new immigrant fresh from the South is much more apt to obtain work suitable for him than the black boy born here and trained in efficiency. Nevertheless it is undoubtedly true that the recent migration has both directly and indirectly increased crime and competition. How is this movement to be checked? Much can be done by correcting misrepresentations as to the opportunities of city life made by designing employment bureaus aud thoughtless persons; a more strict surveillance of criminals might prevent the influx of undesirable elements. Such efforts, however, would not touch the main stream of immigration. Back of that stream is the world-wide desire to rise in the world, to escape the choking narrowness of the plantation, and the lawless repression of the village, in the South. It is a search for better opportunities of living, and as such it must be discouraged and repressed with great care and delicacy, if at all. The real movement of reform is the raising of economic standards and increase of economic opportunity in the South. Mere land and climate without law and order, capital and skill, will not develop a country. When Negroes in the South have a larger opportunity to work, accumulate property, be protected in life and limb, and encourage pride and self-respect in their children, there will be a diminution in the stream of immigrants to Northern cities. At the same time if those cities practice industrial exclusion against these immigrants to such an extent that they are forced to become paupers, loafers and criminals, they can scarcely complain of conditions in the South. Northern cities should not, of course, seek to encourage and invite a poor quality of labor, with low standards of life and morals. The standards of wages and respectability should be kept up; but when a man reaches those standards in skill, efficiency and decency no question of color should, in a civilized community, debar him from an equal chance with his peers in earning a living.

"Funeral of nineteen year old Negro sawmill worker in Heard County, Georgia." Photograph by Jack Delano, 1941. Courtesy of the Library of Congress.

"I Hope My Mother Will be There, " included in *Religious Folk Songs of the Negro as Sung on the Plantations* (Hampton, Virginia: The Institute Press, 1909), p. 46.

XI

Of the Passing of the First-Born

O sister, sister, thy first-begotten,
The hands that cling and the feet that follow,
The voice of the child's blood crying yet,
Who hath remembered me? who hath forgotten?
Thou hast forgotten, O summer swallow,
But the world shall end when I forget.

Swinburne.[1]

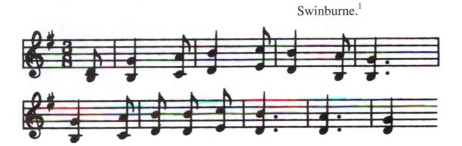

"Unto you a child is born," sang the bit of yellow paper that fluttered into my room one brown October morning.[2] Then the fear of fatherhood mingled wildly with the joy of creation; I wondered how it looked and how it felt,—what were its eyes, and how its hair curled and crumpled itself.[3] And I thought in awe of her,—she who had slept with Death to tear a man-child from underneath her heart, while I was unconsciously wandering. I fled to my wife and child, repeating the while to myself half-wonderingly, "Wife and child? Wife and child?"—fled fast and faster than boat and steam-car, and yet must ever impatiently await them; away from the hard-voiced city, away from the flickering sea into my own Berkshire Hills that sit all sadly guarding the gates of Massachusetts.

---

[1] The poem included by Du Bois is from the final stanza of the English poet Algernon Charles Swinburne's (1837–1909) *Itylus* (1866).

[2] Du Bois begins this chapter by rewriting *Isaiah* 9:6, which prophesizes the birth of Christ saying: "For unto us a child is born." The quote from Isaiah becomes one of the most important lyrics in the German composer George Frederic Handel's (1685–1759) oratorio *The Messiah*.

[3] Burghardt Gomer Du Bois was born in 1897. He died of dysentery on May 24, 1899, and was buried in Great Barrington, Massachusetts.

Du Bois's wife Nina Gomer Du Bois with their son Burghardt, who died as an infant in Atlanta, Georgia, from dysentery. Courtesy of Special Collections and Archives, W. E. B. DuBois Library, University of Massachusetts at Amherst.

Up the stairs I ran to the wan mother and whimpering babe, to the sanctuary on whose altar a life at my bidding had offered itself to win a life, and won. What is this tiny formless thing, this newborn wail from an unknown world,—all head and voice? I handle it curiously, and watch perplexed its winking, breathing, and sneezing. I did not love it then; it seemed a ludicrous thing to love; but her I loved, my girl-mother, she whom now I saw unfolding like the glory of the morning—the transfigured woman. Through her I came to love the wee thing, as it grew strong; as its little soul unfolded itself in twitter and cry and half-formed word, and as its eyes caught the gleam and flash of life. How beautiful he was, with his olive-tinted flesh and dark gold ringlets, his eyes of mingled blue and brown, his perfect little limbs, and the soft voluptuous roll which the blood of Africa had moulded into his features! I held him in my arms, after we had sped far away to our Southern home,—held him, and glanced at the hot red soil of Georgia and the breathless city of a hundred hills, and felt a vague unrest. Why was his hair tinted with gold? An evil omen was golden hair in my life. Why had not the brown of his eyes crushed out and killed the blue?—for brown were his father's eyes, and his father's father's. And thus in the Land of the Color-line I saw, as it fell across my baby, the shadow of the Veil.

Within the Veil was he born, said I; and there within shall he live,—a Negro and a Negro's son. Holding in that little head—ah, bitterly!—the unbowed pride of a hunted race, clinging with that tiny dimpled hand—ah, wearily!—to a hope not hopeless but unhopeful, and seeing with those bright wondering eyes that peer into my soul a land whose freedom is to us a mockery and whose liberty a lie. I saw the shadow of the Veil as it passed over my baby, I saw the cold city towering above the blood-red land. I held my face beside his little cheek, showed him the star-children and the twinkling lights as they began to flash, and stilled with an even-song the unvoiced terror of my life.

So sturdy and masterful he grew, so filled with bubbling life, so tremulous with the unspoken wisdom of a life but eighteen months distant from the All-life,—we were not far from worshipping this revelation of the divine, my wife and I. Her own life builded and moulded itself upon the child; he tinged her every dream and idealized her every effort. No hands but hers must touch and garnish those little limbs; no dress or frill must touch them that had not wearied her fingers; no voice but hers could coax him off to Dreamland, and she and he together spoke some soft and unknown tongue and in it held communion. I too mused above his little white bed; saw the strength of my own arm stretched onward through the ages through the newer strength of his; saw the dream of my black fathers stagger a step onward in the wild phantasm of the world; heard in his baby voice the voice of the Prophet that was to rise within the Veil.

And so we dreamed and loved and planned by fall and winter, and the full flush of the long Southern spring, till the hot winds rolled from the fetid Gulf, till the roses shivered and the still stern sun quivered its awful light over the hills of Atlanta. And then one night the little feet pattered wearily to the wee white bed, and the tiny hands trembled; and a warm flushed face tossed on the pillow, and we knew baby was sick. Ten days he lay there,—a swift week and three endless days, wasting, wasting away. Cheerily the mother nursed him the first days, and laughed into the little eyes that smiled again. Tenderly then she hovered round him, till the smile fled away and Fear crouched beside the little bed.

Then the day ended not, and night was a dreamless terror, and joy and sleep slipped away. I hear now that Voice at midnight calling me from dull and dreamless trance,—crying, "The Shadow of Death! The Shadow of Death!" Out into the starlight I crept, to rouse the gray physician,—the Shadow of Death, the Shadow of Death. The hours trembled on; the night listened; the ghastly dawn glided like a tired thing across the lamplight. Then we two alone looked upon the child as he turned toward us with great eyes, and stretched his string-like hands,— the Shadow of Death! And we spoke no word, and turned away.

He died at eventide, when the sun lay like a brooding sorrow above the western hills, veiling its face; when the winds spoke not, and the trees, the great green trees he loved, stood motionless. I saw his breath beat quicker and quicker, pause, and then his little soul leapt like a star that travels in the night and left a world of darkness in its train. The day changed not; the same tall trees peeped in at the windows, the same green grass glinted in the setting sun. Only in the chamber of death writhed the world's most piteous thing—a childless mother.

I shirk not. I long for work. I pant for a life full of striving. I am no coward, to shrink before the rugged rush of the storm, nor even quail before the awful shadow of the Veil. But hearken, O Death! Is not this my life hard enough,—is not that dull land that stretches its sneering web about me cold enough,--is not all the world beyond these four little walls pitiless enough, but that thou must needs enter here,—thou, O Death? About my head the thundering storm beat like a heartless voice, and the crazy forest pulsed with the curses of the weak; but what cared I, within my home beside my wife and baby boy? Wast thou so jealous of one little coign of happiness that thou must needs enter there,—thou, O Death?

A perfect life was his, all joy and love, with tears to make it brighter,—sweet as a summer's day beside the Housatonic. The world loved him; the women kissed his curls, the men looked gravely into his wonderful eyes, and the children hovered and fluttered about him. I can see him now, changing like the sky from sparkling laughter to darkening frowns, and then to wondering thoughtfulness as he watched the world. He knew no color-line, poor dear,—and the Veil, though it shadowed him, had not yet darkened half his sun. He loved the white matron, he loved his black nurse; and in his little world walked souls alone, uncolored and unclothed. I—yea, all men—are larger and purer by the infinite breadth of that one little life. She who in simple clearness of vision sees beyond the stars said when he had flown, "He will be happy There; he ever loved beautiful things." And I, far more ignorant, and blind by the web of mine own weaving, sit alone winding words and muttering, "If still he be, and he be There, and there be a There, let him be happy, O Fate!"

Blithe was the morning of his burial, with bird and song and sweet-smelling flowers. The trees whispered to the grass, but the children sat with hushed faces. And yet it seemed a ghostly unreal day,—the wraith of Life. We seemed to rumble down an unknown street behind a little white bundle of posies, with the shadow of a song in our ears. The busy city dinned about us; they did not say much, those pale-faced hurrying men and women; they did not say much,—they only glanced and said, "Niggers!"

"African American Children on Porch in Georgia." Photograph included in the Exhibit of the American Negroes at the 1900 Paris Exposition. Courtesy of the Library of Congress.

We could not lay him in the ground there in Georgia, for the earth there is strangely red; so we bore him away to the northward, with his flowers and his little folded hands. In vain, in vain!—for where, O God! beneath thy broad blue sky shall my dark baby rest in peace,—where Reverence dwells, and Goodness, and a Freedom that is free?

All that day and all that night there sat an awful gladness in my heart,—nay, blame me not if I see the world thus darkly through the Veil,—and my soul whispers ever to me, saying, "Not dead, not dead, but escaped; not bond, but free." No bitter meanness now shall sicken his baby heart till it die a living death, no taunt shall madden his happy boyhood. Fool that I was to think or wish that this little soul should grow choked and deformed within the Veil! I might have known that yonder deep unworldly look that ever and anon floated past his eyes was peering far beyond this narrow Now. In the poise of his little curl-crowned head did there not sit all that wild pride of being which his father had hardly crushed in his own heart? For what, forsooth, shall a Negro want with pride amid the studied humiliations of fifty million fellows? Well sped, my boy, before the world had dubbed your ambition insolence, had held your ideals unattainable, and taught you to cringe and bow. Better far this nameless void that stops my life than a sea of sorrow for you.

Idle words; he might have borne his burden more bravely than we,—aye, and found it lighter too, some day; for surely, surely this is not the end. Surely there shall yet dawn some mighty morning to lift the Veil and set the prisoned free. Not for me,—I shall die in my bonds,—but for fresh young souls who have not known the night and waken to the morning; a morning when men ask of the workman, not "Is he white?" but "Can he work?" When men ask artists, not "Are they black?" but "Do they know?" Some morning this may be, long, long years to come. But now there wails, on that dark shore within the Veil, the same deep voice, *Thou shalt forego!* And all have I foregone at that command, and with small complaint,—all save that fair young form that lies so coldly wed with death in the nest I had builded.

If one must have gone, why not I? Why may I not rest me from this restlessness and sleep from this wide waking? Was not the world's alembic, Time, in his young hands, and is not my time waning? Are there so many workers in the vineyard that the fair promise of this little body could lightly be tossed away? The wretched of my race that line the alleys of the nation sit fatherless and unmothered; but Love sat beside his cradle, and in his ear Wisdom waited to speak. Perhaps now he knows the All-love, and needs not to be wise. Sleep, then, child,—sleep till I sleep and waken to a baby voice and the ceaseless patter of little feet—above the Veil.

Document Number 12, Chapter XI

Du Bois's *Credo* originally appeared in *The Independent*, Vol. 57, October 6, 1904, p. 787. It is a remarkable statement that speaks for itself. According to David Levering Lewis, the document was read differently by different audiences. For mainstream whites the text suggested that Du Bois "was not a rash and godless intellectual, but a committed exponent of Judeo-Christian harmony and justice. Perceptive readers heard in its words "a staccato modeled on Zola's J'accuse, distinct sounds of white supremacy crumbling. A good many black people heard the thunder of avenging racial parity."[4] The *Credo* was eventually included in Du Bois's 1920 work *Darkwater*. According to Lewis, it was an inspiration to blacks in the 1920s—frequently hung in a prominent place in many African-American homes—in much the same way that Martin Luther King's "I Have a Dream" speech was an inspiration to African-Americans during the 1960s and 1970s.[5]

*   *   *

Credo[6]

I BELIEVE in God who made of one blood all races that dwell on earth. I believe that all men, black and brown and white, are brothers, varying, through Time and Opportunity, in form and gift and feature, but differing in no essential particular, and alike in soul and in the possibility of infinite development. Especially do I believe in the Negro Race; in the beauty of its genius, the sweetness of its soul, and its strength in that meekness which shall yet inherit this turbulent earth.

I believe in pride of race and lineage and self; in pride of self so deep as to scorn injustice to other selves; in pride of lineage so great as to despise no man's father; in pride of race so chivalrous as neither to offer bastardy to the weak nor beg wedlock of the strong, knowing that men may be brothers in Christ, even tho they be not brothers-in-law.

I believe in Service—humble reverent service, from the blackening of boots to the whitening of souls; for Work is Heaven, Idleness Hell, and Wage is the "Well done!" of the Master who summoned all them that labor and are heavy laden, making no distinction between the black sweating cotton-hands of Georgia and the First Families of Virginia, since all distinction not based on deed is devilish and not divine.

---

[4] David Levering Lewis, *W. E. B. Du Bois: Biography of a Race* (New York: Henry Holt and Company, 1993), p. 312.

[5] Ibid.

[6] Source: W. E. B. Du Bois, "Credo," *The Independent*, Vol. 57, October 1904, p. 787.

I believe in the Devil and his angels, who wantonly work to narrow the opportunity of struggling human beings, especially if they be black; who spit in the faces of the fallen, strike them that cannot strike again, believe the worst and work to prove it, hating the image which their Maker stamped on a brother's soul.

I believe in the Prince of Peace. I believe that War is Murder. I believe that armies and navies are at bottom the tinsel and braggadocio of oppression and wrong; and I believe that the wicked conquest of weaker and darker nations by nations whiter and stronger but foreshadows the death of that strength.

I believe in Liberty for all men; the space to stretch their arms and their souls; the right to breathe and the right to vote, the freedom to choose their friends, enjoy the sunshine and ride on the railroads, uncursed by color; thinking, dreaming, working as they will in a kingdom of God and love.

I believe in the training of children black even as white; the leading out of little souls into the green pastures and beside the still waters, not for pelf or peace, but for Life lit by some large vision of beauty and goodness and truth; lest we forget, and the sons of the fathers, like Esau, for mere meat barter their birthright in a mighty nation.

Finally, I believe in Patience—patience with the weakness of the Weak and the strength of the Strong, the prejudice of the Ignorant and the ignorance of the Blind; patience with the tardy triumph of Joy and the mad chastening of Sorrow —patience with God.

ATLANTA UNIVERSITY, ATLANTA, GA.

Portrait of Alexander Crumell, from William J. Simmons, *Men of Mark: Eminent, Progressive and Rising* (Cleveland, Ohio: Geo. M. Rewell, 1887), p. 530.

"Swing Low Sweet Chariot, " included in J. B. T. Marsh, *The Story of the Jubilee Singers* (Cleveland, Ohio: The Cleveland Printing and Publishing Company, 1892), p. 160.

XII

Of Alexander Crummell

Then from the Dawn it seemed there came, but faint
As from beyond the limit of the world,
Like the last echo born of a great cry,
Sounds, as if some fair city were one voice
Around a king returning from his wars.

Tennyson.[1]

This is the history of a human heart,—the tale of a black boy who many long years ago began to struggle with life that he might know the world and know himself. Three temptations he met on those dark dunes that lay gray and dismal before the wonder-eyes of the child: the temptation of Hate, that stood out against the red dawn; the temptation of Despair, that darkened noonday; and the temptation of Doubt, that ever steals along with twilight. Above all, you must hear of the vales he crossed,—the Valley of Humiliation and the Valley of the Shadow of Death.

I saw Alexander Crummell first at a Wilberforce commencement season, amid its bustle and crush. Tall, frail, and black, he stood, with simple dignity and an un-mistakable air of good breeding. I talked with him apart, where the storming of the lusty young orators could not harm us. I spoke to him politely, then curiously, then eagerly, as I began to feel the fineness of his character,—his calm courtesy, the sweetness of his strength, and his fair blending of the hope and truth of life. Instinctively I bowed before this man, as one bows before the prophets of the world.

---

[1] The verse is from Alfred Lord Tennyson's poem "The Passing of Arthur" included in his 1869 work *The Idylls of the King.*

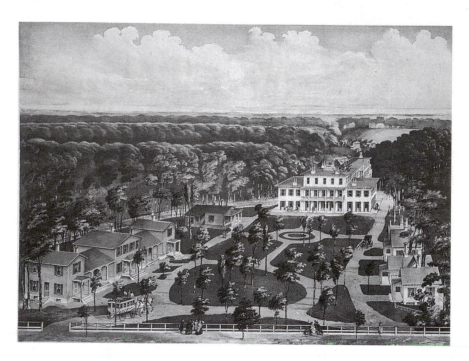

Wilberforce University, Xenia, Ohio. Drawn, lithographed and printed in oil colors by Middleton Wallace & Co., c. 1860. Courtesy of the Library of Congress.

Some seer he seemed, that came not from the crimson Past or the gray To-come, but from the pulsing Now,—that mocking world which seemed to me at once so light and dark, so splendid and sordid. Four-score years had he wandered in this same world of mine, within the Veil.

He was born with the Missouri Compromise[2] and lay a-dying amid the echoes of Manila[3] and El Caney: stirring times for living, times dark to look back upon, darker to look forward to. The black-faced lad that paused over his mud and marbles seventy years ago saw puzzling vistas as he looked down the world. The slave-ship still groaned across the Atlantic, faint cries burdened the Southern breeze, and the great black father whispered mad tales of cruelty into those young ears. From the low doorway the mother silently watched her boy at play, and at nightfall sought him eagerly lest the shadows bear him away to the land of slaves.

---

[2] The compromise passed by Congress in 1820 that admitted Missouri into the Union as a slave state together with Maine as a free state.
[3] Sites of American victories during the Spanish American War.

So his young mind worked and winced and shaped curiously a vision of Life; and in the midst of that vision ever stood one dark figure alone,—ever with the hard, thick countenance of that bitter father, and a form that fell in vast and shapeless folds. Thus the temptation of Hate grew and shadowed the growing child,—gliding stealthily into his laughter, fading into his play, and seizing his dreams by day and night with rough, rude turbulence. So the black boy asked of sky and sun and flower the never-answered Why? and loved, as he grew, neither the world nor the world's rough ways.

Strange temptation for a child, you may think; and yet in this wide land today a thousand thousand dark children brood before this same temptation, and feel its cold and shuddering arms. For them, perhaps, some one will some day lift the Veil,—will come tenderly and cheerily into those sad little lives and brush the brooding hate away, just as Beriah Green strode in upon the life of Alexander Crummell. And before the bluff, kind-hearted man the shadow seemed less dark. Beriah Green had a school in Oneida County, New York, with a score of mischievous boys. "I'm going to bring a black boy here to educate," said Beriah Green, as only a crank and an abolitionist would have dared to say. "Oho!" laughed the boys. "Ye-es," said his wife; and Alexander came. Once before, the black boy had sought a school, had travelled, cold and hungry, four hundred miles up into free New Hampshire, to Canaan. But the godly farmers hitched ninety yoke of oxen to the abolition schoolhouse and dragged it into the middle of the swamp. The black boy trudged away.

The nineteenth was the first century of human sympathy,—the age when half-wonderingly we began to descry in others that transfigured spark of divinity which we call Myself; when clodhoppers and peasants, and tramps and thieves, and millionaires and—sometimes—Negroes, became throbbing souls whose warm pulsing life touched us so nearly that we half gasped with surprise, crying, "Thou too! Hast Thou seen Sorrow and the dull waters of Hopelessness? Hast Thou known Life?" And then all helplessly we peered into those Other-worlds, and wailed, O World of Worlds, how shall man make you one?"

So in that little Oneida school there came to those schoolboys a revelation of thought and longing beneath one black skin, of which they had not dreamed before. And to the lonely boy came a new dawn of sympathy and inspiration. The shadowy, formless thing—the temptation of Hate, that hovered between him and the world—grew fainter and less sinister. It did not wholly fade away, but diffused itself and lingered thick at the edges. Through it the child now first saw the blue and gold of life,—the sun-swept road that ran 'twixt heaven and earth until in one far-off wan wavering line they met and kissed. A vision of life came to the growing boy,—mystic, wonderful. He raised his head, stretched himself, breathed deep of the fresh new air. Yonder, behind the forests, he heard strange sounds; then glinting through the trees he saw, far, far away, the bronzed hosts of a nation calling,—calling faintly, calling loudly. He heard the hateful clank of their chains; he felt them cringe and grovel, and there rose within him a protest and a prophecy. And he girded himself to walk down the world.

A voice and vision called him to be a priest,—a seer to lead the uncalled out of the house of bondage. He saw the headless host turn toward him like the whirling of mad waters,—he stretched forth his hands eagerly, and then, even as he stretched them, suddenly there swept across the vision the temptation of Despair.

They were not wicked men,—the problem of life is not the problem of the wicked,—they were calm, good men, Bishops of the Apostolic Church of God, and strove toward righteousness. They said slowly, "It is all very natural—it is even commendable; but the General Theological Seminary of the Episcopal Church cannot admit a Negro." And when that thin, half-grotesque figure still haunted their doors, they put their hands kindly, half-sorrowfully, on his shoulders, and said, "Now,—of course, we—we know how *you* feel about it; but you see it is impossible,—that is—well—it is premature. Sometime, we trust— sincerely trust—all such distinctions will fade away; but now the world is as it is."

This was the temptation of Despair; and the young man fought it doggedly. Like some grave shadow he flitted by those halls, pleading, arguing, half-angrily demanding admittance, until there came the final *No*: until men hustled the disturber away, marked him as foolish, unreasonable, and injudicious, a vain rebel against God's law. And then from that Vision Splendid all the glory faded slowly away, and left an earth gray and stern rolling on beneath a dark despair. Even the kind hands that stretched themselves toward him from out the depths of that dull morning seemed but parts of the purple shadows. He saw them coldly, and asked, "Why should I strive by special grace when the way of the world is closed to me?" All gently yet, the hands urged him on,—the hands of young John Jay, that daring father's daring son; the hands of the good folk of Boston, that free city. And yet, with a way to the priesthood of the Church open at last before him, the cloud lingered there; and even when in old St. Paul's the venerable Bishop raised his white arms above the Negro deacon—even then the burden had not lifted from that heart, for there had passed a glory from the earth.

And yet the fire through which Alexander Crummell went did not burn in vain. Slowly and more soberly he took up again his plan of life. More critically he studied the situation. Deep down below the slavery and servitude of the Negro people he saw their fatal weaknesses, which long years of mistreatment had emphasized. The dearth of strong moral character, of unbending righteousness, he felt, was their great shortcoming, and here he would begin. He would gather the best of his people into some little Episcopal chapel and there lead, teach, and inspire them, till the leaven spread, till the children grew, till the world hearkened, till—till—and then across his dream gleamed some faint after-glow of that first fair vision of youth—only an after-glow, for there had passed a glory from the earth.

One day—it was in 1842, and the springtide was struggling merrily with the May winds of New England—he stood at last in his own chapel in Providence, a priest of the Church. The days sped by, and the dark young clergyman labored; he wrote his sermons carefully; he intoned his prayers with a soft, earnest voice; he haunted the streets and accosted the wayfarers; he visited the sick, and knelt beside the dying. He worked and toiled, week by week, day by day, month by month. And yet month by month the congregation dwindled, week by week the hollow walls echoed more sharply, day by day the calls came fewer and fewer, and day by day the third temptation sat clearer and still more clearly within the Veil; a temptation, as it were, bland and smiling, with just a shade of mockery in its smooth tones. First it came casually, in the cadence of a voice: "Oh, colored folks? Yes." Or perhaps more definitely: "What do you *expect*?" In voice and gesture lay the doubt—the temptation of Doubt. How he hated it, and stormed at it furiously! "Of course they are capable," he cried; "of course they can learn and strive and achieve—" and "Of course," added the temptation softly, "they do nothing of the sort." Of all the three temptations, this one struck the deepest. Hate? He had outgrown so childish a thing. Despair? He had steeled his right arm against it, and fought it with the vigor of determination. But to doubt the worth of his life-work,—to doubt the destiny and capability of the race his soul loved because it was his; to find listless squalor instead of eager endeavor; to hear his own lips whispering, "They do not care; they cannot know; they are dumb driven cattle,—why cast your pearls before swine?"—this, this seemed more than man could bear; and he closed the door, and sank upon the steps of the chancel, and cast his robe upon the floor and writhed.

The evening sunbeams had set the dust to dancing in the gloomy chapel when he arose. He folded his vestments, put away the hymn-books, and closed the great Bible. He stepped out into the twilight, looked back upon the narrow little pulpit with a weary smile, and locked the door. Then he walked briskly to the Bishop, and told the Bishop what the Bishop already knew. "I have failed," he said simply. And gaining courage by the confession, he added: "What I need is a larger constituency. There are comparatively few Negroes here, and perhaps they are not of the best. I must go where the field is wider, and try again." So the Bishop sent him to Philadelphia, with a letter to Bishop Onderdonk.

Bishop Onderdonk lived at the head of six white steps,—corpulent, red-faced, and the author of several thrilling tracts on Apostolic Succession. It was after dinner, and the Bishop had settled himself for a pleasant season of contemplation, when the bell must needs ring, and there must burst in upon the Bishop a letter and a thin, ungainly Negro. Bishop Onderdonk read the letter hastily and frowned. Fortunately, his mind was already clear on this point; and he cleared his brow and looked at Crummell. Then he said, slowly and impressively: "I will receive you into this diocese on one condition: no Negro priest can sit in my church convention, and no Negro church must ask for representation there."

I sometimes fancy I can see that tableau: the frail black figure, nervously twitching his hat before the massive abdomen of Bishop Onderdonk; his threadbare coat thrown against the dark woodwork of the bookcases, where Fox's "Lives of the Martyrs" nestled happily beside "The Whole Duty of Man." I seem to see the wide eyes of the Negro wander past the Bishop's broadcloth to where the swinging glass doors of the cabinet glow in the sunlight. A little blue fly is trying to cross the yawning keyhole. He marches briskly up to it, peers into the chasm in a surprised sort of way, and rubs his feelers reflectively; then he essays its depths, and, finding it bottomless, draws back again. The dark-faced priest finds himself wondering if the fly too has faced its Valley of Humiliation, and if it will plunge into it,—when lo! It spreads its tiny wings and buzzes merrily across, leaving the watcher wingless and alone.

Then the full weight of his burden fell upon him. The rich walls wheeled away, and before him. lay the cold rough moor winding on through life, cut in twain by one thick granite ridge,—here, the Valley of Humiliation; yonder, the Valley of the Shadow of Death. And I know not which be darker,—no, not I. But this I know: in yonder Vale of the Humble stand today a million swarthy men, who willingly would

... bear the whips and scorns of time,
The oppressor's wrong, the proud man's contumely,
The pangs of despised love, the law's delay,
The insolence of office, and the spurns
That patient merit of the unworthy takes,—

all this and more would they bear did they but know that this were sacrifice and not a meaner thing. So surged the thought within that lone black breast. The Bishop cleared his throat suggestively; then, recollecting that there was really nothing to say, considerately said nothing, only sat tapping his foot impatiently. But Alexander Crummell said, slowly and heavily: "I will never enter your diocese on such terms." And saying this, he turned and passed into the Valley of the Shadow of Death. You might have noted only the physical dying, the shattered frame and hacking cough; but in that soul lay deeper death than that. He found a chapel in New York,—the church of his father; he labored for it in poverty and starvation, scorned by his fellow priests. Half in despair, he wandered across the sea, a beggar with outstretched hands. Englishmen clasped them,—Wilberforce and Stanley, Thirwell and Ingles, and even Froude and Macaulay; Sir Benjamm Brodie bade him rest awhile at Queen's College in Cambridge, and there he lingered, struggling for health of body and mind, until he took his degree in '53. Restless still and unsatisfied, he turned toward Africa, and for long years, amid the spawn of the slave-smugglers, sought a new heaven and a new earth.

So the man groped for light; all this was not Life,—it was the world-wandering of a soul in search of itself, the striving of one who vainly sought his place in the world, ever haunted by the shadow of a death that is more than death,—the passing of a soul that has missed its duty. Twenty years he wandered,—twenty years and more; and yet the hard rasping question kept gnawing within him, "What, in Gods name, am I on earth for?" In the narrow Now York parish his soul seemed cramped and smothered. In the fine old air of the English University he heard the millions wailing over the sea. In the wild fever-cursed swamps of West Africa he stood helpless and alone.

You will not wonder at his weird pilgrimage,—you who in the swift whirl of living, amid its cold paradox and marvellous vision, have fronted life and asked its riddle face to face. And if you find that riddle hard to read, remember that yonder black boy finds it just a little harder; if it is difficult for you to find and face your duty, it is a shade more difficult for him; if your heart sickens in the blood and dust of battle, remember that to him the dust is thicker and the battle fiercer. No wonder the wanderers fall! No wonder we point to thief and murderer, and haunting prostitute, and the never-ending throng of unhearsed dead! The Valley of the Shadow of Death gives few of its pilgrims back to the world.

But Alexander Crummell it gave back. Out of the temptation of Hate, and burned by the fire of Despair, triumphant over Doubt, and steeled by Sacrifice against Humiliation, he tarned at last home across the waters, humble and strong, gentle and determined. He bent to all the gibes and prejudices, to all hatred and discrimination, with that rare courtesy which is the armor of pure souls. He fought among his own, the low, the grasping, and the wicked, with that unbending righteousness which is the sword of the just. He never faltered, he seldom complained; he simply worked, inspiring the young, rebuking the old, helping the weak, guiding the strong.

So he grew, and brought within his wide influence all that was best of those who walk within the Veil. They who live without know not nor dreamed of that full power within, that mighty inspiration which the dull gauze of caste decreed that most men should not know. And now that he is gone, I sweep the Veil away and cry, Lo! the soul to whose dear memory I bring this little tribute. I can see his face still, dark and heavy-lined beneath his snowy hair; lighting and shading, now with inspiration for the future, now in innocent pain at some human wickedness, now with sorrow at some hard memory from the past. The more I met Alexander Crummell. the more I felt how much that world was losing which knew so little of him. In another age he might have sat among the elders of the land in purple-bordered toga; in another country mothers might have sung him to the cradles.

He did his work,—he did it nobly and well; and yet I sorrow that here be worked alone, with so little human sympathy. His name, today, in this broad land, means little, and comes to fifty million ears laden with no incense of memory or emulation. And herein lies the tragedy of the age: not that men are poor,—all men know something of poverty; not that men are wicked,—who is good? not that men are, ignorant,—what is Truth? Nay, but that men know so little of men.

He sat one morning gazing toward the sea. He smiled and said, "The gate is rusty on the hinges." That night at star-rise a wind came moaning out of the west to blow the gate ajar, and then the soul I loved fled like a flame across the Seas, and in its seat sat Death.

I wonder where he is today? I wonder if in that dim world beyond, as he came gliding in, there rose on some wan throne a King,—a dark and pierced Jew, who knows the writhings of the earthly damned, saying, as he Laid those heart-wrung talents down, "Well done!" while round about the morning stars sat singing.

Document 13, Chapter XII

On March 5, 1897, Alexander Crummell delivered his address, "Civilization, the Primal Need of the Race," before the first meeting of the American Negro Academy. The Academy was the outgrowth of a meeting held in December of the previous year by Crummell, the teacher Walter B. Hayson (?–1905), the poet Paul Laurence Dunbar (1872–1906), and Kelly Miller (1863–1939), a mathematics professor at Howard University. The purpose of the Academy was to publish and promote the work of "Colored authors, scholars, and artists." The academy's first meeting was attended by eighteen of the most prominent African American men in the United States, including the Presbyterian minister Francis J. Grimké and W. E. B. Du Bois. Crummell's speech is important for its recognition that African Americans needed to establish an intellectual and cultural vanguard at the highest level of the culture. In doing so, Crummell anticipated Du Bois's conception of the Talented Tenth.

* * *

Civilization, The Primal Need of the Race[4]

GENTLEMEN:

There is no need, I apprehend, that I should undertake to impress you with a sense either of the need or of the importance of our assemblage here today. The fact of your coming here is, of itself, the clearest evidence of your warm acquiescence in the summons to this meeting, and of your cordial interest in the objects which it purposes to consider.

Nothing has surprised and gratified me so much as the anxiousness of many minds for the movement which we are on the eve of beginning. In the letters which our Secretary, Mr. Cromwell, has received, and which will be read to us, we are struck by the fact that one cultured man here and another there,—several minds in different localities,—tell him that this is just the thing they have desired, and. have been looking for.

I congratulate you, therefore, gentlemen, on the opportuneness of your asscmblage here. I felicitate you on the superior and lofty aims which have drawn you together. And, in behalf of your compeers, resident here in the city of Washington, I welcome you to the city and to the important deliberations to which our organization invites you.

Just here, let me call your attention to the uniqueness and specialty of this conference. It is unlike any other which has ever taken place in the history of the

---

[4] Source: Alexander Crummell, "Civilization, The Primal Need of the Race," The American Negro Academy, Occasional Papers, No. 3 (Washington: The American Negro Academy, 1898).

Negro, on the American Continent. There have been, since the landing of the first black cargo of slaves at Jamestown, Va., in 1619, numerous conventions of men of our race. There have been Religious Assemblies, Political Conferences, suffrage meetings, educational conventions. But our meeting is for a purpose which, while inclusive, in some respects, of these various concerns, is for an object more distinct and positive than any of them.

What then, it may be asked, is the special undertaking we have before us, in this Academy? My answer is the civilization of the Negro race in the United States, by the scientific processes of literature, art, and philosophy, through the agency of the cultured men of this same Negro race. And here, let me say, that the special race problem of the Negro in the United States is his civilization.

I doubt if there is a man in this presence who has a higher conception of Negro capacity than your speaker; and this of itself, precludes the idea, on my part, of race disparagement. But, it seems manifest to me that, as a race in this land, we have no art; we have no science; we have no philosophy; we have no scholarship. Individuals we have in each of these lines; but mere individuality cannot be recognized as the aggregation of a family, a nation, or a race; or as the interpretation of any of them. And until we attain the role of civilization, we cannot stand up and hold our place in the world of culture and enlightenment. And the forfeiture of such a place means, despite, inferiority, repulsion, drudgery, poverty, and ultimate death! Now gentlemen, for the creation of a complete and rounded man, you need the impress and the moulding of the highest arts. But how much more so for the realizing of a true and lofty *race* of men. What is true of a man is deeply true of a people. The special need in such a case is the force and application of the highest arts; not mere mechanism; not mere machinery; not mere handicraft; not the mere grasp on material things; not mere temporal ambitions. These are but incidents; important indeed, but pertaining mainly to man's material needs, and to the feeding of the body. And the incidental in life is incapable of feeding the living soul. For "man cannot live by bread alone, but by every word that proceedeth out of the mouth of God." And civilization is the *secondary* word of God, given for the nourishment of humanity.

To make *men* you need civilization; and what I mean by civilization is the action of exalted forces, both of God and man. For manhood is the most majestic thing in God's creation; and hence the demand for the very highest art in the shaping and moulding of human souls.

What is the great difficulty with the black race, in this era, in this land? It is that both within their ranks, and external to themselves, by large schools of thought interested in them, material ideas in divers forms are made prominent, as the master-need of the race, and as the surest way to success. Men are constantly dogmatizing theories of sense and matter as the salvable hope of the race. Some of our leaders and teachers boldly declare, now, that *property* is the source of power; and then, that *money* is the thing which commands respect. At one time it is the *official position* which is the masterful influence in the elevation of the race; at another, men are disposed to fall back upon *blood* and *lineage*, as the root (source) of power and progress.

Blind men! For they fail to see that neither property, nor money, nor station, nor office, nor lineage, are fixed factors, in so large a thing as the destiny of man; that they are not vitalizing qualities in the changeless hopes of humanity. The greatness of peoples springs from their ability to grasp the grand conceptions of being. It is the absorption of a people of a nation, of a race, in large majestic and abiding things which lifts them up to the skies. These once apprehended, all the minor details of life follow in their proper places, and spread abroad in the details and the comfort of practicality. But until these gifts of a lofty civilization are secured, men are sure to remain low, debased and groveling.

It was the apprehension of this great truth which led Melancthon, 400 years ago, to declare, "Unless we have the scientific mind we shall surely revert again to barbarism." He was a scholar and a classic, a theologian and a philosopher. With probably the exception of Erasmus, he was the most erudite man of his age. He was the greatest Grecian of his day. He was rich "with the spoils of time." And so running down the annals of the ages, he discovered the majestic fact, which Coleridge has put in two simple lines:-

"We may not hope from outward things to win

The passion and the life shows fountains are within";

which Wordsworth, in grand style, has declared,

"By the soul only the nations shall be free."

But what is this other than the utterance of Melancthon,—"Without the scientific mind, barbarism." This is the teaching of history. For 2,000 years, Europe has been governed, in all its developments, by Socrates, and Aristotle, and Plato, and Euclid. These were the great idealists; and as such, they were the great progenitors of all modern civilization, the majestic agents of God for the civil upbuilding of men and nations. For civilization is, in its origins, ideal; and hence, in the loftiest men, it bursts forth, producing letters, literature, science, philosophy, poetry, sculpture, architecture, yea, all the arts; and brings them with all their gifts, and lays them in the lap of religion, as the essential condition of their vital permanence and their continuity.

But civilization never seeks permanent abidance upon the heights of Olympus. She is human, and seeks all human needs. And so she descends, re-creating new civilizations; uplifting the crudeness of laws, giving scientific precision to morals and religion, stimulating enterprise, extending commerce, creating manufactures, expanding mechanism and mechanical inventions; producing revolutions and reforms; humanizing labor; meeting the minutest human needs, even to the manufacturing needles for the industry of seamstresses and for the commonest uses of human fingers. All these are the fruits of civilization.

Who are to be the agents to lift tip this people of ours to the grand plane of civilization? Who are to bring them up to the height of noble thought, grand civility, a chaste and elevating culture, refinement, and the impulses of irrepressible progress? It is to be done by the scholars and thinkers, who have secured the vision which penetrates the center of nature, and sweeps the circles of historic enlightenment; and who have got insight into the life of things, and learned the art by which men touch the springs of action.

For to transform and stimulate the souls of a race or a people is a work of intelligence. It is a work which demands the clear induction of world-wide facts, and the perception of their application to new circumstances. It is a work which will require the most skillful resources, and the use of the scientific spirit.

But every man in a race cannot be a philosopher: nay, but few men in any land, in any age, can grasp ideal truth. Scientific ideas however must be apprehended, else there can be no progress, no elevation.

Just here arises the need of the trained and scholarly men of a race to employ their knowledge and culture and teaching and to guide both the opinions and habits of the crude masses. The masses, nowhere are, or can be, learned or scientific. The scholar is exceptional, just the same as a great admiral like Nelson is, or a grand soldier like Caesar or Napoleon. But the leader, the creative and organizing mind, is the master-need in all the societies of man. But, if they are not inspired with the notion of leadership and duty, then with all their Latin and Greek and science they are but pedants, trimmers, opportunists. For all true and lofty scholarship is weighty with the burdens and responsibilities of life and humanity.

But these reformers must not be mere scholars. They must needs be both scholars and philanthropists. For this, indeed, has it been in all the history of men. In all the great revolutions, and in all great reforms which have transpired, scholars have been conspicuous; in the re-construction of society, in formulating laws, in producing great emancipations, in the revival of letters, in the advancement of science, in the rennaissance of art, in the destruction of gross superstitions and in the restoration of true and enlightened religion.

And what is the spirit with which they are to come to this work? My answer is, that *disinterestedness* must animate their motives and their acts. Whatever rivalries and dissensions may divide man in the social or political world, let generosity govern *us*. Let us emulate one another in the prompt recognition of rare genius, or uncommon talent. Let there be no tardy acknowledgment of worth in our world of intellect. If we are fortunate enough, to see, of a sudden, a clever mathematician of our class, a brilliant poet, a youthful, but promising scientist or philosopher, let us rush forward, and hail his coming with no hesitant admiration, with no reluctant praise.

It is only thus, gentlemen, that we can bring forth, stimulate, and uplift all the latent genius, garnered up, in the by-places and sequestered corners of this neglected Race.

It is only thus we can nullify and break down the conspiracy which would fain limit and narrow the range of Negro talent in this caste-tainted country. It is only thus, we can secure that recognition of genius and scholarship in the republic of letters, which is the rightful prerogative of every race of men. It is only thus we can spread abroad and widely disseminate that culture and enlightment which shall permeate and leaven the entire social and domestic life of our people and so give that civilization which is the nearest ally of religion.

African American man, half-length portrait, facing front, included in album of photographs of African Americans in Georgia for the Georgia Negro Exhibit, included as part of the Exhibit of American Negroes compiled by W. E. B. Du Bois for the 1900 Paris Exposition.

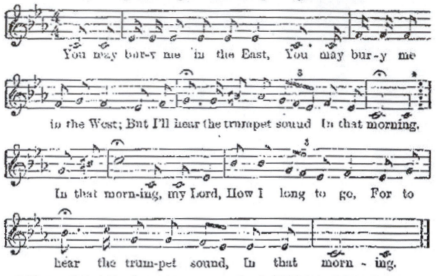

No. 11. I'll hear the Trumpet Sound.

You may bur-y me in the East, You may bur-y me in the West; But I'll hear the trumpet sound In that morning. In that morn-ing, my Lord, How I long to go, For to hear the trum-pet sound, In that morn - ing.

2 Father Gabriel in that day,
   He'll take wings and fly away,
   For to hear the trumpet sound
   In that morning.
   You may bury him in tho East,
   You may bury him in the West;
   But he'll hear the trumpet sound,
   In that morning.

   Cho.—In that morning, &c.

3. Good old christians in that day,
   They'll take wings and fly away,&c.
   Cho.—In that morning, &c.

4. Good old preachers in that day,
   They'll take wings and fly away,&c.
   Cho.—In that morning, &c.

5. In that dreadful Judgment day,
   I'll take wings and fly away, &c.
   Cho.—In that morning, &c.

* Repeat the music of the first strain for all the verses but the first.

Musical notation from the spiritual "I'll Hear the Trumpet Song," also known under the title "You May Bury Me in the East," included in J. B. T. Marsh, *The Story of the Jubilee Singers* (Cleveland, Ohio: The Cleveland Printing and Publishing Company, 1892), p. 170.

XIII

Of the Coming of John[1]

What bring they 'neath the midnight,
    Beside the River-sea?
They bring the human heart wherein
    No nightly calm can be;
That droppeth never with the wind,
    Nor drieth with the dew;
O calm it. God; thy calm is broad
    To cover spirits too.
      The river floweth on.

                    Mrs. Browning.[2]

Carlisle Street runs westward from the centre of Johnstown, across a great black bridge, down a hill and up again, by little shops and meat-markets, past single-storied homes, until suddenly it stops against a wide green lawn. It is a broad, restful place, with two large buildings outlined against the west. When at evening the winds come, swelling from the east, and the great pall of the city's smoke hangs wearily above the valley, then

---

[1] This short story is among the earliest of Du Bois's efforts at fiction, an area for which his substantial contributions are less well-recognized than his work as a social theorist.

[2] "What bring they 'neath the midnight," is taken from Elizabeth Barrett Browning's 1838 poem "A Romance of the Ganges."

"Rice Culture in the South," *Harper's Weekly*, July 5, 1884.

the red west glows like a dreamland down Carlisle Street, and, at the tolling of the supper-bell, throws the passing forms of students in dark silhouette against the sky. Tall and black, they move slowly by, and seem in the sinister light to flit before the city like dim warning ghosts. Perhaps they are; for this is Wells Institute, and these black students have few dealings with the white city below.

And if you will notice, night after night, there is one dark form that ever hurries last and late toward the twinkling lights of Swain Hall,—for Jones is never on time. A long, straggling fellow he is, brown and hardhaired, who seems to be growing straight out of his clothes, and walks with a half-apologetic roll. He used perpetually to set the quiet dining-room into waves of merriment, as he stole to his place after the bell had tapped for prayers; he seemed so perfectly awkward. And yet one glance at his face made one forgive him much,—that broad, good-natured smile in which lay no bit of art or artifice, but seemed just bubbling good-nature and genuine satisfaction with the world.

He came to us from Altamaha, away down there beneath the gnarled oaks of Southeastern Georgia, where the sea croons to the sands and the sands listen till they sink half-drowned beneath the waters, rising only here and there in long, low islands. The white folk of Altamaha voted John a good boy,—fine plough-hand, good in the rice-fields, handy everywhere, and always good-natured and respectful. But they shooktheir heads when his mother wanted to send him off to school. "It'll spoil him,—ruin him," they said; and they talked as though they knew. But full half the black folk followed him proudly to the station, and carried his queer little trunk and many bundles. And there they shook and shook hands, and the girls kissed him shyly and the boys clapped him on the back. So the train came, and he pinched his little sister lovingly, and put his great arms about his mother's neck, and then was away with a puff and a roar into the great yellow world that flamed and flared about the doubtful pilgrim. Up the coast they hurried, past the squares and palmettos of Savannah, through the cotton-fields and through the weary night, to Millville, and came with the morning to the noise and bustle of

Hoeing Rice, South Carolina. Keystone View Company, c1904. Courtesy of the Library of Congress.

Johnstown.

And they that stood behind, that morning in Altamaha, and watched the train as it noisily bore playmate and brother and son away to the world, had thereafter one ever-recurring word,—"When John comes." Then what parties were to be, and what speakings in the churches; what new furniture in the front room, perhaps even a new front room; and there would be a new schoolhouse, with John as teacher; and then perhaps a big wedding; all this and more—when John comes. But the white people shook their heads.

At first he was coming at Christmas-time,—but the vacation proved too short; and then, the next summer,—but times were hard and schooling costly, and so, instead, he worked in Johnstown. And so it drifted to the next summer, and the next,—till playmates scattered, and mother grew gray, and sister went up to the Judge's kitchen to work. And still the legend lingered,—"When John comes."

Up at the Judge's they rather liked this refrain; for they too had a John—a fair-haired, smooth-faced boy, who had played many a long summer's day to its close with his darker namesake. "Yes, sir! John is at Princeton,[3] sir," said the broad-shouldered gray-haired Judge every morning as he marched down to the post-office. "Showing the Yankees what a Southern gentleman can do," he added; and strode home again with his letters and papers. Up at the great pillared house they lingered long over the Princeton letter,—the Judge and his frail wife, his sister and growing daughters. "It'll make a man of him," said the Judge, "college is the place." And then he asked the shy little waitress, "Well, Jennie, how's your John?" and added reflectively, "Too bad, too bad your mother sent him off,—it will spoil him. And the waitress wondered.

Thus in the far-away Southern village the world lay waiting, half-consciously, the coming of two young men, and dreamed in an inarticulate way of new things that would be done and new thoughts that all would think. And yet it was singular that few thought of two Johns,—for the black folk thought of one John, and he was black; and the white folk thought of another John, and he was white. And neither world thought the other world's thought, save with a vague unrest.

Up in Johnstown, at the Institute, we were long puzzled at the case of John Jones. For a long time the clay seemed unfit for any sort of moulding. He was loud and boisterous, always laughing and singing, and never able to work consecutively at anything. He did not know how to study; he had no idea of thoroughness; and with his tardiness, carelessness, and appalling good-humor, we were sore perplexed. One night we sat in faculty-meeting, worried and serious; for Jones was in

---

[3] Princeton University founded in 1746.

trouble again. This last escapade was too much, and so we solemnly voted "that Jones, on account of repeated disorder and in-attention to work, be suspended for the rest of the term."

It seemed to us that the first time life ever struck Jones as a really serious thing was when the Dean told him he must leave school. He stared at the gray-haired man blankly, with great eyes. "Why—why," he faltered, "but—I haven't graduated!" Then the Dean slowly and clearly explained, reminding him of the tardiness and the carelessness, of the poor lessons and neglected work, of the noise and disorder, until the fellow hung his head in confusion. Then he said quickly, "But you won't tell mammy and sister,--you won't write mammy, now will you? For if you won't I'll go out into the city and work, and come back next term and show you something." So the Dean promised faithfully, and John shouldered his little trunk, giving neither word nor look to the giggling boys, and walked down Carlisle Street to the great city, with sober eyes and a set and serious face.

Perhaps we imagined it, but someway it seemed to us that the serious look that crept over his boyish face that afternoon never left it again. When he came back to us he went to work with all his rugged strength. It was a hard struggle, for things did not come easily to him,—few crowding memories of early life and teaching came to help him on his new way; but all the world toward which he strove was of his own building, and he builded slow and hard. As the light dawned lingeringly on his new creations, he sat rapt and silent before the vision, or wandered alone over the green campus peering through and beyond the world of men into a world of thought. And the thoughts at times puzzled him sorely; he could not see just why the circle was not square, and carried it out fifty-six decimal places one midnight,—would have gone further, indeed, had not the matron rapped for lights out. He caught terrible colds lying on his back in the meadows of nights, trying to think out the solar system; he had grave doubts as to the ethics of the Fall of Rome, and strongly suspected the Germans of being thieves and rascals, despite his text-books; he pondered long over every new Greek word, and wondered why this meant that and why it couldn't mean something else, and how it must have felt to think all things in Greek. So he thought and puzzled along for himself,—pausing perplexed where others skipped merrily, and walking steadily through the difficulties where the rest stopped and surrendered.

Thus he grew in body and soul, and with him his clothes seemed to grow and arrange themselves; coat sleeves got longer, cuffs appeared, and collars got less soiled. Now and then his boots shone, and a new dignity crept into his walk. And we who saw daily a new thoughtfulness growing in his eyes began to expect something of this plodding boy.

Palmettoes on Tybee Island, near Savannah, Georgia. Detroit Publishing Company, William Henry Jackson, Photographer, ca. 1900. Courtesy of the Library of Congress.

Thus he passed out of the preparatory school into college, and we who watched him felt four more years of change, which almost transformed the tall, grave man who bowed to us commencement morning. He had left his queer thought-world and come back to a world of motion and of men. He looked now for the first time sharply about him, and wondered he had seen so little before. He grew slowly to feel almost for the first time the Veil that lay between him and the white world; he first noticed now the oppression that had not seemed oppression before, differences that erstwhile seemed natural, restraints and slights that in his boyhood days had gone unnoticed or been greeted with a laugh. He felt angry now when men did not call him "Mister," he clenched his hands at the "Jim Crow" cars, and chafed at the color-line that hemmed in him and his. A tinge of sarcasm crept into his speech, and a vague bitterness into his life; and he sat long hours wondering and planning a way around these crooked things. Daily he found himself shrinking from the choked and narrow life of his native town. And yet he always planned to go back to Altamaha,—always planned to work there. Still, more and more as the day approached he hesitated with a nameless dread; and even the day after graduation he seized with eagerness the offer of the Dean to send him North with the quartette during the summer vacation, to sing for the Institute. A breath of air before the plunge, he said to himself in half apology.

It was a bright September afternoon, and the streets of New York were brilliant with moving men. They reminded John of the sea, as he sat in the square and watched them, so changelessly changing, so bright and dark, so grave and gay. He scanned their rich and faultless clothes, the way they carried their hands, the shape of their hats; be peered into the hurrying carriages. Then, leaning back with a sigh, he said, "This is the World." The notion suddenly seized him to see where the world was going; since many of the richer and brighter seemed hurrying all one way. So when a tall, light-haired young man and a little talkative lady came by, he rose half-hesitatingly and followed them. Up the street they went, past stores and gay shops, across a broad square, until with a hundred others they entered the high portal of a great building.

He was pushed toward the ticket-office with the others, and felt in his pocket for the new five-dollar bill he had hoarded. There seemed really no time for hesitation, so he drew it bravely out, passed it to the busy clerk, and received simply a ticket but no change. When at last he realized that he had paid five dollars to enter he knew not what, he stood stockstill amazed. "Be careful," said a low voice behind him; "you must not lynch the colored gentleman simply because he's in your way," and a girl looked up roguishly into the eyes of her fair-haired escort. A shade of annoyance passed over the escort's face. "You *will* not understand us at the South," he said half impatiently, as if continuing an argument. "With all your professions, one never sees in the North so cordial and intimate relations between white and black as are everyday occurrences with us. Why, I remember my closest playfellow in boyhood was a little Negro named after me, and surely no two,—well!" The man stopped short and flushed to the roots of his hair, for there directly beside his reserved orchestra chairs sat the Negro he had stumbled over in the hallway. He hesitated and grew pale with anger, called the usher and gave, him his card, with a few peremptory words, and slowly sat down. The lady deftly changed the subject.

All this John did not see, for he sat in a half-maze, minding the scene about him; the delicate beauty of the hall, the faint perfume, the moving myriad of men, the rich clothing and low hum of talking seemed all a part of a world so different from his, so strangely more beautiful than anything he had known, that he sat in dreamland, and started when, after a hush, rose high and clear the music of Lohengrin's swan.[4] The infinite

---

[4] The Swan represents a guide in Richard Wagner's 1850 opera *Lohengrin.*

beauty of the wail lingered and swept through every muscle of his frame, and put it all a-tune. He closed his eyes and grasped the elbows of the chair, touching unwittingly the lady's arm. And the lady drew away. A deep longing swelled in all his heart to rise with that clear music out of the dirt and dust of that low life that held him, prisoned and befouled. If he could only live up in the free air where birds sang and setting suns had no touch of blood! Who had called him to be the slave and butt of all? And if he had called, what right had he to call when a world like this lay open before men?

Then the movement changed, and fuller, mightier harmony swelled away. He looked thoughtfully across the hall, and wondered why the beautiful gray-haired woman looked so listless, and what the little man could be whispering about. He would not like to be listless and idle, he thought, for he felt with the music the movement of power within him. If he but had some master-work, some life-service, hard,—aye, bitter hard, but without the cringing and sickening servility, without the cruel hurt that hardened his heart and soul. When at last a soft sorrow crept across the violins, there came to him the vision of a far-off home,—the great eyes of his sister, and the dark drawn face of his mother. And his heart sank below the waters, even as the sea-sand-sinks by the shores of Altamaha, only to be lifted aloft again with that last ethereal wail of the swan that quivered and faded away into the sky.

It left John sitting so silent and rapt that he did not for some time notice the usher tapping him lightly on the shoulder and saying politely, "Will you step this way please, sir?" A little surprised, he arose quickly at the last tap, and, turning to leave his seat, looked full into the face of the fair-haired young man. For the first time the young man recognized his dark boyhood playmate, and John knew that it was the Judge's son. The White John started, lifted his hand, and then froze into his chair; the black John smiled lightly, then grimly, and followed the usher down the aisle. The manager was sorry, very, very sorry,—but he explained that some mistake had been made in selling the gentleman a seat already disposed of; he would refund the money, of course,—and indeed felt the matter keenly, and so forth, and before he had finished John was gone, walking hurriedly across the square and down the broad streets, and as he passed the park he buttoned his coat and said, "John Jones, you're a natural-born fool." Then he went to his lodgings and wrote a letter, and tore it up; he wrote another, and threw it in the fire. Then he seized a scrap of paper and wrote: "Dear Mother and Sister—I am coming—John."

"Perhaps," said John, as he settled himself on the train, "perhaps I am to blame myself in struggling against my manifest destiny[5] simply because it looks hard and unpleasant. Here is my duty to Altamaha plain before me; perhaps they'll let me help settle the Negro problems there,—perhaps they won't. 'I will go in to the King, which is not according to the law; and if I perish, I perish.'"[6] And then he mused and dreamed, and planned a life-work; and the train flew south.

Down in Altamaha, after seven long years, all the world knew John was coming. The homes were scrubbed and scoured,—above all, one; the gardens and yards had an unwonted trimness, and Jennie bought a new gingham. With some finesse and negotiation, all the dark Methodists and Presbyterians were induced to join in a monster welcome at the Baptist Church; and as the day drew near, warm discussions arose on every corner as to the exact extent and nature of John's accomplishments. It was noontide on a gray and cloudy day when he came. The black town flocked to the depot, with a little of the white at the edges,—a happy throng, with "Good-mawnings" and "Howdys" and laughing and joking and jostling. Mother sat yonder in the window watching; but sister Jennie stood on the platform, nervously fingering her dress, tall and lithe, with soft brown skin and loving eyes peering from out a tangled wilderness of hair. John rose gloomily as the train stopped, for he was thinking of the "Jim Crow" car; he stepped to the platform, and paused: a little dingy station, a black crowd gaudy and dirty, a half-mile of dilapidated shanties along a straggling ditch of mud. An overwhelming sense of the sordidness and narrowness of it all seized him; he looked in vain for his mother, kissed coldly the tall, strange girl who called him brother, spoke a short, dry word here and there; then, lingering neither for hand-shaking nor gossip, started silently up the street, raising his hat merely to the last eager old aunty, to her open-mouthed astonishment. The people were distinctly bewildered. This silent, cold man,—was this John? Where was his smile and hearty hand-grasp? "Peared kind o' down in the mouf," said the Methodist preacher thoughtfully. "Seemed monstus stuck up," complained a Baptist sister. But the white postmaster from the edge of the crowd expressed the opinion of his folks plainly. "That damn Nigger," said he, as he shouldered the mail and arranged his tobacco, "has gone North and got plum full o' fool notions; but they won't work in Altamaha." And the crowd melted away.

The meeting of welcome at the Baptist Church was a failure. Rain spoiled the barbecue, and thunder turned the milk in the ice-cream. When the speaking came at night, the house was crowded to overflowing. The

---

[5] "Manifest Destiny" refers to the idea that the United States would eventually spread its border across the North American continent.
[6] A reference to Esther 4:16.

three preachers had especially prepared themselves, but somehow John's manner seemed to throw a blanket over everything,—he seemed so cold and preoccupied, and had so strange an air of restraint that the Methodist brother could not warm up to his theme and elicited not a single "Amen"; the Presbyterian prayer was but feebly responded to, and even the Baptist preacher, though he wakened faint enthusiasm, got so mixed up in his favorite sentence that he had to close it by stopping fully fifteen minutes sooner than he meant. The people moved uneasily in their seats as John rose to reply. He spoke slowly and methodically. The age, he said, demanded new ideas; we were far different from those men of the seventeenth and eighteenth centuries,—with broader ideas of human brotherhood and destiny. Then he spoke of the rise of charity and popular education, and particularly of the spread of wealth and work. The question was, then, he added reflectively, looking at the low discolored ceiling, what part the Negroes of this land would take in the striving of the new century. He sketched in vague outline the new Industrial School that might rise among these pines, he spoke in detail of the charitable and philanthropic work that might be organized, of money that might be saved for banks and business. Finally he urged unity, and deprecated especially religious and denominational bickering. "Today," he said, with a smile, "the world cares little whether a man be Baptist or Methodist, or indeed a churchman at all, so long as he is good and true. What difference does it make whether a man be baptized in river or washbowl, or not at all? Let's leave all that littleness, and look higher." Then, thinking of nothing else, he slowly sat down. A painful hush seized that crowded mass. Little had they understood of what he said, for he spoke an unknown tongue, save the last word about baptism; that they knew, and they sat very still while the clock ticked. Then at last a low suppressed snarl came from the Amen corner, and an old bent man arose, walked over the seats, and climbed straight up into the pulpit. He was wrinkled and black, with scant gray and tufted hair; his voice and hands shook as with palsy; but on his face lay the intense rapt look of the religious fanatic. He seized the Bible with his rough, huge hands; twice he raised it inarticulate, and then fairly burst into words, with rude and awful eloquence. He quivered, swayed, and bent; then rose aloft in perfect majesty, till the people moaned and wept, wailed and shouted, and a wild shrieking arose from the corners where all the pent-up feeling of the hour gathered itself and rushed into the air. John never knew clearly what the old man said; he only felt himself held up to scorn and scathing denunciation for trampling on the true Religion, and he realized with amazement that all unknowingly he had put rough, rude hands on something this little world held sacred. He arose silently, and passed out into the night. Down toward the sea he went, in the fitful starlight, half conscious of the girl, who followed timidly after him. When at last he stood upon the bluff, he turned to his little sister and looked upon her sorrowfully, remembering with sudden pain how little thought he had given her. He put his arm about her and let her passion of tears spend itself on his shoulder.

Long they stood together, peering over the gray unresting water.

"John," she said, "does it make everyone—unhappy when they study and learn lots of things?"

He paused and smiled. "I am afraid it does," he said.

"And, John, are you glad you studied?"

"Yes," came the answer, slowly but positively.

She watched the flickering lights upon the sea, and said thoughtfully, "I wish I was unhappy,—and—and," putting both arms about his neck, "I think I am, a little, John."

It was several days later that John walked up to the Judge's house to ask for the privilege of teaching the Negro school. The Judge himself met him at the front door, stared a little hard at him, and said brusquely, "Go 'round to the kitchen door, John, and wait." Sitting on the kitchen steps, John stared at the corn, thoroughly perplexed. What on earth had come over him? Every step he made offended some one. He had come to save his people, and before he left the depot he had hurt them. He sought to teach them at the church, and had outraged their deepest feelings. He had schooled himself to be respectful to the Judge, and then blundered into his front door. And all the time he had meant right,—and yet, and yet, somehow he found it so hard and strange to fit his old surroundings again, to find his place in the world about him. He could not remember that he used to have any difficulty in the past, when life was glad and gay. The world seemed smooth and easy then. Perhaps,—but his sister came to the kitchen door just then and said the Judge awaited him.

The Judge sat in the dining-room amid his morning's mail, and he did not ask John to sit down. He plunged squarely into the business. "You've come for the school, I suppose Well, John, I want to speak to you plainly. You know I'm a friend to your people. I've helped you and your family, and would have done more if you hadn't got the notion of going off. Now I like the colored people, and sympathize with all their reasonable aspirations; but you and I both know, John, that in this country the Negro must remain subordinate, and can never expect to be the equal of white men. In their place, your people can be honest and respectful; and God knows, I'll do what I can to help them. But when they want to reverse nature, and rule white men, and marry white women, and sit in my parlor, then, by God! we'll hold them under if we have to lynch every Nigger in the land. Now, John, the question is, are you, with your education and Northern notions, going to accept the situation and teach the darkies to be faithful servants and laborers as your fathers were,—I knew your father, John, he belonged to my brother, and he was a good Nigger. Well—well, are you going to be like him, or are you going to try to put fool ideas of rising and equality into these folks' heads, and make them discontented and unhappy?"

"I am going to accept the situation, Judge Henderson," answered John, with a brevity that did not escape the keen old man. He hesitated a moment, and then said shortly, "Very well,—we'll try you awhile. Good-morning."

It was a full month after the opening of the Negro school that the other John came home, tall, gay, and headstrong. The mother wept, the sisters sang. The whole white town was glad. A proud man was the Judge and it was a goodly sight to see the two swinging down Main Street together. And yet all did not go smoothly between them, for the younger man could not and did not veil his contempt for the little town, and plainly had his heart set on New York. Now the one cherished ambition of the Judge was to see his son mayor of Altamaha, representative to the legislature, and—who could say?—governor of Georgia. So the argument often waxed hot between them. "Good heavens, father," the younger man would say after dinner, as he lighted a cigar and stood by the fireplace, "you surely don't expect a young fellow like me to settle down permanently in this—this God-forgotten town with nothing but mud and Negroes?" "I did," the Judge would answer laconically; and on this particular day it seemed from the gathering scowl that he was about to add something more emphatic, but neighbors had already begun to drop in to admire his son, and the conversation drifted.

"Heah that John is livenin' things up at the darky school," volunteered the postmaster, after a pause.

"What now?" asked the Judge, sharply.

"Oh, nothin' in particulah,—just his almight air and uppish ways. B'lieve I did heah somethin' about his givin' talks on the French Revolution, equality, and such like. He's what I call a dangerous Nigger."

"Have you heard him say anything out of the way?"

"Why, no,—but Sally, our girl told my wife a lot of rot. Then, too, I don't need to heah a Nigger what won't –say 'sir' to a white man, or—"

"Who is this John?" interrupted the son.

"Why, it's little black John, Peggy's son,—your old playfellow."

The young man's face flushed angrily, and then he laughed.

"Oh," said he, "it's the darky that tried to force himself into a seat beside the lady I was escorting ""."

But Judge Henderson waited to hear no more. He had been nettled all day, and now at this he rose with a half-smothered oath, took his hat and cane, and walked straight to the schoolhouse.

Of the Coming of John

For John, it had been a long, hard pull to get things started in the rickety old shanty that sheltered his school. The Negroes were rent into factions for and against him, the parents were careless, the children irregular and dirty, and books, pencils, and slates largely missing. Nevertheless, he struggled hopefully on, and seemed to see at last some glimmering of dawn. The attendance was larger and the children were a shade cleaner this week. Even the booby class in reading showed a little comforting progress. So John settled himself with renewed patience this afternoon.

"Now, Mandy," he said cheerfully, "that's better; but you mustn't chop your words up so: "If—the—man—goes." Why, your little brother even wouldn't tell a story that way, now would he?"

"Naw, suh, he cain't talk. "

"All right; now let's try again: 'If the man—'"

"John! "

The whole school started in surprise, and the teacher half arose, as the red, angry face of the Judge appeared in the open doorway.

"John, this school is closed. You children can go home and get to work. The white people of Altamaha are not spending their money on black folks to have their heads crammed with impudence and lies. Clear out! I'll lock the door myself."

Up at the great pillared house the tall young son wandered aimlessly about after his father's abrupt departure. In the house there was little to interest him; the books were old and stale, the local newspaper flat, and the women had retired with headaches and sewing. He tried a nap, but it was too warm. So he sauntered out into the fields, complaining disconsolately, "Good Lord! how long will this, imprisonment last!" He was not a bad fellow,—just a little spoiled and self-indulgent, and as headstrong as his proud father. He seemed a young man pleasant to look upon, as he sat on the great black stump at the edge of the pines idly swinging his legs and smoking. "Why, there isn't even a girl worth getting up a respectable flirtation with," he growled. Just then his eye caught a tall, willowy figure hurrying toward him on the narrow path. He looked with interest at first, and then burst into a laugh as he said, "Well, I declare, if it isn't Jennie, the little brown kitchen-maid! Why, I never noticed before what a trim little body she is. Hello, Jennie! Why, you haven't kissed me since I came home," he said gaily. The young girl stared at him in surprise and confusion,—faltered something inarticulate, and attempted to pass. But a wilful mood had seized the young idler, and he caught at her arm. Frightened, she slipped by; and half mischievously he turned and ran after her through the tall pines.

Yonder, toward the sea, at the end of the path, came John slowly, with his head down. He had turned wearily homeward from the schoolhouse; then thinking to shield his mother from the blow, started to meet his sister as she came from work and break the news of his dismissal to her. "I'll go away," he said slowly;—"I'll go away and find work, and send for them. I cannot live here longer. And then the fierce, buried anger surged up into his throat. He waved his arms and hurried wildly up the path.

The great brown sea lay silent. The air scarce breathed. The dying day bathed the twisted oaks and mighty pines in black and gold. There came from the wind no warning, not a whisper from the cloudless sky. There was only a black man hurrying on with an ache in his heart, seeing neither sun nor sea, but starting as from a dream at the frightened cry that woke the pines, to see his dark sister struggling in the arms of a tall and fair-haired man.

He said not a word, but, seizing a fallen limb, struck him with all the pent-up hatred of his great black arm; and the body lay white and still beneath the pines, all bathed in sunshine and in blood. John looked at it dreamily, then walked back to the house briskly, and said in a soft voice, "Mammy, I'm going away,—I'm going to be free."

She gazed at him dimly and faltered, "No'th, honey, is yo' gwine No'th agin?"

He looked out where the North Star glistened pale above the waters, and said, "Yes, mammy, I'm going—North."[7]

Then, without another word, be went out into the narrow lane, up by the straight pines, to the same winding path, and seated himself on the great black stump, looking at the blood where the body had lain. Yonder in the gray past he had played with that dead boy, romping together under the solemn trees. The night deepened; he thought of the boys at Johnstown. He wondered how Brown had turned out, and Carey? And Jones,—Jones? Why, *he* was Jones, and he wondered what they would all say when they knew, when they knew in that great long dining-room with its hundreds of merry eyes. Then as the sheen of the starlight stole over him, he thought of the gilded ceiling of that vast concert hall, and heard stealing toward him the faint sweet music of the swan. Hark! was it music, or the hurry and shouting of men? Yes, surely! Clear and high the faint sweet melody rose and fluttered like a living thing, so that the very earth trembled as with the tramp of horses and murmur of angry men.

He leaned back and smiled toward the sea, whence rose the strange melody, away from the dark shadows where lay the noise of horses galloping, galloping on. With an effort he roused himself, bent forward,

---

[7] The North Star as a guiding light was a symbol of freedom for the Abolitionist Movement.

and looked steadily down the pathway, softly humming the "Song of the Bride,"—

"Freudig gefurht, ziehet dahin."

Amid the trees in the dim morning twilight he watched their shadows dancing and heard their horses thundering toward him, until at last they came sweeping like a storm, and he saw in front that haggard white-haired man, whose eyes flashed red with fury. Oh, how he pitied him,—pitied him,—and wondered if he had the coiling twisted rope. Then, as the storm burst round him, he rose slowly to his feet and turned his closed eyes toward the Sea.

And the world whistled in his ears.

George Meadows, "murderer & rapist," lynched on scene of his last crime. L. Horgan, Jr. Photograph, c. 1889. Courtesy of the Library of Congress.

Document 14, Chapter XIII

W. E. B. Du Bois would probably be much more well-known as a literary figure if it were not for the prominence of his other work. A prolific poet, among his most famous verses is "The Song of Smoke."

*   *   *

The Song and the Smoke[8]

I am the Smoke King!
I am Black!
I am swinging in the sky,
I am wringing worlds awry:
I am the thought of the throbbing mills,
I am the soul of the soul-toil kills,
Wraith of the ripple of the trading rills;
Up I'm curling from the sod,
I am whirling home to God;
I am the Smoke King
I am Black.
I am the Smoke King,
I am Black!
I am wreathing broken hearts
I am sheathing love's light darts
Insipration of iron times
Wedding the toil of toiling climes,
Shedding the blood of bloodless crimes—
Lurid lowering 'mid the blue,
Torrid towering toward the true,
I am the Smoke King,
I am Black.
I am the Smoke King,
I am Black!
I am darkening with song,
I am hearkening to wrong!
I will be Black as Blackness can—
The blacker the mantle, the mightier the man!
For Blackness was ancient ere whiteness began.
I am daubing God in night,
I am swabbing Hell in white;
I am the Smoke King,
I am Black!

---

[8] This poem was published for the first time in Du Bois's magazine *The Horizon: A Journal of the Color Line*, in February 1907, p. 7.

The Original Jubilee Singers. Source: *The Story of the Jubilee Singers; With Their Songs* (Boston; Houghton, Osgood and Company, 1880).

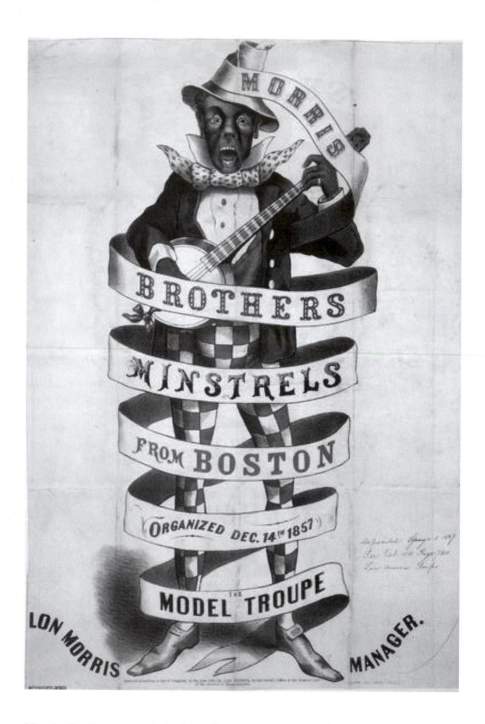

Morris Brothers minstrels from Boston, organized Dec. 14th, 1857—The model troupe / Ledger Job Print, Philadelphia. Courtesy of the Library of Congress.

XIV

Of the Sorrow Songs

I walk through the churchyard
    To lay this body down;
I know moon-rise, I know star-rise;
I walk in the moonlight, I walk in the starlight;
I'll lie in the grave and stretch out my arms,
I'll go to judgment in the evening of the day,
And my soul and thy soul shall meet that day,
    When I lay this body down.

NEGRO SONG.[1]

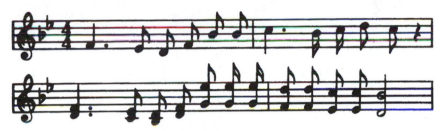

They that walked in darkness sang songs in the olden days—Sorrow Songs—for they were weary at heart. And so before each thought that I have written in this book I have set a phrase, a haunting echo of these weird old songs in which the soul of the black slave spoke to men. Ever since I was a child these songs have stirred me strangely. They came out of the South unknown to me, one by one, and yet at once I knew them as of me and of mine. Then in after years when I came to Nashville I saw the great temple builded of these songs towering over the pale city. To me Jubilee Hall seemed ever made of the songs themselves, and its bricks were red with the blood and dust of toil.[2] Out of them rose for me morning, noon, and night, bursts of wonderful melody, full of the voices of my brothers and sisters, full of the voices of the past.

---

[1] The verse included here is from the spiritual "Lay This Body Down." The two lines of music are from the spirtitual "Wrestlin' Jacob."

[2] Jubilee Hall is the main building at Fisk University in Nashville, Tennessee. It was built with funds obtained by the Fisk Jubilee Singers who began touring the United States and Europe in 1871. Their fund raising efforts were largely responsible for keeping Fisk from going into bankruptcy during its early years.

Jubilee Hall, Fisk University. Detroit Publishing Company, c. 1900. Courtesy of the Library of Congress.

Little of beauty has America given the world save the rude grandeur God himself stamped on her bosom; the human spirit in this new world has expressed itself in vigor and ingenuity rather than in beauty. And so by fateful chance the Negro folk-song—the rhythmic cry of the slave—stands today not simply as the sole American music, but as the most beautiful expression of human experience born this side the seas. It has been neglected, it has been, and is, half despised, and above all it has been persistently mistaken and misunderstood; but notwithstanding, it still remains as the singular spiritual heritage of the nation and the greatest gift of the Negro people.

Away back in the thirties the melody of these slave songs stirred the nation, but the songs were soon half forgotten. Some, like "Near the lake where drooped the willow," passed into current airs and their source was forgotten; others were caricatured on the "minstrel" stage and their memory died away. Then in wartime came the singular Port Royal experiment after the capture of Hilton Head, and perhaps for the first time the North met the Southern slave face to face and heart to heart with no third witness. The Sea Islands of the Carolinas, where they met, were filled with a black folk of primitive type, touched and moulded less by the world about them than any others outside the Black Belt. Their appearance was uncouth, their language funny, but their hearts were human and their singing stirred men with a mighty power. Thomas Wentworth Higginson hastened to tell of these songs, and Miss McKim and others urged upon the world their rare beauty. But the world listened only half credulously until the Fisk Jubilee Singers sang the slave songs so deeply into the world's heart that it can never wholly forget them again.

There was once a blacksmith's son born at Cadiz, New York, who in the changes of time taught school in Ohio and helped defend Cincinnati from Kirby Smith. Then he fought at Chancellorsville and Gettysburg and finally served in the Freedmen's Bureau at Nashville. Here he formed a Sunday-school class of black children in 1866, and sang with them and taught them to sing. And then they taught him to sing, and when once the glory of the Jubilee songs passed into the soul of George L. White, he knew his life-work was to let those Negroes sing to the world as they had sung to him. So in 1871 the pilgrimage of the Fisk Jubilee Singers began. North to Cincinnati they rode,—four half-clothed black boys and five girl-women,—led by a man with a cause and a purpose. They stopped at Wilberforce, the oldest of Negro schools, where a black bishop blessed them. Then they went, fighting cold and starvation, shut out of hotels, and cheerfully sneered at, ever northward; and ever the magic of their song kept thrilling hearts, until a burst of applause in the Congregational Council at Oberlin revealed them to the world. They came to New York and Henry Ward Beecher dared to welcome them, even though the metropolitan dailies sneered at his "Nigger Minstrels." So their songs conquered till they sang across the land and across the sea, before Queen and Kaiser, in Scotland and Ireland, Holland and Switzerland. Seven years they sang, and brought back a hundred and fifty thousand dollars to found Fisk University.

Since their day they have been imitated—sometimes well, by the singers of Hampton and Atlanta, sometimes ill, by straggling quartettes. Caricature has sought again to spoil the quaint beauty of the music, and has filled the air with many debased melodies which vulgar ears scarce know from the real. But the true Negro folk-song still lives in the hearts of those who have heard them truly sung and in the hearts of the Negro people.

What are these songs, and what do they mean? I know little of music and can say nothing in technical phrase, but I know something of men, and knowing them, I know that these songs are the articulate message of the slave to the world. They tell us in these eager days that life was joyous to the black slave, careless and happy. I can easily believe this of some, of many. But not all the past South, though it rose from the dead, can gainsay the heart-touching witness of these songs. They are the music of an unhappy people, of the children of disappointment; they tell of death and suffering and unvoiced longing toward a truer world, of misty wanderings and hidden ways.

The songs are indeed the siftings of centuries; the music is far more ancient than the words, and in it we can trace here and there signs of development. My grandfather's grandmother was seized by an evil Dutch trader two centuries ago; and coming to the valleys of the Hudson and Housatonic, black, little, and lithe, she shivered and shrank in the harsh north winds, looked longingly at the hills, and often crooned a heathen melody to the child between her knees, thus:

The child sang it to his children and they to their children's children, and so two hundred years it has travelled down to us and we sing it to our children, knowing as little as our fathers what its words may mean, but knowing well the meaning of its music.

This was primitive African music; it may be seen in larger form in the strange chant which heralds "The Coming of John":

You may bury me in the East,
You may bury me in the West,
But I'll hear the trumpet sound in that morning,

—the voice of exile.

Ten master songs, more or less, one may pluck from this forest of melody-songs of undoubted Negro origin and wide popular currency, and songs peculiarly characteristic of the slave. One of these I have just mentioned. Another whose strains begin this book is "Nobody knows the trouble I've seen." When, struck with a sudden poverty, the United States refused to fulfill its promises of land to the freedmen, a brigadier-general went down to the Sea Islands to carry the news. An old woman on the outskirts of the throng began singing this song; all the mass joined with her, swaying. And the soldier wept.

The third song is the cradle-song of death which all men know,—"Swing low, sweet chariot,"—whose bars begin the life story of "Alexander Crummell." Then there is the song of many waters, "Roll, Jordan, roll," a mighty chorus with minor cadences. There were many songs of the fugitive like that which opens "The Wings of Atalanta," and the more familiar "Been a-listening." The seventh is the song of the End and the Beginning—"My Lord, what a mourning! when the stars begin to fall"; a strain of this is placed before "The Dawn of Freedom." The song of groping—"My way's cloudy"—begins "The Meaning of Progress"; the ninth is the song of this chapter—"Wrestlin' Jacob, the day is a-breaking,"—a paean of hopeful strife. The last master song is the song of songs—"Steal away,"—sprung from "The Faith of the Fathers."

There are many others of the Negro folk-songs as striking and characteristic as these, as, for instance, the three strains in the third, eighth, and ninth chapters; and others I am sure could easily make a selection on more scientific principles. There are, too, songs that seem to be a step removed from the more primitive types: there is the maze-like medley, "Bright sparkles," one phrase of which heads "The Black Belt"; the Easter carol, "Dust, dust and ashes"; the dirge, "My mother's took her flight and gone home"; and that burst of melody hovering over "The Passing of the First-Born"—"I hope my mother will be there in that beautiful world on high."

These represent a third step in the development of the slave song, of which "You may bury me in the East" is the first, and songs like "March on" (chapter VI) and "Steal away" are the second. The first is African music, the second Afro-American, while the third is a blending of Negro music with the music heard in the foster land. The result is still distinctively Negro and the method of blending original, but the elements are both Negro and Caucasian. One might go further and find a fourth step in this development, where the songs of white America have been distinctively influenced by the slave songs or have incorporated whole phrases of Negro melody, as "Swanee River" and "Old Black Joe." Side by side, too, with the growth has gone the debasements and imitations—the Negro "minstrel" songs, many of the "gospel" hymns, and some of the contemporary "coon" songs,—a mass of music in which the novice may easily lose himself and never find the real Negro melodies.

In these songs, I have said, the slave spoke to the world. Such a message is naturally veiled and half articulate. Words and music have lost each other and new and cant phrases of a dimly understood theology have displaced the older sentiment. Once in a while we catch a strange word of an unknown tongue, as the "Mighty Myo," which figures as a river of death; more often slight words or mere doggerel are joined to music of singular sweetness. Purely secular songs are few in number, partly because many of them were turned into hymns by a change of words, partly because the frolics were seldom heard by the stranger, and the music less often caught. Of nearly all the songs, however, the music is distinctly sorrowful. The ten master songs I have mentioned tell in word and music of trouble and exile, of strife and hiding; they grope toward some unseen power and sigh for rest in the End.

The words that are left to us are not without interest, and, cleared of evident dross, they conceal much of real poetry and meaning beneath conventional theology and unmeaning rhapsody. Like all primitive folk, the slave stood near to Nature's heart. Life was a "rough and rolling sea" like the brown Atlantic of the Sea Islands; the "Wilderness" was the home of God, and the "lonesome valley" led to the way of life. "Winter'll soon be over," was the picture of life and death to a tropical imagination. The sudden wild thunder-storms of the South awed and impressed the Negroes,—at times the rumbling seemed to them "mournful," at times imperious:

My Lord calls me,
He calls me by the thunder,
The trumpet sounds it in my soul.

The monotonous toil and exposure is painted in many words. One sees the ploughmen in the hot, moist furrow, singing:

Dere's no rain to wet you,
Dere's no sun to burn you,
    Oh, push along, believer,
I want to go home.

The bowed and bent old man cries, with thrice-repeated wail:

O Lord, keep me from sinking down,

and he rebukes the devil of doubt who can whisper:

Jesus is dead and God's gone away.

Yet the soul-hunger is there, the restlessness of the savage, the wail of the wanderer, and the plaint is put in one little phrase:

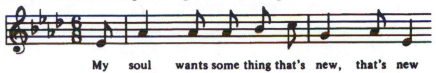

My   soul   wants some thing that's   new,   that's new

Over the inner thoughts of the slaves and their relations one with another the shadow of fear ever hung, so that we get but glimpses here and there, and also with them, eloquent omissions and silences. Mother and child are sung, but seldom father; fugitive and weary wanderer call for pity and affection, but there is little of wooing and wedding; the rocks and the mountains are well known, but home is unknown. Strange blending of love and helplessness sighs through the refrain:

Poor   Ro - sy, poor   gal;   Poor   Ro - sy,
poor   gal;   Ro - sy break my   poor   heart.
Heav'n   shall - a - be   my   home.

A black woman said of the song, "It can't be sung without a full heart and a troubled sperrit." The same voice sings here that sings in the German folk-song:

Jetz Geh I' an's brunele, trink' aber net.

Receipt for sale of Jane, age 18, and her son, Henry, age 1 and all future children, December 20, 1849." Courtesy of the Library of Congress.

Of death the Negro showed little fear, but talked of it familiarly and even fondly as simply a crossing of the waters, perhaps who knows?—back to his ancient forests again. Later days transfigured his fatalism, and amid the dust and dirt the toiler sang:

Dust, dust and ashes, fly over my grave,
But the Lord shall bear my spirit home.

The things evidently borrowed from the surrounding world undergo characteristic change when they enter the mouth of the slave. Especially is this true of Bible phrases. "Weep, O captive daughter of Zion," is quaintly turned into "Zion, weep-a-low," and the wheels of Ezekiel are turned every way in the mystic dreaming of the slave, till he says:

There's a little wheel a-turnin' in-a-my heart.

As in olden time, the words of these hymns were improvised by some leading minstrel of the religious band. The circumstances of the gathering, however, the rhythm of the songs, and the limitations of allowable thought, confined the poetry for the most part to single or double lines, and they seldom were expanded to quatrains or longer tales, although there are some few examples of sustained efforts, chiefly paraphrases of the Bible. Three short series of verses have always attracted me,—the one that heads this chapter, of one line of which Thomas Wentworth Higginson has fittingly said, "Never, it seems to me, since man first lived and suffered was his infinite longing for peace uttered more plaintively." The second and third are descriptions of the Last Judgment,—the one a late improvisation, with some traces of outside influence:

Oh, the stars in the elements are falling,
And the moon drips away into blood,
And the ransomed of the Lord are returning unto God,
Blessed be the name of the Lord.

And the other earlier and homelier picture from the low coast lands:

Michael, haul the boat ashore,
Then you'll hear the horn they blow,
Then you'll hear the trumpet sound,
Trumpet sound the world around,
Trumpet sound for rich and poor,
Trumpet sound the Jubilee,
Trumpet sound for you and me.

Through all the sorrow of the Sorrow Songs there breathes a hope—a faith in the ultimate justice of things. The minor cadences of despair change often to triumph and calm confidence. Sometimes it is faith in life, sometimes a faith in death, sometimes assurance of boundless justice in some fair world beyond. But whichever it is, the meaning is always clear: that sometime, somewhere, men will judge men by their souls and not by their skins. Is such a hope justified? Do the Sorrow Songs sing true? The silently growing assumption of this age is that the probation of races is past, and that the backward races of today are of proven inefficiency and not worth the saving. Such an assumption is the arrogance of peoples irreverent toward Time and ignorant of the deeds of men. A thousand years ago such an assumption, easily possible, would have made it difficult for the Teuton to prove his right to life. Two thousand years ago such dogmatism, readily welcome, would have scouted the idea of blond races ever leading civilization. So wofully unorganized is sociological knowledge that the meaning of progress, the meaning of "swift" and "slow" in human doing, and the limits of human perfectability, are veiled, unanswered sphinxes on the shores of science. Why should Aeschylus have sung two thousand years before Shakespeare was born? Why has civilization flourished in Europe, and flickered, flamed, and died in Africa? So long as the world stands meekly dumb before such questions, shall this nation proclaim its ignorance and unhallowed prejudices by denying freedom of opportunity to those who brought the Sorrow Songs to the Seats of the Mighty?

Your country? How came it yours? Before the Pilgrims landed we were here. Here we have brought our three gifts and mingled them with yours: a gift of story and song—soft, stirring melody in an ill-harmonized and unmelodious land; the gift of sweat and brawn to beat back the wilderness, conquer the soil, and lay the foundations of this vast economic empire two hundred years earlier than your weak hands could have done it; the third, a gift of the Spirit. Around us the history of the land has centred for thrice a hundred years; out of the nation's heart we have called all that was best to throttle and subdue all that was worst; fire and blood, prayer and sacrifice, have billowed over this people, and they have found peace only in the altars of the God of Right. Nor has our gift of the Spirit been merely passive. Actively we have woven ourselves with the very warp and woof of this nation,—we fought their battles, shared their sorrow, mingled our blood with theirs, and generation after generation have pleaded with a headstrong, careless people to despise not Justice, Mercy, and Truth, lest the nation be smitten with a curse. Our song, our toil, our cheer, and warning have been given to this nation in blood-brotherhood. Are not these gifts worth the giving? Is not this work and striving? Would America have been America without her Negro people?

Even so is the hope that sang in the songs of my fathers well sung. If somewhere in this whirl and chaos of things there dwells Eternal Good, pitiful yet masterful, then anon in His good time America shall rend the Veil and the prisoned shall go free. Free, free as the sunshine trickling down the morning into these high windows of mine, free as yonder fresh young voices welling up to me from the caverns of brick and mortar below—swelling with song, instinct with life, tremulous treble and darkening bass. My children, my little children, are singing to the sunshine, and thus they sing.

And the traveller girds himself, and sets his face toward the Morning, and goes his way.

Document Number 15, Chapter XIV

Thomas Wentworth Higginson (1823–1911) was a widely published author, a radical theologian, defender of equal rights for women, and a highly respected abolitionist. During the Civil War he served as a Captain of the Fifty-first Massachusetts Regiment, and eventually as a Colonel in the United States's first regiment of African Americans, the First South Carolina Volunteers (which later became the thirty-third U.S. Colored Troops. Higginson is most well-known for his correspondence with the poetess Emily Dickinson, whose *Poems* he edited in 1891 with Mabel Loomis Todd. The following article, "Negro Spirituals," from the June 1867 edition of *The Atlantic Monthly*, is among the earliest explorations of Negro Spirituals, and represents a pioneering study in the field of ethnomusicology.

Negro Spirituals[3]

The war brought to some of us, besides its direct experiences, many a strange fulfilment of dreams of other days. For instance, the present writer has been a faithful student of the Scottish ballads, and had always envied Sir Walter Scott the delight of tracing them out amid their own heather, and of writing them down piecemeal from the lips of aged crones. It was a strange enjoyment, therefore, to be suddenly brought into the midst of a kindred world of unwritten songs, as simple and indigenous as the Border Minstrelsy, more uniformly plaintive, almost always more quaint, and often as essentially poetic.

This interest was rather increased by the fact that I had for many years heard of this class of songs under the name of "Negro Spirituals," and had even heard some of them sung by friends from South Carolina. I could now gather on their own soil these strange plants, which I had before seen as in museums alone. True, the individual songs rarely coincided; there was a line here, a chorus there,—just enough to fix the class, but this was unmistakable. It was not strange that they differed, for the range seemed almost endless, and South Carolina, Georgia, and Florida seemed to have nothing but the generic character in common, until all were mingled in the united stock of camp-melodies.

Often in the starlit evening I have returned from some lonely ride by the swift river, or on the plover-haunted barrens, and, entering the camp, have silently approached some glimmering Ore, round which the dusky figures moved in the rhythmical barbaric dance the negroes call a "shout," chanting, often harshly, but always in the most perfect time, some monotonous refrain. Writing down in the darkness, as I best could—perhaps with my hand in the safe covert of my pocket,—the words of the song, I have afterwards carried it to my tent, like some captured bird or insect, and then, after examination, put it by. Or, summoning one of the men at some period of leisure,—Corporal Robert Sutton,

---

[3] Source: "Negro Spirituals," *The Atlantic Monthly*, Vol. 19, No. 116, June 1867, pp. 685–694.

for instance, whose iron memory held all the details of a song as if it were a ford or a forest,—I have completed the new specimen by supplying the absent parts. The music I could only retain by ear, and though the more common strains were repeated often enough to fix their impression, there were others that occurred only once or twice.

The words will be here given, as nearly as possible, in the original dialect; and if the spelling seems sometimes inconsistent, or the misspelling insufficient, it is because I could get no nearer. I wished to avoid what seems to me the only error of Lowell's "Biglow Papers" in respect to dialect,—the occasional use of an extreme misspelling, which merely confuses the eye, without taking us any closer to the peculiarity of sound.

The favorite song in camp was the following,—sung with no accompaniment but the measured clapping of hands and the clatter of many feet. It was sung perhaps twice as often as any other. This was partly due to the fact that it properly consisted of a chorus alone, with which the verses of other songs might be combined at random.

I. HOLD YOUR LIGHT.

Hold your light, Brudder Robert,—
Hold your light,
Hold your light on Canaan's shore.

What make ole Satan for follow me so?
Satan ain't got notin' for do wid me.
Hold your light,
Hold your light,
Hold your light on Canaan's shore.

This would be sung for half an hour at a time, perhaps, each person present being named in turn. It seemed the simplest primitive type of "spiritual." The next in popularity was almost as elementary, and, like this, named successively each one of the circle. It was, however, much more resounding and convivial in its music.

II. BOUND TO GO.

Jordan River, I'm bound to go,
Bound to go, bound to go,—
Jordan River, I 'm bound to go,
And bid 'em fare ye well.

My Brudder Robert, I 'm bound to go,
Bound to go, &c.

> My Sister Lucy, I 'm bound to go,
> Bound to go, &c.

Sometimes it was "tink 'em " (think them) "fare ye well." The *ye* was so detached, that I thought at first it was "very" or "vary well."

Another picturesque song, which seemed immensely popular, was at first very bewildering to me. I could not make out the first words of the chorus, and called it the "Romandàr," being reminded of some Romaic song which I had formerly heard. That association quite fell in with the Orientalism of the new tent-life.

III. ROOM IN THERE.

> O, my mudder is gone! my mudder is gone!
> My mudder is gone into heaven, my Lord!
> I can't stay behind!
> Dere's room in dar, room in dar,
> Room in dar, in de heaven, my Lord!
> I can't stay behind,
> Can't stay behind, my dear,
> I can't stay behind !

> O, my fader is gone! &c.

> O, de angels are gone! &c.

> O, I'se been on de road! I'se been on de road!
> I'se been on de road into heaven, my Lord!
> I can't stay behind!
> O, room in dar, room in dar,
> Room in dar, in de heaven, my Lord!
> I can't stay behind!

By this time every man within hearing, from oldest to youngest, would be wriggling and shuffling, as if through some magic piper's bewitchment; for even those who at first affected contemptuous indifference would be drawn into the vortex erelong.

Next to these in popularity ranked a class of songs belonging emphatically to the Church Militant, and available for camp purposes with very little strain upon their symbolism. This, for instance, had a true companion-in-arms heartiness about it, not impaired by the feminine invocation at the end.

IV. HAIL MARY.

One more valiant soldier here,
One more valiant soldier here,
One more valiant soldier here,
To help me bear de cross.
O hail, Mary, hail!
Hail!, Mary, hail!
Hail!, Mary, hail!
To help me bear de cross.

I fancied that the original reading might have been "soul," instead of "soldier,"
—with some other syllable inserted, to fill out the metre,—and that the "Hail,
Mary," might denote a Roman Catholic origin, as I had several men from St.
Augustine who held in a dim way to that faith. It was a very ringing song,
though not so grandly jubilant as the next, which was really impressive as the
singers pealed it out, when marching or rowing or embarking.

V. MY ARMY CROSS OVER.

My army cross over,
My army cross over.
O, Pharaoh's army drownded!
My army cross over.

We'll cross de mighty river,
My army cross over;
We'll cross de river Jordan,
My army cross over;
We'll cross de danger water,
My army cross over;
We'll cross de mighty Myo,
My army cross over. (*Thrice.*)
O, Pharaoh's army drownded!
My army cross over.

I could get no explanation of the "mighty Myo," except that one of the old
men thought it meant the river of death. Perhaps it is an African Word. In the
Cameroon dialect, "Mawa" signifies "to die."

The next also has a military ring about it, and the first line is well matched
by the music. The rest is conglomerate, and one or two lines show a more
Northern origin. "Done" is a Virginia shibboleth, quite distinct from the "been"
which replaces it in South Carolina. Yet one of their best choruses, without any
fixed words, was, "De bell done ringing," for which, in proper South Carolina
dialect, would have been substituted, "De bell been a-ring." This refrain may
have gone South with our army.

VI. RIDE IN, KIND SAVIOR.

Ride in, kind Saviour!
No man can hinder me.
O, Jesus is a mighty man!
No man, &c.
We 're marching through Virginny fields.
No man, &c.
O, Satan is a busy man,
No Man, &c.
And he has his sword and shield,
No man, &c.
O, old Secesh done come and gone!
No man can hinder me.

Sometimes they substituted "hinder *we*," which was more spicy to the ear, and more in keeping with the usual head-over-heels arrangement of their pronouns.

Almost all their songs were thoroughly religious in their tone, however quaint their expression, and were in a minor key, both as to words and music. The attitude is always the same, and, as a commentary on the life of the race, is infinitely pathetic. Nothing but patience for this life,—nothing but triumph in the next. Sometimes the present predominates, sometimes the future; but the combination is always implied. In the following, for instance, we hear simply the patience.

VII. THIS WORLD ALMOST DONE.

Brudder, keep your lamp trimmin' and a-burnin',
Keep your lamp trimmin' and a-burnin',
Keep your lamp trimmin' and a-burnin',
For dis world most done.
So keep your lamp, &c.
Dis world most done.

But in the next, the final reward of patience is proclaimed as plaintively.

VIII. I WANT TO GO HOME.

Dere's no rain to wet you,
O, yes, I want to go home.
Dere's no sun to burn you,
O, yes, I want to go home ;
O, push along, believers,
O, yes, &c.

Dere's no hard trials,
O, yes, &c.
Dere's no whips a-crackin',
O, yes, &c.
My brudder on de wayside,
O, yes, &c.
O, push along, my brudder,
O, yes, &c.
Where dere's no stormy weather,
O, yes, &c.
Dere's no tribulation,
O, yes, &c.

This next was a boat-song, and timed well with the tug of the oar.

IX. THE COMING DAY.

I want to go to Canaan,
I want to go to Canaan,
I want to go to Canaan,
To meet 'em at de comin' day.
O, remember, let me go to Canaan, (*Thrice.*)
To meet 'em, &c.
O brudder, let me go to Canaan, (*Thrice.*)
To meet 'em, &c.
My brudder, you-oh!—remember (*Thrice.*)
To meet 'em at de comin' day.

The following begins with a startling affirmation, yet the last line quite outdoes the first. This, too, was a capital boat-song.

X. ONE MORE RIVER.

O, Jordan bank was a great old bank!
Dere ain't but one more river to cross.
We have some valiant soldier here,
Dere ain't, &c.
O, Jordan stream will never run dry,
Dere ain't, &c.
Dere's a hill on my leff, and he catch on my right,
Dere ain't but one more river to cross.

I could get no explanation of this last riddle, except, "Dat mean, if you go on de leff, go to 'struction, and if you go on de right, go to God, for sure."
In others, more of spiritual conflict is implied, as in this next.

XI. O THE DYING LAMB!

I wants to go where Moses trod,
O de dying Lamb!
For Moses gone to de promised land,
O de dying Lamb!
To drink from springs dat never run dry,
O, &c.
Cry O my Lord!
O, &c.
Before I'll stay in hell one day,
O, &c.
I'm in hopes to pray my sins away,
O, &c.
Cry O my Lord!
O, &c.
Brudder Moses promised for be dar too,
O &c.
To drink from streams dat never run dry,
O de dying Lamb!

In the next, the conflict is at its height, and the lurid imagery of the Apocalypse is brought to bear. This book, with the books of Moses, constituted their Bible; all that lay between, even the narratives of the life of Jesus, they hardly cared to read or to hear.

XII. DOWN IN THE VALLEY.

We'll run and never tire,
We'll run and never tire,
We'll run and never tire,
Jesus set poor sinners free.
Way down in de valley,
Who will rise and go with me?
You've heern talk of Jesus,
Who set poor sinners free.

De lightnin' and de flashin',
De lightnin' and de flashin'
De lightnin' and de flashin'
Jesus set poor sinners free.
I can't stand de fire. (*Thrice.*)
Jesus set poor sinners free,
De green trees a-flamin'. (*Thrice.*)
Jesus set poor sinners free,
Way down in de valley,

Who will rise and go with me?
You 've heern talk of Jesus
Who set poor sinners free.

"De valley" and "de lonesome valley" were familiar words in their religious experience. To descend into that region implied the same process with the "anxious-seat" of the camp-meeting. When a young girl was supposed to enter it, she bound a handkerchief by a peculiar knot over her head, and made it a point of honor not to change a single garment till the day of her baptism, so that she was sure of being in physical readiness for the cleansing rite, whatever her spiritual mood might be. More than once, in noticing a damsel thus mystically kerchiefed, I have asked some dusky attendant its meaning, and have received the unfailing answer,—framed with their usual indifference to the genders of pronouns,-"He in de lonesome valley, sa."

The next gives the same dramatic conflict, while its detached and impersonal refrain gives it strikingly the character of the Scotch and Scandinavian ballads.

XIII. CRY HOLY.

Cry holy, holy!
Look at de people dat is born of God.
And I run down de valley, and I run down to pray,
Says, look at de people dat is born of God.
When I get dar, Cappen Satan was dar,
Says, look at, &c.
Says, young man, young man, dere 's no use for pray,
Says, look at, &c.
For Jesus is dead, and God gone away,
Says, look at, &c.
And I made him out a liar and I went my way,
Says, look at, &c.
Sing holy, holy!

O, Mary was a woman, and he had a one Son,
Says, look at, &c.
And de Jews and de Romans had him hung,
Says, look at, &c.
Cry holy, holy!

And I tell you, sinner, you had better had pray,
Says look at, &c.
For hell is a dark and dismal place,
Says, look at, &c.
And I tell you, sinner, and I wouldn't go dar!
Says, look at, &c.
Cry holy, holy!

Here is an infinitely quaint description of the length of the heavenly road:—

XIV. O'ER THE CROSSING.

Yonder's my old mudder,
Been a-waggin' at de hill so long.
It 's about time she 'll cross over;
Get home bimeby.
Keep prayin', I do believe
We 're a long time waggin' o'er de crossin'.
Keep prayin' I do believe
We 'll get home to heaven bimeby.

Hear dat mournful thunder
Roll front door to door,
Calling home God's children;
Get home bimeby.
Little chil'en, I do believe
We're a long time, &c.
Little chil'en, I do believe
We'll get home, &c.

See dat forked lightning
Flash from tree to tree,
Callin' home God's chil'en;
Get home bimeby.
True believer, I do believe
We 're a long time, &c.
O brudders, I do believe,
We'll get home to heaven bimeby.

One of the most singular pictures of future joys, and with a fine flavor of hospitality about it, was this:—

XV. WALK 'EM EASY.

O, walk 'em easy round de heaven,
Walk 'em easy round de heaven,
Walk 'em easy round de heaven,
Dat all de people may join de band.
Walk 'em easy round de heaven. (*Thrice.*)
O, shout glory till 'em join dat band!

The chorus was usually the greater part of the song, and often came in paradoxically, thus:—

XVI. O YES, LORD.

O, must I be like de foolish mans?
O yes, Lord!
Will build de house on de sandy hill.
O yes, Lord!
I'll build my house on Zion hill,
O yes, Lord!
No wind nor rain can blow me down
O yes, Lord!

The next is very graceful and lyrical, and with more variety of rhythm than usual:—

XVII. BOW LOW, MARY.

Bow low, Mary, bow low, Martha,
For Jesus come and lock de door,
And carry de keys away.
Sail, sail, over yonder,
And view de promised land.
For Jesus come, &c.
Weep, O Mary, bow low, Martha,
For Jesus come, &c.
Sail, sail, my true believer;
Sail, sail over yonder;
Mary bow low, Martha, bow low,
For Jesus come and lock de door
And carry de keys away.

But of all the "spirituals" that which surprised me the most, I think—perhaps because it was that in which external nature furnished the images most directly,—was this. With all my experience of their ideal ways of speech, I was startled when first I came on such a flower of poetry in that dark soil.

XVIII. I KNOW MOON-RISE.

I know moon-rise, I know star-rise,
Lay dis body down.
I walk in de moonlight, I walk in de starlight,
To lay dis body down.
I'll walk in de graveyard, I'll walk through de graveyard,
To lay dis body down.
I'll lie in de grave and stretch out my arms;
Lay dis body down.
I go to de judgment in de evenin' of de day,

When I lay dis body down;
And my soul and your soul will meet in de day
When I lay dis body down.

"I'll lie in de grave and stretch out my arms." Never, it seems to me, since man first lived and suffered, was his infinite longing for peace uttered more plaintively than in that line.

The next is one of the wildest and most striking of the whole series: there is a mystical effect and a passionate striving throughout the whole. The Scriptural struggle between Jacob and the angel, which is only dimly expressed in the words, seems all uttered in the music. I think it impressed my imagination more powerfully than any other of these songs.

XIX. WRESTLING JACOB.

O wrestlin' Jacob, Jacob, day's a-breakin';
I will not let thee go!
O wrestlin' Jacob, Jacob, day's a-breakin';
He will not let me go!
O, I hold my brudder wid a tremblin' hand;
I would not let him go!
I hold my sister wid a tremblin' hand;
I would not let her go!

O, Jacob do hang from a tremblin' limb,
He would not let him go!
O, Jacob do hang from a tremblin' limb;
De Lord will bless my soul.
O wrestlin' Jacob, Jacob, &c.

Of "occasional hymns," properly so called, I noticed but one, a funeral hymn for an infant, which is sung plaintively over and over, without variety of words.

XX. THE BABY GONE HOME.

De little baby gone home,
De little baby gone home,
De little baby gone along,
For to climb up Jacob's ladder.
And I wish I'd been dar,
I wish I'd been dar,
I wish I'd been dar, my Lord,
For to climb up Jacob's ladder

Still simpler is this, which is yet quite sweet and touching.

XXI. JESUS WITH US.

He have been wid us, Jesus,
He still wid us, Jesus,
He will be wid us, Jesus,
Be wid us to the end.

The next seemed to be a favorite about Christmas time, when meditations on "de rollin' year" were frequent among them.

XXII. LORD, REMEMBER ME!

O do Lord, remember me!
O do, Lord, remember me!
O, do remember me, until de year roll round!
Do, Lord, remember me!

If you want to die like Jesus died,
Lay in de grave,
You would fold your arms and close your eyes
And die wid a free good will.

For Death is a simple ting,
And he go from door to door
And he knock down some, and he cripple up some,
And he leave some here to pray.

O do, Lord, remember me!
O do, Lord, remember me!
My old fader 's gone till de year roll round;
Do, Lord, remember me!

The next was sung in such an operatic and rollicking way that it was quite hard to fancy it a religious performance, which, however, it was. I heard it but once.

XXIII. EARLY IN THE MORNING.

I meet little Rosa early in de mornin',
O Jerusalem! early in de mornin' ;
And I ax her, How you do, my darter?
O Jerusalem! early in de mornin'.

I meet my mudder early in de mornin',
O Jerusalem! &c.
And I ax her, How you do, my mudder?
O Jerusalem! &c.

I meet Brudder Robert early in de mornin'
O Jerusalem! &c.
And I ax him, How you do, my sonny?
O Jerusalem! &c.

I meet Tittawisa early in de mornin',
O Jerusalem! &c.
And I ax her, how you do, my darter?
O Jerusalem! &c.

"Tittawisa" means "Sister Louisa." In songs of this class the name of every person present successively appears.

Their best marching song, and one which was invaluable to lift their feet along, as they expressed it, was the following. There was a kind of spring and *lilt* to it, quite indescribable by words.

XXIV. GO IN THE WILDERNESS.

Jesus call you. Go in de wilderness,
Go in de wilderness, go in de wilderness,
Jesus call you. Go in de wilderness
To wait upon de Lord.
Go wait upon de Lord,
Go wait upon de Lord,
Go wait upon de Lord, my God,
He take away de sins of de world.

Jesus a-waitin'. Go in de wilderness,
Go, &c.
All dem chil'en go in de wilderness
To wait upon de Lord.

The next was one of those which I had heard in boyish days, brought North from Charleston. But the chorus alone was identical; the words were mainly different, and those here given are quaint enough.

XXV. BLOW YOUR TRUMPET, GABRIEL.

O, blow your trumpet, Gabriel,
Blow your trumpet louder;
And I want dat trumpet to blow me home
To my new Jerusalem.

De prettiest ting dat ever I done
Was to serve de Lord when I was young.
So blow your trumpet, Gabriel, &c.

O, Satan is a liar, and he conjure too,
And if you don't mind, he 'll conjure you.
So blow your trumpet, Gabriel, &c.

O, I was lost in de wilderness,
King Jesus hand me de candle down.
So blow your trumpet, Gabriel, &c.

The following contains one of those odd transformations of proper names with which their Scriptural citations were often enriched. It rivals their text, "Paul may plant, and may polish wid water," which I have elsewhere quoted, and in which the sainted Apollos would hardly have recognized himself.

XXVI. IN THE MORNING.

In de mornin',
In de mornin',
Chil'en? Yes, my Lord!
Don't you hear de trumpet sound?
If I had a-died when I was young,
I never would had de race for run.
Don't you hear de trumpet sound?

O Sam and Peter was fishin' in de sea,
And dey drop de net and follow my Lord.
Don't you hear de trumpet sound?

Dere's a silver spade for to dig my grave
And a golden chain for to let me down.
Don't you hear de trumpet sound?
In de mornin',
In de mornin',
Chil'en? Yes, my Lord!
Don't you hear de trumpet sound?

These golden and silver fancies remind one of the King of Spain's daughter in "Mother Goose," and the golden apple, and the silver pear, which are doubtless themselves but the vestiges of some simple early composition like this. The next has a humbler and more domestic style of fancy.

XXVII. FARE YE WELL.

My true believers, fare ye well,
Fare ye well, fare ye well,
Fare ye well, by de grace of God,
For I 'm going home.

Massa Jesus give me a little broom
For to sweep my heart clean,
And I will try, by de grace of God,
To win my way home.

Among the songs not available for marching, but requiring the concentrated enthusiasm of the camp, was "The Ship of Zion," of which they had three wholly distinct versions, all quite exuberant and tumultuous.

XXVIII. THE SHIP OF ZION.

Come along, come along,
And let us go home,
O, glory, hallelujah!
Dis de ole ship o' Zion,
Halleloo! Halleloo!
Dis de ole ship o' Zion,
Hallelujah!

She has landed many a tousand,
She can land as many more.
O, glory, hallelujah! &c.

Do you tink she will be able
For to take us all home?
O, glory, hallelujah! &c.

You can tell 'em I'm a coming,
Halleloo! Halleloo!
You can tell 'em I'm a coming
Hallelujah!
Come along, come along, & c.

XXIX. THE SHIP OF ZION. (*Second version.*)

Dis de good ole ship o' Zion,
Dis de good ole ship o' Zion,
Dis de good ole ship o' Zion,
And she 's makin' for de Promise Land.
She hab angels for de sailors, (*Thrice.*)
And she's, &c.
And how you know dey 's angels? (*Thrice.*)
And she's, &c.
Good lord, shall I be de one? (*Thrice.*)
And she's, &c.

Dat ship is out a-sailin', sailin', sailin',
And she's, &c.
She's a-sailin' mighty steady, steady, steady,
And she's, &c.
She'll neither reel nor totter, totter, totter,
And she's, &c.
She's a-sailin' away cold Jordan, Jordan, Jordan,
And she's, &c.
King Jesus is de captain, captain, captain,
And she's making for de Promise Land.

XXX. THE SHIP OF ZION. (*Third Version.*)

De Gospel ship is sailin',
Hosann-sann.
O, Jesus is de captain,
Hosann-sann.
De angels are de sailors,
Hosann-sann.
O, is your bundle ready?
Hosann-sann.
O, have you got your ticket?
Hosann-sann.

This abbreviated chorus is given with unspeakable unction.

The three just given are modifications of an old camp-meeting melody; and the same may be true of the three following, although I cannot find them in the Methodist hymnbooks. Each, however, has its characteristic modifications, which make it well worth giving. In the second verse of this next, for instance, "Saviour" evidently has become "soldier."

337

XXXI. SWEET MUSIC.

Sweet music in heaven,
Just beginning for to roll.
Don't you love God?
Glory, hallelujah!

Yes, late I heard my soldier say,
Come, heavy soul, I am de way.
Don't you love God?
Glory, hallelujah!

I'll go and tell to sinners round
What a kind Saviour I have found.
Don't you love God?
Glory, hallelujah!

My grief my burden long has been,
Because I was not cease from sin.
Don't you love God?
Glory, hallelujah!

XXXII. GOOD NEWS.

O, good news! O, good news!
De angels brought de tidings down,
Just comin' from de trone.

As grief from out my soul shall fly,
Just comin' from de trone;
I'll shout salvation when I die,
Good news, O, good news!
Just comin' from de trone.

Lord, I want to go to heaven when I die,
Good news, O, good news! &c.

De white folks call us a noisy crew,
Good news, O, good news!
But dis I know, we are happy too,
Just comin' from de trone.

XXXIII. THE HEAVENLY ROAD.

You may talk of my name as much as you please,
And carry my name abroad,
But I really do believe I'm a child of God
As I walk in de heavenly road.
O, won't you go wid me? (*Thrice.*)
For to keep our garments clean.

O, Satan is a mighty busy ole man,
And roll rocks in my way;
But Jesus is my bosom friend,
And roll 'em out of de way.
O, won't you go wid me? (*Thrice.*)
For to keep our garments clean.

Come, my brudder, if you never did pray,
I hope you may pray to-night;
For I really believe I'm a child of God
As I walk in de heavenly road.
O, won't you, &c.

Some of the songs had played an historic part during the war. For singing the next, for instance, the negroes had been put in jail in Georgetown, S. C., at the outbreak of the Rebellion. "We'll soon be free," was too dangerous an assertion; and though the chant was an old one, it was no doubt sung with redoubled emphasis during the new events. "De Lord will call us home," was evidently thought to be a symbolical verse; for, as a little drummer-boy explained to me, showing all his white teeth as he sat in the moonlight by the door of my tent, "Dey tink *de Lord* mean for say *de Yankees*."

XXXIV. WE 'LL SOON BE FREE.

We'll soon be free,
We'll soon be free,
We'll soon be free,
When de Lord will call us home.
My brudder, how long,
My brudder, how long,
My brudder, how long,
'Fore we done sufferin' here?
It won't be long (*Thrice.*)
'Fore de Lord will call us home.
We'll walk de miry road (*Thrice.*)
Where pleasure never dies.
We'll walk de golden street (*Thrice.*)

Where pleasure never dies.
My brudder, how long (*Thrice.*)
'Fore we done sufferin' here?
We'll soon be free (*Thrice.*)
When Jesus sets me free.
We'll fight for liberty (*Thrice.*)
When de Lord will call us home.

The suspicion in this case was unfounded, but they had another song to which the Rebellion had actually given rise. This was composed by nobody knew whom,—though it was the most recent, doubtless, of all these "spirituals,"—and had been sung in secret to avoid detection. It is certainly plaintive enough. The peck of corn and pint of salt were slavery's rations.

XXXV. MANY THOUSAND GO.

No more peck o' corn for me,
No more, no more,—
No more peck o' corn for me,
Many tousand go.

No more driver's lash for me, (*Twice.*)
No more, &c.

No more pint o' salt for me, (*Twice.*)
No more, &c.

No more hundred lash for me, (*Twice.*)
No more, &c.

No more mistress' call for me,
No more, No more,—
No more mistress' call for me,
Many tousand go.

Even of this last composition, however, we have only the approximate date, and know nothing of the mode of composition. Allan Ramsay says of the Scotch songs, that, no matter who made them, they were soon attributed to the minister of the parish whence they sprang. And I always wondered, about these, whether they had always a conscious and definite origin in some leading mind, or whether they grew by gradual accretion in an almost unconscious way. On this point I could get no information, though I asked many questions, until at last, one day when I was being rowed across from Beaufort to Ladies' Island, I found myself, with delight, on the actual trail of a song. One of the oarsmen, a brisk young fellow, not a soldier, on being asked for his theory of the matter, dropped out a coy confession. "Some good sperituals," he said, "are start jess out o' curiosity. I been a-raise a sing, myself, once."

My dream was fulfilled, and I had traced out, not the poem alone. but the poet. I implored him to proceed.

"Once we boys." he said, "went for tote some rice, and de nigger-driver, he keep a-callin' on us; and I say, 'O, de ole nigger-driver!' Den anudder said, 'Fust ting my mammy tole me was, notin' so bad as nigger-driver.' Den I made a sing, just puttin' a word, and den anudder word."

Then he began singing and the men, after listening a moment, joined in at the chorus as if it were an old acquaintance, though they evidently had never heard it before. I saw how easily a new "sing" took root among them.

XXXVI. THE DRIVER.

O, de ole nigger-driver!
O, gwine away!
Fust ting my mammy tell me,
O, gwine away!
Tell me 'bout de nigger-driver,
O, gwine away!
Nigger-driver second devil,
O, gwine away!
Best ting for do he driver,
O, gwine away!
Knock he down and spoil he labor,
O, gwine away!

It will be observed that, although this song is quite secular in its character, its author yet called it a "spiritual." I heard but two songs among them, at any time, to which they would not, perhaps, have given this generic name. One of these consisted simply in the endless repetition—after the manner of certain college songs—of the mysterious line,

Rain fall and wet Becky Martin.

But who Becky Martin was, and why she should or should not be wet, and whether the dryness was a reward or a penalty, none could say. I got the impression that, in either case, the event was posthumous and that there was some tradition of grass not growing over the grave of a sinner; but even this was vague, and all else vaguer.

The other song I heard but once, on a morning when a squad of men came in from picket duty, and chanted it in the most rousing way. It had been a stormy and comfortless night, and the picket station was very exposed. It still rained in the morning when I strolled to the edge of the camp, looking out for the men, and wondering how they had stood it. Presently they came striding along the road, at a great pace, with their shining rubber blankets worn as cloaks around them, the rain streaming from these and from their equally shining faces, which were almost all upon the broad grin, as they pealed out this remarkable ditty:

XXXVII. HANGMAN JOHNNY.

O, dey call me Hangman Johnny!
O, ho! O, ho!
But I never hang nobody,
O, hang, boys, hang!
O, dey call me Hangman Johnny!
O, ho! O, ho!
But we'll all hang togedder,
O, hang, boys, hang!

My presence apparently checked the performance of another verse, beginning, "De buckra 'list for money," apparently in reference to the controversy about the pay-question, then just beginning, and to the more mercenary aims they attributed to the white soldiers. But "Hangman Johnny" remained always a myth as inscrutable as "Becky Martin."

As they learned all their songs by ear, they often strayed into wholly new versions, which sometimes became popular, and entirely banished the others. This was amusingly the case, for instance, with one phrase in the popular camp-song of "Marching Along," which was entirely new to them until our quartermaster taught it to them, at my request. The words, "Gird on the armor," were to them a stumbling-block, and no wonder, until some ingenious ear substituted, "Guide on de army," which was at once accepted, and became universal.

"We'll guide on de army, and be marching along," is now the established version on the Sea Islands. These quaint religious songs were to the men more than a source of relaxation; they were a stimulus to courage and a tie to heaven. I never overheard in camp a profane or vulgar song. With the trifling exceptions given, all had a religious motive, while the most secular melody could not have been more exciting. A few youths from Savannah, who were comparatively men of the world, had learned some of the "Ethiopian Minstrel" ditties, imported from the North. These took no hold upon the mass; and, on the other hand, they sang reluctantly, even on Sunday, the long and short metres of the hymnbooks, always gladly yielding to the more potent excitement of their own "spirituals." By these they could sing themselves, as had their fathers before them, out of the contemplation of their own low estate, into the sublime scenery of the Apocalypse. I remember that this minor-keyed pathos used to seem to me almost too sad to dwell upon, while slavery seemed destined to last for generations; but now that their patience has had its perfect work, history cannot afford to lose this portion of its record. There is no parallel instance of an oppressed race thus sustained by the religious sentiment alone. These songs are but the vocal expression of the simplicity of their faith and the sublimity of their long resignation.

THE AFTERTHOUGHT

Hear my cry, O God the Reader; vouchsafe that this my book fall not still-born into the world wilderness. Let there spring, Gentle One, from out its leaves vigor of thought and thoughtful deed to reap the harvest wonderful. Let the ears of a guilty people tingle with truth, and seventy millions sigh for the righteousness which exalteth nations, in this drear day when human brotherhood is mockery and a snare. Thus in Thy good time may infinite reason turn the tangle straight, and these crooked marks on a fragile leaf be not indeed.

THE END

Index